General Practice under the
National Health Service
1948–1997

General Practice
under the
National Health Service
1948–1997

Edited by

IRVINE LOUDON

JOHN HORDER

and

CHARLES WEBSTER

CLARENDON PRESS · LONDON

1998

Oxford University Press, Great Clarendon Street, Oxford OX2 6DP

Oxford New York

Athens Auckland Bangkok Bogota Bombay Buenos Aires
Calcutta Cape Town Dar es Salaam Delhi Florence Hong Kong Istanbul
Karachi Kuala Lumpur Madras Madrid Melbourne Mexico City
Nairobi Paris Singapore Taipei Tokyo Toronto Warsaw
and associated companies in
Berlin Ibadan

Oxford is a registered trade mark of Oxford University Press

Published in the United States
by Oxford University Press Inc., New York

British Library Cataloguing in Publication Data
Data available

Library of Congress Cataloging in Publication Data
Data applied for

ISBN 0–19–820675–5

1 3 5 7 9 10 8 6 4 2

Typeset by Best-set Typesetter Ltd., Hong Kong
Printed in Great Britain
on acid-free paper by
Bookcraft Ltd., Midsomer-Norton
Nr. Bath, Somerset

Preface

The first steps in the production of this book took place in 1991, when a meeting was held in London to discuss some ideas about a publication on the development of general practice. Realizing that there was no comprehensive history of general practice and primary care, a steering committee (whose membership is listed below) was established to discuss the form such a history should take. A history of general practice from 1750 to 1850 had been published in 1986, and the committee decided that this should be followed by two volumes. The first, covering the period 1850 to the beginning of the National Health Service in 1948, would be written by a single author. Professor Anne Digby of Oxford Brookes University was invited to write this volume; she accepted, and is close to completing this work. The second—this volume—would consist of a series of essays on general practice and primary care under the National Health Service which would be edited by John Horder, Irvine Loudon, and Charles Webster. The history of general practice would thus consist of three volumes, as follows:

1. Irvine Loudon, *Medical Care and the General Practitioner, 1750–1850* (Oxford: Clarendon Press, 1986).
2. Anne Digby, *The Evolution of British General Practice 1850–1948* (Oxford: Clarendon Press, in preparation)—the title is provisional.
3. Irvine Loudon, John Horder, and Charles Webster (eds.), *General Practice under the National Health Service, 1948–1997* (Oxford: Clarendon Press, 1998).

A great deal of the planning of this volume was carried out by the steering committee, and the editors would like to acknowledge their invaluable help in the design, the choice of authors, and getting the work off the ground.

The steering committee consisted of John Horder (Chairman), Charles Webster (Vice-Chairman), Anne Crowther, Tony Delamothe, Sally Irvine, Margot Jefferys, Irvine Loudon, Marshall Marinker, Kenneth Morgan, Denis Pereira Gray, Richard M. Smith, Richard S. W. Smith, Ian Tait, and David Wilkin.

Acknowledgements

The editors are grateful to the Office of Health Economics (OHE) for permission to reproduce a large number of tables and graphs published in the OHE *Compendium of Health Statistics* (8th edn., 1992; 9th edn., 1995). They are also grateful to Professor Niels Bentzen, Odense, Denmark; Professor Hendryk van den Bussche, Hamburg, Germany; Dr Donald Crombie; Professor Jan van Es, Amersfoort, Netherlands; Dr Douglas Fleming; Professor George Freeman; Dr Jean Friedel, Châlon-sur-Saône; Dr Douglas Garvie; Professor Keith Hodgkin; Professor Michael Modell; Professor Gordon Moore, Boston; Dr Philalithis, WHO, Copenhagen; Dr Alan Rowe; Mme S. Sandier, Paris; and Ms Val Whelan, Assistant Librarian, the Royal College of General Practitioners. In the writing of Chapter 11, a particular debt is owed to the work of the late Dr John Fry, Professor Barbara Starfield, and Dr John Stephen.

Contents

List of Figures

List of Tables

Abbreviations

ACT	Additional Cost of Teaching
Aids	acquired immune deficiency syndrome
ASME	Association for the Study of Medical Education
BCG	Bacille Calmette-Guérin
BMA	British Medical Association
BPMF	British Postgraduate Medical Federation
CHSC	Central Health Services Council
CME	Continuing Medical Education
CMO	Chief Medical Officer
CPCR	Centre for Primary Care Research (in Manchester)
CPD	Continuing Professional Development
CRAGPIE	Committee of Regional Advisers in General Practice in England
DHSS	Department of Health and Social Security
EBM	Evidence Based Medicine
EEC	European Economic Community
EGPRW	European General Practice Research Workshop
FBA	Fellowship by Assessment
FHSA	Family Health Service Authority
FPC	Family Practitioner Committee
FHSA	Family Health Service Authority
FPS	Family Practitioner Services
FRCP	Fellow of the Royal College of Physicians
GMC	General Medical Council
GMSC	General Medical Services Committee (of the BMA)
GPRF	General Practice Research Framework
HCHS	Hospital and Community Health Services
HEFC	Higher Education Funding Council
HMO	Health Maintenance Organization
ICD	International Classification of Disease
ICFM	International Centre for Family Medicine
ICRF	Imperial Cancer Research Fund
IFFASP	International Forum on Family Medicine for the Americas, Spain, and Portugal
IOM	Institute of Medicine
IVP	intravenous pyelogram/pyelography

JCPTGP	Joint Committee on Postgraduate Training for General Practice
LRCP	Licentiate of the Royal College of Physicians
LSA	Licence of the Society of Apothecaries
MCGP	Membership of the College of General Practitioners
MO	Medical Officer
MPU	Medical Practitioners' Union
MRC	Medical Research Council
MRCGP	Membership of the Royal College of General Practitioners
MRCP	Member of the Royal College of Physicians
MRCS	Membership of the Royal College of Surgeons
NHI	National Health Insurance
NI	National Insurance
NHS	National Health Service
NHS R&D	National Health Service, Research and Development
OECD	Organization for Economic Cooperation and Development
OHE	Office of Health Economics
OPCS	Office of Population Censuses and Surveys
OSCE	Objective Structure Clinical Examination
PGEA	Post-Graduate Education Attendance
PHLS	Public Health Laboratory Service
PRO	Public Record Office
QUALYS	quality adjusted life years
RAE	Research Assessment Exercise
RAWP	Resource Allocation Working Party
RCGP	Royal College of General Practitioners
RCOG	Royal College of Obstetricians and Gynaecologists
RCP	Royal College of Physicians
RCS	Royal College of Surgeons
SHARE	Scottish Health Authorities Resource Equalization
SHHD	Scottish Home and Health Department
SIFT	Service Increment for Teaching
SIMG	Societas Internationalis Medicinae Generalis
SMAC	Standing Medical Advisory Committee
STA	Specialist Training Authority
TUC	Trades Union Congress
UEMO	Union Européenne de Médecins Omnipraticiens (the European Union of General Practitioners)
WHO	World Health Organization
WONCA	World Organization of National Colleges, Academies, and Academic Associations of General Practitioners/Family Physicians (after 1992 World Organization of Family Doctors)

List of Contributors

Nick Bosanquet, BA, M.Sc., Professor of Health Policy, Department of Primary Health Care and General Practice, Imperial College School of Medicine at St Mary's, London, since 1993. Formerly Senior Research Fellow, Centre for Health Economics, University of York. With Brenda Leese, he carried out surveys in 1986–7 and 1992–3 of how general practitioners take decisions. Publications include *Family Doctors and Economic Incentives*.

Mark Drury, MB, MRCGP, general practitioner, Wantage, Oxfordshire, and Research Fellow, ICRF General Practitioner Research Group, Oxford University Department of Public Health and Primary Care. Upjohn Lectureship in Therapeutics, 1983. Katherina von Kuenssberg Award, 1995. Publications on palliative and shared care.

Sir Michael Drury, OBE, FRCP, FRCGP, FRACGP, Hon. FRCPCH. Thirty-eight years in general practice in Bromsgrove. Professor, now Emeritus, of General Practice at the University of Birmingham. Past President of the Royal College of General Practitioners. Held a number of visiting professorships and served on bodies such as the General Medical Council, the Prescription Pricing Authority, and the Standing Committee on Postgraduate Medical Education. Author of research papers and books on therapeutics, general practice, and the work of staff in general practice.

Susanna Graham-Jones, MA, MB, BS, D.Phil., MRCGP. Trained at St Mary's Hospital, London. Worked in Nepal for three years before becoming Lecturer in the Department of General Practice, Liverpool University, and principal at the Prince's Park Health Centre in Liverpool. Appointed to a Lectureship in General Practice in the University of Oxford in 1993 to help establish an integrated course in public health and primary care for medical students. Her current research is in mental health and she is a member of Women in Medicine.

David Hannay, MA, MD, Ph.D., FRCGP, FFPHM, DCH. Professor of General Practice, University of Sheffield, 1987–96, currently Senior Research Fellow and Emeritus Professor. Following junior hospital posts in London and Manchester, he was appointed Lecturer in Community Medicine, and then Senior Lecturer in General Practice, University of Glasgow; also Research Fellow at McMaster University, Ontario, and Principal in General Practice in Glasgow, rural south-west Scotland, and Sheffield. Co-author of the

Mackenzie Report on University Departments of General Practice. Author of *The Symptom Iceberg* and *Lecture Notes on Medical Sociology* as well as papers on medical education and primary care.

John Horder, CBE, MA (Oxon.), BM, B.Ch., MD hon. (Amsterdam), FRCP, FRCP (Edinburgh), FRCGP, FRCPsych., Honorary Fellow, Green College, Oxford, and Queen Mary and Westfield College, London University. Previously general practitioner, London, NW1. President of the Royal College of General Practitioners, 1979–82, Vice-President, 1987–9, and Honorary Fellow, the Royal Society of Medicine. Visiting Professor, the Royal Free Hospital School of Medicine, 1983–91. Visiting Fellow, the King's Fund College, 1982–4. Editor and co-author of *The Future General Practitioner: Learning and Teaching* (1972), and co-author of *Primary Care in an International Context* (1994).

John Howie, CBE, MD, Ph.D., FRCPE, FRCGP. Professor of General Practice in the University of Edinburgh since 1980, previously Principal in General Practice in Glasgow, and Senior Lecturer in General Practice in the University of Aberdeen. His research interests have included the fields of clinical decision-making (antibiotics in respiratory illness) and the definition and delivery of quality of care. He has published widely on research in general practice, including two editions of the monograph *Research in General Practice*.

Margot Jefferys, B.Sc. (Econ.), FRCGP, FFPHM, FHC (Lond.). Emeritus Professor of Medical Sociology (London). Since 1992 Visiting Professor, Centre of Medical Law and Ethics, King's College, London. Previously lectured in Social Aspects of Public Health, London School of Hygiene and Tropical Medicine, 1953–65; Professor of Medical Sociology, Bedford College, 1968–82. Chaired BMA's Planning Unit's Working Party on Primary Medical Care, 1968–70. Member of the GMC Working Party on General Practice, Epidemiology, and Behavioural Science Teaching in the Medical Curriculum, 1986–7. Author of *An Anatomy of Social Welfare Services* (1965) and (with H. Sachs) *Re-thinking General Practice: Dilemmas in Primary Care* (1983); editor of *Growing Old in the Twentieth Century* (1989).

Irvine Loudon, DM, BM, B.Ch. (Oxon), FRCGP, D(Obst.)RCOG, ARE. Medical Historian, previously general practitioner, Wantage, Oxfordshire, 1952–1981. Wellcome Research Fellow in the History of Medicine at the University of Oxford (1981–6) and subsequently Research Associate at the Wellcome Unit for the History of Medicine in Oxford. Publications on the history of disease, historical epidemiology, maternal care, and the history of medical institutions and the medical profession include *Medical Care and the General Practitioner, 1750–1850* (Oxford, 1986), *Death in Childbirth: An International Study of Maternal Care and Maternal Mortality, 1800–1950* (Oxford, 1992), and (ed.) *Western Medicine. An Illustrated History* (Oxford, 1997).

Marshall Marinker, OBE, MD, FRCGP, has been Visiting Professor of General Practice at the United Medical and Dental Schools of Guy's and St Thomas's Hospital Medical School since 1991, chairs the Research and Development Committee of the High Security Psychiatric Services Commissioning Board, and also acts as an independent consultant in health-care education and policy. He was Foundation Professor of General Practice and Head of Department of Community Health, University of Leicester Medical School, 1973–82; Director, the MSD Foundation, 1982–92, and Director of Medical Education, MSD Ltd, 1992–5. He was a member of Council of the Royal College of General Practitioners, 1974–89, and among other posts was Chairman of its Education Division and Committee on Medical Ethics. He has lectured and published widely on the theory of general medical practice, medical education, the patient–doctor relationship, medical ethics, and health-care policy.

David Morrell, OBE, KSG, MB, BS, FRCP, FRCGP, FFPHM. General Practitioner, Hoddesdon, 1957–63. Lecturer in General Practice, University of Edinburgh, 1963–7. Senior Lecturer in General Practice, St Thomas's Hospital Medical School, 1967–74, Wolfson Professor, 1974–93. Sub-dean, St Thomas's Hospital Medical School, 1984–9. Emeritus Professor of General Practice, University of London, 1993. President, British Medical Association, 1994–5. Author of *The Art of General Practice* (1966; 4th edn., 1991), editor of *Epidemiology in General Practice* (1988), and co-editor of *Practice: A Handbook of Primary Medical Care*, (1976).

Chris Salisbury, M.Sc., MB.ChB., FRCGP, Consultant Senior Lecturer in General Practice at the University of Bristol since 1998. Previously Senior Lecturer, Imperial College, 1995–8 and General Practitioner in Reading 1985–98. Author of papers on practice nursing, consumerism in medicine, reaccreditation, and out-of-hours care, and co-author of *The Handbook of Practice Nursing* (1992).

Ian Tait, MD, MA, MB, B.Chir., FRCGP, DCH. Retired. Previously general practitioner, Aldeburgh, Suffolk. Associate Regional Adviser in General Practice, East Anglia. Jeffcoate Visiting Professor, UCH Medical School, 1977. Publications on general practice, medical education, and medical history.

Charles Webster, MA, B.Sc., M.Sc., D.Sc., Lond., FBA. Since 1988 Senior Research Fellow, All Souls College, Oxford. Previously taught at Leeds University, and in Oxford, where he was, from 1972 to 1988, a Fellow of Corpus Christi College, Reader in the History of Medicine, and Director of the Wellcome Unit for the History of Medicine. Author of books on medicine and science in the early modern period, and the two-volume official history of the NHS from its origins to 1979, published in 1988 and 1996.

Denis Pereira Gray, OBE, MA, FRCGP, Hon.FRSH, General Practitioner, St Leonard's Medical Practice, Exeter, Professor of General Practice at the Institute of General Practice, University of Exeter, and President of the Royal College of General Practitioners. Former Chairman of the Joint Committee on Postgraduate Training for General Practice (1994–7) and Chairman of Council of the Royal College of General Practitioners (1987–90).

Chronology

Dec. 1949 National Health Service (Amendment) Act

23 Feb. 1950 General election: Labour majority 6. Prime Minister, Clement Attlee; Minister of Health, Aneurin Bevan

1950 BMA, *General Practice and the Training of the General Practitioner* (Second BMA Cohen Report)

1950 The Collings Report, published in the *Lancet*

Jan. 1951 Aneurin Bevan, Minister of Labour; Hilary Marquand, Minister of Health

April 1951 Resignation of Bevan, Wilson, and Freeman over the imposition of health-service charges

May 1951 Imposition of direct charges for dentures and spectacles

25 Oct. 1951 General election: Conservative majority 17. Prime Minister, Winston Churchill; Minister of Health, Harry Crookshank

May 1952 Crookshank replaced by Iain Macleod as Minister of Health

1952 Danckwerts award. Uprated the pay of general practitioners, and later led to the maximum list size for a single-handed general practitioner being reduced from 4,000 to 3,500

June 1952 Introduction of charges for prescriptions and dental treatment

1952 C. A. H. Watts and B. M. Watts, *Psychiatry in General Practice*

1952 College of General Practitioners founded

1953 S. Hadfield, 'A Field Survey of General Practice, 1951–52'

1954 S. Taylor, *Good General Practice*

1954 Central Health Services Council, *Report of the Committee on General Practice within the National Health Service* (The Cohen Report)

26 May 1955 General election: Conservative majority 58. Prime Minister, Sir Anthony Eden; Minister of Health, Iain Macleod

Dec. 1955 Macleod replaced by Robert Turton as Minister of Health

Jan. 1956 *Report of the Committee of Enquiry into the Cost of the National Health Service*, Cmd. 9663 (The Guillebaud Report)

1956 Foundation of the Netherlands College of General Practice

10 Jan. 1957 Resignation of Eden following Suez Invasion and replacement as Prime Minister by Harold Macmillan; Minister of Health, Dennis Vosper

1957 M. Balint, *The Doctor, his Patient and the Illness*

May 1957 *Report of the Royal Commission on the Law Relating to Mental Illness and Mental Deficiency*, Cmnd. 169 (The Percy Report)

March 1957 Treaties of Rome establishing EEC and Euratom

Sept. 1957 Replacement of Vosper by Derek Walker-Smith as Minister of Health

1958 W. P. D. Logan and A. A. Cushion, *Morbidity Statistics from General Practice* (The First National Morbidity Study)

Feb. 1959 *Report of the Maternity Services Committee* (The Cranbrook Report)

July 1959 Mental Health Act

8 Oct. 1959 General election: Conservative majority 100. Prime Minister, Harold Macmillan; Minister of Health, Derek Walker-Smith

1960–9

Feb. 1960 *Report of the Royal Commission on Doctors' and Dentists' Remuneration*, Cmnd. 939 (The Pilkington Report)

1960 J. Spence, *The Purpose and Practice of Medicine*

July 1960 Replacement of Walker-Smith by Enoch Powell as Minister of Health

1960–4 WHO Expert Committee reports on general practice

1961 Foundation of the Consumers' Association

1961 The recognition of foetal deformities due to thalidomide (the 'thalidomide disaster') led to a new concern about the safety of medicines

1961 J. Fry, *The Catarrhal Child*

Jan. 1962 *A Hospital Plan for England and Wales*, Cmnd. 1604

1962 Foundation of Societas Internationalis Medicinae Generalis (SIMG)

Nov. 1962 Medical Services Review Committee, *A Review of the Medical Services in Great Britain* (The Porritt Report)

1963 Foundation of the Patients' Association

1963 R. Scott, appointed in Edinburgh as Professor of General Practice, the first such post to be created

April 1963 *Health and Welfare: The Development of Community Care*, Cmnd. 1973

1963 K. Hodgkin, *Towards Earlier Diagnosis*

1963 Central Health Services Council, Standing Medical Advisory Committee, *The Field of Work of the Family Doctor: Report of the Sub-Committee* (The Gillie Report)

Oct. 1963 Resignation of Harold Macmillan owing to ill health. Prime Minister, Sir Alec Douglas-Home; Minister of Health, Anthony Barber

1963 K. F. Clute, *The General Practitioner: A Study of Medical Education and Practice in Ontario and Nova Scotia*

15 Oct. 1964 General election: Labour majority 5. Prime Minister, Harold Wilson; Minister of Health, Kenneth Robinson

1964 Declaration of Helsinki: a landmark in medical ethics

1965 College of General Practitioners, *Special Vocational Training for General Practice: Report from General Practice No. 1*

1965 D. Morrell, *The Art of General Practice*

31 March 1966 General Election: Labour majority 95. Prime Minister, Harold Wilson; Minister of Health, Kenneth Robinson

May 1966 *Report of the Committee on*

1966 Family Doctors' Charter led to a

Senior Nursing Staff Structure (The Salmon Report)

Oct. 1967 Abortion Act

July 1968 *Report of the Committee on Local Authority and Allied Personal and Social Services*, Cmnd. 3703 (The Seebohm Report)

July 1968 *The Administrative Structure of Medical and Related Services in England and Wales* (First Green Paper)

Nov. 1968 Robinson stands down as Minister of Health; Richard Crossman Secretary of State for Social Services of the combined Department of Health and Social Security

Oct. 1969 *The Functions of the District General Hospital* (The Bonham-Carter Report)

June 1969 *Report of the Royal*

new system of payment of general practitioners.

1966 R. Stevens, *Medical Practice in Modern England, the Impact of Specialization and State Medicine*

1966 First Dutch Professorial Chair in General Practice (Utrecht)

1966 *The Graduate Education of Physicians* (The Millis Report)

1967 College of General Practitioners receives its Royal charter

1967 Dame Cecily Saunders opened the St Christopher's Hospice in London, thereby starting the hospice movement.

*c.*1967 The beginning of a sudden increase in the building of health centres

1967 J. Berger and J. Mohr, *A Fortunate Man*

1967 Royal College of General Practitioners, *The Implementation of Vocational Training: Report from General Practice No. 6*

1967 A. Cartwright, *Patients and their Doctors*

1967 Foundation of the European Union of General Practitioners (UEMO)

1968 *Report of the Royal Commission on Medical Education*, Cmnd. 3569 (The Todd Report)

1969 J. Fry, *Medicine in Three Societies*

Commission on Local Government in England 1966–1969, Cmnd. 4040 (The Redcliffe-Maud Report)

1970–9

Feb. 1970 *The Future Structure of the National Health Service* (Second Green Paper)

May 1970 Local Authority Social Services Act

18 June 1970 General election: Conservative majority 33. Prime Minister, Edward Heath; Secretary of State for Social Services, Sir Keith Joseph

June 1971 *Better Services for the Mentally Handicapped*, Cmnd. 4683

May 1971 *National Health Service Reorganisation: Consultative Document*

August 1972 *National Health Service Reorganisation. England*, Cmnd. 5055 (Reorganization White Paper)

Sept. 1972 *Management Arrangements for the Reorganised National Health Service* (The Grey Book)

Oct. 1972 *Report of the Committee on Nursing*, Cmnd. 5115 (The Briggs Report)

Jan. 1973 UK, Denmark, and Ireland become full members of EEC

July 1973 National Health Service Reorganisation Act

Oct. 1973 *Report of the Royal Commission on the Constitution*, Cmnd. 5460 (The Kilbrandon Report)

Dec. 1973 *Report of the Committee on*

1971 A. Cochrane, *Effectiveness and Efficiency*, The Rock Carling Fellowship

Oct. 1971 *The Organisation of Group Practice* (The Harvard Davis Report)

1971 J. Tudor Hart, 'The Inverse Care Law', *Lancet*, i. 405–12

1972 RCGP, *The Future General Practitioner: Learning and Teaching*

1972 Inauguration of the World Organization of National Colleges, Academies, and Academic Associations of General Practitioners/Family Physicians (WONCA)

1973 J. Fry, *Common Diseases: Their Nature, Incidence and Care*

1973 Medical Research Council establishes the 'General practice research framework'

Hospital Complaints Procedure (The Davies Report)

28 Feb. 1974 General election: Labour minority Government, 301 seats out of 635. Prime Minister, Harold Wilson; Secretary of State for Social Services, Barbara Castle

1 April 1974 Reorganization of the National Health Service. Establishment of Community Health Councils

May 1974 Consultative Document, *Democracy in the National Health Service*

10 Oct. 1974 General election: Labour majority 4. Prime Minister Harold Wilson; Secretary of State for Social Services, Barbara Castle

Oct. 1975 *Better Services for the Mentally Ill*, Cmnd. 6233.

April 1975 *Report of the Committee of Enquiry into the Regulation of the Medical Profession*, Cmnd. 6018 (The Merrison Report)

5 June 1975 Referendum on EEC Membership

April 1976 Retirement of Harold Wilson. Prime Minister, James Callaghan; Secretary of State for Social Services, David Ennals

Sept. 1976 *Sharing Resources for Health in England: Report of the Resource Allocation Working Party*

Dec. 1976 *Report of the Committee on Child Health Services. Fit for the Future* (The Court Report)

March 1976 *Priorities for Health and*

1974 Leeuwenhorst Group formed. European definition of the general practitioner's role proposed. European General Practice Research Workshop formed.

1974 Creation of the Association of University Teachers of General Practice, now the Association of University Departments of General Practice

1974 With the reorganization of the NHS, the Executive Councils became the Family Practitioner Committees

1975 Establishment of the Joint Committee on Postgraduate Training for General Practice. Vocational training for general practice became mandatory

1975 European Directives 75/362 and 363, concerning registration and access to social-security systems, allowing migration of doctors

1975 I. Illich, *Medical Nemesis: The Expropriation of Health*

1976 D. Hicks, *Primary Health Care*

1976 P. S. Byrne and B. E. L. Long, *Doctors Talking to Patients*

1976 Vocational Training Act

Personal Social Services in England: A
Consultative Document

March 1976 *Prevention and Health:*
Everybody's Business: A Reassessment of
Public and Personal Health

Sept. 1977 *Priorities in the Health*
and Social Services: The Way Forward

1977 Council of Europe Symposium,
Strasbourg

1977 RCGP *Trends in General Practice*

June 1978 *A Happier Old Age: A*
Discussion Document on Elderly People in
our Society

1978 F. J. A. Huygen, *Family Medicine:*
The Medical Life History of Families
(Nijmegen, 1978; Eng. trans., London,
1990)

1978 The Alma Ata Declaration,
'Health for All by the Year 2,000',
promulgated by WHO

1978 The Medical Act which
reconstituted the GMC and increased
general-practitioner membership of the
Council

March 1979 *Report of the Committee of*
Enquiry into Mental Handicap Nursing
and Care (The Jay Report)

1 March 1979 Referendum on Scottish
and Welsh Devolution

3 May 1979 General election:
Conservative majority 43. Prime
Minister, Margaret Thatcher; Secretary
of State for Social Services, Patrick
Jenkin

July 1979 *Report of the Royal*
Commission on the National Health Service,
Cmnd. 7615 (The Merrison Report)

Dec. 1979 *Patients First: Consultative*
Paper on the Structure and Management
of the National Health Service in
England and Wales

1980–9

August 1980 *Report of a Research*
Working Group on Inequalities in Health
(The Black Report)

March 1981 *Growing Older, White Paper*
on the Elderly, Cmnd. 8173

1981 A. Cartwright and R. Anderson,
General Practice Revisited: A Second
Study of Patients and their Doctors

April 1981 *Care in Action: A Handbook*

1981 *The Primary Care Team: Report of*

of Policies and Priorities for the Health and Personal Social Services in England

July 1981 *Care in the Community, a Consultative Document on Moving Resources for Care in England*

Sept. 1981 Replacement of Jenkin by Norman Fowler as Secretary of State for Social Services

April 1982 Restructuring of the NHS in England; abolition of AHAs; statutory status for FPCs

9 June 1983 General election: Conservative majority 144. Prime Minister, Margaret Thatcher; Secretary of State for Social Services, Norman Fowler

Oct. 1983 *NHS Management Inquiry Report* (The Griffiths Report) leading to withdrawal of general management, and establishment of Supervisory Board (later Policy Board) and NHS Management Board (later NHS Executive)

June 1984 HC (84) 13, *Health Services Management: Implementation of the NHS Management Inquiry Report*

April 1986 *Neighbourhood Nursing: A Focus for Care* (The Cumberlege Report)

11 June 1987 General election: Conservative majority 102. Prime Minister, Margaret Thatcher; Secretary of State for Social Services, John Moore

Feb.–Dec. 1988 Prime Minister's Confidential Review of NHS

March 1988 *Community Care: Agenda*

a Joint Working Group (The Harding Report)

1981 London Health Planning Consortium, Primary Health Care Study Group, *Primary Health Care in Inner London* (The Acheson Report)

1982 The Department of Health supports a pilot scheme for the use of computers in general practice

1983 M. Jefferys and H. Sachs, *Rethinking General Practice*

1984 Journal, *Family Practice*, launched

1985 RCGP, *Quality in General Practice*

1986 European Economic Community. European Directive on Specific Training in General Medical Practice, 86/457/EEC

1986 *Primary Health Care: An Agenda for Discussion*, Cmnd. 9771 (Primary Care Green Paper)

1987 *Promoting Better Health: The Government's Programme for Improving Primary Health Care*, Cm. 249 (Primary Care White Paper)

1988 J. Tudor Hart, *A New Kind of Doctor*

1988 *Report of the Working Group on*

for Action (The Griffiths Report)

July 1988 Split of Departments of
Health and Social Security. Secretary of
State for Health, Kenneth Clarke

Jan. 1989 *Working for Patients*, Cm. 555

April 1989 Introduction of charges for
eye tests and dental inspections

Nov. 1989 *Caring for People:
Community Care in the Next Decade and
Beyond*, Cm. 849

*Research in Health Care in the
Community* (The Howie Report)

1989 I. R. McWhinney, *Introduction to
Family Medicine*

1989 *General Practice in the NHS: The
1990 Contract. The Government's
Programme for Changes in GPs' terms of
service and remuneration system*

1990–7

1990 *Care in the Community: Making it
Happen*

June 1990 NHS and Community Care
Act

28 Nov. 1990 Replacement of Thatcher
by John Major as Prime Minister;
Secretary of State for Health, William
Waldegrave

April 1991 Implementation of the NHS
and Community Care Act.
Commencement of the Purchaser/
Provider and Fundholding system

June 1991 *The Health of the Nation: A
Consultative Document*, Cm. 1523

April 1992 Introduction of the Patient's
Charter

9 April 1992 General Election:
Conservative majority 21. Prime
Minister, John Major; Secretary of State
for Health, Virginia Bottomley

July 1992 *The Health of the Nation: A
Strategy for Health in England*, Cm. 1986

April 1993 Implementation of
Community Care provisions of the NHS
and Community Care Act

1990 Family Practitioner Committees
were reconstituted as Family Health
Service Authorities

1990 D. L. Crombie, J. van der Zee,
and P. Backer, *The Interface Study*
(RCGP)

1992 B. Starfield, *Primary Care:
Concept, Evaluation and Policy*

Nov. 1993 Implementation of
Maastricht Treaty establishing the
European Union

May 1994 *Being Heard: The Report of a
Review Committee on NHS Complaints
Procedures*

1994 Dept. of Health, *Developing NHS
Purchasing and GP Fundholding: Towards
a Primary Care-Led NHS*

1994 J. Fry and J. P. Horder, *Primary
Health Care in an International Context*

March 1995 Health Authorities Act.
Permits abolition of RHAs;
amalgamation of FHSAs and DHAs

1995 A. McCormick, D. Fleming, and J.
Charlton, *Morbidity Statistics from
General Practice, Fourth National Study
1991–1992*

July 1995 Stephen Dorrell replaces
Bottomley as Secretary of State for
Health

1995 JCPTGP was appointed by
Government as the Competent
Authority for General Practice in
Europe

April 1996 Abolition of Regional Health
Authorities. Merger of District Health
Authorities and Family Health Services
to form Health Authorities.

1996 *Choice and Opportunity: Primary
Care, the Future*, Cm. 3390

April 1996 Introduction of new
Complaints Procedure

1996 Secretary of State for Health,
Primary Care: Delivering the future

Oct. 1996 *The NHS: A Service with
Ambition*, Cm. 3425

March 1997 Primary Care Act

1 May 1997 General election: Labour
majority, 179. Prime Minister, Anthony
Blair; Secretary of State for Health,
Frank Dobson

Introduction and Overview

DAVID MORRELL

I entered medical school in 1947, qualified in 1952, entered general practice in 1957, retired in 1993, and have continued as a consultant in this field. My career therefore almost spans the first fifty years of the National Health Service. Active in the College of General Practitioners since 1958, and involved in academic general practice since its inception, I have been privileged to work with most of the leaders in general practice over this period of time. It is from this very personal perspective that I will try to set the scene for this book. Against this background other authors with experience of general practice will describe in detail different aspects of this most exciting experiment in the delivery of medical care encapsulated in the term British general practice.

The early years, c.1948–1957

When a plebiscite was taken by the British Medical Association (BMA) in January 1948, 84 per cent of general practitioners voted against the introduction of a National Health Service (NHS). Despite this, owing to the determination and political skill of Aneurin Bevan, the NHS was launched in July 1948. It is difficult to describe accurately the immediate response of general practitioners to the NHS, but it appears that, in spite of continuing resentment, most considered it their duty to make it work for the sake of their patients. The political background to the introduction of the NHS is described in detail in Chapter 1.

Information about the clinical care provided in general practice at this time and the problems encountered is overshadowed by the constant controversies over remuneration. To get a feel for the benefits and difficulties which the NHS brought to the lives of general practitioners it is necessary to resort to anecdotes from doctors living through that time, leading articles, letters in the medical journals, and a limited number of biographies.

The one great financial benefit which the NHS conferred on many general practitioners was relieving them from the burden of bad debts and the need to employ debt collectors. There is abundant evidence of the relief which the profession experienced in this regard. Although general practitioners had traditionally tried to provide care to those in need, irrespective of financial resources, the new NHS gave welcome support, particularly for those working in areas of poverty and deprivation. There is some evidence from the medical journals about new problems arising from the new NHS. The increase in work-load following the provision of primary care, free at the time of demand, figures prominently in the writings of the time. Many of the complaints were of inap-propriate demands for care particularly out of hours, unrealistic expectations of patients, the regulations concerning certification for sickness benefit, and the need for certificates for eye tests and prescriptions for corsets and similar items. Factual information about consultation and visit rates for general prac-titioners during the early years of the NHS is difficult to find and of variable quality. It is also difficult to find data collected prior to the NHS with which it may be compared.

In 1936–7 Bradford Hill had carried out a study of general-practitioner workload at the request of the BMA. He drew a random sample of 6,000 practitioners and asked 500 each month to record the demands of their National Health Insurance (NHI) patients, as these were the only patients for whom he had a reliable denominator. The results of this study were not published until many years later.[1] These revealed that the average consultation rate per NHI patient per year was 5.4, which included home-visit rates of 1.3 per patient per year. In 1947 Pemberton measured the number of consultations undertaken by eight general practitioners in Sheffield.[2] He collected data for one week in the summer and one week in the winter of 1947. These doctors were consulted on average by 350 patients per week in the winter and 260 per week in the summer. Thirty-three per cent of the consultations took place in the patients' homes. This represents a very high workload. As most doctors worked a six-day week, it suggests that, in the winter, the average doctor was conducting thirty-four surgery consultations and sixteen home visits per day.

During the early years of the NHS, data on workload in general practice came from the Annual Survey of Sickness based on home interviews with patients. A random sample of 3,000 people over the age of 16 years was inter-viewed, and their sickness experience in the preceding three months was recorded. This was reviewed by Logan and Brook.[3] Based on these data, it was estimated that the average consultation rate per person per year rose from 4.8 in 1947 to 5.6 in 1950. Consultation rates varied widely in different parts of the country, from 4.4 per patient per year in East Anglia to 7.8 in Wales. Stephen Taylor, in a survey of general practice in 1953, found that consulta-tion rates varied from 3.5 to 9.6 per patient per year and that the average size of registered list was 2,500, varying from 1,500 to 3,600.[4] He estimated that

[1] A. Bradford Hill, Presidential Address, *Journal of the Royal Statistical Society*, 114 (1951), 1–34.
[2] J. Pemberton, 'Illness in General Practice', *British Medical Journal* (1949), i. 306–8.
[3] W. Logan and E. Brook, *The Survey of Sickness 1943–1952* (Studies of Medical and Population Subjects, 12; London: HMSO, 1957).
[4] S. Taylor, *Good General Practice* (London, 1954), 77–81.

home visits per day per doctor could vary from 12 to 30 and surgery consultations from 15 to 50 per day.

There can be little doubt that in the early days of the NHS the workload of general practitioners was substantial. Evidence suggests that a decade later demands had fallen, although it is always difficult to be sure that data recorded at different times can be reliably compared. The first National Morbidity Study, conducted in 1956, recorded an average consultation rate of 3.8 consultations per patient per year, and home visits accounted for about 25 per cent of these consultations.[5] With average list sizes in the region of 2,500, this still represented a heavy workload. A striking feature of consultations at that time was their short duration, in some cases averaging less than five minutes per patient.

This evidence supports the extensive anecdotal reports of excessive demands on general practitioners in the first decade of the NHS. But what about the quality of care delivered? Three reports in the early 1950s present conflicting evidence. Collings, in 1950, carried out a survey of general practice, which is described in detail in Chapter 4.[6] He concluded that 'The overall state of general practice in England is bad and still deteriorating. Some working conditions are bad enough to require condemnation in the public interest. Inner city practice is at the best unsatisfactory and at the worst a source of public danger.'[7] The most useful recommendation arising from this report was that 'An attempt should be made to define the function of general practice within the National Health Service.' Others had reached a similar conclusion without carrying out a survey. There is no doubt, however, that this report both provoked an immediate angry response from the profession and stimulated research.

In response to this damning report, the BMA launched a survey of general practice carried out by Hadfield,[8] who was an assistant secretary in the Association. He visited a random sample of general practitioners and reported that

17 per cent of GPs were working from good well-equipped premises.
49 per cent had adequate premises.
24 per cent worked from premises lacking essential facilities.
10 per cent had totally unsuitable and inadequate premises.[9]

The report by Stephen Taylor, referred to previously, focused on good general practice and was carried out for educational purposes to highlight what could be achieved within the NHS. In conducting his survey he did, however, have the opportunity to review general practice more widely. He concluded:

---

[5] W. Logan and A. Cushion, *Morbidity Statistics from General Practice* (Studies of Medical and Population Subjects, 14; London: HMSO, 1958).
[6] J. S. Collings, 'General Practice in England Today: A Reconnaissance', *Lancet* (1950), i. 555–85.
[7] Ibid. 563.
[8] S. Hadfield, 'Field Survey of General Practice 1951–52', *British Medical Journal* (1953), ii. 683–706.
[9] Ibid. 700.

About one quarter of general practitioners are very good indeed.
About one half are good, sound and reliable and one would not hesitate to call them
in for one's family.
About one quarter are unsatisfactory with poor equipment and no records.[10]

Perceptions of a young general practitioner, c.1958–1964

I entered general practice in 1957 in a country town in Hertfordshire. I became
the third partner in a practice providing care for 8,500 patients from a converted house in the centre of the town and three branch surgeries in surrounding villages. The only paramedical support was one receptionist. Entry
into practice in the 1950s was difficult, with up to 100 applicants for good partnership vacancies. Interviews for a post always included the doctor's wife and
there were very few female applicants at that time. In many practices the
doctor's wife became an integral part of the practice organization. Partnership
agreements usually offered parity of income with the existing partners in about
twelve years. It was also common for the incoming doctor to be asked to live
over the surgery and answer the doorbell outside working hours. The terms of
employment offered to new partners at the time did not reflect very well on
the profession, but it must be remembered that income was dependent almost
entirely on capitation payments. Competition for patients was intense, and
there were few opportunities to increase income by the increased productivity
which a new partner might provide.

On entering practice, I had two and a half years' experience as a house officer
in medicine, surgery, and obstetrics and three years' experience as a physician
in the Royal Air Force. My vocational training lasted three days, because one
of the partners was in desperate need of a holiday and left a week after my
arrival. The training consisted of instruction on writing prescriptions and
certificates for sickness benefit, and on the location and access to the lock-up
surgeries. A list of specialists to whom patients should or should not be referred
was also provided.

The early weeks and months in the consulting room were confused and I
was filled with feelings of guilt. The knowledge and skills acquired in hospital just did not seem relevant to many of the problems presented, and when a
proper 'hospital-type' patient presented, there was never time to carry out the
type of examination which I had learnt in house-officer posts. I was not aware
of the political battles over general practice at the time, but was simply
conscious of my own inadequacies and the constant demand for care. Even in
1957, forty surgery consultations and twenty home visits in a day in the winter
were not uncommon. The high number of home visits was not due simply to
irresponsibility among the patients, although, like the doctors, they had never

---

[10] Taylor, *Good General Practice* (London, 1954), 8.

been taught how to use the NHS. A major factor was that few possessed tele-phones or cars. Domiciliary maternity care, which was common in general practice at the time, although extremely satisfying in human terms, was very demanding, and my practice was then delivering about fifty patients each year in the home.

General practitioners responded to this situation in different ways. They could become desperate and depressed at the demands being made on them, which differed so much from their expectations and training. They complained 'this is not the medicine for which I was trained'. They were, of course, right, but they assumed that it was the medicine which was wrong and failed to realize that it was the training which was at fault. Many emigrated to Australia, Canada, or the USA, where the terms and conditions of service were more attractive. Others became overwhelmed, demoralized, and accepted that they were functioning as second-class doctors, a label which had been applied to them. Others accepted the challenge and tried to do something about their problems.

In 1952 the College of General Practitioners was established by a group of doctors who had responded to the challenge of providing good general-practitioner care.

The College encouraged energetic and able general practitioners to get together and not only counter the pervading gloom, but also challenge spe-cialist opposition, which was not just neutral to general practice but actively hostile. It set up faculties in local areas, which became centres for change. They were largely apolitical and concerned with education, research, and improving patient care. I had the good fortune to join the Northern Home Counties faculty in 1959. Here I met a number of angry young doctors who were trying to analyse and resolve the problems they were encountering in their practices. These doctors included John Horder, subsequently to become President of the College, Basil Slater, subsequently College Secretary, Marshall Marinker, Paul Freeling, John and Valerie Graves, and Tom McKane, all of whom became household names in academic general practice in later years.

This was indeed an exciting time to enter general practice. The terms and conditions of service precluded any radical initiatives to improve the service, but a spirit of enquiry was abroad and early research into the content of general practice was beginning to provide facts on the basis of which general-practitioner care could be developed.

The problems of delivering primary care as revealed by careful analysis were formidable. It was apparent that many of the tasks undertaken by doctors could be equally well carried out by nurses, secretaries, or receptionists. However, there were no financial incentives for doctors to employ ancillary staff to under-take these tasks. In fact, they could do so only at their own expense. This was indeed one of the most perverse incentives of all time. District nurses, health visitors, and midwives were employed by the local authorities and were answer-able to the Medical Officer of Health and not to the general practitioners whose patients they were treating. Practice premises often consisted of a room in the doctor's home or a converted shop or private house. Many premises, as reported in the surveys described, were inadequate to provide primary care to the whole population free at the time of demand, but there were no financial resources to develop new ones. In the cities devastated by bombing, buildings and land were expensive and difficult to acquire. The health-centre building programme which had been promised in the first enthusiasm at the inauguration of the NHS resulted in only ten centres being completed in the first decade.

The problems of staffing and facilities represented just one aspect of the challenges faced by general practitioners in the 1950s. Many clinical problems coexisted. Pulmonary tuberculosis was still taking young lives, poliomyelitis was a constant anxiety in the summer months. There was no effective treatment for hypertension, schizophrenia, asthma, or depression, and the management of peptic ulcer was bedrest, alkali, and very often surgery. The management of heart failure depended on digitalis and painful injections of mersalyl, and rheumatic heart disease was still responsible for many being crippled by cardiac failure.

Obstetric care was still largely in the hands of general practitioners and midwives, partly from tradition, but also because there were not enough obstetric beds in the hospitals to cope with the post-war baby boom. Most primigravidae expected to have normal deliveries and had home births. Toxaemia of pregnancy was, however, still a common problem and eclampsia a source of anxiety.

In hospital practice, doctors had become accustomed to use X-rays and laboratory tests to help resolve clinical problems. In many areas of the country, particularly in the immediate vicinity of teaching hospitals, these facilities were denied to general practitioners, because the specialists were not convinced that they would use them responsibly, or be capable of interpreting the results. It was not surprising that in the 1950s there were many angry general practitioners, expected to undertake an excessive workload and deprived of adequate resources in order to fulfil a role which had not been properly defined and for which they had not been trained.

The turning point, c.1965–1967

In the late 1950s, and early 1960s, many studies had been reported about the content of the work of the general practitioner. Important contributions to this literature included the first National Morbidity Study in General Practice, already referred to. John Fry, a general practitioner in Beckenham, led the field in personally undertaking research into the work carried out in general practice.[11] Richard Scott, the first Professor of General Practice in the

[11] J. Fry, 'Five Years in General Practice: A Study in Simple Epidemiology', *British Medical Journal* (1957), ii. 1453–7.

world, made invaluable contributions to systematic enquiry and analysis.[12] Donald Crombie and Robin Pinsent set up the College research unit in Birmingham, and Ian Watson and Hope Simpson made important contributions to infectious-disease epidemiology. Keith Hodgkin's meticulous collection of data about illness in general practice compared with hospital practice was published in 1963, under the title *Towards Earlier Diagnosis*.[13] These were among the most outstanding, but there were many other reports of systematic research undertaken by individual general practitioners throughout the country.

In 1947 the BMA curriculum committee, under the chairmanship of Professor Henry Cohen, had reviewed medical education. It had concluded for the first time that the purpose of undergraduate medical education should be to produce not merely a competent general practitioner but a 'basic doctor' who, before entering general practice, would undertake appropriate postgraduate training. In 1950 the committee was reconvened to consider how to implement its earlier conclusions. It recommended that all doctors should undertake a one-year residency programme prior to registration by the General Medical Council (GMC) and that in future general practitioners should undertake a further three years of postgraduate vocational training. The former recommendation was incorporated in the Medical Act of 1950, but it was to be two decades later before compulsory vocational training was introduced. These educational developments are described in detail in Chapter 8. In 1961 the Standing Medical Advisory Committee of the Central Health Services Council set up a special subcommittee to advise on the future field of work of the general practitioner. This was chaired by Annis Gillie and reported in 1963 (The Gillie Report).[14] It described general practice as a 'cottage industry', pointing out many of the features described in the preceding paragraphs of this chapter. In response, the government set up a working party headed by Sir Bruce Fraser to review all aspects of general practice except remuneration. As this working party began its discussions, the Review Body appointed to report on the remuneration of general practitioners produced a report which greatly angered the profession and the BMA. As a result the BMA invited all general practitioners to submit signed resignations from the NHS to the British Medical Guild, set up some years earlier for this specific purpose. With this, the majority of general practitioners complied.

Into this political cauldron stepped Kenneth Robinson as Minister of Health. He was described by John Horder in an obituary as follows: 'Kenneth brought to this crisis a mind that was well prepared and the calmness, consideration and personality which we all have known . . . In James Cameron and his colleagues from the British Medical Association with whom he conducted

---

[12] R. Scott, J. Anderson, and A. Cartwright, 'Just What the Doctor Ordered: An Analysis of Treatment in General Practice', *British Medical Journal* (1960), ii. 293–9.

[13] K. Hodgkin, *Towards Earlier Diagnosis* (Edinburgh, 1963).

[14] Central Health Services Council, Standing Medical Advisory Committee, *The Field of Work of the Family Doctor: Report of the Sub-Committee* (The Gillie Report; London: HMSO, 1963).

negotiations, he met the same positive qualities.'[15] He told them they were pushing at an open door. Negotiations led quickly to agreement on a series of changes in the terms of service for general practitioners, proposed by the BMA, and known as the Family Doctor Charter of 1966.

The Charter, based on the work of the Gillie Report and the Fraser working party, produced major changes in the way in which practice premises could be improved, ancillary staff remunerated, and vocational training introduced. Most importantly, the Treasury provided new money for these developments.

I felt it was a great pleasure and privilege to work in general practice during the decade following the Charter. So many of the hopes and ambitions, particularly of young general practitioners, had been frustrated by the terms and conditions of employment. Suddenly they were able to improve their working conditions, to employ secretaries to type their letters, receptionists to organize appointment systems, and practice nurses to undertake delegated tasks in the surgery. As a result morale recovered and general practitioners began to feel they were respected by both patients and most hospital specialists. Academic departments of general practice were established in a number of universities and medical schools (see Chapter 7), and significant research began to explore in more detail the role of the general practitioner and the knowledge, skills, and attitudes needed by those who aspired to this career (see Chapter 6).

A major problem faced by general practitioners was that they had been trained in medicine in hospital settings. Important new research was concerned with interpreting symptoms presenting at the primary- as opposed to the secondary-care level—in terms of the probability of disease and appropriate management. This was described in the first edition of my book *The Art of General Practice*, published in 1965 and developed in subsequent editions.[16] Hodgkin's book *Towards Earlier Diagnosis* and much of the research by John Fry focused on the same issue.[17] This was later developed by Wright and McAdam in their seminal work *Clinical Thinking and Practice*,[18] and by Ian McWhinney.[19] The term 'problem-solving' replaced the term 'diagnosis' in some primary-care situations. Incorporation of nurses, social workers, and health visitors in the primary-care team was being explored in this decade and the effects of a team approach to primary care was investigated.

---

[15] J. Horder, 'An Important Episode', *Journal of the Royal College of Physicians*, 31 (1997), 206.

[16] D. Morrell, *The Art of General Practice* (Edinburgh, 1965). This went to four editions, the fourth published by OUP in 1991. They reflect the evolution of the 'Art' over a period of twenty-five years.

[17] J. Fry, *Common Diseases: Their Nature, Incidence and Care* (Lancaster, 1973). The 5th edition was published by Kluwer Academic Publications in 1993. These editions summarize much of Fry's research over a period of thirty years.

[18] J. Wright and I. McAdam, *Clinical Thinking and Practice* (Edinburgh, 1979).

[19] I. McWhinney, 'Problem Solving and Decision Making in Family Practice', *Canadian Family Physician*, 25 (1979), 1473–7.

Exciting developments in clinical care also occurred apace at this time. These included the prevention of poliomyelitis and the effective prevention and treatment of tuberculosis. Drugs were introduced which reduced raised blood pressure and injectable phenothiazines facilitated the control of schizophrenia. The role of steroids in the management of asthma and eczema was investigated. The introduction of oral contraceptives, oral diuretics, and oral hypoglycaemic drugs extended the doctor's pharmaceutical resources. Developments in reconstructive orthopaedic, cardiac, and vascular surgery provided new challenges in decisions about referral to specialists.

Years of growth, c.1968–1977

All these organizational and clinical advances were very exciting, but it soon became clear that, if full advantage was to be taken of them, a period of vocational training, as described and advocated a decade earlier by the Cohen Committee, would be essential for new entrants to general practice. Experiments in vocational training for general practice, combining hospital and practice appointments, had commenced as far back as 1952 in Inverness and later developed in Winchester through the efforts of George Swift, and in Ipswich, Canterbury, and other centres. As these courses were developed, it became apparent that many of the skills of particular importance to general practitioners, such as communication skills, could not be taught by traditional methods. Led by the now Royal College of General Practitioners, and the new academic departments, a great deal of research was devoted to exploring new teaching methods, and general practitioners became widely accepted as leaders in this academic field. Even before vocational training was established, it was argued that some form of assessment and recognition of the special knowledge and skills required by general practitioners should be expected of doctors seeking to become members of the Royal College. This caused some resentment among general practitioners, who felt that the College was becoming too élitist. Following much debate and finally a vote of College members, an examination was introduced.

In its early days predictably the examination was imperfect, but a great deal of effort was devoted to devising one which would be a fair test of the special knowledge and skills required to practise this branch of medicine. The task was greatly facilitated by the publication of a College document entitled *The Future General Practitioner* in 1972.[20] This spelt out clearly the objectives of vocational training, and clarified the content of an examination.

The original examination consisted of a multiple-choice question paper to test knowledge. Problem-solving was tested by a modified essay question in which the candidate was presented with a series of clinical problems. In the

---

[20] RCGP, *The Future General Practitioner: Learning and Teaching* (London: RCGP, 1972).

early days a traditional essay question was included, but it was later abandoned. The oral examination included the presentation of a practice diary, describing the candidate's practice and the content of one surgery session, about which the candidate was questioned. The final part of the oral consisted of the exploration of clinical problems. As one of the first examiners, I found it interesting to observe how the examination developed and the enormous commitment of those involved. Examiners' meetings and examiners' weekend retreats were held and the content of the examination and the behaviour of the examiners constantly reviewed. In the early days, mock oral examinations were videotaped and the examiners taking part exposed themselves to the criticism of their peers. It could be a traumatic experience for them and was at the time quite unique in terms of quality control of medical examinations.

During the 1970s many advances were made in practice organization. The attachment of local-authority nurses and health visitors to general practices was first reported by Swift and McDougall in 1964,[21] and the advantages to both the nurses and the doctors of such attachments was demonstrated by Lisbeth Hockey, in a publication entitled *Feeling the Pulse*.[22] These experiments were replicated widely in the next decade. The introduction of appointment systems in general practice was resisted by some doctors and some patients, as limiting access to care. Research, however, by Bevan and Draper revealed that they reduced waiting time for patients and produced better-organized surgery sessions for doctors.[23] It was also demonstrated that they led to a redistribution of care from care led by acute demand to more care for the chronic sick and aged.[24] By the end of the decade, more than one half of all practices were seeing most patients by appointment.

The role of the practice nurse was also being investigated at this time. In many practices this was at first restricted to delegated care, but it very soon became apparent that patients valued direct access to the nurse, when they, the patients, considered this appropriate. A major constraint on general practitioners in the early days of the service was the design of the records system originating from the time of Lloyd George and known as the Lloyd George envelope. This was, in fact, the property of the Secretary of State for Health, and, as patients moved from one practice to another, the doctor was obliged to ensure that this envelope went with them. Over time the envelope bulged with records and split at the edges. A number of entrepreneurs, at their own expense, replaced these archaic envelopes with A4-sized records. These were demonstrated to offer considerable benefits,[25] but government resisted all demands to make them universally available.

[21] G. Swift and I. McDougall, 'The Family Doctors and the Family Nurse', *British Medical Journal* (1964), i. 1697–9.

[22] L. Hockey, *Feeling the Pulse* (London, 1966).

[23] H. Bevan and G. Draper, *Appointment Systems in General Practice* (Oxford, 1967).

[24] D. Morrell and H. Kasap, 'The Effects of an Appointment System on Demand for Medical Care', *International Journal of Epidemiology*, 1 (1972), 143–51.

[25] L. Zander, S. Beresford, and P. Thomas, 'Medical Records in General Practice', *Journal of the Royal College of General Practitioners*, Occasional Paper 5 (1978).

The extensive research in primary care which took place at this time was meticulously documented by Donald Hicks, in his book entitled *Primary Health Care*.[26] Trained as a chemical engineer, and later developing an operational research group, he was commissioned by the Department of Health to write a review of the primary-health-care services in the UK. Published in 1976, and containing 430 references, it provides a unique guide to research in primary care at that time.

Perhaps the most important development during these years of growth was the disappearance of the spirit of competition for patients between general practitioners and its replacement by a spirit of cooperation. This led to the development of rota systems between practices to cover out-of-hours work, and close cooperation in education and training.

Advances in the organization of general practice were unfortunately not uniform throughout the profession. There were areas, particularly in the inner cities, where many single-handed doctors, working from very inadequate premises, were unable to develop a primary-care team, simply owing to lack of suitable accommodation. There were many appointments to single-handed vacancies in the inner cities of doctors, trained in totally different medical cultures, who did not fully embrace the new concepts of primary care in the UK and were inadequately supported. There were also doctors with NHS lists of patients who devoted a significant amount of their time to private medicine, usually working as industrial medical advisers, and who for many hours each day were not available to their patients. As previously described, in the early years of the NHS general practitioners were exposed to an enormous workload and were not trained to undertake the tasks demanded of them. Some of them, particularly in the inner cities, were worn down by their working conditions. They often had no rota systems for out-of-hours care and no holidays. They became dejected and demoralized. They could not make time to stand back and evaluate their problems and possible solutions. They simply survived and the care they provided was suboptimal. For all these reasons some practices became an embarrassment to the profession, because most general practitioners had accepted the new discipline of general practice and left them behind. They became an excuse for a government in subsequent years to introduce a rigid system of accountability in general practice which had disastrous consequences.

Many of these doctors worked in the vicinity of the teaching hospitals and took advantage of the easy access to the casualty departments to solve their clinical problems, as had been the practice before general practice was available to the whole population. Some of these referrals were judged to be inappropriate and these were used by consultants and registrars in the teaching hospitals to demonstrate to their students the inadequacies of general practitioners. This led to widespread denigration of general practice in the teaching hospitals. It took some years to convince the hospital staff, who had no

---

[26] D. Hicks, *Primary Health Care* (London, 1976).

appreciation of the problems of providing primary medical care, that the responsibility for deficiencies in the quality of care provided lay largely with the medical schools which had trained the doctors and the lack of resources, both service and educational, which they provided for the general practitioners in their catchment areas. A major influence in bringing about this change was the increasing enthusiasm of students and house officers for careers in general practice.

During this decade advances continued in medical science. In ophthalmology improved management of cataract, glaucoma, retinal detachment, and diabetic retinopathy occurred. Reconstructive orthopaedic surgery developed apace, hip replacements being followed by knee replacements and the reconstruction of small joints in rheumatoid arthritis. Arterial surgery pioneered in the 1950s now became commonplace, and early diagnosis by the general practitioner of such conditions as coronary artery disease, aortic aneurysm, and peripheral vascular disease were rewarded by advances in management and improved prognosis. At the same time, gastric surgery declined, to be replaced by drugs effective in the management of peptic ulcer. Advances in the understanding of immune disorders improved not only the management of these conditions but also the outcome of transplant surgery. Cancer, despite advances in surgery, radiotherapy, and chemotherapy, continued to present major problems in management to general practitioners, and one of the great advances in the care of patients with terminal illness came from research carried out in the hospice movement. This is described in detail in Chapter 4.

At a practice level, new technology made it possible for diabetics to monitor their own blood glucose levels and for asthmatics to monitor their peak expiratory flow rate. Simple 'stick' tests became available for identifying abnormal constituents in the urine. Many hospitals offered facilities for measuring the blood levels of drugs such as phenytoin, phenobarbitone, and lithium, which helped in the management of epilepsy and manic depressive disorders.

The treatment of many diseases, however, became more complex with the advent of a multiplicity of new drugs for the management of hypertension, ischaemic heart disease, asthma, Parkinson's disease, migraine, and psoriasis, to mention just a few examples. General practitioners needed to assess the cost, benefits, and side effects of a wide variety of drugs all claiming to offer some unique advantage. At the same time they had the satisfaction of being able to manage an ever wider range of disorders.

The happy years, c.1978–1987

The late 1970s and early 1980s were perhaps some of the happiest years for general practitioners this century. They understood their role and research and education had helped them to solve many of the clinical and organizational problems presented to them. Many practised from purpose-built premises with teams of other primary-care professionals.

Research during this decade focused on such issues as the doctor–patient relationship and the development of skills in the consultation. Many years earlier, Balint had drawn attention to the importance of this subject and made a great impression on general practice in the 1950s.[27] Stott and Davis described the exceptional potential of the consultation.[28] Others, such as Byrne and Long and Pendleton explored in more detail the dynamics of the consultation.[29] All this information found its way into vocational training, leading to a special emphasis on training in communication skills.

A major constraint, however, was the lack of time available in the average consultation in general practice. This had been a criticism by overseas doctors visiting this country, and many specialists considered that lack of time was responsible for high prescribing and high referral rates in general practice. In an experiment, Morrell and Roland were not able to show a relationship between prescribing and referral rates and the duration of consultations, but demonstrated that better communications and more preventive medicine were practised in longer consultations.[30] This was later confirmed by Howie, who went on to postulate that the ratio of long to short consultations in a practice might be a proxy for quality of care.[31] Continuity of care over a period of time was also regarded as important to the general practitioner's diagnostic and management decisions, and research by Pereira Gray and Hjortdahl appeared to support this contention.[32] Much of this research reinforced the role of the general practitioner as the provider of personal and continuing care for patients in the NHS.

At the same time as the special skills of the general practitioner in the consultation were being explored, there was increasing interest in the potential for greater cooperation between the providers of primary and secondary care. In the early 1970s, obstetric care had been largely taken over by the hospital specialists, and yet the ongoing care of the family rested with the primary-care

[27] M. Balint, *The Doctor, his Patient and the Illness* (London, 1957).

[28] N. Stott and R. Davis, 'The Exceptional Potential for each Primary Care Consultation', *Journal of the Royal College of General Practitioners*, 29 (1979), 201–5.

[29] P. S. Byrne and B. E. L. Long, *Doctors Talking to Patients* (London: HMSO, 1976); D. Pendleton, T. Schofield, P. Tate, and P. Havelock, *The Consultation: An Approach to Learning and Teaching* (Oxford, 1984).

[30] D. Morrell, M. Evans, R. Morris, and M. Roland, 'The Five Minute Consultation: Effect of Time Constraint on Clinical Content and Satisfaction', *British Medical Journal*, 292 (1986), 870–3; M. Roland, J. Bartholomew, M. Courtenay, R. Morris, and D. Morrell, 'The Five Minute Consultation: Effect of Time Constraint on Verbal Communication in the Consultation', *British Medical Journal*, 292 (1986), 874–6.

[31] J. Howie, A. Porter, D. Heaney, and J. Hopton, 'Long to Short Consultation Ratio: A Proxy Measure of Quality of Care for General Practice', *Journal of the Royal College of General Practitioners*, 41 (1991), 48–54.

[32] D. Pereira Gray, 'The Key to Personal Care', *Journal of the Royal College of General Practitioners*, 29 (1979), 666–8; P. Hjortdahl, 'Continuity of Care: General Practitioners' Knowledge and Sense of Responsibility to their Patients', *Family Practice*, 1 (1992), 3–7.

team. There was a lot of criticism of hospital antenatal clinics and the lack of continuity in the provision of post-natal care. Experiments in community-based antenatal care with delivery in hospital demonstrated considerable advantages,[33] and this practice began to develop in a number of areas. The care of diabetes was another subject which had in the 1970s been taken over by hospitals in many places, and yet the day-to-day care of diabetics was assumed to be the responsibility of the primary-care team. The development of community clinics for the care of diabetes was therefore examined, and the results of general-practice-based or hospital-based diabetic care appeared to be equally good as long as there was close cooperation between generalists and specialists.[34] The advantages to the patients of attending their general practitioner rather than a large hospital clinic were self-evident. Further experiments took place in shared care of patients suffering from asthma and psychiatric disorders. These examples are included here to demonstrate that cooperation between primary and secondary care was being actively pursued, and the results of initiatives to achieve closer cooperation were being measured long before the reforms of the NHS in 1990 and would doubtless have continued to develop irrespective of changes introduced in the Act of 1990. The big difference was that the 1980s experiments developed from the grass roots, were properly monitored, and were not imposed from above.

Prevention and health education were activities which began seriously to concern general practitioners at the cutting edge of their branch of medicine at this time. The simultaneous evolution of the primary-care team based on group general practice facilitated many developments. Most practices ran their own well-baby clinics, and these usually included immunization procedures. Developmental tests for infants were at this time a constant source of controversy as some were very time-consuming and of uncertain predictive value. The greatest value of these clinics was seen by many as providing an opportunity for new parents to spend some time with different members of the primary-care team and explore their problems and anxieties. Special clinics were also commonly provided for cervical cytology and family planning. There was little research evidence at this time of the benefits of special clinics to prevent smoking or obesity. There was no evidence for the benefits of multiphasic screening for healthy adults.[35]

Most doctors practised what they described as opportunistic prevention and health education. This entailed taking advantage of occasions presented in the consultation to undertake preventive actions or to provide advice. There was good evidence that specific advice about smoking in this situation, with proper

[33] L. Zander, M. Watson, R. Taylor, and D. Morrell, 'Integration of General Practitioner and Specialist Ante-Natal Care', *Journal of the Royal College of General Practitioners*, 22 (1978), 455–8.
[34] B. Singh, M. Holland, and P. Thorn, 'Metabolic Control of Diabetes in General Practice Clinics: Comparison with a Hospital Clinic', *British Medical Journal*, 289 (1984), 726–30.
[35] W. Holland and S. Stewart, *Screening in Health Care* (London, 1990), 115.

follow-up, could alter behaviour,[36] and some evidence that advice about diet could lead to weight reduction in patients suffering from ischaemic heart disease and osteoarthritis. It was generally agreed that the measurement of blood pressure every five years in all adults was useful in identifying hypertension at an early stage. It was argued that opportunistic prevention could involve those unlikely to attend routine screening clinics, which tend to attract unduly the worried well.[37] The weakness of depending on this approach was that it called for more time in the consultation, and for the doctors' judgement of the best use of their time.

During this period the medical schools were becoming increasingly aware of the importance of general practice in medical education. By then every university and medical school with the exception of Oxford and Cambridge had appointed a professor of general practice. In many, students were introduced to general practice from their earliest years, and in all schools there were clinical clerkships in general practice. Members of academic departments of general practice were increasingly involved in curriculum-planning and many chaired the education committees in their schools. It became clear that the educational skills of academics in general practice, acquired in the early 1970s, were valued by their schools and other departments, even if this was not reflected in funding.

The decade was characterized by high morale in general practice, recruitment of high-quality graduates, and large numbers of applicants for vocational training courses. It saw the increasing influence of general practice in medical education, with the appointment of general practitioners as sub-deans and deans of medical schools and to such prestigious bodies as the medical sub-committee of the University Grants Committee and the Medical Research Council. By the end of the decade, however, there were clouds on the horizon which were to burst with considerable ferocity in the next few years.

The National Health Service reforms, c.1988–1996

The thinking behind the NHS reforms was complex. There was undoubtedly anxiety about the increasing cost of the NHS due to a combination of technological and pharmaceutical advances in medical care and demographic changes in the population. Doubts were expressed as to whether the country could continue to provide health care according to need and free at the time of delivery to the entire population and paid for out of general taxation. There was an ideological conviction in government that market forces might be as

[36] M. Russell, C. Wilson, C. Taylor, and C. Baker, 'Effect of General Practitioner Advice against Smoking', *British Medical Journal*, 292 (1979), 231–5.

[37] R. Pill, T. Flench, K. Harding, and N. Stott, 'Invitation to Attend a Health Check in a General Practice Setting: Comparison of Attenders and Non-Attenders', *Journal of the Royal College of General Practitioners*, 38 (1988), 53–6.

relevant to demand for health care as to demand for any other commodity, and that, if only they were allowed to operate in medicine, the care provided would be more cost effective. The government appeared to distrust the professions and to question their ability to set their own standards and monitor their performance. This was not limited to medicine, but exhibited in due course to teachers at all levels, the police, and the legal profession. It was questionable whether all the issues of self-governing professions were properly thought through by the politicians, and they were certainly not debated soberly within the medical profession. It was accused of protectionism, and the reforms were forced through uncompromisingly by a government with a comfortable parliamentary majority.

The decision to reintroduce the market-place philosophies and practices into the NHS resulted in the purchaser/provider split, with the creation of Hospital and Community Health Service Trusts from which the health authorities and later the general practitioners purchased services. The Trusts competed with each other for customers. This programme, even when it appeared to health professionals to be misconceived, because health care could not be regarded as a commodity like cars, shoes, or baked beans, seemed to satisfy the ideological philosophy of the reformers.

The reforms in general practice were even less easy to understand. The introduction of Family Health Service Authorities (FHSAs), with a strategic role in planning primary care, seemed logical. Up to that time little strategic planning had seemed possible in this field. The powers given to these authorities to require general practitioners to account for individual services which had previously been accepted as part of their contract reflected the government's distrust of self-governing professionals. They led, however, to a burgeoning bureaucracy to police the provision of health care and increased demands on general practitioners in terms of the paperwork to be carried out.

Competition for patients among general practitioners, ideologically conceived of as a way to improve primary care, was encouraged by attaching a greater proportion of income to capitation payments. To those with experience of the 1960s there seemed no evidence that competition had improved the quality of care at that time, and in the 1980s most general practitioners, in the interests of quality of their services, were demanding smaller lists of registered patients.

In the reformed contracts general practitioners were expected to provide and account for a variety of new services. These included prescribed medical examinations at the time of registering new patients, screening of patients who had not consulted in the last three years, and a variety of health-education clinics, despite the fact that none of these new initiatives had been shown by research to improve health.[38] General practitioners were expected to achieve certain

---

[38] D. Morrell, 'Role of Research in Development of Organisation and Structure of General Practice', *British Medical Journal*, 309 (1991), 1313–16.

targets in terms of the number of cervical smears taken or immunizations performed, with no reference to the type of population for whom they were providing care, or the validity of the data upon which their performance would be judged.

Late on the scene of the 1990 reforms came 'budget-holding' for general practitioners. Limited as an option at first to larger practices, it was later offered to smaller ones too. This gave general practitioners the opportunity of accepting budgets to purchase specialist medical care for their patients from either NHS or private sources. At first the budgets were designed to pay for additional practice staff, prescribing, and non-acute hospital referrals. Later, it was, as an experiment, offered to selected practices to cover all forms of care. Budget-holding gave doctors the opportunity to determine their own priorities in the care they purchased for their patients, and some interesting experiments have emerged. For patients of those practices not holding budgets, non-acute hospital care and community care were purchased by the health authorities. Unfortunately, in some situations the budgets of the health authorities were not as robust as those of fundholding general practices, and there were occasions when patients of fundholders received priority in treatment.

The 1990 reforms in the NHS coincided with many changes in the values of society. In many fields this led to a more materialistic society with increasing litigation. The Patient's Charter, introduced in 1992, encouraged a consumerist approach in medical care. Patient demands for care from general practitioners, particularly out of normal working hours, increased. At the same time, cultural expectations were taking place in the profession itself. Doctors no longer expected medicine to consume their whole life at the expense of the family and leisure activities which appeared to be enjoyed by contemporaries in other walks of life. The old stereotyped pattern of a male general practitioner and wife committing their lives to a defined community and deriving their satisfaction from fulfilling this role no longer remotely applied. Increasing numbers of women were entering general practice and they needed space to develop not just their medical, but also their maternal careers. Many of them were married to partners also pursuing professional careers, and pressure on the family became intense. Pressure on men to be different kinds of husbands and fathers was also occurring. Violence in the community and even in the surgery presented new problems, particularly for those undertaking out-of-hours care in inner cities. There were many reports about stress in the profession, sometimes accompanied by greater recourse to drugs and alcohol. It is difficult to understand why the stresses in general practice which were formidable in the 1950s did not lead to similar problems or cries of distress. Doubtless this will provide a fruitful source for research for sociologists and psychologists. There is, however, no doubt that one of the special changes affecting general practice has been that doctors, so often described as independent contractors, have, between 1990 and 1995, had diminishing control of their lives and professional activities. They have become constrained by detailed accountability for all their actions, whether or not they believed these contributed to health, and economic issues have increasingly determined their practice plans. The general practitioner was at one time free to provide an excellent or a second-rate service. Fortunately most opted for the former. The adoption of a standard predetermined level of care limits initiative and freedom, although it may ensure basic levels of care.

The first half of the 1990s in the NHS witnessed unremitting change which brought with it insecurity and confusion about the role of the general practitioner in society. It was indeed feared that the pace and extent of the reforms threatened the core values of the medical profession. The BMA in 1994 ran a two-day meeting of all the Presidents of the Royal Medical Colleges, the undergraduate and postgraduate deans, and officers of the Association to debate this issue.[39] At this unprecedented gathering of senior doctors from all specialities, it was agreed that the patient–doctor relationship should be a partnership of mutual trust, with the personal consultation remaining the bedrock of medical practice. It was reaffirmed that the profession's ancient values distilled over time remained a vital asset. These values were described as commitment, integrity, confidentiality, caring, competence, responsibility, compassion, spirit of enquiry, and advocacy. There was no doubt that the meeting considered that these were being challenged by many of the new developments in the NHS. It was, however, concluded that, if these ancient virtues could be retained by the profession and shared with patients, managers, and other health professionals, it could lead to increased understanding and cooperation within the service and a resurgence of high morale.

Envoi

Over a period of forty years, the role of the general practitioner has changed dramatically as a result of changes in the patterns of illness in the community, advances in therapeutics and medical technology, and, perhaps most importantly, a better understanding of the knowledge and skills required by general practitioners to carry out their work. It is perhaps time to review this role. In the 1970s and 1980s this was widely accepted as providing accessible primary care; solving the problems presented by their patients usually as symptoms of illness; providing continuity of care often over a period of years; and providing appropriate preventive care. Of all these, the provision of personal, primary, and continuing care to patients in the context of an ongoing doctor–patient relationship was always regarded as an essential characteristic of general practice in the UK. The special skills needed to fulfil this role were agreed to be communicating with patients, understanding the physical, psy-

---

[39] Editorial, *British Medical Journal*, 309 (1994), 1247–8.

chological, and social factors which can lead to symptoms of illness and disease, and acquiring the knowledge and experience necessary to solve problems and initiate appropriate management. These encapsulate the characteristics of the doctors vocationally trained for general practice from the mid-1970s to the mid-1990s. Are they still relevant today?

Looking back to the 1950s, a crisis occurred because the role of general practitioners was undefined and it appeared that all important clinical decisions were made by specialists. I have tried to trace how these general practitioners evolved in the ensuing years. In the crisis in general practice in the 1990s, the clinical role of doctors and their relationships with their patients have been threatened by the increasing demands of business management, bureaucratic accountability, and information overload.

In 1960 James Spence, in a book entitled *The Purpose and Practice of Medicine*, wrote, 'The essential unit of medical practice is the occasion when, in the intimacy of the consulting room or the sick room, a person who is ill or believes himself to be ill, seeks advice from a doctor whom he trusts. This is a consultation and all else in medicine derives from it'.[40] This is perhaps the vision which attracted so many young doctors to general practice in the 1970s and 1980s. It is a memory which the elderly doctors look back on with nostalgia. I believe that it is still central to the work of the general practitioner, but can it survive the winds of change which are destabilizing general practice close to the end of the twentieth century?

[40] J. Spence, *The Purpose and Practice of Medicine* (Oxford, 1960), 276.

1

The Politics of General Practice

CHARLES WEBSTER

This chapter will outline the course of central government intervention respecting general medical practice and primary health care since the beginning of the NHS. Limitations of space naturally preclude comprehensive coverage. For instance, policy developments connected with pay negotiations will be considered only where these were particularly important.[1] Nevertheless, it is hoped to supply a broader political context for specific topics discussed in greater depth in other contributions to this volume. It is too soon to analyse historically the phase of dramatic change taking place in the NHS since 1991, but some preliminary observations will be offered concerning the longer-term perspective for these events.

Architects of the National Health Service

Although general medical practice was hardly the leading edge of the early NHS, this was not the design of its architects. Evidence regarding wartime preparations for a comprehensive health service, or more distant plans dating from the inter-war period, confirm the importance attached to the revival of general medical practice, which was accorded a central place in all the rival schemes for a future health service. One of the most ambitious plans emerged as long ago as 1920, when the celebrated Dawson Report granted general practitioners a key role in Dawson's newly invented 'primary health centres'.[2] The Dawson Report thereby gave currency to the health centre, and it also introduced the germ of the primary/secondary/tertiary care distinction. The health centre and the concept of primary care were destined to become central to thinking about general practice.

During the Second World War plans for a new comprehensive health service again gave primacy to general medical practice and revisited the idea of the health centre. By this date, enterprises such as the Peckham Health Centre,

---

[1] Remuneration issues are considered by the present author in greater detail in the two volumes of the official history of the NHS, *The Health Services since the War*, i. *Problems of Health Care: The National Health Service before 1957* (London: HMSO, 1988); ii. *Government and Health Care: The British National Health Service 1958–1979* (London: The Stationery Office, 1996).

[2] Consultative Council on Medical and Allied Services, *Interim Report on the Future Provision of Medical and Allied Services*, Cmd. 693 (The Dawson Report; London: HMSO, 1920).

and the new concept of Social Medicine, endowed the health centre with even greater potentialities than were evident to Dawson. However, the idea of general practitioners working collaboratively, using the superior resources supplied by publicly provided health centres, became irrevocably associated with the proposal for their employment as full-time salaried officers, thereby subservient to Medical Officers of Health of local authorities. Given the attachment of general practitioners to their status as independent contractors, and their history of bad relations with Medical Officers of Health and local government agencies, the government's proposals for the development of general practice became one of the most bitterly contested aspects of policy regarding the new health service.

By 1945 many concessions to the profession had been granted by the Coalition health ministers, but it was anticipated that the new Labour Government would return to an uncompromising line. Indeed, Labour's initial scheme for the health service envisaged maximization of the salary component, although in the course of lengthy negotiations with the profession this idea was gradually abandoned. With shrewd political judgement, Aneurin Bevan, the new Minister of Health, accepted that it was unrealistic to impose a unified administration on the NHS. The huge hospital sector was nationalized under a regional system of administration. General medical practitioners, dentists, pharmacists, and opticians retained their independence as independent contractors, regulated by Executive Councils, which were little more than reincarnations of the Insurance Committees inherited from the NHI system. The third and smallest sector in the new health service comprised the rump of miscellaneous services administered by local government. Important among the powers of local health authorities was provision of health centres, which gave grounds for the suspicion in medical circles that this was the thin end of the wedge to salaried employment of general practitioners. Although in its initial plans for the new health service Labour insisted that health centres would be a key feature, in reality there was no expectation that sufficient cooperation from the medical profession would be forthcoming for this promise to become a reality. Reticence on the part of the medical profession was in fact a relief to the planners, since the new health service was overwhelmed by urgent demands for its services; there were neither building materials nor financial resources available to support large-scale capital projects in either the hospital or primary-care sectors.[3]

Stagnation, 1948–1960

By the date of introduction of the new NHS on 5 July 1948, promises about health centres were being expressed in only the most guarded terms. Granted,

[3] F. Honigsbaum, *Health, Happiness, and Security: The Creation of the National Health Service* (London, 1989), 105–7.

a leaflet delivered to all homes devoted its last paragraph to the proposed health
centres, but only as a distant and vague prospect.[4] When this leaflet was revised
later in 1948, the paragraph about health centres was completely eliminated.[5]
The constructive energies of the Ministry of Health were dedicated to the hospital sector, where the first priority was building up a comprehensive consultant and specialist service. Notwithstanding slender resources, this objective
was secured with remarkable speed and efficiency. But this magnificent
achievement was not without its costs; the regional hospital service absorbed
a steadily increasing share of the human and material resources available to
the NHS; of necessity, the two other arms of the NHS service became treated
as a lesser priority. The dominance of the hospital service added to the
disadvantage already experienced within the field of general practice. Not only
were general practitioners pushed out of hospitals by the new generation of
salaried specialists and consultants, but increasingly the dominant hospital
medical profession looked upon general practitioners as minor functionaries,
suitable for little more than sorting out patients for referral. The positive
strengths of the early NHS therefore exacerbated the already serious problems
of low morale in general practice. As pointed out elsewhere in this volume,
the Collings Report published in 1950 gave credence to the view that the
low quality of service under the 'panel' was not much altered by the arrival of
the NHS.[6]

Health-centre policy, upon which hopes for the revival of general practice
had traditionally rested, reverted to the status of an untried experiment,
and the health departments displayed no enthusiasm for commencing the
experiment. Consequently, in the first ten years of the NHS, only a handful
of health centres were opened. This policy failure perplexed early analysts
of the NHS and it was widely discussed by them. Eckstein's thoughtful
and persuasive discussion of this problem draws attention to the seriousness
of this policy retreat.[7] He concluded that the absence of health centres
and group practices 'must be reckoned as perhaps the greatest failure of the
Service'.[8]

In the first phase of the NHS, despite formulaic expressions of good intentions by Ministers, it is difficult to avoid the conclusion that general medical
practice was treated by the health departments as a receding backwater.
This was due not only to crowding out by other priorities, but also to medico-
political sensitivities peculiar to general practice. A continuous succession
of bruising encounters with the BMA, beginning in 1943 and extended by

---

    [4] Central Office of Information, *The New National Health Service* [1948].
    [5] Central Office of Information, *The National Health Service: Who can Use the National Health
Service?* [1948]. The government's retraction on health centres was confirmed in Circular 3/48, issued
in Feb. 1948.
    [6] J. S. Collings, 'General Practice in England Today: A Reconnaissance', *Lancet* (1950), i. 555–85.
    [7] H. Eckstein, *The English Health Service: Its Origins, Structure and Achievements* (Cambridge, Mass.,
1958), 247–52.
    [8] Ibid. 252.

confrontations over pay, associated with the Danckwerts award in 1952 and the Royal Commission on Doctors' and Dentists' Remuneration in 1956–7, induced an atmosphere of mutual suspicion.[9] Rather than risk provoking further outbreaks of hostilities, the little shell-shocked garrison within the Ministry of Health was inclined to retreat into its bunker and maintain the status quo. The small size of the Whitehall forces concerned with the general-practitioner services is not always appreciated. It was, for instance, pointed out that even in 1961, out of the 2,320 headquarters staff of the Ministry of Health, only fourteen were dedicated to general medical practice. At this date there were five under-secretaries and twenty-four assistant secretaries in the department; of these, one under-secretary and one assistant secretary devoted half their time to general medical practice; they were assisted by one principal and one principal part-time. Division 3, in which all Executive Council and local-authority functions were located, was very much the poor relation with respect to Division 4, the division responsible for hospitals.[10] This slightly understates the support for general practice within the Ministry of Health, since the medical and professional staff were also relevant. However, the Chief Medical Officer and his staff were also heavily engaged with hospital work, and their best efforts were made in this direction.

Further grounds of justification for inaction were provided by administrative precedent. Traditionally the Ministry of Health had been primarily concerned with routine regulation of services provided by autonomous bodies such as local authorities, which fiercely guarded their freedom of action in the use of funds provided by their rate-payers. The same attitude carried over into the NHS with respect to services administered by Executive Councils and local health and welfare authorities. Hence substantial local variations in the provision of service, including striking evidence of inequity, were tolerated as one of the inevitable consequences of the devolved system of health-service administration.

Complete evasion of responsibility for planning was not possible owing to the inevitable attention to terms and conditions of employment on every occasion the profession and the government negotiated over remuneration. As a consequence of the recommendations of the joint working party on distribution following the Danckwerts award of 1952, the maximum list size for a single-handed doctor was reduced from 4,000 to 3,500. Also a small sum was set aside annually from the central pool for loans to support the improvement of group-practice premises. Similarly, following the comprehensive review of pay arrangements conducted by the Royal Commission chaired by Sir Harry Pilkington, further small modifications were introduced, the main being introduction of 'loading' designed to give advantages to doctors with moderate numbers of patients on their lists, some small payments for designated

---

[9] Webster, *The Health Services since the War*, i. 227–32.
[10] L. Pavitt, HC Debates, vol. 644, cols. 278–9, 11 July 1961; Webster, *The Health Services since the War*, ii. app. 2.8.

improvements in practitioner skills, and an addition to the fund supporting the development of group-practice facilities.

Although Danckwerts and Pilkington produced fine tuning of working arrangements, their main effect was conservative. Indeed, the Royal Commission offered authoritative support for the old system and suggested its suitability for the future without essential change. It therefore reinforced a system of rewards that had changed little since it was introduced in 1911. This pay mechanism most benefited large-list doctors who incurred minimum practice expenses and exploited any opportunities for earning additional fees. On account of these perverse incentives, the pay structure was disadvantageous to younger doctors struggling to provide an enlightened quality of service conducted from well-equipped premises.

Given the disinclination for significant constructive intervention on the part of the government, changes in general practice were generated through the haphazard operation of a variety of forces mainly originating from within the profession itself, partly stimulated by frustration owing to lack of initiative and leadership from the Ministry of Health. Ministers turned up at events like the Annual Conference of the Executive Councils Association and delivered statements about the priority they attached to general practice, teamwork, and cooperation. These messages typically echoed policies that constituted the common denominator of planning documents from the Dawson Report onwards. Inevitably, many official reports impinged on general practice, especially notable being those on the cost of the NHS, prescribing practice, the maternity services, and medical staffing structure in the hospital service.[11] These exercises served to underline the need for more active policy leadership from the centre.

Indicative of the sensitivity of its relationship with the BMA, the Ministry of Health tended to remit questions relating to general practice to the central advisory machinery, the relevant committees of which were largely dominated by appointees of the BMA. These committees were slow acting and generally ineffective. Indicative of the importance of the health-centre idea at the outset of the NHS, this constituted the topic selected for the first significant intervention of the Central Health Services Council (CHSC) in the field of primary care. The CHSC health-centre committee was established in December 1948, but its report was not published until April 1951 and then only obscurely as part of the annual report of the CHSC.[12] By this stage, the detailed recommendations of the CHSC committee on organization and design of health

---

[11] *Report of the Committee of Enquiry into the Cost of the National Health Service*, Cmd. 9663 (The Guillebaud Report; London: HMSO, 1956); *Report of the Maternity Services Committee* (The Cranbrook Report; London: HMSO, 1959); *Final Report of the Committee on the Cost of Prescribing* (London: HMSO, 1959); *Report of the Joint Working Party on Medical Staffing Structure in the Hospital Service* (The Platt Report; London: HMSO, 1961).

[12] 'Health Centres', in *Central Health Services Council: Report for 1950* (London: HMSO, 1951), 9–31.

centres was largely irrelevant, since there were no opportunities for such schemes. However, the committee insisted that there was a place for health centres, especially in new housing developments, and it advised against providing accommodation for single-handed practice in such circumstances.[13] The CHSC expressed irritation when the government failed to heed this advice and recommended the provision of conventional surgery accommodation for general practitioners located in housing estates and new towns.[14]

The most relevant intervention of the CHSC in the field of general practice was the *Report of the Committee on General Practice within the National Health Service* published in 1954.[15] This was not a spontaneous initiative by the CHSC and it was a less radical assessment than originally intended. Responding to neglect of primary care by the CHSC, in the spring of 1950 the Labour-affiliated Medical Practitioners' Union (MPU) and the Trades Union Congress (TUC) pressed the government to institute a CHSC investigation into the modernization of general practice. Urgency for this investigation was suggested by the Collings Report. Bevan's officials were unsympathetic, but Bevan insisted on the enquiry being instituted along the lines advocated by the MPU. Reference to the CHSC took the matter outside the control of the Minister. Although the committee contained a small element reflecting the views of the MPU, it was dominated by BMA appointees, and it was cautious about offending BMA interests. The Chairman, Sir Henry Cohen, was relied on by officials to suppress any tendency to radical recommendations.[16] Accordingly the Report, although containing useful information, was largely a sanction for the status quo, offensive neither to the BMA nor to the Ministry of Health. Indeed, the latter feared that 'the main criticism of the report will be that it does not say anything momentous and that it keeps very closely to what is known to be Ministry policy'.[17] Contrary to the aspirations of the MPU and its allies, and in line with official thinking, the Cohen Report pronounced an adverse verdict regarding health centres and concluded that group practice would achieve most of the same objectives. Although pious exhortations concerning cooperation were a prominent feature of the Report, it conveyed only a limited impression of the notion of the general practitioner as the leading figure within the 'domiciliary team', which was a greatly favoured idea within the Ministry. An alternative and superior opportunity to advance the concept of the domiciliary team emerged, and it was grasped with enthusiasm by the Guillebaud Committee, which welcomed 'efforts made in recent years to build up the idea of a "domiciliary team" of local authority workers [home nurses,

---

[13] Ibid., para. 139. See also CHSC(HC)50, 6th mtg, 8 June 1950, Department of Health, 94152/1/1C.

[14] Department of Health, 94151/2/2D.

[15] Central Health Services Council, *Report of the Committee on General Practice within the National Health Service* (The Cohen Report; London: HMSO, 1954).

[16] Department of Health, 94157/1/1.

[17] Ministry of Health minute, 3 May 1954, PRO MH 94157/4/10.

midwives, health visitors, social workers, and home helps] under the clinical leadership of the general practitioner'.[18]

Notwithstanding official encouragement of cooperation between Executive Council and local health-authority services, realization of this objective was impeded by the long legacy of mutual distrust between general practitioners and Medical Officers of Health. The separate administration of the family practitioner and local-authority services was in fact engineered to keep these enemies apart. It was only slowly that traditional animosities subsided. New generations were more open to reasonable suggestions concerning cooperation and generally more constructive in their attitudes. The coincidence of innovative group practices and a less imperious Medical Officer of Health was nevertheless rare. Consequently, even obvious opportunities for cooperation, with respect to the School Health Service, the maternity and child-welfare services, or attachment of local-authority district nurses, health visitors, and midwives to general practices, were confined to a small number of authorities. Given the greater bureaucratic obstacles involved, establishment of a health centre was rendered a virtual impossibility before 1960.

Revitalization, 1960–1974

After a long period of stagnation, more active leadership on the part of the Ministry of Health with respect to the development of general practice became evident during the 1960s. Indeed, this change was dramatic, almost revolutionary. Crucial to the development was the change of leadership within the Ministry that occurred in 1960. Important was the arrival of a new Permanent Secretary, Sir Bruce Fraser, who was recruited from the Treasury; this initiated a phase of better relations between the Ministry of Health and the Treasury. Of decisive importance was the promotion of the experienced George Godber to the office of Chief Medical Officer (CMO). Godber immediately set about introducing an innovative ethos into the division responsible for general practice. This was essential in order to prevent an embarrassing lacuna opening up in medical planning. In 1960 the department obtained approval to launch its ten-year hospital plan. In order to keep this expensive undertaking within reasonable cost limits, it was essential to optimize community and primary care. The two were, of course, inseparably related. Once the hospital plan was near to completion, preparations were made for a ten-year plan for local-authority services. The final part of the planning tripod was general medical practice. A further incentive for a general-practice planning exercise was provided by the committee established by nine leading medical organizations, including the College of General Practitioners, under the chairmanship of Sir Arthur Porritt, to conduct a comprehensive review of the medical ser-

[18] *Report of the Committee of Enquiry into the Cost of the National Health Service*, Cmd. 9663.

vices. The report of this committee was published in November 1962.[19] It was essential for the credibility of the Ministry of Health to have come to its own conclusions on the issues likely to be raised by the Porritt Report.

Godber's influence was exercised through both formal and informal agencies. For instance, a series of informal meetings were convened to discuss improving cooperation between local authorities and general practitioners. Although much latent hostility was evident, many examples of local cooperation were cited; all the evidence suggested that barriers to progress were breaking down; and there was evident expectation of much greater activity on this front in the near future. Various practical improvements were suggested, the most important being adoption as a model of the Hampshire scheme for attachment of local-authority staff to group practices. It was accepted by all concerned that this development offered a realistic basis for realization of the domiciliary team.[20]

Although there was greater optimism about the prospects for unguided development, the need for a more specific policy directive was appreciated, especially in the light of the above-mentioned and much-publicized ten-year hospital and local-authority services plans that were published in 1962 and 1963 respectively. After some hesitation, the obvious expedient of a parallel ten-year plan for general practice was not adopted, partly on account of the need to avoid further capital expenditure commitments, but also because of traditional medico-political sensitivities. Accordingly, once again this problem was remitted to the central medical advisory machinery. On this occasion the CHSC was rejected in favour of the more expert Standing Medical Advisory Committee (SMAC). The Cohen Committee, which was chaired by a powerful hospital physician, had comprised ten members from the CHSC and thirteen co-opted members. By contrast, the new general-practice committee was headed by the woman general practitioner, Annis Gillie. The Gillie Committee was a more compact and expert affair, comprising five members from the SMAC, together with eight co-opted members. The report of the Gillie Committee was published in October 1963.[21] The Gillie Report illustrates the extent of the change in ethos that had occurred in general practice since the Cohen Report. It reaffirmed Cohen's support for the general-practitioner obstetrician, but gave rather more prominence to general-practice psychiatry, something which Cohen had ignored. It also attached a new level of importance to research by general practitioners. One of the most elaborate sets of proposals by the Gillie Committee related to the service by general practitioners in hospital, but more importantly exploitation of hospital diagnostic facilities by general practitioners.

---

[19] *A Review of the Medical Services in Great Britain* (The Porritt Report; London: Social Assay, 1962).
[20] Meetings of CMO with MOHs, 30 Jan. 1961, and with Chairmen of Local Medical Committees, 15 Mar. 1961, PRO MH 133/268.
[21] Central Health Services Council, Standing Medical Advisory Committee, *The Field of Work of the Family Doctor: Report of the Sub-Committee* (The Gillie Report; London: HMSO, 1963).

With respect to capital development and practice organization, the Gillie
Report was noticeably more ambitious and enterprising than Cohen; the new
report also gave definitive support for the rehabilitation of the health centre.
Although the Gillie Report is often remembered for its advocacy of the
primary-health-care team, this idea was not particularly well developed and
this particular terminology was not used. The chief emphasis of the sections
on teamwork related to closer cooperation between general practitioners
engaged in group practice. The benefits of the domiciliary team were recognized, but this concept was not considered in detail, and the passing references
to the usefulness of 'his ancillary staff' suggest lack of regard for the level of
contribution offered by other professionals.[22]

Reforms of medical education at all levels were demanded in order to
provide for the vocational training and continuing education of general practitioners. For this purpose university departments and chairs of general practice were regarded as essential. Although remuneration was outside the remit
of the Gillie Committee, some of its recommendations questioned the suitability of the existing system to reward the qualities desired from the practitioner of the future.

The Gillie Report briefly considered whether achievement of its aims
required administrative unification of the NHS. It decided that this was neither
necessary nor desirable, a conclusion diametrically opposite to the Porritt
Report, which concluded that administrative unification was an essential prerequisite for the development of all services.[23] In most other respects the Porritt
Report was more cautious and conventional than Gillie. The Gillie Report was
welcomed as reflecting the new spirit of innovation within the Ministry of
Health. The failure to back the Porritt scheme for administrative reorganization at this time came as a relief to officials, since there was little support for
this proposition within the department.

The Gillie Report demonstrated the possibility of a good working relationship between the Ministry of Health and leaders of the profession. More
specifically, it showed that the officials were receptive to the view of general
practice advocated within the College of General Practitioners, within which
Annis Gillie was a leading figure. However, there was not perfect consensus. A
conference called by the MPU criticized the Gillie Report for being too timid.
Among the speakers drawing attention to the perilous state of general practice
was John Brotherston of Edinburgh, who was soon to be appointed Chief
Medical Officer in Scotland.[24] Also more critical of the state of general practice and more radical than the Gillie Report was a survey of health centres and
group practices undertaken by two Medical Officers from the Ministry of
Health. The Chief Medical Officer was in favour of publication of this report,
but this was vetoed by his administrative colleagues in Division 3 on account

[22] Central Health Services Council:, paras. 137–8.
[23] Ibid., para. 206.
[24] The Times, 21 Oct. 1963.

of likely embarrassment to the government.[25] The Lees–Carr Report concluded that, even at their best, group practices rarely came near to the department's ideals concerning domiciliary teams. The Report drew attention to the extremely limited extent of cooperation between general practitioners and neighbouring local-authority and hospital services. It even asserted that the planning of health centres was fundamentally flawed, and had therefore obstructed rather than assisted cooperation. The authors put forward a comprehensive programme involving exploiting the most successful features of existing health centres and group practices, greater access to the facilities of hospitals, reforming the system of remuneration, and improving education and training. By this means the domiciliary team could be developed into the leading edge of the NHS. The Lees–Carr Report was in fact a shadow to the Gillie Report, but on account of the freedom it offered for expression of an independent opinion it was considerably more radical than its more formal counterpart.

The Gillie episode is instructive in demonstrating broad agreement on the means to effect improvements in general practice, but also a sense of frustration about uneven professional standards, and awareness of the political sensitivity of the process of reform. Within most sections of the leadership of the profession there was a much greater level of receptivity to reform than had been the case even a few years earlier. Although lacking White Paper status, the Gillie Report emerged as the credible counterpart to the ten-year hospital and community-care plans. The Gillie Report was even heralded as the 'Charter for Britain's Family Doctors'.[26]

The Gillie Report enjoyed sufficiently broad support to merit immediate further action on the part of the Ministry of Health.[27] Following informal preparatory talks with the leadership of the BMA, it was agreed that the best way forward was to institute a working party under the chairmanship of the Permanent Secretary to examine issues raised by the Gillie Report as well as other contentious problems, many of them relating to remuneration. The Fraser Working Party was announced in February 1964. This immediately split into two panels, with a separate working group addressing the problem of practice expenses. Between them, these groups dealt with most of the problems worrying general practitioners, and most aspects of professional development.[28] These constructive negotiations, involving the health departments, the BMA, and the College of General Practitioners conducted under the umbrella of the Fraser Working Party, were suddenly interrupted by the crisis over general practitioners' pay provoked by unpalatable pay awards announced by

[25] W. Lees and T. E. A. Carr, 'Survey of Health Centres and Group Practices 1960', PRO MH 133/270.

[26] Daily Telegraph, 4 Oct. 1963.

[27] PRO MH 153/247.

[28] R. Stevens, Medical Practice in Modern England, the Impact of Specialization and State Medicine (New Haven, Conn., 1966) 298–9; Webster, The Health Services since the War, ii. 270–1. PRO MH 153/271–2; Treasury, 2SS 1289/01A.

the new Kindersley Review Body in February 1963 and February 1965.[29] These
two awards were not particularly inadequate in themselves, but they took on
the appearance of unfairness owing to the perverse operation of the method
of distribution. The traditional system of remuneration therefore failed at its
first test by the Kindersley Review Body. A renewed outburst of militancy
within the profession disrupted negotiations within the Fraser Working Party.
The profession countered with its own demands, which it called the 'Family
Doctor Charter', which was presented in the spirit of an ultimatum.[30] However,
the threat to harmony proved more apparent than real. The Fraser Working
Party had already brought the government and profession within sight of the
objectives contained in the Charter. The two sides were generally in accord
over such fundamental issues as the scrapping of the central pool and over the
need for direct reimbursement of practice expenses. If anything, the outburst
of militancy on the part of the profession strengthened the Minister's hands
in persuading his colleagues to accept further negotiation, and in reducing their
inclination to intervene unhelpfully. Accordingly, after some intensive discussions, in June 1965 basic agreement on implementing the Family Doctor
Charter had been reached. The new contract was introduced in the following
year. With little alteration, this remained in force until 1990. It proved both
durable and popular; the revival of general practice is popularly ascribed to the
influence of the Family Doctor Charter, and the succeeding years are often
regarded as something of a golden age.

This estimate is something of an exaggeration, but the 1966 contract represented a genuine liberation from an obsolete and inegalitarian system of
remuneration. This was encouraging for younger and innovative practitioners,
without unduly threatening the position of their more conventional colleagues.
Even the general practitioners who benefited least from the new arrangements
were better off on account of the overall substantial increases in pay that
accompanied the new contract. The discredited pool system was abolished and
the cost of the general medical service was borne by the Exchequer without
any imposed ceiling.

A substantial part of the general practitioner's income continued to derive
from the capitation fee, but equal prominence was assumed by a new basic practice allowance and its authorized supplements, which were estimated according to a variety of factors relating to the services delivered by the practitioner,
and the nature and size of the practice. The basic practice allowance itself was
paid on a graduated scale, and only at the full rate for lists above 1,000. The
capitation fee was paid at a higher rate with respect to elderly patients. Separate payments were introduced for out-of-hours service, while more generous
payments were available for continuing education. Other services such as
supervision of maternity cases continued to be subject to separate fees, and the

[29] Webster, *The Health Services since the War*, ii. 162–5, 264–6.
[30] Stevens, *Medical Practice*, 298–312; Webster, *The Health Services since the War*, ii. 266–7.

range of fee-for-service payments was increased. Opportunities for deputizing arrangements were increased.

In an important departure from the previous scheme for practice expenses, the new contract offered direct payments towards offsetting the cost of employing ancillary staff or to offset rent and rates. A new General Practice Finance Corporation was established to make loans available on a more substantial scale for the acquisition and improvement of practice premises.[31] This initiative permitted group practices to develop their accommodation in line with the facilities available to groups opting to work in publicly funded health centres.

Some significant brakes on progress in general practice were left unaffected by the new contract. Significant among these were the problems associated with education and training. At all levels, medical education was dictated by the needs of hospital specialities. By the 1960s, general practitioners were demanding greater parity of treatment, and recognition of their needs in the undergraduate curriculum, in postgraduate vocational training, and in continuing education. As noted above, this problem was recognized by the Gillie Report. The report of the Working Party on Medical Staffing Structure in the Hospital Service chaired by Sir Robert Platt also called for intending general practitioners to spend at least two years of training in the hospital service. The demand for more systematic and dedicated vocational training was led by the College of General Practitioners. By the mid-1960s pilot vocational training schemes were in place in centres as far apart as Inverness and Wessex. This issue was taken up by the Fraser Working Party, which evolved a comprehensive scheme for vocational training designed for all entrants into general practice.[32] The Ministry of Health was supportive of this objective but regarded it as inexpedient on account of the growing shortage of doctors. A convenient opportunity to advance discussions, but also to defer action, was presented by the establishment of the Royal Commission on Medical Education in 1965. The Todd Report was of definitive importance in establishing the principle that general practitioners required professional training on a level with other specialities. Although this Commission, chaired by Lord Todd, was primarily concerned with the expansion of the medical schools, it also dealt with a range of other sensitive issues, among them education and training for general practice, where its report recommended implementation of the plans evolved by the College of General Practitioners and reflected in the Gillie Report, or the papers of the Fraser Working Party.[33] As noted elsewhere in this volume, the full implementation of the new vocational training system proved to be a lengthy process requiring legislation in 1976 and further preparations which

[31] *Family Doctor Service: Second Report of Joint Discussions between the General Practitioner Representatives and the Ministry of Health* (London: BMA, October 1965).
[32] PRO MH 153/370–2.
[33] *Royal Commission on Medical Education 1965–68: Report*, Cmnd. 3569 (London: HMSO, 1968), 59–62.

lasted until 1982.[34] Accordingly, improvements in general practice attributable
to innovations in training were much in arrears of changes associated with
incentives contained in the new contract.

As already noted, health centres provide a further area where administrative
intervention on the part of the health departments was used to defer developments for which there was growing national and local demand. Despite the
many disincentives placed in the way of health-centre schemes, resistance to
this idea within the profession notably declined, and the number of proposals
presented to the health departments steadily increased. However, such was the
success of the health departments in stemming the tide of demand that by the
end of 1965 there were only twenty-five health centres in England and Wales,
and three in Scotland. By this date it had become evident that continuing resistance to this form of collective practice was unrealistic. The Scottish Home
and Health Department (SHHD) frankly admitted that in the last few years
there had occurred a 'remarkable upsurge of interest not only among family
doctors but among Executive Councils and other interested bodies'.[35] At this
point the Scottish planners sharply reversed their policy; health centres became
the preferred basis for general practice in new towns and housing redevelop-
ments. The prime centre for experimentation was Livingston New Town,
where it was proposed to establish an 'area health board' to supervise the coordinated provision of health care, based on health centres and a new district
general hospital. All the medical personnel were employed in both health
centre and hospital. This bold plan for breaking down traditional professional
boundaries and for integrating the administration of health care soon became
regarded as an ideal model for replication elsewhere. Indeed, the Livingston
experiment constituted one of the sources for the early Scottish lead in thinking about health-service reorganization.[36]

In England, bureaucratic obstruction was slower to break down and leadership over health-centre development was less pronounced.[37] However, demand
for health-centre provision steadily escalated, and the case for this alternative
was particularly effectively presented by the MPU.[38] Although the new contract was not directly relevant to health centres, it provided an indirect stimulus, since local authorities were able for the first time to charge economic rents
for facilities provided for general practitioners, which the latter could then
reclaim from Exchequer sources. Since local authorities therefore incurred a
smaller rate subsidy for health centres, they were less reluctant to embark on
these ventures. Enthusiasm of local authorities for health centres received a
further boost when they appreciated that NHS reorganization would provide

---

[34] The basis for this new training system was the NHS (Vocational Training) Act 1976.

[35] SHHD to Treasury, 6 Apr. 1965, Treasury, 2SS 461/01.

[36] Webster, *The Health Services since the War*, ii. 346–8.

[37] M. Ryan, 'Health Centre Policy in England and Wales', *British Journal of Sociology*, 19 (1968)
34–46; P. Hall, 'The Development of Health Centres', in P. Hall, H. Land, R. Parker, and A. Webb
(eds.), *Change, Choice and Conflict in Social Policy* (London, 1975), 277–310.

[38] See e.g. Bruce Cardew, *The Future of the Family Doctor* (London: Fabian Society, 1959).

them with an opportunity to hand over their health-centre debts to the new health-service administration.[39]

Health centres finally received the imprimatur of the Chief Medical Officer, whose report accepted that there was a fresh realization that health centres offered, 'as no other project could offer, a means of providing groups of doctors with suitable premises adequately staffed, with ancillary help and with the opportunity to work in the closest cooperation with the professional staffs of the local health authorities'.[40] Once the idea was embraced, health centres soon took on the symbolic importance they had possessed at the inception of the NHS. The Treasury was advised that the recent explosion of interest in health centres reflected 'profound changes . . . taking place in the profession and organization of medical care outside hospital', indicating the growing realization of the need to break down the 'historical and administrative barriers between the preventive and curative health services and of the benefits to be gained from the professional staffs concerned working closely together in a single team'.[41] Health centres were, of course, neither a necessary nor a sufficient condition for the development of teamwork. In recognition of this, the Department of Health and Social Security (DHSS) increasingly attached importance to the desirability of local authorities negotiating attachment schemes with group practices. The first circular giving effect to this idea dates from 1969.[42]

Once the new health-centre policy was under-way, the health departments were required for the first time to invest substantial energies in health-centre planning and deflect material resources towards this objective. In England, the first circular giving positive encouragement to health-centre planning was issued in 1967 and the first Design Guide in 1970. As in the case of the Gillie Report, a main planning role was remitted to the SMAC. At the instigation of two general practitioners working in a health centre, in December 1967 the Chief Medical Officer convened a conference of health-centre medical staffs, after which this issue was referred to the SMAC. The latter established an expert committee containing fifteen members, of which only two were drawn from the SMAC, to examine practical problems of the organization of group practice, with particular reference to health centres. This committee was chaired by Harvard Davis, a senior academic in general practice from the Welsh National School of Medicine.[43] By this stage health centres were accepted as an uncontroversial variety of group practice. The practical report of this committee was published in the summer of 1971.[44] By the date of NHS

[39] The first guidance to local authorities on the new health-centre policy was LHA Circular 7/67.

[40] *Report of the Chief Medical Officer on the State of Public Health for the Year Ended 31 December 1966* (London: HMSO, 1967), 206.

[41] DHSS to Treasury, 22 Apr. 1971, Treasury, 2SS 461/01D.

[42] LHA Circular 13/69.

[43] Department of Health, F/C 50/10A.

[44] *The Organisation of Group Practice: A Report of a Sub-Committee of the Standing Medical Advisory Committee* (London: HMSO, 1971).

reorganization in 1974 there were 566 health centres in operation in England and fifty-nine in Scotland.

The language of official publications changed to reflect the newer thinking regarding the role of general practitioners as key members of groups involving various professions engaged in providing the first line of contact with the health service. Explicit reference to 'primary health care' and 'primary-health-care team' was virtually unknown before 1970, but in 1974 the relevant sections of both the DHSS and SHHD annual reports gave prominence to this terminology in describing the future goals of general practice.[45] This terminology was also taken for granted in the Godber Report, published in the same year.[46]

Retrenchment, 1974–1979

The period ending in 1974 provided increasing grounds for optimism that general practice was capable of maintaining its place among the major medical specialities. As evident in other sections of this book, the process of incremental improvement was evident on many fronts.

The 1974 reorganization constituted the biggest policy initiative in the NHS since 1948. This was the fruit of a long and confused planning process extending back to the mid-1960s.[47] Through its management and organizational changes, reorganization was intended to bring substantial benefits to all parts of the NHS. However, most of the expected advantages failed to materialize, and in practice the 1974 reorganization proved to be the dawn of an age of uncertainty and loss of confidence.

This adverse trend was in part occasioned by economic factors. The date selected for reorganization coincided with the major international oil crisis, which dealt a particularly hard blow to an already weak UK economy. The oil crisis brought immediate pressures for cuts in public expenditure. From this date, the UK, in common with other Western economies, set about urgent reassessment of its welfare-state commitments. This brought about a sudden end to the long period of incremental growth in NHS spending. Henceforth the NHS was forced to accustom itself to growth levels insufficient to meet the demands of demographic change or medical advance. In order to soften the impact of this new phase of retrenchment, there commenced an ever more desperate search for efficiency savings or policy options calculated to generate a greater volume of service from the limited available resources.

The impact of the cold economic climate was quickly evident in NHS planning. Initially, the Labour Administration hoped to maintain the rate of growth at the traditional average level of 2 per cent a year. For the first time since the

[45] *DHSS Report 1974*, 36; *SHHD Report 1974*, 51–5.
[46] *General Medical Services: Report of the Joint Working Party* (London: HMSO, 1974).
[47] Webster, *The Health Services since the War*, ii. chs. IV and VI.

beginning of the NHS, the Service embarked on a systematic priorities exercise. The consultative document stemming from this review, published in March 1976, acknowledged the enhanced importance attached to primary care. Consequently, whereas acute services were to be held down to a growth rate of 1.2 per cent a year, the family practitioner and community services were to be permitted to expand at the rate of 3.7 and 6 per cent respectively.[48]

Indicative of the crisis facing the priorities exercise, in September 1977 the government issued yet another consultative document covering the same ground, maintaining its stated priorities, but across the board diluting its promises. The Secretary of State warned that progress could not be resumed until there was 'an improvement in the general economic situation. I hope that we shall not have to wait too long.'[49] In fact, the norms published in 1976 have never effectively been reinstated. In the Scottish consultation document, it was conceded that the 'input of additional funds into the primary care services can only be achieved if there is a slackening of demand on the acute hospital services'.[50] However, the Scottish document was noticeably more positive in its commitment to the health-centre programme than its English equivalent. Whereas in England it was expected that there would be a sharp rundown in the provision of purpose-built health centres, in Scotland the cuts were not allowed to interfere with the new health-centre policy: 'the Secretary of State is anxious that Boards should continue to accord priority to the provision of health centres as the most effective means of promoting the development of primary care.'[51]

It was initially hoped that the benefits of reorganization would soften the impact of this new wave of retrenchment. From the outset of preparation for reorganization it was expected that unification of the NHS would bring particular benefits to general practice, particularly by facilitating integration of effort, removing the sense of isolation felt by independent contractors, and opening up fresh opportunities for planning. It was hoped that the new unified health authorities would effectively promote teamwork and health-centre development. As a consequence there would result 'a better balanced service, in which community facilities, including the family doctor service, and the hospitals would be developed with regard for each other's needs and capacities and would provide for continuity of care'.[52]

Since the proposals adopted by the government were the linear descendant of the profession's own plan announced in the Porritt Report, there was some confidence that it would be received more sympathetically than the scheme devised by Bevan. In Scotland the plan for integration was generally supported.

[48] *Priorities for Health and Personal Social Services in England: A Consultative Document* (London: HMSO, 1976), para. 9.
[49] *Priorities in the Health and Social Services: The Way Forward* (London: HMSO, 1977), foreword.
[50] *The Health Service in Scotland: The Way Ahead* (Edinburgh: HMSO, 1977), para. 4.5.
[51] Ibid., para. 4.4.
[52] *National Health Service: The Administrative Structure of the Medical and Related Services in England and Wales* (London: HMSO, 1968), para. 36.

But with respect to England, the government's confidence proved to be mis-placed; it failed to reckon with the Adullamite instincts of the professional leadership. In fact the Porritt Report had not been ratified by the BMA in London. As soon as they were challenged to support integration, the general practitioners responded, as in 1948, by retreating to the certainties of the old order. They demanded and were soon granted a guarantee that their traditional rights and privileges would be respected and that the separate administration adopted in 1948 would be imported into the reorganized NHS with as little alteration as possible.

At the time the BMA was widely criticized for its antediluvianism. The con-tinuing administrative separation of the family-practitioner services was identified as one of the main weaknesses of the reorganized NHS. However, capitulation by the government on this point adroitly avoided a potentially damaging confrontation with the most militant interest group within the NHS. It also provided a single point of certainty in the system, about which few areas of settled agreement could be located in the course of labyrinthine negotia-tions. In the reorganized NHS in England and Wales, the new Area Health Authorities took over former local-authority functions and thereby became responsible for health-centre planning and the administration of community services. Executive Councils were reincarnated as Family Practitioner Com-mittees, continuing with their regulatory function, but with little else. General practitioners therefore continued as before, although they were also granted a wholly new opportunity to participate along with other medical colleagues in the new NHS management and advisory hierarchies.

In view of the rapid evaporation of confidence in the 1974 reorganization, general practitioners were in some respects fortunate in their location as adven-titious elements in the system. They thereby avoided some of the demoraliza-tion and uncertainty experienced by other professional groups. They were also not affected by the state of paralysis generated by the new management system. They were also exempt from the system of cash limits and the Resource Avo-cation Working Party (RAWP) redistribution scheme, both of which in 1976 were applied to the hospital and community services. However, they were not entirely immune from adverse consequences stemming from the effects of redistribution, retrenchment, and reorganization. The health-centre pro-gramme was a prime target for cuts in capital expenditure, while community nursing and related staff were victims of reductions in the current budget. These economies immediately threatened to undermine the continuing devel-opment of primary-care teams and health centres, both of which were common in more prosperous locations, but were still not sufficiently widely established in centres of multi-deprivation.

Suspicions concerning the continuing perilous state of primary care in the inner city were amply confirmed by the study group of the London Health Planning Consortium chaired by Donald Acheson. Inner London in particu-lar had proved immune to the striking advances in health care that had taken root elsewhere. Indeed, the catalogue of defects drawn up in the Acheson Report was uncannily reminiscent of the Collings Report produced thirty years previously.[53]

In view of the widespread evidence that, especially in inner cities, health visitors and nurses were being employed on a geographical rather than an attachment basis, and suspicion that attachment schemes were being dismantled, this problem was referred by the DHSS to the relevant Standing Advisory Committees.[54] The medical and nursing and midwifery committees responded by establishing a small committee under the chairmanship of Wilfrid Harding to examine this question. The report of this committee, like the Acheson Report, was not completed until after the change of government.[55] This committee confirmed fears that the primary-health-care-team concept was losing momentum and it called for reduplication of effort towards this objective. By contrast with previous reports from central advisory sources, the Harding Report placed the blame for this situation largely on the general-practitioner leadership. In particular it attacked the continuing 'isolated administration of general practitioner services' which created a 'clash of interest between independent contractors whose prime interest must be for the patients on their practice list and nurse managers whose prime duty is to organise nursing services as effectively as possible for the whole population of a particular geographical area'. The Harding Committee therefore concluded that health authorities should 'actively strive to integrate the planning and organization of Family Practitioner Committee and health authority-provided services', and it boldly criticized the new Conservative Administration for announcing that it would strengthen the separation of the operational management of these two branches of the health service.[56]

Although not citing the Royal Commission on the National Health Service as its source, the Harding Report was reiterating many of the conclusions of the Merrison Commission. I have argued elsewhere that the Commission chaired by Sir Alexander Merrison did not possess quite the authority that has sometimes been assumed.[57] This exercise was largely a concession reluctantly offered to the medical profession by the Labour Administration to assist its troubled relations with this group. The Commission began work in 1976 and its report was published in July 1979, just after the fall of the Labour Administration. The report possesses no great importance and it exercised little influence, but it provides a convenient review of the state of the NHS on the eve of the assumption of power by Mrs. Thatcher. The Merrison

[53] London Health Planning Consortium, Primary Health Care Study Group, *Primary Health Care in Inner London* (The Acheson Report; London: DHSS, 1981). The Consortium was a non-executive body formed in 1977 to promote cooperation across the boundaries of the four Thames regions.
[54] SAC(M)(78) 3rd mtg, 4 July 1978, Department of Health, F/C 50/76.
[55] *The Primary Care Team: Report of a Joint Working Group* (The Harding Report; London: HMSO, 1981).
[56] Ibid., paras. 66.9, 66.16.
[57] Webster, *The Health Services since the War*, ii. 613–20.

Commission contained two general practitioners, Christopher Wells from
Sheffield and Cyril Taylor from Liverpool. This compared with only one hospital medical specialist and one hospital dental specialist. General practice was
therefore well represented. As already noted, the findings of the Royal Commission ran along the same lines as the Harding Report, but it was more specific
in its emphasis on health-centre provision for inner-city areas. It also called for
experiments with salaried service in deprived areas. Other proposals likely to
be sensitive to the general-practitioner leadership were the call for a compulsory retirement age, the introduction of a limited drug list, and obligatory
generic prescribing. In its proposals for simplifying the administrative
structure of the NHS, the Commission gave first preference to abolition of the
area tier and termination of the separate administration of family-practitioner
services.[58]

Thatcherization, 1979–1997

Mrs. Thatcher's Administration represented a strong lurch to the right, which
among other things promised a radical reappraisal of all facets of the welfare
state. However, despite many forebodings, implications for the NHS were far
from evident. Although the whole period was characterized by substantial
changes, it was not until near the end of her tenure that the final formula was
devised for applying a distinctive Thatcherist stamp on the NHS.

The 1979 Conservative general-election manifesto merely promised to 'simplify and decentralise the service and cut back bureaucracy'. Such themes as
cutting red tape and maximizing local devolution were a common denominator of Conservative policy at this date. Paradoxically, in the case of the NHS,
the proposed cure entailed unceremonious dismantling of Sir Keith Joseph's
monument to 1970s Conservative fashion in management thinking.

The Thatcher Administration's new blueprint for the NHS was produced
after only a few months in office and these changes were introduced in 1982.[59]
They proved to be remarkably uncontentious. The main preoccupation was
removing some of the complications of Joseph's system, primarily abolition of
the area tier of hospital and community health services administration. This
had the awkward consequence of undermining the coterminosity of boundaries between these services, family-practitioner services, and local-authority
social-service departments. Hitherto, this principle of coterminosity was
regarded as sacrosanct. It was now abandoned. Rather than pursue the further
simplification advocated by the Royal Commission and Harding Committee by
creating a unitary health-service administration at district level, the Thatcher

[58] *Royal Commission on the National Health Service Report*, Cmnd. 7615 (The Merrison Report;
London: HMSO, 1979), chs. 7 and 20.
[59] *Patients First: Consultative Paper on the Structure and Management of the National Health Service
in England and Wales* (London: HMSO, 1979), para. 25.

Administration elected to reinforce the independence of the Family Practitioner Committees according to their existing area boundaries. This was merely one of many points upon which the Thatcher team declined to adopt a more radical interpretation of its election commitment. The new arrangements scarcely assisted integrated planning of primary-care or health-centre planning. However, the latter was not a problem, since, with the issue of circular HC(80)6, health centres were once again demoted to a low priority.

The 1982 changes could be seen as a response to the Family Practitioner Committee lobby, and as appeasement of the BMA, meeting its traditional objective of maximizing the statutory separation of family-practitioner services. This solution was therefore politically helpful to the DHSS in purchasing political credit with the BMA. It also adroitly sidestepped a further potential source of confrontation with the BMA by thwarting the Treasury objective of imposing a combined cash limit covering family practitioners and hospital services.

It is difficult to avoid the impression that during the first phase of the Thatcher Administration, on account of preoccupation with the riddle of health-authority administration, general medical practice was allowed to slip down the policy agenda. This conclusion is confirmed by the important priorities policy document, *Care in Action*, which devoted only one short paragraph to primary health care, the main import of which was to pour further cold water over any residual plans for health-centre development.[60] However, it was not realistic to allow primary health care to drift again into a backwater. Given the primacy of the policy of retrenchment in the public sector, the demand-led expenditure of the FPS sector stood out increasingly as an anomaly. High levels of direct charges on recipients satisfactorily reduced the financial burden of the eye and dental services, but this drew even greater attention to the anomalous status of the general-practitioner and pharmaceutical sectors, which in the course of the 1980s were the only parts of the NHS to witness buoyant growth in their expenditure. Regular increases in the prescription charge compensated for this trend to only a limited extent. Accordingly, at Treasury insistence, many old ideas for reining back general medical practitioner and pharmaceutical expenditure were revived, but with a new intensity of purpose.

Consistent with the Thatcher style, the family-practitioner 'problem' was remitted to the accountants, Binder Hamlyn, whose confidential report was completed in the summer of 1983 but was not reported until early in 1984.[61] This again examined the cash-limit option but concluded that this was impracticable given the current contractual situation. Building on recent estimates of future medical manpower requirements, the Binder Hamlyn Report regarded measures to control general-practitioner numbers as the most likely path to

---

[60] *Care in Action: A Handbook of Policies and Priorities for the Health and Personal Social Services in England* (London: HMSO, 1981), para. 4.11.
[61] N. Timmins, *The Times*, 7 Mar. 1984.

secure major economies. Ministers were divided over this issue. On grounds
of maximizing competition, they opted against limiting numbers. Following
the Binder Hamlyn Report, the government returned to the problem of controlling the drug bill, by restrictions on either general practitioners or the
profits of drug companies. It considered but, responding to clever propaganda
from the pharmaceutical industry and its allies, rejected generic substitution
or abolition of the Pharmaceutical Price Regulation Scheme. The Thatcher
team was, however, more courageous than its predecessors in raising the
prospect of a 'white' or limited drug list. When this idea was floated in 1984,
it was greeted by a furore on the part of the BMA and the pharmaceutical
industry, forcing the government into an immediate retreat, with the result that
only minor restrictions on prescribing were introduced, yielding only trivial
savings. The limited list exercise was quietly buried and the Conservative
Administration ended without it being again disinterred. This represented an
apparent humiliation for a government increasingly renowned for its success
in confrontation with corporate interests. But this experience constituted a
valuable learning exercise for the Thatcher team. It demonstrated that it was
practicable to undertake radical policy initiatives without prior consultation
with the profession, or the customary rigmarole of enquiries by expert committees. It also indicated that even radical and unpalatable measures were
unlikely to be met by united opposition from within the medical profession.
The limited-list initiative therefore constituted a firm platform for further and
more audacious forays into the primary-care-policy arena.

The government's drive to transform the quality of management in the
NHS provided a further stimulus to intervention within primary care. The
Griffiths Report of 1983 led to sweeping away consensus management teams
and their replacement by general management. This was symptomatic of a
general transformation taking place in the culture of the NHS which was
giving increasing precedence to management and market considerations. Few
of these changes were welcomed by the medical profession, and they eroded
the dominance of the profession within the hospital sector. Nevertheless, the
Griffiths philosophy took hold without active opposition. Emboldened by
success in turning the screw on hospital medical staffs, and armed with the
Binder Hamlyn assessment, the government gave further thought to control
and management within the family-practitioner services. First, steps were
taken to transform Family Practitioner Committees from minor regulatory
bodies into more aggressive management agencies. Secondly, as in 1946 and
1966, it was recognized that the only practicable means to securing improved
performance from general medical practitioners themselves lay in renegotia-
tion of their contract. By contrast with the Family Doctor Charter, the pace
was set by the government rather than the independent contractors.

Production of a new charter for primary care required cautious preparation.
Early expectations of a Green Paper by the summer of 1984 were disap-

pointed.[62] Although the Thatcher Administration was primarily preoccupied with preventing continuing escalation of FPS costs and squeezing a greater volume of work out of general practitioners, it was essential to avoid an overtly repressive presentation of its plans for radical shake-up. The new policy orientation revived the notion that the future health service should be primary-care led. The idea that the effective primary care would save recourse to expensive hospital facilities was a theme at least as old as the NHS, and indeed it can be located in the Dawson Report. Such factors as demographic change, advances in therapy, decarceration, community care, and changing expectations of patients, discussed elsewhere in this volume, added to the strength of this argument. During the 1980s this message was reinforced by such agencies as the World Health Organization (WHO). As indicated by such evidence as the 115 recommendations of the Acheson Report, the profession itself was sensitive to the unhappy state of general practice, especially in areas of deprivation. The profession also recognized weaknesses of the existing contract and the need for greater management intervention. Finally, 1980s initiatives in the USA, especially the proliferation of Health Maintenance Organizations (HMOs) of various types, seemed to constitute a repository of experimentation appropriate for transference to the UK situation.[63]

The government's new programme was finally announced in its Green Paper, *Primary Health Care: An Agenda for Discussion*, published in April 1986. Reflecting the fashion of the moment, this contained a section on HMOs. After full consultation, involving some concessions to its critics, the government issued its revised ideas as the White Paper, *Promoting Better Health*, issued in November 1987.[64] After further protracted negotiations, representative bodies of the profession failed to ratify the new contract. Disregarding this setback, the details of a new contract based on the White Paper were circulated by the government in August 1989 and this contract became operative on 1 April 1990.[65]

The stated objective of the 1990 contract was to reward 'high-quality services', guarantee better value for money, and give greater consumer satisfaction. Although involving some significant changes, the new contract preserved and indeed enhanced many traditional features. It eliminated some fees and allowances introduced in 1966, made other payments conditional on meeting stated targets, while adding new responsibilities and incentives for carrying out

[62] N. Timmins, *The Times*, 4 Apr. 1984.

[63] See, for instance, the prominence given to HMOs and the ideas of A. C. Enthoven in N. Macrae, 'Health Care International', *The Economist*, 28 Apr. 1984.

[64] *Primary Health Care: An Agenda for Discussion*, Cmnd. 9771 (London: HMSO, 1986); *Promoting Better Health: The Government's Programme for Improving Primary Health Care*, Cm. 249 (London: HMSO, 1987).

[65] *General Practice in the NHS: The 1990 Contract. The Government's Programme for Changes in GPs' Terms of Service and Remuneration System* (London: Health Departments of Great Britain, 1989).

a greater range of services for patients. The effect of these adaptations was considerably to increase, indeed almost double, the proportion of the income derived from capitation. This was at the expense of the basic practice allowance, which had hitherto increased in importance since its introduction in 1966. The basic practice allowance was itself converted into a capitation payment. Successful practices were implicitly encouraged to compete more actively to build up their lists, and fewer obstacles were placed in the way of patients who wished to change to another practice. By this means it was hoped to generate a market situation within general practice. For general practitioners working in adverse circumstances who were likely to be disadvantaged by the new arrangements, some compensation was provided by a new deprivation supplement. Symbolic of the profession's declining ability to veto changes offensive to its members, for the first time since the introduction of NHI in 1911, a compulsory retirement age of 70 was introduced.

Building on more limited changes introduced in 1985 to give FPCs greater powers to manage and plan their services, under the 1990 contract the FPCs were granted further authority, while under the more general reforms of 1989 they were radically strengthened in their management functions and in 1990 renamed Family Health Service Authorities (FHSAs). As a consequence of these changes, for the first time since they were inaugurated as Insurance Committees before the First World War, the committees responsible for independent contractor services were accorded more than routine powers of regulation. Particularly controversial and important among the new powers of FHSAs was the introduction of the indicative drug budget. This in fact represented the culmination of a lengthy drive to introduce more effective monitoring of general practitioners' prescribing habits. The indicative budget was presented as a source of useful intelligence to practices and as an aide to better prescribing, but it was also recognized as a further step towards the Treasury's long-term objective of cash-limiting the general medical practitioner and pharmaceutical services.

Imposition of the 1990 contract provided further evidence of the greater assertiveness and briskness of the Thatcher Administration in its dealings with the unions and professions. This audacious move was also justified on account of the need to avoid warfare with the profession on two fronts simultaneously.

Residual disagreements concerning the contract paled into insignificance when compared with the government's package of more radical NHS changes. By contrast with the contract affair, the wider reforms were sprung on the profession as a complete surprise, and the consequences were more uncertain and potentially greatly more disadvantageous.

The new threat was more ominous because it possessed no settled name and no defined limitations to its operations. This danger arose when, without prior warning in its 1987 general-election manifesto and with few signs of prior preparation, in January 1988 Mrs. Thatcher embarked on a confidential review of the NHS.[66] This review was addressed primarily to the question of funding, and it was expected to result in measures to increase resources available to the NHS. Instead, it reaffirmed support for the traditional method of financing the NHS. This signalled continuation of the government's ongoing campaign of retrenchment, and it necessitated the application of even greater ingenuity than previously in evolving means to yield greater volume of services from the static level of financial inputs.

The fruits of this review emerged as the White Paper, *Working for Patients*, published in January 1989.[67] Despite widespread scepticism and vociferous opposition from the profession, the White Paper scheme was quickly confirmed by the government; the relevant NHS and Community Care Act received its Royal Assent in June 1990, and the reforms were introduced in April 1991. In almost every respect—the spontaneity of the policy initiative, the confidentiality of the review, the peremptory nature of the government's policy documents, the telescoped timetable for implementation, the lack of consideration for opposition from major pressure groups and expert bodies, and absence of clarity concerning the outcome of the reforms—the 1991 exercise was a complete contrast from its 1948 and 1974 predecessors. The 1991 changes were arguably the biggest shock to the NHS since its establishment, and they had less support than any previous significant change in policy. Assiduous commentators since the event have succeeded in discovering precedents and premonitory signs, but at the time the government's intervention seemed at odds with the evolutionary drift that had in the past characterized change within the NHS. The failure of the BMA to arrest or even modify the course of the reforms constituted a second big rebuff from the government within a short span of time, and it added to the sense of humiliation within the medical profession.

The 'purchaser-provider', 'internal market', or 'managed-market' reforms affected every corner of the system. The main item of relevance to general practitioners was the introduction of the fundholding option.[68] Fundholders might have been granted total responsibility for purchasing services for their patients from providers inside and outside the NHS. This radical option was seriously considered, but ultimately rejected by the government. It was initially unclear whether fundholding would be more than a limited experiment affecting only large practices and a small range of non-emergency services. Encouraged by the unexpectedly favourable response to fundholding at the grass roots, the government has relaxed conditions of entry and increased the

---

[66] For a full discussion of this review, see J. Butler, *Patients, Policies and Politics: Before and After 'Working for Patients'* (Buckingham: Open University Press, 1992).

[67] *Working for Patients*, Cm. 555 (London: HMSO, 1989).

[68] For recent assessments of the 1991 reforms and fundholding, see J. Allsop, *Health Policy and the NHS: Towards 2000* (2nd edn., London, 1995); R. Klein, *The New Politics of the NHS* (3rd edn., London, 1995); H. Glennerster, M. Matsaganis, and P. Owens, with S. Hancock, *Implementing GP Fundholding: Wild Card or Winning Hand* (Buckingham: Open University Press, 1994); R. Robinson and J. Le Grand (eds.), *Evaluating the NHS Reforms* (London: King's Fund Institute, 1993).

sphere of influence of fundholders. The business organization of both fund-holders and non-fundholders is a rapidly evolving phenomenon. It has already been noted that the new system added greatly to the status of FHSAs. By contrast, with the encouragement of opting out for NHS providers, who were quickly assembled into NHS Trusts, the once-dominant regional and local-health authorities went into visible decline. Accordingly, the 1991 shake-up destabilized the NHS administrative system. Among the anomalies, it was evident that there was no place for two separate and parallel purchasing authorities in each district, one being the recently aggrandised FHSA and the other the residual district health authority. The government therefore set in motion the amalgamation of these bodies, thereby achieving an objective that had defeated Sir Keith Joseph in 1974. The analogy is, of course, not complete, since the new amalgams are concerned with service provision only to a limited extent. The 1991 reforms also provide a parallel with 1948, which was the last big political intervention in policy regarding general medical practice and the NHS generally. The changes of 1948 represented the fruits of continuous preparations beginning at least as early as 1941. The political ethos for the changes of 1991 is rooted in policy reappraisals extending back at least to the Griffiths and Binder Hamlyn reports of 1983. General practitioners entered the NHS in 1948 reluctantly and with the greatest misgivings; they have displayed scarcely less concern over the 1991 changes. Both great political interventions have exercised a profound impact on general medical practice. We are now familiar with the shortcomings of the 1948 system; it remains for historians of the future to adjudicate on the capacity of the current wave of changes to address the remaining intractable and endemic problems of primary care.

2

The Practice

NICK BOSANQUET and CHRIS SALISBURY

A general practice can be viewed in various ways. The term 'the practice' can refer to a surgery building, a team of professionals, a model of organization, or a set of business accounts. We examine how premises, staffing, activities, and finances have changed under three different policy regimes which have shaped the local strategy and response of family doctors. The first is that of the eighteen years between the start of the NHS (1948) and 1966; then there are the long twenty-four years of the Family Doctor Charter (1966–90). The third phase opened in 1990 with a new contract and a new range of choices and opportunities for general practitioners, particularly in relation to fundholding.

We see family doctors as 'owners' of small enterprises who have to take decisions about how to develop their services. Their response and strategy can vary from a dogged determination to retain traditional routines, through passive acceptance, to a strong drive towards innovation and investment. In each of the three policy regimes there have been a few innovators who have been driven by temperament or personal values even in a restrictive environment. However, the number of innovators, and the strategies and developments in local practices, are shaped by the influence of forces from the wider environment.

These forces could be categorized at length. We shall simplify them into those which have had key importance in determining the organization of the practice as it exists today. The first key force is that of changes in the scope of treatment in general practice, due to changing morbidity patterns, improved therapeutic options, and access to technology. The introduction of antibiotics greatly increased the effectiveness of treatment for common infectious diseases, and the rise of the contraceptive pill created a new area of prescribing and activity in general practice. As most practices acquired electrocardiograms and gained open access to radiography and laboratory services, it became possible to manage conditions in general practice which had previously been the province of hospital medicine.

The second key force is that of professional models or definitions of good practice which affect aspirations and professional identity. Thus the 1970s saw the growth of a new perspective in general practice, particularly through the work of the Royal College of General Practitioners. This in turn helped to produce changes in practice development and in vocational training which had further effects on the practice.

Thirdly, there is the impact of financial incentives which shape decisions on partnership size, list size, and practice activities. The system post-1948 created incentives to keep lists long and costs low. The Family Doctors' Charter reduced the costs of teamwork and gave a declining return to additional patients. The changes introduced in 1990 created opportunities for considerable practice development, with some fundholding practices providing a wide range of services from larger premises, housing an extensive and multi-professional team of staff.

The first phase of the National Health Service, 1948–1966

The NHS inherited a system which had been shaken by six years of war. For hospitals, wartime conditions had led to the development of a new vision of improving access and investment in technology; for general practice it meant increased use of retired doctors, as younger general practitioners joined the forces, and a further strain on premises. The panel system had provided little incentive to improve the quality of care, and the problems of maintaining service in face of wartime shifts in population had left little time for developing any spacious visions of general practice. The one-minute consultation, the bottle of medicine, and the long queue around the corner out of the surgery door were the daily reality of a service under great strain. Doctors' workload was much more concerned with respiratory illness and with infectious disease. There were few palliatives for the respiratory effects of an industrial environment where winter fogs could lead to significant increases in mortality. Increased smoking during the war further increased respiratory illness. The conscientious doctor in industrial areas also had to respond to the needs of families with children, even though many were not formally covered by the panel system. Improving child health as a result of a better wartime diet and immunization had done something to reduce the burden of infectious disease but the pressures were still heavy even in the 1940s.

The NHS inherited practices which were often within the doctor's own home. A leading general practitioner in the mid-1950s described the inter-war practice of an elderly doctor which he had joined in 1937. 'The surgery was a room leading off from his smoke room; the walls were distempered in a dirty dark red; the floor was of bare boards and the room ill-lit by a small gas jet from his own plant. It contained a desk which was rarely used, half a dozen chairs, on one wall a dresser-like collection of shelves. . . . There was no examination couch and no washbasin.'[1] There had been some development of new

---

[1] D. M. Hughes, '25 Years in Country Practice', *Journal of the Royal College of General Practitioners*, 1 (1958), 5.

surgeries in suburban and rural areas, but these conditions were typical of practices in the older industrial areas. For help the doctor looked to his wife, who acted as an unpaid receptionist. General practice had a domestic focus, with the surgery in the doctor's own home, and more than 25 per cent of consultations being carried out in the patients' homes. The notion of the 'family doctor' was based in reality. With many single-handed and small practices and less social mobility, most patients would identify 'the practice' with a particular doctor whom they and their family had known over many years.

The immediate problems in the post-war transition—pay and the abolition of the sale of practices—loomed much larger than any vision of the future of general practice. General practice was put further on the defensive by the powerful critique in 1950 of Collings, a visiting Australian general practitioner backed by the authority of the Nuffield Provincial Hospitals Trust and the *Lancet*.[2] This study was based on a limited selection of practices in industrial areas and painted a picture of poor conditions and inadequate professional standards. It drew rebuttals and counter-surveys, but these did little to offset the first impression. The first three years of the NHS were taken up mainly with financial concerns about the sale of vacancies and about fees. Once these were settled temporarily by the Danckwerts award of 1952, the scene was set for a decade of conflict between negative forces cramping practice development and more positive changes in the environment. The negative forces were mainly those to do with the professional prestige of general practice and of the funding system.

- The general practitioner lost power and prestige relative to the increasing numbers of hospital consultants. The hospital system expanded. For the first time there was a national network of consultants which stretched beyond the cities into smaller centres and country areas. This was attractive to young doctors and offered improved pay, so that by the early 1960s the lifetime earnings of consultants were estimated to be 45 per cent higher than those of general practitioners. By 1966 a general practitioner at the BMA's annual conference summed the profession up as 'broke and bored'.[3] General practitioners felt themselves to be trapped in an inexorable decline in their status and pay. Against such a background, only the very confident would seek to raise the range of activities at practice level or to leave the relative safety of established routines and relationships with patients.
- The new payment system created a direct conflict between extra spending on the practice and additional income. Practices were paid gross mainly on a capitation basis and they were left free to decide whether to spend the money on improving the practice, employing staff, or investing in

[2] J. S. Collings, 'General Practice in England Today: A Reconnaissance', *Lancet* (1950), i. 555–85.
[3] Report of General Medical Services Committee, *British Medical Journal* (1965), ii, suppl., p. 178.

premises. The level of costs rose and there was no increase in fee levels from 1951 through to the early 1960s. The pooling system also worked to the disadvantage of doctors who worked full-time in the NHS, compared to those who had outside earnings, as these were deducted from the amount available for distribution before average fees were calculated. As the memory of the bad old days faded, there was an increasing sense of resentment that people's incomes were being reduced to pay for basic practice costs.

- There was increasing difficulty in filling vacancies in older industrial areas. This created even higher list sizes, until a national system of designated areas aimed to block movement of doctors into well-doctored areas and to promote movement into areas where the average list size was 3,000 or more.

Many of these problems were most strongly felt by a new generation of doctors who had entered practice after the war. There was a shortage of practice vacancies, with 150 or more applicants for practices in more attractive areas. Senior partners were able to raise their income by setting long terms to parity: and in areas of expanding population and overspill towns shrewd general practitioners in established practices were able to raise income from additional patients faster than the costs from additional partners. The system rewarded those who increased list size to 3,000 or more and provided the minimum of services. The consultation rate could be kept down by the length of the queue and the feeble warmth of a one-bar fire in the dilapidated waiting room. Older doctors also saw the most benefit from the new superannuation system.

Against these strong negative pressures limiting innovation there were some forces making for change at the practice level. The payment system was also a stimulus to the formation of partnership so as to share costs and out-of-hours cover. By 1964 doctors in partnerships were more satisfied than those in single-handed practice.[4] In 1952 the proportion of single-handed practitioners was 43 per cent; by 1965 it had fallen to 24 per cent. The rise of partnerships led to some movement in premises away from the home, although most surgeries were still in converted houses. There was less reliance on the doctor's wife, and partnerships were more likely to employ receptionists, although by 1964 only 12 per cent of practices employed nurses.[5] Having moved out of the doctor's home, general practice also began to move away from the patient's home through a reduced number of home visits. General practice was becoming professional and specialized rather than an activity linked to domestic environments. The change to partnerships was most striking among younger doctors: in 1964 only 4 per cent of doctors under 40 were in single-handed practice.

[4] A. Cartwright, *Patients and their Doctors* (London, 1967), 150.
[5] Ibid. 160.

In his autobiography, the BMA's main negotiator in the 1960s described the networks involved in development.

Baffer had a letter from a Dr Robert Forbes . . . to say that his son, James, would like to practise in or near Winchester. I thought there was no harm in us seeing him, even if we could offer him only the now traditional blood, tears, toil and sweat, and he duly arrived for interview. He had been trained at St Mary's (he was an excellent rugger player) but had done his house jobs at Bart's. He also wore an old school tie with which I was familiar. . . . By mutual consent Jimmy Forbes joined the practice and in no time at all the three of us had moved to roomier accommodation. We found a four-story Georgian house down the road . . . Each floor became a separate consulting unit with waiting and consulting rooms; reception and filing were on the ground floor . . . We decided to spare no expense on furniture and equipment. Looking back, I do not know how or why we did it. It all came from our own pockets. We were poor and money which we could have spent on our families was put into the practice.[6]

There were pressures too on the practice from new visions of general practice in the Cohen BMA Report of 1950,[7] later promoted by the Royal College of General Practitioners, as well as by some individual innovators such as Fry in Beckenham. Key contributions were those of Irvine in Ashington and Horder and Faulkner in north London: but apart from these well-known leaders there was perhaps one innovative practice every twenty or thirty miles.[8] These practices had a distinctive organization involving employment of practice nurses, appointment systems, the use of records in age-sex registers, and special clinics with a specific disease focus. Some of these practices were to be found in areas such as south Birmingham and Ashington, where they drew on an older tradition of innovation. In a few new towns health centres also supplied a further source of innovation with the attachment of district nurses and health visitors. The strongest rebuttal of the Collings Report came from Harlow, a new town with a number of health centres.

By the early 1960s it was possible to speak of two different styles of practice. These were well summed up in the stereotypes used to test patient opinion in a major survey of general practice carried out by Cartwright in 1964.

The first doctor has his surgery attached to his house. He works mainly on his own, but he has an arrangement with a nearby doctor for some weekends and some night calls. His waiting room is comfortable, which is a good thing because patients often have to wait a long time. He knows his patients and their families well, and when you do see him, he takes his time, doesn't hurry you and listens to what you say. He prescribes well established drugs and sends patients to hospital if they need anything more complicated.

The second doctor works in a partnership. There are four of them altogether and they share a well equipped surgery where they have a nurse and a secretary. This doctor takes turns with his partners to be on duty for surgeries and for weekend and night calls. They all examine you carefully, and are very up to date, and only send patients to hospital if they need very complicated investigation or treatment.[9]

In 1964 51 per cent of patients felt that their doctor was more like the first and 38 per cent the second. Patients tended to prefer whatever style they happened to have, and, whatever their professional travails, in the 1950s the doctors retained the support and esteem of their patients. Critical remarks were few: 44 per cent of patients saw the doctor as a personal friend and home visiting was still common.[10] Most doctors recorded this close contact with patients as one of the most satisfying aspects of the job.

Lastly there were pressures for change from new therapies and new methods of practice. Innovation in pharmaceuticals was creating a range of new drugs so that family doctors could treat (for example) hypertension, infections, and anxiety much more effectively in the mid-1960s than they could in the early 1950s. There were also new services, such as in family planning due to the availability of the oral contraceptive pill.[11] The 1950s were a time of confidence in the growth of hospital medicine. Changes in therapy tended to increase general practitioners' sense of what could be done in general practice. The medicine bottles of the panel system now began to seem a quaint heritage of the past, even though this had been a common style of practice only fifteen years earlier.

General practice by the early 1960s was experiencing a growing tension between professional aspiration and economic reality. Family doctors, 'broke and bored', felt penalized in both professional and financial terms. General practitioners seemed one of the rejected groups of the newly affluent society. For some the remedy lay in exit, with a rising rate of medical emigration usually to Canada, Australia, or the USA. Others became involved in the long-running negotiations over a new Family Doctor Charter. This radically changed both the financial and the professional incentives affecting the local practice.

The period of radical change, 1966–1990

The Family Doctor Charter introduced a number of fundamental changes to remuneration, which were to have a profound effect on the development of general practice. The main changes which had an impact on practice organization and structure included the following.

First, overall pay was increased substantially, and the proportion of income which was dependent on the number of registered patients decreased. There

---

[9] Cartwright, *Patients and their Doctors*, 165–6.
[10] Ibid. 111.
[11] Family-planning services were available under the NHS from the outset. The contraceptive pill was available from 1960, at first on private prescriptions only, but from 1974 on NHS prescription.

was a new balance between capitation-based income, basic practice allowances, and fees for specific tasks such as contraception and immunizations. Secondly, each general practitioner was reimbursed for 70 per cent of the wages costs of employing nursing and ancillary staff, up to a maximum of two whole-time equivalent staff. Thirdly, several schemes were devised to reimburse general practitioners for the cost of providing adequate premises. Doctors who paid rent could have this directly reimbursed, those who owned buildings could receive a 'notional rent', and doctors borrowing money to finance the building of new premises or substantial conversion of existing premises could receive reimbursement of interest payments on loans. Fourthly, extra allowances encouraged general practitioners to work in groups, and vocational training payments encouraged young doctors to undertake specific training before entering practice.

The Family Doctor Charter was devised in 1965 and implemented in 1966. There is overall agreement that it created important economic incentives, which were essential to the growth of general practice over the following two decades. However, these economic incentives cannot be understood in isolation. They came about in response to proposals from the medical profession, which were borne out of frustration with the limitations and disincentives created by the pre-existing contractual arrangements. The new economic incentives facilitated changes which had been sought because of underlying assumptions about the role of general practice and the type of practice which should be encouraged.

The developments in practice organization which occurred during this 'second phase' from 1966 to 1990 came about because of the combined effect of economic incentives, the emerging culture of general practice, and evolving social expectations and political imperatives. These factors are strongly inter-related, as will be seen through discussion of issues such as premises, work-load, and general practitioners' perceived identity. The Family Doctor Charter was primarily concerned with structural issues such as premises and staffing. By resolving these issues it ensured the survival of general practice as an important part of the NHS. While this process was occurring, various other developments were influencing general practitioners' understanding of their role.

Some years earlier, Lord Moran had said that general practitioners were doctors who had fallen 'off the ladder'.[12] Although much ridiculed, his assertion was not without foundation. In 1963 Curwen had interviewed a random sample of general practitioners and found that over half had wanted to be specialists.[13] Both Cartwright and Mechanic had recorded the frustrations that many general practitioners felt at the large number of trivial problems

---

[12] This notorious statement was made by Lord Moran, in March 1958, in his evidence (Q. 1323) to the Royal Commission on Doctors' and Dentists' Remuneration, published in 1960.

[13] M. Curwen, 'Lord Moran's Ladder: A Study of Motivation in the Choice of General Practice as a Career', *Journal of the College of General Practitioners*, 7 (1964), 38–65.

presented to them by patients.[14] Starting from this low base, a number of general practitioners began to question the assumptions that lay beneath these attitudes. The most important influence was the work of Michael Balint, who with small groups of doctors began to redefine the appropriateness of existing medical models when applied to general practice.[15] General practitioners began to develop their own ideology and sense of identity, with their own particular skills needing specific training. The creation of university departments of general practice and of vocational training schemes made it necessary to define what general practice was, what skills and attitudes needed to be taught, and what was the particular contribution of general practice to medicine. This process is best illustrated by the influential document *The Future General Practitioner: Learning and Teaching*, published in 1972.[16] By 1953 the College of General Practitioners had been instituted, providing a professional structure to support these emerging ideas.

In Tudor Hart's words, the Family Doctor Charter 'underwrote the College by giving its independent ideologies of general practice a material base'.[17] Without the structural changes enabled by the Charter, the aspirations of idealistic thinkers in the College could not be widely fulfilled. Armstrong has described 'the emancipation of biographical medicine',[18] in which general practice developed a medical model distinct from that of hospital medicine. This led to the articulation of core values in general practice such as the importance of continuity of care, understanding the social context of patients' problems, formulating diagnoses in physical, social, and psychological terms, and the role of the doctor in providing health promotion and disease prevention as well as treatment. Only by appreciating these professional incentives can one understand the ways that general practitioners chose to organize their practices. This includes the arrangements they made for appointments, the number and range of staff they employed, and the type of premises they built.

Although the new ideology of general practice influenced the development of organizational structures, these structures in turn had an effect on the ideology. Practices became larger, encouraged by incentives for doctors to work in groups and by subsidies for staff and premises. This enabled practices to take on new roles, and working in groups with attached nursing staff raised issues about the importance of teamwork. The concept of the primary-health-care team became increasingly important in the rhetoric of general practice, even if this importance was not always evident in reality. These issues are further explored elsewhere in this book.

[14] Cartwright, *Patients and their Doctors*, 44–52; D. Mechanic, 'Correlates of Frustration among British General Practitioners', *Journal of Health and Social Behaviour*, 11 (1970), 87–104.

[15] M. Balint, *The Doctor, his Patient and the Illness* (London, 1957).

[16] RCGP, *The Future General Practitioner: Learning and Teaching* (London: RCGP, 1972).

[17] J. Tudor Hart, *A New Kind of Doctor* (London, 1988), 95.

[18] D. Armstrong, 'The Emancipation of Biographical Medicine', *Social Science and Medicine*, 13A (1979), 1–8.

The interaction between economic incentives and professional values can be seen most easily by considering the size and characteristics of general-practice partnerships and the types of premises from which they worked. The Charter was based on the belief that the future lay with groups of general practitioners working together in purpose-built premises with full supporting staff. A group-practice allowance provided a financial incentive for doctors to work in groups of three or more practitioners in one building. In 1952, 43 per cent of doctors were in single-handed practice, and a further 33 per cent had only one partner. Practices of five or six doctors were very rare. Although there was a slight decline in single-handed practice before the Charter, most doctors still worked in partnerships containing less than four partners. Following the Charter there was a gradual increase in partnership size, so that by 1990 only 12 per cent of practitioners were single-handed and 22 per cent worked in partnerships of six or more doctors (see fig. D1).

This change in partnership size was accompanied by a gradual change in the medical workforce. The most important change was the increasing proportion of women becoming general practitioners, following the increasing number of female entrants to medical schools from the late 1960s onwards. The proportion of female general practitioners more than doubled between 1970 and 1990, from 12 per cent to 25 per cent of the total (see Table D3). However, far fewer of these women doctors worked as general-practitioner principals. Whereas 90 per cent of men who entered general practice became general-practitioner principals within ten years of graduation, this was true of only 61 per cent of women general practitioners.[19] The remainder worked as assistants, associates, or trainees. It is also noteworthy that less than half of the women working in general practice in 1990 were working full time. The age profile of general practitioners showed a shift towards younger doctors. In 1979 28 per cent of doctors were aged under 40, which rose to 37 per cent in 1989.[20]

Provision of adequate surgery premises to house larger partnerships, surrounded by supporting staff, was a high priority for the authors of the Family Doctor Charter. The building of purpose-built health centres, able to house a range of health professionals, had been espoused ever since the Dawson Report of 1920.[21] The Gillie Report of 1963 re-emphasized the advantages of group practice and suggested that district nurses and health visitors should be attached to practices rather than geographical areas.[22] However, the concept of health centres took off only after the Charter made arrangements for the reimbursement of rent paid by general practitioners for premises. The advantages of practising from purpose-built premises, at little or no cost, were

---

[19] J. Parkhouse, *Doctors' Careers* (London, 1991).

[20] J. Fry, *General Practice: The Facts* (London, 1992), 36.

[21] Ministry of Health Consultative Council on Medical and Allied Service, *Interim Report on the Future Provision of Medical and Allied Services*, Cmd. 693 (The Dawson Report; London: HMSO, 1920).

[22] Central Health Services Council, Standing Medical Advisory Committee, *The Field of Work of the Family Doctor: Report of the Sub-Committee* (Chairman: Annis Gillie; London: HMSO, 1963).

obvious to doctors who had previously practised from inadequately converted rooms, often in their own homes. Earlier misgivings about a loss of independence were overcome. Only twenty-eight health centres had been built between 1948 and 1967, but over the following decade over 700 new health centres were built.[23] Many centres housed not only general practices but also district nurses, midwives, health visitors, social workers, and dentists. Treatment rooms were provided so that nurses, employed by health authorities, could see patients at the centre who did not need home visits. Centres usually served a number of separate medical partnerships, and were managed by health-authority staff.

By the beginning of the 1980s, general practitioners' enthusiasm for local-authority-owned health centres had waned. Problems became apparent in different centres with recurring themes. The idea that simply housing various professional groups in one building would create a team was naïve, and ignored the historical rivalries between different professional groups. This was reinforced by the different management structures of different disciplines. Doctors felt powerless to influence important aspects of the organization of their practice, as they did not employ the reception or administrative staff.

Not only were there tensions between different professional groups, but often between different medical partnerships in the same building, none of whom had ownership or responsibility for the centre. Genuine teamwork was rarely achieved, and the external management of health centres was too inflexible to respond to the rapidly changing needs of practices. Practice development which depended on alterations to premises were hindered by the external control of distant committees, excessive bureaucracy, and under-investment. In 1974 the responsibility for health centres was transferred from local authorities to Area Health Authorities as part of a major NHS reorganization. Within health authorities, health centres were rarely a high priority for resources, when in competition with the hospital and emergency services. However, the aspirations of those who had proposed a multi-disciplinary team working in purpose-built premises were gradually being achieved in a different guise.

The Family Doctor Charter did not only allow for the reimbursement of rent to landlords. It also led to the setting-up of the General Practice Finance Corporation, a body set up by government to help doctors finance the building and alteration of premises. Doctors could borrow money at a commercial rate and be reimbursed for interest payments on loans up to pre-set limits under the 'cost-rent' scheme. Such arrangements enabled partnerships to design and build surgeries which they would own and control. During the 1980s this became an increasingly popular option, and many excellent surg-

---

[23] RCGP, *Trends in General Practice* (London: RCGP, 1977), 144.

eries were built. These often provided facilities equal or superior to local-authority health centres, and also included room for attached district nurses and health visitors, without the complications of external management or multi-practice involvement. Some partnerships left health authorities to establish their own premises. In other areas doctors purchased health centres from health authorities, as the doctors sought control over their future and health authorities were keen to raise capital.

The design of general-practice premises reflects the prevailing medical ideology of their time. The early health centres reflected a desire to build efficient and technological structures, which would resemble mini-hospitals. As part of their struggle for professional recognition, general practitioners hoped that by surrounding themselves with the trappings of a hospital consultant, with large buildings and teams of subordinates, they would gain credibility.[24] By the time of the 1980s boom in cost-rent-financed owner-occupied surgeries, general practice had developed its own more self-confident view of medicine. This incorporated the notion of a general practitioner as a personal family doctor. Cost-rent surgeries became less clinical and more informal than their health-centre forebears. Rooms were arranged so that patients could sit beside their doctor, instead of facing them across a desk. Some doctors proposed removing the desk altogether, and practising from an easy chair. Practices began to provide space for health-promotion activities, common rooms, and consulting rooms for practice nurses.

In owner-occupied surgeries the doctors employed the reception and administrative staff, and from the mid-1980s they increasingly employed nurses to work in rapidly expanding roles. Despite the rhetoric of continuity of care as a core tenet of general practice, most practices abandoned personal lists, whereby patients saw the doctor with whom they were registered, and allowed patients to see any doctor or nurse they chose. The concept of 'the practice' therefore gradually changed, and became less identified with a particular doctor or doctors. The practice developed an identity of its own, not linked to any specific personality but related to the team and the building from which it worked. Practices were referred to not as 'Dr Smith and partners' but as 'the Willows surgery' or the 'Valley Medical Centre'.

As general practitioners moved into purpose-built or adapted premises, they acquired a new level of organization, and this led to new ways of working. Larger partnerships allowed doctors to attempt to regularize their working day, by sharing work and arranging cross-cover. The employment of reception staff enabled patient demand to be channelled and structured. The organizational changes enabled by the Charter meant that general practitioners increasingly saw patients by appointment, rather than seeing all those people who turned up at a given surgery on a 'first-come, first-served' basis. In 1964 only 15 per

---

[24] J. G. Beales, *Sick Health Centres and How to Make Them Better* (London, 1978), 18.

cent of a sample of doctors interviewed by Cartwright consulted by appointment.[25] By the time of her follow-up study in 1977, this had risen to 75 per cent of general practitioners.[26]

Appointment systems had advantages for doctors because they enabled them to organize their working week flexibly to suit personal arrangements, and for patients they meant less time waiting in a queue. This also enabled large practices to have a smaller waiting room. It was claimed that dedicating a specified length of time to each patient should enhance quality of care, without the sense of time pressure created by a waiting room filled with patients. The growth in appointment systems was not, however, universally welcomed. Several submissions were made to the Merrison Royal Commission on the NHS criticizing such systems.[27] Interestingly two major studies found that patients preferred the system they were used to, whether their practice used an appointment or an open system.[28] One great virtue of the appointment system was that it allowed a general practitioner who was faced with a complex, but not immediately urgent problem, to arrange for the patient to come back in one or two days' time and to book a double or triple appointment. This allowed adequate time to deal with the problem at length and without feeling hurried. It was something which was generally appreciated by the patient.

Appointment systems have been extensively studied and written about, reflecting the search for a solution to the constant problem of trying to deal with a large number of patients in a limited length of time. The median appointment time for general practitioners has consistently been found to be between six and seven minutes per patient. It has long been argued that this is insufficient to provide adequate care, and that general practitioners need smaller lists of patients in order to offer longer consultations to each one.

During the 1970s and 1980s 'the consultation' became an important issue for research, with many studies of the process, content, and style of general-practice consultations using audio and videotape recordings. This reflected the changing conceptualizations in general practice, particularly following the influence of Balint, and later the work of Pendleton and others.[29] No longer did consultations focus only on symptoms as clues for the detection of organic disease, but increasingly they focused on the doctor–patient relationship and on patients' ideas, concerns, and expectations. Various models of the consultation were developed, describing how each encounter represents an opportunity for health promotion, to review ongoing problems, to deal with the

[25] Cartwright *Patients and their Doctors*, 155.
[26] A. Cartwright and R. Anderson, *General Practice Revisited: A Second Study of Patients and their Doctors* (London, 1981).
[27] *Report of the Royal Commission on the NHS*, Cmnd. 7615 (The Merrison Report; London: HMSO, 1979).
[28] Cartwright and Anderson, *General Practice Revisited*, 32; J. Ritchie, A. Jacoby, and M. Bone, *Access to Primary Health Care* (London: HMSO, 1981).
[29] D. Pendleton *et al.*, *The Consultation: An Approach to Learning and Teaching* (Oxford, 1984).

patients' fears, and to modify their 'health-seeking behaviour', as well as to diagnose and treat the symptom presented.[30]

Such an ambitious agenda could scarcely be tackled adequately in six minutes, and the ideal of the ten-minute consultation was promoted. Longer consultation times have been associated in some (but not all) studies with greater patient satisfaction, lower consultation rates, lower rates of prescribing, and more preventive activities. It was argued that a reduction in the number of patients registered with each general practitioner was a prerequisite for these improvements, although the relationship between smaller list sizes and longer consultations is not straightforward.[31] The importance of reducing average list size became a central plank in the BMA's strategy for improving the quality of care in general practice.[32]

The average number of patients registered with each general practitioner increased from 2,282 in 1961 to 2,360 in 1966, and then declined steadily to 1,812 in 1991 (see Table D1). This was due to an increase in the number of general practitioners from 21,302 in 1966 to 29,560 in 1991 (see Table D2). The reduction in the number of patients cared for by each general practitioner did not appear to increase significantly the length of each consultation, nor did it decrease the general practitioner's hours of work. This is because important changes in patterns of work occurred over the period between 1966 and 1990.

First, there was a dramatic drop in the proportion of patients visited at home, as more people were seen in the doctor's surgery. In 1971 22 per cent of consultations were home visits (see Tables D4 and D5). By 1990 this proportion had more than halved, to only 10 per cent of all consultations. Home visits are time-consuming, therefore a decrease in their frequency should reduce general-practitioner workload. However, during the same period overall consultation rates rose from a low of three per patient in 1976 to five per patient in 1990. Consultation rates are higher for women than for men, except in young children and the elderly, when consultation rates are considerably higher overall for both sexes (see Table D6).

The pattern of a general practitioner's working day, and the proportion of time spent on different activities, also altered in the 'second phase' of general practice from 1966 to 1990. In 1965 the average general practitioner was consulted by approximately thirty-two patients per day, of which six consultations were home visits. These consultations were carried out within an average working week of forty hours (excluding on-call duties). Half of the time was spent in surgery consultations, a quarter on home visits, and a quarter on administrative, hospital work, and other duties.[33] By 1990 the average general

---

[30] N. C. Stott and R. H. Davis, 'The Exceptional Potential in Each Primary Care Consultation', *Journal of the Royal College of General Practitioners*, 29 (1979), 201–5.
[31] J. Butler and M. Calnan, *Too Many Patients?* (Aldershot, 1987).
[32] BMA, *General practice—a British Success* (London: BMA, 1984).
[33] RCGP, *Present State and Future Needs of General Practice* (London: RCGP, 1970), 11.

practitioner spent forty-two hours per week working, and a further twenty-three hours on call.[34] The proportion of time spent in direct patient contact had dropped slightly to 71 per cent, with the remaining 29 per cent of time spent on administration, meetings, and teaching. Although the number of visits had declined, the time spent visiting was almost as high, probably because of the increase in road traffic. The fall in list size was compensated for by the rising consultation rate per patient, and the burden of administration had grown considerably.

The increasing size of partnerships, and the increasing complex organization of practices, led general practitioners to spend more of their time in activities other than patient care. Large partnerships needed regular meetings, and the development of the primary-health-care team necessitated time for liaison, planning, and training.

One aspect of general-practitioner workload which changed dramatically was the arrangements made to provide patient care when surgeries were closed. Between 1966 and 1990 the demand for out-of-hours care appeared to rise considerably, although estimates of workload should be treated with caution, owing to differences in the ways that figures are calculated. The Family Doctor Charter introduced a specific payment for visits to patients requested and made between midnight and 7 a.m. (11 p.m. to 7 a.m. from 1973 onwards). The number of visits claimed per 1,000 patients per annum rose from four in 1967/8 to ten in 1975/6,[35] and then to nineteen in 1988/9.[36]

As demand grew, general practitioners reduced the amount of time they personally spent on call. The emergence of large partnerships meant that, by sharing a rota, each doctor could be on call once or twice a week instead of every night. During the late 1950s several commercial organizations were established offering deputizing services for out-of-hours care. This concept expanded in the 1960s to cover most large towns. In 1972, 28 per cent of general practitioners nationally used deputizing services,[37] which increased to 45 per cent by 1984.[38] In large cities such as Manchester over 90 per cent of general practitioners used deputizing services at least some of the time.[39] Use of these services was particularly common among older, male, single-handed general practitioners, and those with larger list sizes, and was less common in group practices.[40]

The increasing contribution of deputizing services caused controversy

[34] Fry, *General Practice: The facts*, 53.

[35] M. J. Buxton, R. E. Klein, and J. Sayers, 'Variations in GP Night Visiting Rates: Medical Organisation and Consumer Demand', *British Medical Journal* (1977), i. 827–30.

[36] D. R. Klein, and R. Carter, 'Impact of the 1990 Contract for General Practitioners on Night Visiting', *British Journal of General Practice*, 44 (1994), 68–71.

[37] B. T. Williams and J. Knowelden, 'General-Practitioner Deputizing Services—their Spread and Control', *British Medical Journal* (1974) i. suppl., 9–11.

[38] Anon., 'Deputising Services: A Serious Blunder', *British Medical Journal*, 288 (1984), 172.

[39] D. Wilkin, L. Hallam, R. Leavey, and D. Metcalfe, *Anatomy of Urban General Practice* (London, 1987), 131–2.

[40] Williams and Knowelden, 'General-Practitioner Deputizing Services'.

amongst both professionals and the public. Concern about the standard of care provided by deputies led to the introduction in 1984 of constraints on their use. Deputizing services were controversial with the medical profession because they appeared to strike at concepts of continuity of care and the doctor–patient relationship which were seen as central tenets of good general practice. However, by the end of the second phase, in 1990, these services appeared well established. The growth in deputizing services can be seen not as a response to either economic or professional incentives, but as a result of changing expectations of both patients and doctors. It can be seen as one symptom of the increasing professionalization of general practice, a theme which will be discussed later.

As well as a change in the pattern of the general practitioner's working week, there was also a gradual change in the scope of the doctor's working role. The growth in the size of partnerships, working with teams of nurses and administrative staff from adequate and in some cases excellent premises, had a very positive effect on morale. The previously described structural changes, the newly defined identity and role of general practice articulated by leaders in the Royal College and elsewhere, and the influx of bright young vocationally trained doctors formed a powerful combination. This released the ambition of many general practitioners who sought to expand their remit beyond the diagnosis and treatment of minor illness. Pioneers such as Tudor Hart in Wales described the importance of fusing care for individuals with care for groups of people and communities.[41] A series of reports from the Royal College of General Practitioners emphasized the potential role of general practice in preventing illnesses ranging from arterial disease to psychiatric disorders.[42] The implications of these ideas required practices to develop a level of organization that few had yet achieved.

In particular, the identification of patients at risk of certain conditions, or of groups of patients with a given diagnosis, required much better record systems than were commonly found in general practice. The vast majority of practices recorded information about consultations on small cards retained in Lloyd George envelopes, so called because of their association with the 1911 National Insurance Act introduced by Lloyd George. In many cases notes were not in chronological order, and the Lloyd George envelopes contained a jumbled collection of record cards and folded hospital letters. In 1970 a new A4 medical record was designed as a replacement for the hopelessly inadequate Lloyd George envelopes. The project was undertaken, with the support of the DHSS, by a group of general practitioners in Wantage, Berkshire. It met with approval from a sample of general practitioners all over the country who tested it in their practices, and from at least some members of the DHSS. But for reasons which are not certain, but probably because it was

[41] Tudor Hart, *A New Kind of Doctor*.
[42] RCGP, *Prevention of Arterial Disease in General Practice* (London: RCGP, 1981); RCGP, *Prevention of Psychiatric Disorders in General Practice* (London: RCGP, 1981).

believed to be too expensive, the plan to introduce this A4 record throughout the UK was abandoned. Nevertheless, A4 records were provided for quite a large number of practices in England and Wales, and for a much larger number of practices in Scotland, where the new record was made available for all who wanted it.[43]

While the A4 system represented a significant advance, although limited in distribution, many systems were devised to enable doctors to structure their records to make them more useful. Age–sex registers, comprising an index card for each patient sorted according to age and sex, were used by a significant minority of practices. The Royal College of General Practitioners promoted special cards on which doctors could record summaries of important illnesses, and flow charts for the systematic recording of items of care for patients with specific conditions.

Although such systems demonstrated the initiative that people can apply in difficult situations, the task of maintaining them was immense and required considerable clerical help. A survey of urban practices in 1981–2 showed that most doctors had little knowledge of these manual aids to improved note-keeping, and apart from age–sex registers there were very few attempts to create effective systems. Many records were inadequate and illegible.[44] The limitations of manual record systems, and the extent to which they hindered the further development of general practice, became increasingly obvious. During the 1980s attention moved to the potential of computers.

Computers were first used in general practice in the 1970s and the Department of Industry supported a pilot scheme, 'Micros for general practitioners', in 1982. However the use of computers in general practice escalated after 1987 owing to a combination of factors. During the mid-1980s the first single-user computer systems became available at an affordable price. These were initially used to replace the previous manual systems such as age–sex registers and card-index recall systems. Computers were commonly used for repeat prescribing, thus automating a repetitive and time-consuming task. In 1987 two large computer companies offered practices multi-user computer systems free of charge in return for access to anonymous data about prescribing patterns, which the companies could in turn market to pharmaceutical companies. For the first time practices could afford to have a computer on each consulting-room desk. Although both 'free' computer schemes soon foundered, they had facilitated the growth of a critical mass of computerized practices, so that by 1990 about half of the practices in England and Wales were computerized. Practices used their computers for patient registration, repeat and acute prescribing, call and recall systems, audit, running appointment systems, and some began to use them to replace manual notes altogether.

What themes characterize the organization of practices in this period

[43] J. K. Hawkey, I. S. L. Loudon, G. P. Greenhalgh, and G. T. Bungay, 'New Record Folder for Use in General Practice', *British Medical Journal* (1971), ii. 667–70.
[44] D. Wilkin *et al.*, *Anatomy of Urban General Practice*, 45.

between the Family Doctor Charter and the 1990 general-practitioner contract? There is a consistent theme of increasing professionalization and of a growing separation between the doctor's personal and work life. The decline in single-handed practice, the move from surgeries at the doctor's home to purpose-built centres (largely removing the involvement of doctors' wives), the growth in appointment systems and deputizing services, the reduction in home visiting, the increasing emphasis on teamwork, and the increasing number of doctors working part-time, are all examples of this trend.

Before the Charter, concerns were about the basic structure and organization of practices—issues such as premises, staff, and pay. Without fundamental reorganization, the survival of general practice was in serious doubt. The Charter reforms were effective because the contractual economic incentives reinforced the professional incentives, and allowed general practice to flourish. As a new and self-confident ideology of general practice developed distinct from the hospital model of medical care, there were attempts to regain control over areas which had been ceded to hospitals. Practices established diabetic and asthma clinics, and developed protocols for the management of other chronic diseases. Vocational training schemes produced a substantial core of élite practices which were assessed against criteria which were constantly made more rigorous. These practices were generally well equipped and well staffed, with high levels of organization, and they made up a quarter of all practices. At the other extreme there were a substantial minority of practices offering standards of care little different from that available before the Family Doctor Charter.

Debate in the 1980s therefore moved on from standards of organization to the quality of care provided in general practice. Great variability was identified in all measures of activity, from prescribing costs and hospital referral rates to childhood immunization rates. Particular concern was expressed about seemingly intractable problems in general practice in deprived urban areas, especially in Inner London.

These issues were addressed in the 1985 Royal College of General Practitioners 'Quality Initiative'. This identified the inconsistency of standards in general practice, and emphasized the importance of audit as a means of raising quality. The policy document explicitly pointed out the lack of incentives in the existing contract for high-quality care.[45] This view was an influential force in the gestation of a new general-practitioner contract. In contrast to the Royal College of General Practitioners' approach of creating incentives for quality, the BMA proposed measures to improve training for general practice and again emphasized the centrality of reducing list sizes. They argued that rewarding high standards of care would increase the diversity in standards, and that it was more important to focus resources on removing the root causes of poor quality care.

[45] RCGP, *Quality in General Practice* (London: RCGP, 1985).

This view was not in keeping with current political orthodoxy, which emphasized competition as the main force leading to improved standards. Practices were not seen as sufficiently responsive, and empowering consumers was seen as an important priority. In direct contrast to the BMA's view that smaller list sizes were necessary to improve quality, it was proposed that an increased capitation element in the fee structure would improve standards of care, as practices competed to attract patients. The stage was therefore set for the third policy regime, from 1990 to the present.

From 1990 onwards

The 1990 contract and the introduction of fundholding had the effect of reinforcing and accelerating change in all aspects of the practice. A survey comparing practices in 1986–7 with 1992–3 showed more change in premises and staffing in these five years than in the previous 25.[46] The pressure for more space in practice premises, which had already been increasing under the Family Doctor Charter, accelerated further. Partnership size increased, with many more practices comprising five or more partners and the range of contribution within the primary-care team also increased. Practice nurses began to play a more independent role with some acting as nurse practitioners in seeing patients directly. The family doctor's job came to be less task orientated and more concerned with communication and management with patients, staff, and professionals from outside under contract to the practice. From the one receptionist of the late 1950s a practice could employ 40–50 people in differing roles including nurses, social workers, counsellors and physiotherapists, dieticians and chiropodists. There was further expansion in the role of the practice nurse in running health-promotion clinics and other services. There were also closer relationships to the wider primary-care team of community nurses with the old arguments for and against attachment falling into the background. For premises and staffing some of the changes could be seen as an intensification and acceleration of change which had already started under the Family Doctor Charter. Some of the inequalities in standards were reduced as FHSAs targeted their support at practices which were most in need of improvement. The main new direction of change was in the range of services and in the activities within the practice.

Many family doctors were now seeking to carry out four different jobs. There were the old demand-led consultations: and the overall consultation rate had shown a 10 per cent increase by 1991 compared with 1981.[47] There were new roles in disease management which had developed furthest in diabetes and

[46] B. Leese and N. Bosanquet, 'Change in General Practice and its Effects on Service Provision in Areas with Different Socio-Economic Characteristics', *British Medical Journal*, 311 (1995), 546–50.

[47] Office of Population Censuses and Surveys (OPCS), and *Morbidity Statistics from General Practice: Fourth National Study* (London: HMSO, 1995).

asthma. The primary-care team aims to manage care for patients with chronic illness over time. There was a third area of activity in reducing risk factors. And finally many general practitioners were involved in purchasing secondary care. With this widening of role went an increase in workload and hours of work, which rose by 15–20 per cent in the early 1990s.[48] In 1987 only 12 per cent of GPs had felt that they were under great pressure and continually short of time; by 1993 this proportion had risen to 43 per cent.[49] In practice many general practitioners were having to delegate. Increasingly they were coming to accept that they could not do everything. So, for example, they might leave involvement in maternity care, counselling, or health promotion to others. New local approaches to running out-of-hours service supplied one of the few extra elements in relief: it seemed by 1997 that these had been quite successful in reducing demand through giving more patients the option of coming up to special out-of-hours centres. The old role of twenty-four-hour care was a casualty of the increased workload during the normal day.

These changes were helped by government policy and by stronger local management of family health services: but they were also assisted by change in therapy and in the process of care. The 1990s were a period of rapid development in home-based care and in new drug therapy. There were more new and powerful drugs available on prescription. It became more common for frail elderly patients to live at home. Even though hospital admissions rose, they were for shorter periods, so that there were many more people with high levels of disability living in the community. At the same time, technology was changing the process of care at the practice most obviously with the introduction of computerization. British family doctors were world leaders in the use of local computer systems in primary care, and much of the initiative came from practices themselves with government coming in later to reinforce this. Some practices were going 'paperless', and many more were using IT links with the health authority for registration and financial claims. Soon there would be links with hospital pathology for results to be downloaded directly into patients' electronic notes.

Lastly there was change in professionals' models and professional pressures. The old models of general practice, based on the importance of consultation skills and the doctor–patient relationship, were giving way to detailed protocols and guidelines of care in specific diseases. The practice had to face audit and external review much more often than in the past. Professional identity had passed from ideals to detailed processes shown by care programmes for specific groups of patients and proved by a computer print-out.

By 1997 general practice had been through an intense phase of development. For some the signs pointed forward in a positive direction towards a primary-care-led NHS in which family doctors would have the confidence to develop

[48] Leese and Bosanquet, 'Change in General Practice and its Effects on Service Provision'.
[49] B. Leese and N. Bosanquet, 'Changes in General Practice Organisation: Survey of GPs' Views on the 1990 Contract and Fundholding', *British Journal of General Practice*, 46 (1996), 95–9.

care on a more integrated basis close to patients' homes. Others pointed to the difficulties that might be involved in filling practice vacancies and in serving the investment that had already been made. For experienced family doctors the job may well have become more interesting, reducing middle-aged burn-out; but for new recruits it was more intimidating, so that by 1997 there were serious recruitment problems for many partnership vacancies. As the proportion of women in general practice increased, there seemed likely to be more interest in flexible contracts and salaried employment. Some practices had expanded premises so rapidly that they now had substantial negative equity; others faced hidden long-term costs from staff pensions and increased pay bills. There was an underlying conflict between the drive forward of the secondary-care machine and the investments required for primary and ambulatory care. Behind the concerns about morale there was already solid evidence of success in reaching targets and in improving the care process; but more evidence seemed likely to lead to new concerns about improved care in many areas such as prevention, care of people with severe mental illness, and palliative care. For doctors the drama of tension between practice resources and professional aspiration was now playing out over weeks and months rather than the years of the past. Access to funding and quality of leadership seemed likely to bring about a future of expansion : but more expectant and informed patients could bring new challenges. Family doctors were moving into an era of local innovation as contracts seemed likely to become more flexible; for family doctors a new era was opening of achievement in care but of greater professional and financial risk as activities increased and with it investment in premises and staffing. One model to cope with these expanding responsibilities was the development of multi-funds: networks of fundholding practices which group together to negotiate contracts with hospitals. New groups of lead partners might emerge which would be specialists in managing risk, and Trusts might be more directly involved in primary care. Expansion of activities might bring greater diversity in models of care and contractual arrangements. The age of single national models seemed likely to be ending, and family doctors, even before the twenty-first century dawned, would have to work out the logic of their investment in local enterprise. The practice of 2000 might be very different even from that of 1990, let alone the advanced practice of 1964.

3

'What is Wrong' and 'How We Know It': Changing Concepts of Illness in General Practice

MARSHALL MARINKER

In the half-century history of the NHS, unprecedented advances have taken place in the understanding of human biology and morbidity, in the techniques of surgery and clinical investigation, and in the range and power of medicines. Increasingly the means of laboratory and imaging investigations were brought into the ambit of general practice. In Chapter 4 the impact of all this on the recognition, diagnosis, and treatment of disease is examined. Among the consequences of these advances were shifts in the emphasis which doctors placed on different aspects of the medical task. The focus moved from the response to short-term acute illness, to the management of long-term, chronic, and degenerative conditions, and then to earlier and earlier interventions in the natural history of diseases.

For the greater part of this history, however, these advances in the technical aspects of medicine, although dramatic and influential, will form only the backdrop to the examination of other sources of change in the ways in which general practitioners came to see the clinical picture. I will suggest that a number of powerful 'movements' in epidemiology, the social and behavioural sciences, and in the wider politics of the times, changed the doctor's perception of 'what is wrong' and 'how we know it'. I use the former term in order to avoid the (specifically biotechnical) meaning attached to the word 'diagnosis', and the latter term in order to avoid the (specifically rationalistic and mechanistic) meanings associated with 'clinical method'. The changes with which I am concerned in what follows were essentially moral, philosophical, psychological, and, in a special sense, political.

By 'political' I mean to convey not so much the political nature of medicine's role in society, but rather the micro-politics (the checks and balances of power) of the consultation. There were also macro-political changes in society that affected the doctor's perception of the illness. These concerned a debate at the heart of twentieth-century philosophy and policy in health-care planning, between alternative libertarian and collectivist views of the tasks of medicine. These views can be traced back to the eighteenth-century development of the medical profession, at the time of the appearance of the general practitioner of physic, pharmacy, surgery, and man-midwifery. General practice in the NHS became a central arena for these contending ideas, and in the fifth decade of the NHS the paradox of 'self' (the pursuit of autonomy, consumerism, entitlements, transparency of information, and so on) and 'solidarity' (the pursuit of evidence for efficiency, rationing, and distributive justice)[1] surfaced in fierce public debates. These resounded with the echoes of Virchow's plangent trumpet call in Germany a century earlier: 'Medicine is a social science.'[2]

Consideration of what happened to the general practitioner's notion of 'what is wrong' and 'how we know it' cannot be divorced from the spirit of the age in which NHS general practice was developing. For example, what will be described as the coming to the fore of the psychological agenda in the 1960s and early 1970s, the valuing of feelings and intimate relationships in the consultation, cannot be considered unrelated to the fashions of 'flower power' and 'sexual freedoms', 'purple hearts' (a mixture of stimulating amphetamine and sedating barbiturate) from the doctor's surgery, and 'pot' (cannabis) at the Beatles' concerts, and the seemingly socio-lyrical poetry of their popular songs.

Introduced in the early 1960s, the benzodiazepines reached their peak prescription rate (around 30 million per annum) in 1977. The attraction of psychotherapeutic responses to the patients' life situations at this time (discussed below) was in part a reaction to what seemed the unstoppable explosion of tranquillizer prescribing, and the concomitant fashion for psychiatric diagnosis. These therapeutic fashions seem arbitrary without reference to the wider body politic. Medawar quotes the following advertisement by a major pharmaceutical company for the leading brand of benzodiazapine in 1970:

The Sixties. It is ten years since Librium became available. Ten anxious years of aggravation and demonstration, Cuba, Vietnam, assassination and devaluation, Biafra and Czechoslovakia. Ten turbulent years in which the world-wide climate of anxiety and aggression has given Librium—with its specific calming action and its remarkable safety margin—a unique and still growing role in helping man meet the challenge of a changing world.[3]

The emphasis in the later 1970s and early 1980s on preventive medicine and the avoidance of disease and premature death was of a piece in the UK with

---

[1] M. Marinker, 'Sense and Sensibility', in M. Marinker (ed.), *Sense and Sensibility in Health Care* (London, 1996).

[2] Rudolph Virchow, nineteenth-century German pathologist, public-health activist, and revolutionary, formulated the striking slogan 'Medicine is a social science, and politics nothing but medicine on a grand scale'. The sequel would seem to be that, if politics is medicine on a grand scale, medicine is politics on a small scale. See also G. Rosen, *From Medical Police to Social Medicine* (New York, 1974).

[3] C. Medawar, *Power and Dependence* (London, 1992), 110.

a decade of relative general prosperity and a sense of inevitable economic growth. In the Introduction to this book Morrell calls them 'the happy years'. As I shall later argue, the domestic political climate of the late 1980s and the 1990s to date, influenced by the theories of monetarism and competitive markets, further contributed to a redefinition of 'what is wrong' and 'how we know it', in the light of their values.

The tides of change

The changes in the way in which general practitioners viewed and talked about 'what is wrong' with the patient over the past fifty years might well be put down to nothing more substantial than the vagaries of fashion. In the medical literature, for the most part, common terms such as 'disease' or 'diagnosis' or 'illness' or 'case' are rarely qualified. Yet at different times they carry certain inflections of meaning which reflect current preoccupations about the nature of illness and therefore of the clinical task. I shall argue that, in the period under review, there were in effect profoundly radical shifts in the way in which the patient's problem or illness came to be 'understood' by the doctor. These changes in clinical language and discourse, which sometimes resembled the ebb and flow of fashion, were neither trivial nor cosmetic.

They came about because, as the developing NHS made clear the pivotal role of general practice in sustaining a rational and affordable public service, general practitioners became self-confident enough to challenge the sufficiency of their medical school biotechnology training in preparing them for the problems with which their patients presented them forty or fifty times a day. They sought new insights elsewhere, from beyond clinical medicine, in the search for 'what is wrong' with the patient and 'how we know it'.

These new insights were imported into general practice from such diverse fields as epidemiology, psychoanalysis, sociology, social psychology, management theory, political philosophy, and moral theory. Like a succession of tides washing over the foreshore of clinical general practice, each of these disciplines left behind distinct sediments of language, values, and methods, over the fifty years of our purview. I shall attempt to excavate these sedimentary layers under the following headings: 'the patient as diagnosis' (the notion that the patient and not just the disease is the object of enquiry); 'the family as illness' (the extension of the enquiry beyond the individual to the domestic group); 'the illness as risk' (the extension of 'what is wrong' from past and present time, where it has traditionally been sought, to the future); 'the patient as community' (the consequences for the individual of a population-based method of clinical care), and 'the illness as commodity' (the clinical implications of cost-benefit and other analyses from health economics).

Subtly but radically these shifts in emphasis redirected what Foucault described as the doctor's 'gaze'[4]—that is to say, the assumptions about what is to be looked at, and looked for. Paradoxically, as biotechnology began to provide more powerful tools for diagnosis and treatment, the general practitioner became increasingly confident in naming the patient as the true object of the consultation. It became a lapse of good taste to refer to the patient as a 'case'—as though she were (to point to the unconscious root of that word) the receptacle inside which the doctor's true clinical object, the name of the disease, was cunningly concealed.

One caveat before I continue: the evidence of these changes in perception will be drawn from the growing literature on the subject—and here the most vexing problem presents itself. The changes are recorded in the writings and research reports of behavioural scientists and general-practitioner researchers and teachers. The evidence presented is, for the most part, of changes in the *ideas*. Evidence of consequent changes in actual *practice* is less secure.

Pictures and stories

In looking at the ways in which these perceptions have changed over the past half-century, I want to begin with some observations made in a seminal study of general practice published in 1954.[5] Under the aegis of the Nuffield Provincial Hospitals Trust, Stephen Taylor had in 1951–2 carried out a non-statistical survey of ninety-four general practitioners in thirty practices, with a view to answering the trenchant criticisms of British general practice which had been published by an Australian visiting doctor.[6] This had painted a damning picture of general practice in the opening years of the NHS. Here, in his prologue, Taylor is describing a vignette from one of his many practice visits. He gives it as an example of what makes general practice 'the most fascinating and absorbing and rewarding job in the world':

The tiny room is scarcely seven feet square. It is over a stable in a Victorian mews. The horse has gone, but the coster's cart remains, and the smell of old hay wins out against strong competition. A party is in progress. There is an old lady of 88, her lodger of 72, her son aged 65, and, covered with a sheet, the corpse of her late husband, aged 91. They are waiting for the undertaker. 'Have a cup of tea, doctor,' says the old lady, 'lor' but it's a blessing he's gone. More trouble than the old horse he used to be . . .'[7]

[4] M. Foucault, *The Birth of the Clinic* (London, 1963).
[5] S. Taylor, *Good General Practice* (Oxford, 1954).
[6] J. S. Collings, 'General Practice in England Today: A Reconnaissance', *Lancet* (1950), i. 555–85.
[7] Taylor, *Good General Practice*, p. xxi. Similar descriptions of general practice in the early 1930s appear in G. Barber, *Country Doctor* (Ipswich, 1973). Most of the illnesses described were acute and 'surgical' rather than medical, still reflecting the far stronger links that the nineteenth-century apothecaries had with the surgeons than with the physicians. To this day in the UK, general practitioners and their patients refer to the practice premises, and to the doctor's consulting hours, as 'surgeries'.

What does the language used to describe this clinical encounter suggest? A sense of intimacy, of domesticity, but also of the precise social space, the distance, between doctor and patient, indicated by the smells of the room (Taylor was quite obsessed by smell as a marker of health and social status), and the almost comic report of demotic speech. This is a picture of the good squire visiting the deathbed of an old retainer, the kindly parson about his charitable work at the poor end of the parish. As to the doctor's clinical task, the first example in the book has us in a similar domestic milieu, but now with traditionally valued symptoms, diagnoses, and treatments added:

It is a dingy little house in the east end of London. The doctor climbs the narrow stair to the patient's bedroom. Doctor and patient are both wheezing: the one is a chronic asthmatic, the other a chronic bronchitic with cardiac failure and basal bronchopneumonia. By the bed is an oxygen cylinder, a bobbin flow-meter, and a BLB mask . . . 'There wasn't a bed for an old chap like him. He's having mersalyl, digoxin and distaquaine penicillin as well, and he needs the lot. And what's more, he's getting better . . .'[8]

Again the feeling for general practice's peculiar time and place and relationships is strong. The layout of the ward, and the pulmonary distress of the visiting physician, would scarcely have been thought relevant for comment in a report of a patient in hospital with pneumonia and heart failure. But the domestic picture, the suggested social situation, and the description of the doctor are clearly *contextual*. They are parts of the scenery of the drama being enacted and described. They have not yet become *intrinsic*—as they were later to become—to the idea of 'diagnosis'.

As to the patient's psychological health, for Taylor this was still firmly separated from the organic pathology, and clearly labelled 'neurosis' or 'hysteria'—words heavy with pejorative judgement. Taylor warns time and again against the excesses and hazards of a psychotherapeutic approach:

Most patients with organic illnesses react to them with a measure of anxiety . . . At once the psychotherapeutically-inclined doctor starts to hunt for causes of hidden mental tension: and, of course, there are few normal people in whom such causes cannot be unearthed. Meanwhile the bronchiectasis, tuberculosis, or perinephric abscess advances undiagnosed.[9]

For Taylor, the psychological is the antithesis of the physical, and the psychological approach seduces the doctor from fidelity to the clinical task. He asserts that 'There is a substantial element of truth in the hypothesis that the better the clinician, the less often does he diagnose neurosis.'[10] His *ad hoc* psychiatric nosology curiously omits any mention of psychoses. He does, however, recognize 'true mild endogenous depression', quoting C. A. H. Watts, a Leicestershire general practitioner, who had just published his treatise on psychiatric

[8] Taylor, *Good General Practice*, p. xxi.
[9] Ibid. 416.   [10] Ibid.

illness as seen by the general practitioner.[11] Watts was already at work on his important narrative-based study of patients with depression,[12] which was to do so much to counter the then prevalent sense of therapeutic helplessness in the face of psychiatric illness, and so the attendant sense of stigma.

This sense of stigma is reflected in Taylor's categories of psychological illness which included 'neurasthenia', 'neurotic "hang over" from the organic complaint', 'neurotic reactions to difficult or hopeless housing conditions', 'the weaker brethren who need helping over every stile', and 'the familiar compensation neurosis'. Taylor observes that the amount of psychiatric illness with which the doctor is obliged to deal depends on the attitude of the practitioner. In this context he quotes the following from one of his interviews:

I make it an absolute rule never, under any circumstances, to tell a patient what his blood pressure reading is. Instead I say 'Not bad for your age', or 'Quite reasonably satisfactory'. Once a patient knows he or she has hypertension, symptoms multiply enormously, and misery grows . . . If such a patient goes to hospital I always ask the staff *not* to mention the blood pressure reading in front of the patient. But in spite of this some silly HP [*sic*] will say 'My goodness! What a blood pressure you have got!', and all my good work will be undone.'[13]

I have quoted so much from Taylor because this work was a landmark in the renaissance of British general practice following the Collings Report. It reflects a practice of medicine in which the diagnostic prizes to be won by the general practitioner were clearly the major diseases first encountered by him in the wards of the university teaching hospital. I use the masculine pronoun here because Taylor's disdain for the psychological was matched only by his view of women doctors: 'Such (women) doctors get great pleasure out of removing sebaceous cysts and opening whitlows and abscesses; they do it extremely efficiently, with the neatness, aplomb and expertise that might otherwise go into dress-making and embroidery.'[14]

This view of women doctors was all of a piece with the robust masculine instrumentality of medical sentiment, education, and practice at the time. The dominant ethical value was beneficence rather than autonomy (as the above passage on the hypertensive patient illustrates). And there is a feeling of solidity and certainty about all Taylor's diagnostic formulations, including the psychological ones: words such as 'asthma' and 'hypertension' and 'neurosis' and 'endogenous depression' as they are used here appear as the desired and well-recognized destinations of the diagnostic journey. They do not yet, as they would in the years to come, appear also to be points of departure for further exploration of 'what is wrong'.

Some twenty years after Taylor's book appeared, another general-practice

---

[11] C. A. H. Watts and B. M. Watts, *Psychiatry in General Practice* (London, 1952).
[12] C. A. H. Watts, *Depressive Disorders in the Community* (Bristol, 1966).
[13] Taylor, *Good General Practice*, 417.
[14] Ibid. 54.

landmark publication, by a working party of the Royal College of General Practitioners,[15] contained a strikingly different contemporary view of 'what is wrong'. Two 'cases' were described.

The first is of a 30-year-old woman who presents with intermittent choking sensations, palpitations, scant periods, full and staring eyes, tremulous sweating hands, and a number of other salient signs and laboratory findings that indicate an overactive thyroid, with intermittent bleeding into the gland.

The second is of a young mother who attends the doctor's surgery with an irritable 'badly behaved' sleepless 3-year-old child who cries out constantly in the night and keeps her parents awake. Her elderly mother is about to visit and she is worried about what she will think to find the house and the child 'in such a state'. Meanwhile she requests a repeat prescription for some medicine for her husband who is having exacerbated pain from his duodenal ulcer. These descriptions are then used as texts to discuss uncertainty and ambiguity, and the passage ends:

If you are now told that the woman described as the second case has also complained of intermittent choking sensations, that in fact she is the same 30-year-old woman described as the first, you are able to see how much more the applied behavioural sciences may be able to add to the diagnosis 'thyrotoxicosis with recurrent haemorrhages into a retrosternal goitre' which a knowledge of the biological sciences alone revealed.[16]

The biological and the psychosocial elements of the diagnosis are presented here not as coincidental, but as fused. In another chapter of the same report the first of the key goals of vocational training is given as 'To make diagnoses about his patient which are expressed *simultaneously* in physical, psychological and social terms' (emphasis added).[17] *The Future General Practitioner* marked a massive breaking-away from the intellectual and emotional chains of a predominantly instrumental and reductionist hospital-oriented medicine. What had brought this about?

The patient as diagnosis

Only three years separate the publication of *Good General Practice* in 1954 and the appearance in 1957 of *The Doctor, his Patient and the Illness*.[18] Yet the distance between them is great. In 1939 Michael Balint had arrived in the UK as an émigré from Hungary, where a repressive far-right political regime had

[15] RCGP, *The Future General Practitioner: Learning and Teaching* (London: RCGP 1972).
[16] Ibid. 27.
[17] Ibid. 4.
[18] M. Balint, *The Doctor, his Patient and the Illness* (London, 1957).

made the professional life of its Jewish intellectuals, and by association the practice of psychoanalysis, all but untenable.

The son of a general practitioner, Balint had concentrated his early medical researches in the field of biochemistry. As a young man wedded to the advance of medicine by scientific method, he early encountered psychoanalysis (then so fashionable among the middle European intelligentsia, though considered rather suspect by the medical profession), and wrote what he later described as highly ambivalent attacks on Freud's *The Interpretation of Dreams* and *The Psychopathology of Everyday Life*. Within a year he had begun a teaching analysis in Berlin with one of the original group of Freud's disciples, H. Sachs, but completed this later in Budapest with another of the original Freudian group, Sandor Ferenczi. In the Hungarian model of psychoanalytical training, the first case treated by the trainee-analyst was supervised by the trainer, so that attention was paid both to the trainee's relationship with the analyst-trainer, and to the relationship between the trainee-analyst and his patient. It was this sort of 'double-decker' trainer–trainee relationship that shaped Balint's later approach to training general practitioners.

In 1950 he began work with general practitioners at the Tavistock Clinic in London, where he had been appointed consultant. His original intention in advertising what he later came to call his 'training-cum-research' seminars appears to have been the teaching of psychotherapeutic techniques.[19] This sharing of techniques with non-psychiatrists by a psychoanalyst was, to say the least, unusual. Given the profound and pervasive effect that this 'sharing' was to have on general practice, one is intrigued to ask why Balint chose to devote such a large part of his teaching and research energies to this novel task. Perhaps, initially, he turned to general practitioners because of the general rejection of psychoanalysis by much of the psychiatric establishment, in this country—as in his native Hungary.

But another reason suggests itself. Psychoanalysis is not only a form of psychotherapy; it is represented by its adherents primarily as a moral philosophy.[20] It seems likely that Balint saw his work with general practitioners as a powerful vehicle for psychoanalytical 'evangelism' (Balint uses the term 'apostolic function' to describe the doctor's values and style), in pursuit of a moral agenda. In the preface to a monograph on psychoanalytical theory, there is a clear statement of Balint's orientation as a psychiatrist and theorist.[21] It makes visible what later he seems at pains either to deny or to repress—the part played by his psychoanalytical beliefs that lay just beneath the surface of his work with general practitioners. He writes that, from the beginning of his interest in psy-

---

[19] Balint worked with a number of leading psychoanalysts in developing his training methods: for an account of this see M. Balint, E. Balint, R. Gosling, and P. Hildebrand, *A Study of Doctors* (London, 1966).

[20] P. Rieff, *Freud: The Mind of the Moralist* (London, 1960).

[21] M. Balint, *Primary Love and Psycho-analytic Technique* (London, 1952).

choanalysis, the focus of his interest was 'the development of the individual sexual function and the development of human relationships'.[22]

Although in *The Doctor, his Patient and the Illness* there is no explicit use of Freudian terms or theories, they can, I believe, often be detected in what is implied, and in how Balint chooses to construct meaning.[23] The subject of the general-practice seminars is quite clearly the 'development of human relationships'. What then of the other half of his twin focus, 'the development of the individual sexual function'? For the most part this is implied by the sexual 'spin' that Balint put on the patients' stories, and by the inferences he drew, even though the language is virtually free of analytical terms. Summing up the whole of the Balint contribution years, after her husband's death, his wife and collaborator Enid told me: 'We tried to show how important it is for the doctor to listen to the patient.' This was work far distanced from psychoanalytical theory.

The number of general practitioners who worked with Balint and his colleagues in the 1950s, 1960s, and 1970s was relatively small: for the most part they were Londoners, because most of the analyst group leaders were London based, and the seminars were conducted weekly over periods of some years. But among their number were many of the pioneering leaders of the Royal College of General Practitioners, of university departments of general practice, and of vocational training schemes. Four of the six authors of *The Future General Practitioner* had been members of Balint groups.[24] More importantly, because of the influence of the College, many of the professional leaders in the 1970s and 1980s who had had no personal contact with Balint, or membership of any of the seminars associated with his name, became imbued with this philosophical approach to practice, and, as their number grew, were able to achieve far more than the small band of original seminar members to further the teaching and research.

One of Balint's non-analyst psychiatrist collaborators, Sir Desmond Pond, who was later to become President of the Royal College of Psychiatrists, and Chief Scientist to the Department of Health, remarked how profoundly and originally Balint influenced the language of general practice.[25] The greatest mark of success of his insights, he suggested, was that, as a result of his

[22] Ibid., p. vii.

[23] P. Sowerby, 'Balint Reassessed: *The Doctor, his Patient and the Illness*: A Reappraisal', *Journal of the Royal College of General Practitioners*, 27 (1977), 583–9. Sowerby's article, which caused much comment at the time, was highly critical of the Balint approach, on the ground that its diagnoses were implicitly rooted in psychoanalytical theory, and were therefore outside the proper scientific province of modern medicine.

[24] The term 'Balint seminars' is generic: seminars were led by a number of influential psychoanalysts such as Robert Gosling, Tom Main, Pierre Tourquet, and so on. Later they were co-led by general-practitioner 'alumni'. They and their general-practitioner-seminar members and co-researchers were later referred to, with mocking affection, as 'The Tavistocracy'.

[25] P. Hopkins (ed.), *The Human Face of Medicine* (London, 1979).

originality the profession came to the conclusion that 'everybody knew it all the time, anyway'.[26]

But what was it that 'everybody knew . . . all the time'? Consider the following observations from the original book. 'Every illness is also the "vehicle" of a plea for love and affection'; and, linked to this, another: 'The patient develops an illness in order to be able to complain. . . . Complaining is a social phenomenon par excellence. i.e. the person complained to [the doctor] is nearly as important [as the patient].'[27] It was in ideas like this, which were unfamiliar and, at first, difficult to grasp ideas, that the focus of the general practitioner's clinical concern was readjusted, first from the diagnosis of disease to the meaning of the illness, secondly, from the illness to the patient, and, thirdly, from the patient to the doctor–patient relationship.

Despite being thought to do so, Balint was not advancing a covert argument (which was perhaps be expected from psychoanalysis) for the 'psychologizing' of physical illness or the physician's therapeutic response. He reminds the general practitioner that he is 'a family doctor, not an amateur psychiatrist'. Moreover, he gives an intriguing psychological reason for not rejecting the somatic illness. Having noted that, because of their training, doctors prefer diagnosing and treating physical illness, he warns the general practitioner of the reciprocal danger of being 'tempted to brush aside all physical symptoms and make a bee-line for what he thinks may be the psychological root of the trouble'.[28] To do this would be to force the patient to face something too painful.

Other Balint dicta have become amalgamated into the language of general practice—for example, the use of 'the drug doctor', with its attendant pharmacological analogues about dose, timing, toxicity, and so on. This idea became powerfully incorporated into the profession's growing emphasis on personal doctoring and the creation of 'personal lists' as practice partnerships grew larger. Balint's metaphor of the relationship as a 'Mutual Investment Company' underpinned the emphasis that was increasingly given to the benefits of continuity of care, and provided a psychological rationale for it.

A decade after the appearance of *The Doctor, his Patient and the Illness*, and six years before the publication of *The Future General Practitioner*, an important paper by Ian McWhinney, based on his visiting fellowship to the USA, where he studied the emerging 'speciality' of 'family medicine', emphasized the significance, from the general practitioners' point of view, of the social and psychological aspects of 'what is wrong'.[29] The significance of McWhinney's categorizing of the content of general practice as an academic discipline is that the psychosocial dimensions are no longer presented as confined to 'psychiatry' in general practice, but are applied to the whole field of diagnosis. However,

---

[26] Ibid., p. xiii.   [27] Balint, *The Doctor, his Patient and the Illness*, 276–7.
[28] Ibid. 273.
[29] I. R. McWhinney, 'General Practice as an Academic Discipline', *Lancet* (1966), i. 419–23.

he had not yet incorporated them into the very stuff of diagnosis itself. He writes rather that 'The practitioner must be a student of human behaviour, because this determines the way in which illness presents to him'. The patient's social situation and the quality of her personal relationships are not yet recognized here as *part of the diagnosis*, but McWhinney writes presciently that 'parent disciplines must be melted down, amalgamated, and moulded into a new form'.[30]

This sort of 'new form' appeared four years later in a study of patients on long-term medication, or 'repeat prescriptions'—the first time this now much-researched phenomenon is mentioned in the medical literature.[31] This was a narrative description of a large minority of patients in a number of general practices, in whom the original diagnosis (almost invariably a 'physical' illness, though rarely reliably supported by strong clinical evidence) was treated by a regimen of medications, usually in low and sub-therapeutic doses, over very long periods of time.

For the most part these patients had remained remarkably 'well' on such treatment, or at least they did not complain of new symptoms or present with new pathology. In fact, providing there was no interruption of the regimen—which typically involved little contact with the doctor, or at most a highly ritualized contact in which no real clinical work could be done—peace reigned. If the regimen were interrupted or examined, the peaceful 'contract' was breached, and mayhem (new illness and disturbed relationships) ensued. How could this mysterious collection of 'findings' be understood?

The title of the book—Treatment or Diagnosis?—presented in interrogatory form the conclusion of the researchers. There was no orthodox medical name for the diagnoses of 'what is wrong' with these patients. The treatment followed the diagnosis, but not in a way that could be understood in terms of pathology or pharmacology—though the language of both these disciplines was usually employed. These were patients who could not tolerate the intimacy required to examine their problems in more than the most superficial way. Indeed, because of this, the research was carried out despite a deal of resistance from the general-practitioner researchers themselves, who were embarrassed by this hitherto hidden but pervasive aspect of their work. The research findings highlighted, in psychological terms, what was to be confirmed in epidemiological terms twenty-two years later.

Reviewing the variability of the data from the Second National Morbidity Study, Crombie and his colleagues concluded that general practitioners lacked a common diagnostic language—that is to say, agreed criteria for naming very many of the conditions that they saw.[32] This should not suggest that general

---

[30] Ibid. 419.

[31] M. Balint, J. Hunt, R. Joyce, M. Marinker, and J. Woodcock, *Treatment or Diagnosis?* (London, 1970).

[32] D. L. Crombie, K. W. Cross, and D. M. Fleming, 'The Problem of Diagnostic Variability in General Practice', *Journal of Epidemiology and Community Health*, 46 (1992), 447–54.

practitioners were not diagnosing and treating their patients appropriately. It does imply, however, that, although their medical education and the construction of diagnostic rubrics for the purposes of epidemiological studies appeared to constrain general practitioners to express their patients' illnesses in rigid somatic labels, they resisted such oversimplification in practice. In the continued absence of a vocabulary to describe the diagnosis made 'simultaneously in physical, psychological and social terms', doctors appeared to use 'politically correct' language for the purposes of epidemiological recording, although this language could not express the complexity of how general practitioners thought about, and responded to, 'what is wrong'. For the most part this could not be expressed as diagnostic labels or numeric rubrics, but rather as narrative and critical appreciation.

Much credit for popularizing this distinctive general-practice view of the diagnosis belongs to two general-practitioner writers who, in the mid-1960s, published a series of 'case studies'. Browne and Freeling adapted the model of transactional analysis and psychological games to the general-practice encounter.[33] Almost two decades later Neighbour, another general practitioner, taking a similar model-building approach, although referring to a different psychodynamic model, influenced a new generation of doctors.[34]

Two social psychologists whose work was also separated by two decades added to the vocabulary of general practice's psychosocial language. Both, like Balint, worked closely with general-practitioner collaborators. Long, working with Byrne, the first English Professor of General Practice, carried out a detailed analysis of audiotaped consultations and showed the differences between a patient-centred and a doctor-centred style.[35] Pendleton, working with a group of leading general-practitioner trainers in Oxfordshire, carried out a series of experimental analyses of videotaped consultations, deriving a list of key (desirable and undesirable) behaviours.[36] Although essentially reductionist, this method of examining the videotaped consultation was undoubtedly created by its inventors to serve a holistic teaching agenda. But its later use in assessment and accreditation, had (as we shall see) more to do with the 1990s emphasis on explicit standards, protocols, and quantification than with Balint's concern to achieve the 'limited but significant change in the doctor's personality'.[37]

The educational use of documentary (actual and materially unedited) video-

---

[33] K. Browne and P. Freeling, *The Doctor–Patient Relationship* (London, 1967). For the model of transactional analysis, see E. Berne, *Games People Play* (London, 1966).

[34] R. Neighbour, *The Inner Consultation* (London, 1987).

[35] P. S. Byrne and B. E. L. Long, *Doctors Talking to Patients* (London, 1976).

[36] D. Pendleton, D. Schofield, P. Tate, *et al.*, *The Consultation—An Approach to Learning and Teaching* (Oxford, 1984). One of the consequences of this popular and successful approach has been a shift in emphasis throughout the 1980s and 1890s, from reliance on the doctor's memory, feelings, and interpretation (the tools of psychoanalysis), to reliable evidence of observed performance and measurement (the tools of modern psychology). The examination of the doctor's visible performance in the recorded consultation replaced the reflective discussion of the recalled relationship.

[37] Balint, *The Doctor, his Patient and the Illness*, 299.

taped consultations was pioneered in the 1970s by the MSD Foundation,[38] and for the first time opened up the profession's unblinking gaze to the way in which (sometimes very senior and influential) colleagues dealt with their patients. Arguably the very widespread use of these videotapes in vocational training seminars did more than any previous initiative to bring the issues of patient-centredness (a concern and respect for the patient's health beliefs), the use of open- as well as close-ended questions, the tension between the doctor's beneficence and the patient's autonomy, onto the centre stage of clinical teaching.

Alongside the psychoanalytical and psychosocial interpretations of the encounter between the general practitioner and the patient, medical sociology was making its own distinctive and powerful contribution. Sociology directed the doctors' attention first to the power structure of the relationship between patient and doctor, and, secondly, to the power play in the groups concerned with health care. It was medical sociology that advanced the case for patient autonomy, and for more open and democratic primary-health-care teams— causes which, ironically, scarcely prospered until the NHS changes in the 1990s.[39]

In 1970 Margot Jefferys, already the English doyenne of medical sociology, convened a small week-long seminar of some twelve general-practice teachers and researchers.[40] The group included members of the College working party then writing *The Future General Practitioner,* as well as a number of national leaders—Julian Tudor Hart (of whom more later), John Stevens (an original theorist and charismatic teacher), Ian Tait (his practice partner, and a pioneer of vocational training), and Geoffrey Marsh (an influential researcher and practice innovator). Among those who gave us tutorials were Michael Meacher (later a prominent left-wing Member of Parliament and Environment Minister in the 1997 Labour government, but then a young academic researching the bounds between social welfare and health care), George Brown (whose research was demonstrating a sociological aetiology of psychiatric illness),[41] and Ann Cartwright (whose statistical-cum-narrative methodology was revealing some discomforting evidence about the way in which the doctors' benign intentions could be translated into repressive behaviour).[42]

---

[38] The MSD foundation, an independent charitable trust concerned with medical education, was established in 1973, and funded by the multinational pharmaceutical company Merck, Sharp, & Dohme. Its first Chairman was Sir Douglas Black and its first Director the television documentary film-maker Karl Sabbagh. It is Sabbagh who deserves most credit for the widespread educational use of documentary video-recorded consultations.

[39] See Chapter 10 on the growth of patient consumerism, and Chapter 2 on the impact of the 1990 contract and fundholding on the primary-care teams.

[40] M. Jefferys, 'Social Science and Medical Education in Britain', *International Journal of Health Services*, 3 (1974), 549.

[41] Reviewed in G. W. Brown, 'Sociology and the Aetiology of Disease', in R. M. Acheson and L. Aird (eds.), *Seminars in Community Medicine*, i. *Sociology* (Oxford, 1976).

[42] A. Cartwright, *Patients and their Doctors* (London, 1967); A. Cartwright and R. Anderson, *General Practice Revisited: A Second Study of Patients and their Doctors* (London, 1981).

Twenty years later Jeffreys asked me what had then become of the role of medical sociology in the training of general practitioners. I replied that it had become invisible (like the contribution of Balint), because it had been quite internalized, and a generation of doctors would now be relatively unaware of how profoundly these insights had reshaped the very nature of general practice.

As a result of all these inputs, the psychodynamic and psychosocial approaches strongly advocated in *The Future General Practitioner* became, in the 1970s and throughout the 1980s, central to the teaching of future general-practitioner teachers.[43] They formed the basis of small-group teaching in trainee schemes, and courses for trainers became much concerned with small-group dynamics.[44]

The family as illness

The National Health Insurance Act of 1911 provided workers earning a maximum of £2 per week with the free services of a general practitioner of their own choice. The 'panels' of these patients were forerunners of the NHS practitioners' 'lists', created by similar free choice thirty-seven years later. Stevens comments that the 1911 Act 'established throughout society the concept of the "family doctor"'.[45] Yet if, as commentators suggest, the government of the day was following Bismarck's lead in Prussia, state health insurance was introduced not to foster the care of the family, but to ensure the healthy functioning of the workforce, and the soldiery. Indeed, the dependants of those insured under the provisions of the 1911 National Insurance Act were not covered by its provisions, but were eventually covered by sick clubs and friendly societies. None the less, the *idea* of family doctoring was to persist, despite its unclear meaning, ambiguous origins, uncertain support among patients, and potential moral hazards.[46]

In the first years of the NHS, the study of one 'quite ordinary practice' revealed that 60 per cent of 'nuclear families', and 96 per cent of 'mothers with

---

[43] M. Marinker, 'Balint Seminars and Vocational Training for General Practice', *Journal of the Royal College of General Practitioners*, 19 (1970), 79–91. P. Freeling and S. Barry, *In Service Training: A Study of the Nuffield Courses of the Royal College of General Practitioners* (London, 1982). The Nuffield Courses, provocatively and brilliantly led by Paul Freeling, involved many of the leaders of general-practice education in the 1970s, and profoundly influenced vocational training throughout the UK.

[44] M. Courteney, 'Small Groups', in J. Cormack, M. Marinker, and D. Morrell (eds.), *Teaching General Practice* (Brentford, 1981).

[45] R. Stevens, *Medical Practice in Modern England* (New Haven, Conn., 1966). But see also I. Loudon, 'Concept of the Family Doctor', *Bulletin of the History of Medicine*, 58 (1984), 347–62, which demonstrates that the term 'family doctor' in fact appeared around 1850.

[46] M. Marinker, 'The Family in Medicine', *Proceedings of the Royal Society of Medicine*, 69 (1976), 115–24. This argued that the inherent conflicts of interest and confidentiality between different members of the same family and household, relating to the same doctor, rendered 'family medicine' inimical to personal, and advocative, care.

children' were registered with the same practice.[47] Cartwright and Anderson found that in 1964, in the practices they studied, the proportion of people living with relatives who had the same doctor was 72 per cent.[48] By 1977 the figure was virtually unchanged at 74 per cent. There has always been epidemiological support for the sobriquet 'family doctor' in the NHS.

In the USA, as general practice began to re-establish its credentials in the health-care system in the early 1960s, the intense academic and political activity was preceded by a careful marketing exercise. McWhinney, returning from his 1964 visit to the USA reports: 'The American Founders of the Board of Family Medicine have found it necessary to repudiate the name "general practice" because of its association with a type of practice which is deplored in academic circles.'[49] Although stopping short of advocating a change of name in the UK, he advances the argument for it in marketing terms when he observes, '"Family medicine" as a name for our discipline and "family physician" for its members are both descriptive and dignified.'[50] But just how descriptive were they of general practice in the UK, and what did they purport to describe?

In Taylor's case vignettes, and in the delightful clinical anecdotes that enliven Barber's reminiscences of life in an Essex country practice in the 1930s,[51] the families of the patients play important roles. The title 'family doctor' was certainly used by official bodies in the UK,[52] and appears to have been a term of endearment, significant to both doctors and patients. But the term never carried with it the force of a clinical philosophy, which it achieved in the USA.[53] The authors of *The Future General Practitioner* ambiguously phrased its job definition 'a doctor who provides personal, primary and continuing care to individuals *and families*'.[54] Yet, despite the evident conflicts of interest between different members of the family being cared for by the same doctor, the contradiction between advocacy for the individual and justice for the group, the wish to espouse the label, and a notion of family-orientation persisted. Kellner's study of families in a northern England city practice,[55] and

---

[47] E. M. Backett, J. A. Heady, and J. C. G. Evans, 'Studies in a General Practice: The Doctor's Job in an Urban Area', *British Medical Journal* (1954), i. 109.

[48] Cartwright and Anderson, *General Practice Revisited*.

[49] McWhinney, 'General Practice as an Academic Discipline', 421.

[50] Ibid.

[51] Barber, *Country Doctor*.

[52] Central Health Services Council, Standing Medical Advisory Committee, *The Field of Work of the Family Doctor: Report of the Sub-Committee* (London: HMSO, 1963). Known as the Gillie Report, this underpinned the 'family' orientation of the general practitioners and advocated the extension of their clinical responsibility in the anticipatory care of schoolchildren and others, then the concern of public-health or community clinicians. The term 'family' carried an important political message for the development of the NHS.

[53] 'The family physician has chosen the family . . . as his basic interest. The family is the logical unit on which he focuses his attention' (J. Williams and T. L. Leaman, in H. F. Conn, R. E. Rakel, and T. W. Johnson (eds.), *Family Practice* (New York, 1983)), 3–18.

[54] RCGP, *The Future General Practitioner*, 1 (emphasis added).

[55] R. Kellner, *Family Ill Health* (London, 1963).

Huygen's elegant description of families in his semi-rural practice in Holland,[56] both dignified this approach.

Although there were proponents of a family-therapy approach to practice,[57] this never achieved the centrality that it was accorded in the USA. In the late 1970s Cartwright found that enthusiasm for family care (as for continuing care) was inversely related to the age of the doctor, and to the number of partners in the practice.[58] She concluded, 'As single handed practice becomes less common does this mean that family care and continuing care are also declining?'[59] It is noteworthy that in her careful research into the attitudes of patients, Cartwright appears not to have asked them, in her second study (researched in the 1970s), about their attitudes to family care. It would appear that concern for a family framework of clinical thinking was of greater importance to some general-practice theorists and family-oriented doctors than to most practitioners and their patients.

The clue to the importance that many persistently attached to the notion of 'family', during decades that saw a steady decline in the notion of the traditional two-parent family as the societal norm, probably lies less in a belief that doctors might have had in the family's influence on the diagnosis or its management, let alone in any theoretical model of the family as patient, and more in the semantic overtones of intimacy and biography suggested by the word 'family'.

Armstrong traces a close parallel between the spatial and temporal dimensions of general practice, and what happened to the elements of intimacy and biography in the doctor's formulation of 'what is wrong'.[60] Rivington in his description of the metamorphosis of the eighteenth-century apothecary into the nineteenth-century general practitioner, records how, over time, as the advisory (as opposed to the purely dispensing) function of the apothecary became more important and publicly acknowledged, he gradually withdrew from the front of the shop to the rear.[61] Rivington noted: 'As the scale is ascended, the surgery retires more and more into the background until it reaches the interior of the dwelling, where it is no longer exposed to the vulgar gaze.'[62]

Armstrong picks up the story of this spatial migration in the twentieth century, and describes three sequential stages, commenting on their consequences for the clinical task—in fact, for the changing concepts of 'what is

---

[56] F. J. A. Huygen, *Family Medicine: The Medical Life History of Families* (Nijmegen, 1978: Eng. trans. London, 1990).

[57] J. G. Howells, 'Family Psychiatry in Family Practice', *Practitioner*, 205 (1970), 280; P. R. Williams, *Family Problems* (Oxford, 1989).

[58] Cartwright and Anderson, *General Practice Revisited*.

[59] Ibid. 22.

[60] D. Armstrong, 'Space and Time in British General Practice', *Social Science and Medicine*, 20/7 (1985), 659–66. Armstrong's case is surprising and challenging: he appears to argue that the changes in 'space' predicted changes in 'task', and not the other way around.

[61] W. Rivington, *The Medical Profession* (London, 1879).

[62] Ibid.

wrong' and 'how we know it'. The earliest configuration has the doctor's surgery incorporated into the body of the doctor's house: the consulting room opens off the domestic passageway or indeed a sitting- or dining-room, which can serve as waiting areas that are part of the living space of the doctor's family. Strangely, there were still examples of this domestic spatial arrangement, though in rather aristocratic settings, in most of the premises of Harley Street consultants in the 1990s.

The third and most recent stage, coinciding with the years of the NHS, is the purpose-built surgery, the most developed form being the quite elaborate health or medical centres of which today there are widely admired architecturally imaginative examples. The second, intermediary, stage combines elements of the domestic internal, and the public external space, often in the form of surgery adaptations and extensions of the senior doctor's original home.

Armstrong observes that these later spatial realignments involved 'the separation of the illness from the domestic and its subsequent fragmentation'.[63] The more elaborate and differentiated the social spaces of the new buildings, the more possible, indeed necessary, it became to 'map' the patient's illness onto the building, the spaces of the receptionist, the doctors, the nurse, and eventually the extended primary-care teams. Illness, says Armstrong, was no longer located in 'separate domestic bodies'. He concludes that it was this sense of the domestic, characterized in the earlier years of the NHS by the location of much consultation in the patient's home, that explains the meaning given of 'family medicine'.[64]

In place of this domestic space, and the location of the illness in the patient, a new larger territory was claimed by general practice—the community, described as the practice population. At the same time as the biotechnologists were exploring the internal spaces of the patient's body, and the psycho-analysts and behavioural scientists were exploring her feelings and family relationships, the public-health epidemiologists were directing the general practitioner's 'gaze' to the population, and once again redefining 'what is wrong'.

The illness as risk

There were interesting temporal sequelae to this shift in spatial perceptions. Psychology is much concerned with the individual's past and present—the archaeology of thought and feeling, the phenomena of present behaviour. Sociology is much concerned with a description of present social structures, their roots in social history and their impact on contemporary social life and

---

[63] Armstrong, 'Space and Time', 661.
[64] Ibid.

illness behaviour. Epidemiology (by searching for antecedent causes of present morbidity) focuses the general practitioner's attention on the patient's future. It was epidemiology that offered an alternative temporal frame. 'What is wrong' and 'how we know it' were no longer to be confined to the *cause* and *nature* of the present illness, but extended to the *possibility* of future illness.

A number of factors can be identified in the growth of preventive medicine, in the general practitioner's clinical agenda. Early diagnosis was always a valued goal, and the pursuit of this gave rise to one of the earliest and most important epidemiological studies to be published from general practice.[65] Similarly, in the management of established disease, so-called secondary prevention, the attempt to avoid deterioration and the consequences of poorly controlled disease—for example, accelerating damage to eyesight and kidney function in diabetic patients who did not achieve reasonable control of their blood-sugar levels—was a basic aim of treatment. But, at the outset of the NHS, general practitioners were little involved in primary prevention—intervention before the onset or declaration of the disease. They were occasional immunizers and vaccinators of children on their lists, and doubtless they gave *ad hoc* advice on healthy living. But there is scant evidence of the case-finding, pro-active agendas which began to dominate the general-practice literature from the 1970s.[66]

Primary prevention before 1948 was largely the province of Medical Officers of Health and their clinical colleagues in the School Medical Service (see Chapter 5). In relation to the newborn and toddlers, the preventive medicine tasks were the responsibility of health visitors, whose accountability was outside the practice. The increasing involvement in, and responsibility for, these aspects of preventive medicine in the 1970s, and particularly in the developmental assessment of children, were the result of long-fought political and territorial battles, but were powerfully argued for by the representatives of general practitioners on the basis of the growing sense of general practice's holistic philosophy and self-confidence.[67] The successful incorporation of developmental assessment into general practice in the 1970s marks an important step in the subsequent domination of the preventive agenda in general practice, and the consequent further transformation in the march of concepts about 'what is wrong' and 'how we know it'.

The eventual dominance of prevention, especially the diminution of risk, in the clinical intentions of general practice can be traced to a number of interacting influences. As a result of the Family Doctor Charter in 1965[68] there was

[65] K. Hodgkin., *Towards Earlier Diagnosis* (Edinburgh, 1963).
[66] RCGP, *Combined Reports on Prevention: Reports from General Practice Nos. 18–21* (London: RCGP, 1975) This publication brought together the work of a number of College working parties on preventive medicine, convened by Dr John Horder, President of the College. The impact on practice was great, and the recommendations were subsequently believed to have influenced Secretary of State Kenneth Clark in the drafting of the 1990 general-practice contract, with its emphasis on prevention.
[67] RCGP, *Healthier Children: Report from General Practice No. 22* (London: RCGP, 1974).
[68] See Chapter 2 on the impact of the Family Doctor Charter.

an accelerated growth of new premises capable of housing primary-care-team members whose participation in primary health care had been greatly facilitated by it. Health-screening activities, such as blood-pressure checks, urine-testing, developmental assessments, and so on, could be undertaken in other than the doctor's consulting room, and by other than the doctors. The new preventive agenda, which marked a distinct rewriting of the doctor's previous concern to diagnose disease and offer treatment, involved three desiderata. First, a redefinition in future-oriented terms of 'what is wrong'; secondly, a new source of information in regard to 'how we know it'; and, thirdly, the spatial reconfiguration that Armstrong observed,[69] in order to redistribute the clinical tasks among the new team members.

In 1974 Pereira Gray argued that 'the introduction of doctor-initiated consultations for symptom-free people has made the old definition of the word patient inappropriate'.[70] Two years later Marinker took the opposite view and urged that the word patient be reserved for someone in a clinical relationship with a doctor, and that to assume that *persons* on the doctor's list were *patients* 'can only result in a personal invasion of privacy . . . and a loss of integrity in the doctor/patient relationship'.[71] Preventive medicine, by the mid-1970s, had become for many of the most influential thinkers in general practice 'our supreme objective'.[72] In the light of events, not least the 1990 practitioners' contract, it became increasingly clear that Marinker had lost the argument.

The relationship between general-practice and public-health medicine (also called social medicine, epidemiology, community medicine, or community health in the course of the last fifty years, and later still appropriately reowning its original good name) had been ambivalent, at times close and cooperative, at times strangely stressed, as we shall see. The relationship reflected many shared social values, but these were not always similarly interpreted. Many university departments of general practice began as units within public-health departments, and this encouraged and strengthened the epidemiological approach of most early general-practice research (see Chapter 6). It may also have deepened the ambivalence.

A central preoccupation of public-health thinking since the eighteenth century has been the search for causes, and the primacy of prevention over cure. Over the fifty-year period under review, this proactive agenda has been driven by leading general-practice academics,[73] and has been taken up by NHS

[69] Armstrong, 'Space and Time'.

[70] D. J. Pereira Gray, Editorial, 'What is a Patient?' *Journal of the Royal College of Practitioners*, 24 (1974), 513.

[71] M. Marinker, 'The Nature of Continuing Care', in C. Cormack, M. Marinker, and D. Morrell (eds.), *Practice: Clinical Management in General Practice* (London, 1976).

[72] D. J. Pereira Gray, 'Feeling at Home', *Journal of the Royal College of General Practitioners*, 24 (1974), 513–14.

[73] For example, in *The Future General Practitioner* the epidemiological framework and approach in J. N. Morris, *Uses of Epidemiology* (London, 1957; rev. edn., 1964) was incorporated into the core of

policy-makers. The enthusiasm for neurological developmental assessment of children, opportunistic screening for high blood pressure, obesity, diabetes, cancer of the cervix, and latterly for unhealthy behaviour—smoking and excessive alcohol consumption—have substantially affected the conduct of the consultation, and the patient's itinerary in the health centre.

One of the consequences in the 1990s of obliterating the fine distinction between persons on the general practitioner's list, and those who, by consulting, become patients, was that 'what is wrong' was transformed into 'what may happen'. The illness became a prediction, a variable probability, a genetic weakness in the system, or a human frailty of behaviour, in which treatment must be invested now, in the expectation of benefit later.

The risk to be avoided, however, remained impersonal: it was necessarily a risk established in and for very large groups, not for discrete individuals. The difference was between the (unknowable) personal risk, and the calculated risk of persons in the group (of cigarette smokers, hypertensives, the obese, and so on) to which the patient happened to belong. Imperceptibly, 'what is wrong', and the techniques for determining 'how we know it', were no longer to be found here and now in the patient, but were to be distributed over future time in populations.[74]

This quest for early intervention, the diagnosis and treatment of the still well, had strong philosophical and historical links with another precept of public-health medicine—the pursuit of social justice. Nothing better illustrates the attempt to pursue these two goals in general practice than the work of Julian Tudor Hart, a general practitioner most of whose professional life was devoted to the health care of a south Wales (originally coal-mining) village community, where he also directed a research unit funded by the Medical Research Council (a quite remarkable and unique achievement).[75]

The patient as community

The systematic collection of data on mortality and morbidity and health impairment began in the nineteenth century, and the evidence of social and geographical inequalities in health has been unassailable and constant over time. To give one trenchant example from the mid-point of our history, in 1970–2 in Aberdeen the perinatal mortality (stillbirths plus death in the first week) rate for first-born babies in families of 'semi- and un-skilled workers'

the training programme. Subsequently Morris had a profound influence on John Horder's enthusiasm for the 'preventive-medicine' agenda in general practice: 'John, your College examines 1,500 doctors a year. The future is in your hands.'

[74] P. Skrabanek and J. McCormick, *Follies and Fallacies in Medicine* (London, 1990).

[75] J. Tudor Hart, *Hypertension* (London, 1987); J. Tudor Hart, 'The Inverse Care Law', *Lancet* (1971), i. 405–12. Tudor Hart observed that, in any locality, the availability of health care and resources stood in inverse ratio to the estimate of that population's need.

was 28.6 per 1,000 births.[76] The corresponding rate for 'professional and business' families was 10.9. These figures show a difference related to social class. There were also geographical differences: in the same period the corresponding rate for 'professional and business' families in Scotland as a whole was 19.3. In the UK socio-geographical gradients of morbidity and premature mortality were shown to increase approximately from south to north.

Since Chadwick,[77] these morbidity and mortality statistics had driven reform of the public health, of the Poor Laws, and other socio-political attempts to ameliorate not only the suffering of the poor, but also the sense of social injustice. What is remarkable is that the spectacular advances in health-care technology in the second half of the twentieth century, and the advent in 1948 of the NHS with its founding principle of social equity, although accompanied by general improvements in health, appeared to have had little effect on the continuing *relative* social class and geographical differences. These persisted in study after study throughout this period, but came finally to the fore in the debate about how to sustain and develop the NHS with the publication in 1980 of a report from a working group set up by the then Secretary of State for Social Services, and chaired by Sir Douglas Black.[78]

Subsequent debate and analyses suggested that this link between social class and ill health is complex and could not be easily explained away in terms of artefact or intervening variables. Most intriguingly, one commentator concluded that the causes of the differences between the classes go even deeper than the deprivation of material goods: 'The social consequences of people's differing circumstances in terms of stress, self-esteem and social relations may now be one of the most important influences on health.'[79]

Nine years before the appearance of the Black Report, Tudor Hart had published an article on health-care inequalities in the *Lancet*, and coined a ringing phrase of immense political sensitivity: The Inverse Care Law.[80] What was important about this article was the articulation by a successful general-practitioner researcher and influential thinker of the two linked themes of public health—prevention of excess morbidity and social justice. Indeed, all the evidence from public-health epidemiology (about the relationship between poverty, ill health, and premature mortality) pointed inexorably to one remedy: the need for the redistribution of wealth. But this was essentially a socio-political objective. Tudor Hart's great mentor, Cochrane, perhaps the foremost epidemiologist of his day, was critical of this focus on the differences in health

---

[76] I. MacGillivray, quoted in Morris, *Uses of Epidemiology*.

[77] Edwin Chadwick (1800–90) was a major nineteenth-century libertarian reformer, associated with reforms of the Poor Law, the Factory Act of 1833, and the Public Health Act of 1848.

[78] M. Whitehead, *The Health Divide (with The Black Report)* (London, 1987). The Black Report was published as: *Report of a Research Working Group on Inequalities in Health* (London: DHSS, 1980).

[79] R. G. Wilkinson, 'Income Distribution and Life Expectancy', *British Medical Journal*, 304 (1992), 165–8.

[80] Tudor Hart, 'The Inverse Care Law'.

and care between the social classes.[81] While sympathetic with Tudor Hart's political aims, he questioned the priority he accorded to the redistribution of medical resources, and urged rather 'finding out which treatments are effective, and then ensuring that these treatments are efficiently given to all who need them'.[82]

Tudor Hart's philosophy was set out, seventeen years later, when his public-health agenda for general practice became fully developed: the 'fusion of epidemiology with primary care'.[83] This fusion would, again, redefine the general practitioner's understanding of 'what is wrong' and 'how we know it'. What emerged from his arguments was the relocation of the patient's illness from 'in here' (in the body–mind of the individual), to 'out there' (in the socio-economic characteristics of the community). The illness was transformed into a measure of the patient's social and economic deficit. However, once 'out there', the identity of the patient, the differentiation between patient and person, and between person and class, became problematical.

In many ways Tudor Hart offered a stark but coherent alternative to the model that derived from the work of Balint, to whom he none the less paid real respect. He criticized the Balint model on the following three counts. Tudor Hart believed, first, that, despite its claim to be patient-centred, the model was in fact doctor-centred: patients were given scarcely more opportunity than before to define their own problems in their own terms; secondly, that the model, despite its holistic philosophy, separated the psychological from the organic, and all but ignored the latter; and, thirdly, that the approach ignored the social context: that it concerned itself with 'one-person clinical medicine'.

What Tudor Hart's reservation about 'one-person clinical medicine' might mean becomes more clear when he relates the so-called Platt–Pickering controversy. In 1952 Sir George Pickering, a pioneer clinical scientist, demonstrated that high blood pressure was not a discrete condition, an identifiable morbid state like chickenpox (the patient either had the disease or had not), but rather that levels of blood pressure were continuously distributed in populations. Lord Platt, a distinguished physician, and most other members of the then medical establishment, resisted this view for many years, although the evidence for Pickering's findings (and not only in relation to blood pressure) mounted. Platt and his supporters held that high blood pressure was in fact a discrete disease. Eventually, in Tudor Hart's words, 'Pickering's heresy became official wisdom'.[84]

This Tudor Hart portrayed as an example of the historical struggle between scientific discovery (the heroes would include Galileo, Copernicus, Darwin, Harvey, and Jenner) and professional orthodoxy, and from it he drew a

[81] A. Cochrane, *Effectiveness and Efficiency* (London, 1971).
[82] Ibid.
[83] J. Tudor Hart, *A New Kind of Doctor* (London, 1988).
[84] Ibid. 302.

strangely politicized conclusion. The Platt–Pickering controversy was presented as a battle between the natural historians (those like Platt who sought theory through the careful and repeated observation of individual patients over time), and the experimental scientists (of whom Pickering is here the shining example).

Tudor Hart's reservation of the term scientist for Pickering, and denial of it to Platt, however, was very special pleading. Most of the classical diseases that medicine recognizes today resulted from the orderly but imaginative observations of physicians like Graves (overactivity of the thyroid gland), Bright (failure of the kidney), Addison (failure of the adrenal gland), and so on. The fact that Pickering was proven to be right (and in something very important indeed), and Platt wrong, was advanced as part of the argument for fundamentally shifting the doctor's gaze: 'The new concept we need is anticipatory of health rather than treatment of disease.'[85] Crucially he says: 'to be consistent with science, (medicine) must serve whole populations according to their needs, rather than be *merely available to individual demanders* or purchasers of care.'[86] 'Individual demanders' might be thought another term for 'patients': here they were presented as usurpers of a superior client, the community.

Tudor Hart was pretty scathing about natural historians. Swales believed that, even if the two philosophies could not be reconciled, they would at least continue in fruitful conflict.[87] Tudor Hart, the idealist, disagreed. Similarly his own openly Marxist analysis of the role of the doctor in society, and Balint's scarcely concealed Freudian analysis, appeared also to be irreconcilable. Yet somehow, in the general practitioners' practical business of looking after patients, and managing a practice, all these contradictory views had to be, and were, reconciled.

The illness as commodity

Surprisingly, and ironically, Tudor Hart's insistence on the supremacy of quantitative over qualitative descriptions of health care found an unlikely echo in the changes brought about in 1989 by the Thatcher Government's reforms of the NHS,[88] and what followed. He will not be grateful to me for that comparison. The paradox is that, while Tudor Hart's intentions and those of *Working for Patients* were opposite, the language (of producers and consumers) in which they were both couched revealed intriguing similarities. Tudor Hart saw the consultation as 'the point of production of critically important decisions which affect all other (health related)

---

[85] Ibid. 306.
[86] Ibid. 316 (emphasis added).
[87] J. D. Swales, *Platt versus Pickering: An Episode in Recent Medical History* (London, 1985).
[88] Secretaries of State for Health, *Working for Patients* (London, 1989).

consumptions'.[89] It was the language, perhaps one could say the moral arithmetic, of political economics.

The 1989 reforms of the NHS contained in *Working for Patients* were
impelled by a crisis in funding. In all state or private-insurance schemes in
developed economies, increasingly costly biotechnology, rising public expectations, increasing morbidity associated with greater survival into old age, and a
reluctance of electorates to vote for increases in taxation combined to suggest
that the service could not continue without some radical improvements in the
cost–benefit from all health-care expenditure. The different responses in different societies all involved attempts to rationalize the uses of resources, and
to ration the provision of services.

This chapter is *not* concerned with the successes or failures of the solutions
proposed by government concerning the reconfiguration of the NHS, or
the use of resources, or the effect on the morale of general practitioners
and others. It *is* concerned with their consequences for the perception of
'what is wrong'. These consequences were profound, and were driven as much
by new initiatives from the medical profession, as by the policy-makers and
managers.

What was new was the expectation of a high degree of explicitness about
everything—diagnosis, treatment, expected outcome, and entitlements. This
explicitness was to be expressed as quantities, and as costs (of what was to be
purchased, what provided, and what forgone). For general practice, the impact
of all this was disorienting. Explicitness could be, and was, presented as self-
evidently desirable, and a morally sound characteristic of a public service. But,
for the most part, the clinical work of the general practitioner had been characterized by implicitness, not explicitness, and there were compelling reasons
for this, as the foregoing history has suggested.

The Conservative Government's reforms were inspired by the goal of
efficiency, and, given its right-wing political philosophy, this was believed to
be achievable by creating a market—albeit an internal and modified one.
Markets require that their goods be explicitly described, truthfully quantified,
and costed. In the bright new light of accountability, how were the general
practitioners to express and preserve the values of the Balint model—the
complexity and uniqueness of 'what is wrong', and the role of empathy and
intuition, as well as of observation and measurement, in 'how we know it'? In
their totally different ways, what I dare to call the Tudor Hart and Thatcher
models confronted the general practitioners with similar difficulties.

For the first time the relationship between state and clinician in general practice became substantially determined by economic factors and state-defined
controls. Targets were set that referred to rates of performance—for example,
in childhood immunizations, screening for cervical cancer, prevention of coronary heart disease, measurement of health status in old age, and so on. These

---

[89] J. Tudor Hart, *Feasible Socialism: The NHS, Past, Present and Future* (London, 1994).

targets directed the doctor's gaze away from the individual patient to the population, and, with this shift, came the threat of a defocusing or loosening of the personal, implicit contract with the patient, as the public, explicit contract between the doctor and the state was tightened.

The rationing of health care had always been a part of the general practitioner's work, but had previously been implied rather than stated. Now, particularly in fundholding practice, and in the tension between fundholding and non-fundholding, the general practitioner's ethical duty to advocate justice for the individual patient became strained by the additional ethical duty to achieve distributive justice for the community. 'What is wrong' became coloured by new perceptions, by conflicting priorities, and so did 'how we know it'.

Economists, in the search for a moral basis for rationing (that is the rank ordering of the patients' illnesses so as to decide who and what shall be denied), devised an arithmetic of cost and likely benefit from treatment called 'quality adjusted life years' (QUALYS). 'What is wrong' (because it implied 'what should be done') now carried explicit burdens of 'worth' that could be expressed in monetary terms.

Fuzziness could not be tolerated in such a rigorous estate. The medical profession seized the opportunity to move to a science-based clinical practice, since, if choices had to be made, they had better be made on sound statistical evidence. Sackett and colleagues, whose earlier work on clinical epidemiology had demonstrated the value of reliable quantification as an aid to clinical decision-making, introduced what in the 1990s became another 'evangelical' movement—Evidence Based Medicine (EBM).[90] The impact of this on general practice gathers pace as this history is being written. As the criteria for diagnosis and treatment were increasingly to be determined by combing the world research literature, and adducing best evidence, a growth industry was created in the production of clinical guidelines, protocols (strict criteria for diagnosis and choice of action), and algorithms (the setting-out of this information in the form of branching logic or decision-making 'trees').

The response to these developments was mixed. In many ways the advent of EBM and guidelines promised to reduce the wide variations in clinical practice which could best be explained by the idiosyncratic habits of thought and action on the part of doctors, rather than by any responsiveness to the needs and predicaments of individual patients. The anxiety was that, in reducing the former, the latter would be sacrificed. This was the fear expressed by Sweeney, reflecting on discussions of the role of EBM by a group of doctors convened by the Royal College of General Practitioners. He warned that the combined forces of government policies, explicit contract, and guidelines, might force the understanding of 'what is wrong' into procrustean beds of mechanistic and

---

[90] D. L. Sackett, R. B. Haines, and P. Tugwell, *Clinical Epidemiology* (Boston, 1985); Evidence Based Medicine Working Group, 'Evidence Based Medicine: A New Approach to Teaching the Practice of Medicine', *Journal of the American Medical Association*, 268 (1992), 2420–5.

reductionist thought; that 'how we know it' will come to be synonymous only with the information from evidence of a particular kind—that deriving from rigorous randomized controlled trials.[91]

Ending in the middle

My story ends here—in the middle, of course. I conclude it with quotations from a lecture given by a general practitioner in mid-career, practising in an Inner London practice a mile or two from where I live. She calls her lecture *The Mystery of General Practice.*[92] Her insights are interesting for a number of reasons. Her practice was one of the great pioneering practices of the NHS, and many of those associated with it in the past have made significant contributions to the history that this book has attempted to chronicle. The population that it serves exhibits the rich diversity, including the deep deprivations, of so very many NHS practices—and not only in inner cities. And she is also someone who has been much influenced by two of the key actors in this history (Balint and Tudor Hart) who have figured largely in what is here written.

I chose to quote her because in her lecture she captures the contemporary mid-1990s tensions between the paradoxes which are an inevitable part of contemporary medicine in its general-practice mode. On the matters of 'what is wrong' and 'how we know it' she writes:

Illness begins as a subjective sense of bodily unease, an experience of the functioning of the body as being not quite right. It is often very intangible and the sense of unease arises not just from what we have come to recognise as disease but from other forms of distress including tiredness and unhappiness, misery and grief. With the success of scientific medicine has come an emphasis on disease which has tended to invalidate the individual's experience of illness.[93]

Most general practitioners, fifty years into the history of the NHS, would not necessarily use her language, but might identify with her analysis and feelings. Here she describes much that is implicit, if still rarely explicit, in the fifty years of change with which this chapter has been concerned:

We must make available the benefits of scientific medicine but mitigate its dangers through an understanding of anthropology, biography, poetry, myth, philosophy and politics. The skills of anthropology and biography help us with empathy and the use of continuity, and an awareness of poetry and myth can help us find the words to communicate our understanding to the patient. A grasp of philosophy and politics can show us how to be effective partisans on behalf of our patients.[94]

---

[91] K. Sweeney, 'Evidence and Uncertainty', in M. Marinker (ed.), *Sense and Sensibility in Health Care* (London, 1996).

[92] I. Heath, *The Mystery of General Practice* (London, 1995).

[93] Ibid. 17.   [94] Ibid. 35.

At the beginning of this chapter I warned that the bulk of the evidence for changing perceptions would come from the writings of academics, rather than from the observation of practice. In 1996 a study of general practitioners in north-west England found that, for the majority of them, the biomedical model was, in fact, the most 'appropriate'. The authors suggested that the biopsychosocial model was stronger in the rhetoric than in the reality of general practice.[95]

Also, I described the accelerating improvements in the techniques of diagnosis and treatment as only the 'backdrop' to the greater part of this history. Now, another tide of fashion appears to be running in the 1990s, and depositing a new layer of ideas consonant with the advent of medical audit and contract, the electronic exchange of data, the techniques of EBM, and the development of near-patient testing.

Thomas Kuhn suggests that science and technology develop 'paradigms' (theoretical models) in relation both to the tools that we invent, and to the needs of our societies.[96] I have sought to show similar relationships in the doctor's changing perceptions of 'what is wrong' and 'how we know it', over the half-century of the NHS. The political drive for a so-called 'primary-care-led NHS' resulted not only in the involvement of general practitioners in the 'purchase' of hospital care for their patients (as fundholders and subsequently as locality commissioners), but also as advocates for, and guardians of, the quality of the hospital care of their patients.

To become meaningfully involved in contracting for hospital services, the general practitioners of the 1990s were being challenged to find new ways of reconciling their psycho-socio-political models of illness with the highly successful biotechnical models of diseases and treatments which had been developing in the hospital specialisms. At the same time, other primary-health-care workers were becoming increasingly involved in the processes of screening, diagnosis, and treatment.[97] The tasks of the intimate consultation between doctor and patient were being disaggregated and shared with others.

At the conclusion of the first half-century of the NHS, the long-established division between primary and secondary health care was no longer clearly defined. As health-care structures began to realign, and boundaries to shift, so too did the doctors' perceptions of 'what is wrong' and 'how we know it'. As the half-century of the NHS approaches, yet again (to echo McWhinney) the 'parent disciplines must be melted down, amalgamated, and moulded into a new form'.[98]

[95] C. Dowrick, C. May, M. Richardson, and P. Bundred, 'The Biopsychosocial Model of General Practice: Rhetoric or Reality?', *Britsh Journal of General Practice*, 46 (1996), 105–7.

[96] T. Kuhn, *The Structure of Scientific Revolutions* (Chicago, 1962).

[97] Secretary of State for Health, *Primary Health Care: Delivering the Future* (London, 1996).

[98] McWhinney, 'General Practice'.

4

Some Aspects of Clinical Care in General Practice

IRVINE LOUDON and MARK DRURY

In 1950, a report on the state of general practice in England was published in the *Lancet*.[1] Written by Joseph Collings, it was a frank and devastating condemnation of the standard of general practice at the beginning of the NHS which was so influential that it is mentioned in many of the chapters in this book. At the time he wrote this report, Joseph Silver Collings (1918–71), who was born in Sydney, Australia, was Research Fellow at the Harvard School of Public Health in Boston, Mass. His training in medicine had been interrupted by war service in the Far East, and he graduated in medicine at the University of Sydney in 1946, and began his study of health services, in New Zealand, the UK, and then in the USA. In 1954, Collings entered general practice in Melbourne. He later became Director of the Department of Physical Medicine at the Royal Melbourne Hospital, where he developed a special interest in spinal injuries. Collings was an early advocate of 'whole-person medicine' and reform of medical education. His obituarist wrote that 'Teaching was as natural to Collings as breathing' and that 'In many ways he was too far ahead of his time; and many regarded his visions of better medical centres, better medical training, and a position for the general practitioner at the top, rather than the bottom of the hierarchy as merely visionary.' He was a remarkable, often controversial, humane doctor, and an active member of the Australian College of General Practitioners.[2]

To return to the Collings Report, although it was criticized by some on the grounds of being based on too small a sample, it had a compelling ring of truth and was intensely readable with 'the merit of saying plainly what he saw and what he thinks'.[3] As Webster has said, 'most of his shots hit the mark with explosive impact . . . [the Report] was the single most effective factor in mobilising opinion in favour of constructive change.'[4]

---

[1] J. S. Collings, 'General Practice in England Today: A Reconnaissance', *Lancet* (1950), i. 555–85.

[2] For biographical details, see obituary notice, 'Joseph Silver Collings', *Medical Journal of Australia* (1971), i. 1346–50. I am grateful to Brenda Heagney, Librarian, History of Medicine Library, the Royal Australasian College of Physicians, for her assistance in providing information on Collings.

[3] Leading article, 'The Collings Report', *Lancet* (1950), i. 547.

[4] C. Webster, *The Health Services since the War*, i. *Problems of Health Care: The National Health Service before 1957* (London: HMSO, 1988), 356.

Collings described dingy, dirty, ill-equipped surgeries in which the standard of medicine was deplorable. 'Few skilled craftsmen', he said, 'be they plumbers, butchers or motor mechanics, would be prepared to work under such conditions or with equipment so bad . . .'[5]

In one industrial practice of four partners, two assistants, and a list of 20,000 patients:

The surgery consisted of a small dilapidated waiting room, three equally small and untidy consulting rooms, and a kind of cupboard which served as a dispensary . . . The consulting rooms were dirty and ill-equipped. There were no examination couches . . . apart from a few rusty and dusty antique instruments, there was no sign of any sort of equipment. Large stock bottles were standing all over the place, and the desk and floor were littered with papers. Only one of the consulting rooms was equipped with a hand-basin and hot and cold water. I made my visit during an afternoon consulting hour and found a queue of people extending about 200 yards up the street, waiting their turn to see the doctors . . . I was told, not without pride, that 'we have seen 500 already today'; and I have no reason to doubt it.

The bottle of medicine was the *sine qua non* of this practice. 'Notes' (sickness certificates) and 'bottles' were asked for by almost everyone seen and were supplied on request. These practitioners do a considerable amount of midwifery and, I was informed, 'run our own nursing home'. When asked about antenatal work, the senior member of the firm said: 'We don't have much time for that sort of thing.'[6]

Collings found a few general practitioners whose standards were excellent, citing one who had built his own laboratory and whose 'quality of service was far above anything his colleagues could offer. The point I want to make is that these colleagues . . . regarded this doctor as crazy . . . he was mad—merely because he endeavoured to exercise to the limit the skills of which he was capable in the interests of his patients.' This practitioner was in danger of being forced out of practice because of the cost of providing a high-quality service.[7] In an appendix to the report, Collings found that standards as a whole were higher in Scotland than in England,[8] and reserved some of his highest praise for the doctors in the Highlands and Islands Service, who 'were as fine men as I have met anywhere'.[9]

Collings concluded that the knowledge of many general practitioners 'was out of date [and] they worked to a routine and within limits that had long since dulled their curiosity and their sensitivity',[10] so that the 'overall state of general practice is bad and still deteriorating'.[11] It was a stagnant branch of medicine. The NHS did nothing 'to disturb the structure of general practice' or reward

---

[5] Collings, 'General Practice', 557.
[6] Ibid. 583. On midwifery, Collings remarked that 'The few who continued to dabble in midwifery were mostly considered by midwives and other responsible observers to be a menace.'
[7] Ibid. 560.
[8] Ibid., app. 1. General practice in Scotland, pp. 579–82.
[9] Ibid. 580.
[10] Ibid. 560.
[11] Ibid. 568. His general conclusions and recommendations can be found on pp. 578–9.

those who tried to produce work of a high standard while 'increasing the load on the G.P. to the point of near-breakdown, resulting in a depression of the quality of care'.[12]

The response to the Collings Report was decidedly mixed.[13] The BMA was hostile and commissioned another survey, which was carried out by Stephen Hadfield, the Assistant Secretary of the BMA. Published in 1953 with the title 'A Field Survey of General Practice 1951–2', it was bland and soothing.[14] He concluded from his survey that 'Over ninety per cent of the practitioners that I saw are undoubtedly interested and careful in the treatment of their patients.'[15]

A third survey of general practice, considerably more impressive than Hadfield's, was included in Stephen Taylor's book, *Good General Practice*, published in 1954.[16] Taylor remarked that 'The unhappy picture which Dr Collings painted of industrial and urban residential practice had many marks of authority, but he was inclined to represent the worst as typical of general practice in Britain.' He estimated that 'one quarter of practices are of a high standard, and some of these are outstanding. One half are sound and reliable if unexciting. One twentieth are so bad it is hard to find excuses.'[17]

Such was the nature and reputation of general practice in the 1950s. General practitioners alone decided the content and nature of what they considered to be their duties. Many worked in isolation and saw no reason to change the way they practised. There was no postgraduate education in general practice to speak of (see Chapter 8). The system of payment not only failed to encourage a high standard of clinical care, but actually penalized those practitioners who spent money on their practice premises and equipment, or limited the size of their list to have more time for consultations.

Small wonder that, in striking contrast to hospital medicine, which was forging ahead with utter confidence in the rapid advance of medical science, general practice was characterized by low morale and stagnation; or that students were left in no doubt that general practice was scorned by their teachers. The correspondence columns of medical journals revealed deep dissatisfaction.[18] As Marinker declared in 1975, the response of the general

---

[12] Collings, 'General Practice', 578.

[13] See comments in the correspondence columns of the *Lancet* (1950), i, by Lindsay Batten (pp. 780–1) and Anthony Ryle (p. 884). See also the comments by I. C. Gillard in the *British Medical Journal* (1950), i. 956.

[14] S. Hadfield, 'A Field Survey of General Practice 1951–2', *British Medical Journal* (1953), ii. 683–706. The report as a whole was so much at variance with Collings that it is astonishing to find that the Collings Report is never mentioned by Hadfield, either in the text, the references, or the accompanying leading article.

[15] Ibid. 704.

[16] S. Taylor, *Good General Practice* (Oxford, 1954).

[17] Ibid. 7.

[18] 'The more work you do upgrading general practice, the more it costs you' (R. A. Murray Scott, Correspondence, *British Medical Journal* (1950), i. 1079–80); general practitioners were 'sick of the

practitioner to the NHS had been to develop 'the most profound depression from which, a quarter of a century later, he has only now emerged'.[19]

These considerations, and the three reports by Collings, Hadfield, and Taylor, provide a starting point to this chapter, in which we try to answer two very broad questions. In what ways has clinical care in general practice altered since the NHS began, and what were the factors causing change?

These are extremely broad questions. For example, amongst the factors which have influenced the scope and standards of clinical care are pre- and postgraduate education, changes in group practice, practice premises, and the notion of the primary-care team, and the new appreciation of the nature of illness in general practice. Because these are dealt with in other chapters, we have confined ourselves to certain selected subjects. And we begin with changes in the patterns of illness in the UK over the last half-century.

Changes in patterns of illness

Retired general practitioners whose memories go back to medicine in the 1940s nearly always stress two major changes: the enormous changes in the means to diagnose and treat illness, and changes in the pattern of illness which afflict the population.

Two obvious examples are infant and maternal mortality. The former has fallen from a level of thirty-six deaths per 1,000 births in the 1950s to less than eight in the 1990s (see Fig. B1). The fall in maternal mortality has been even more striking. Before the mid-1930s, between 400 and 500 women died of pregnancy-related causes for every 100,000 births, and almost every woman of child-bearing age knew of at least one friend, neighbour, or member of her family who had died in childbirth during her lifetime. Now, in the 1990s, when the maternal mortality rate is less than ten per 100,000 births, few have personal knowledge of such a disaster (see Fig. B2).[20]

But the most striking change in patterns of disease since the 1940s is the shift away from acute infectious diseases to chronic degenerative disease associated with the ageing of the population. These can be seen in detail in Table 4.1.[21] These changes have had a profound effect on the clinical content of

NHS, being run off their feet and ordered about [and] with surgeries so crowded that it was impossible to examine a patient carefully' (J. T. Maclachlan, ibid. 1202). 'The doctor now feels he is chasing his practice downhill all the time with no hope at present of ever catching up' (Dr D. Anthony, ibid. 1077–8).

[19] M. Marinker, *The Doctor and his Patient: An Inaugural Lecture Delivered in the University of Leicester, 4 February 1975* (Leicester University Press, 1975), 5.

[20] This applies to most countries in the Western world. The rate of maternal deaths in many developing countries today is as high as it was in the UK in the nineteenth century. It has been said that there is no aspect of health in which the disparity between the developed and the developing countries is as large as their respective rates of maternal mortality.

[21] See also Appendix B.

TABLE 4.1 *Changes in the pattern of diseases in the UK between 1950 and the mid-1990s*

Part 1 Disorders which are *less* common in the mid-1990s than they were in 1950, grouped according to the following most likely reasons for their decline in prevalence.

Routine immunization

Tuberculosis (all forms): BCG
Diphtheria
Tetanus
Whooping cough
Poliomyelitis
Measles
Mumps

Rubella (German measles) and congenital
　abnormalities due to rubella
Haemophilus influenza B (epiglottitis and
　meningitis)

By the screening of target populations, therapy, or improved clinical care

Cretinism
Phenylketonuria
Rubella antibody screening
Haemolytic disease of the newborn
Downs Syndrome
Spina bifida
Hydrocephalus
Hypertensive heart disease
Malignant hypertension
Eclampsia
Tuberculosis (all forms)
Lupus vulgaris

Addison's disease
Chronic bronchitis and emphysema
Bronchiectasis
Lung abscess
Tertiary and congenital syphilis
Puerperal fever
Obstetric haemorrhage
Birth injuries
Stillbirths
Retinal damage in premature infants
Acute mastoiditis
Pink disease in children

Because of changes in the nature or virulence of infective organisms

Scarlet fever
Erysipelas
Rheumatic fever

Mitral stenosis
Acute nephritis
Influenza

Because of improvements in social and environmental conditions

Tuberculosis (all forms)
Chronic bronchitis and emphysema
Bronchiectasis
Vomiting and failure to thrive in
　infancy (from underfeeding)
Rickets
Scurvy in children
Anaemia in children

Lead poisoning in children
Ringworm
Scabies
Impetigo
Chilblains
Pneumoconiosis
Many industrial diseases

For unknown reasons

Gastric and duodenal ulcer
Gastric antral carcinoma
Congenital pyloric stenosis

da Costa's syndrome
'Varicose' ulcers?

TABLE 4.1 *Continued*

Part 2 Disorders which are *more* common in the mid-1990s than they were in 1950, or have appeared as new diseases in the intervening period, grouped according to the following most probable reasons for their increase in prevalence.

New diseases, or diseases partly or wholly unrecognized in 1950

Aids	Child abuse
Legionnaire's disease	Autism
Lyme disease	Dyslexia
Alzheimer's disease	Bulimia nervosa
Creutzfeldt-Jakob disease	Chronic fatigue syndrome/myalgic
Hepatitis B and C	encephalomyelitis
Extrinsic allergic alveolitis (farmer's	Polymyalgia rheumatica
lung, bird fancier's lung)	
Sudden Infant Death Syndrome	
('cot deaths')	

Because of adverse social or environmental factors

Cancer of the lung	Infertility in females
Malignant melanoma	Teenage pregnancy
Other skin cancers	Minor salmonella infections
Drug overdoses	Gonococcal infection
Drug abuse	Herpes genitalis
Suicide in young males	Obesity
Anorexia nervosa	Mesothelioma
Bulimia nervosa	Alcohol-related diseases such as cirrhosis and
Road Traffic Injuries (not deaths)	pancreatitis

Because of increasing longevity

Osteoarthritis	Cancer of the pancreas
Alzheimer's disease	Cancer of the colon
Cancer of the breast	Heart disease in general
Cancer of the prostate	Parkinson's disease

Because of tourism and immigration

Traveller's malaria	Sickle-cell disease
Giardia lamblia	Thalassaemia
Lassa fever	G6PD deficiency
Ebola virus	

Iatrogenic—that is, caused by medical treatment

Congenital disorders due to	Addiction to tranquillizers
thalidomide	
Steroid purpura	Many other drug side effects
Gastric ulcer in the elderly	

For unknown reasons

Cancer of the testis (seminoma)	Aortic aneurysm
Motor neurone disease	Crohn's disease

TABLE 4.1 *Continued*

Fibrosing alveolitis	Systemic Lupus Erythematosus
Asthma, especially in children	Sjögren's syndrome
Atopic eczema	
Insulin-dependent diabetes mellitus of childhood onset	

Notes: In this list of diseases, no indication is given of the magnitude of change. Some disorders which were common in the 1950s have virtually disappeared—poliomyelitis for example. Others have diminished only to a relatively slight extent.

Some of the 'new diseases' which are listed as having become more common in the mid-1990s may only appear to have become more common because of increased recognition or because of changes in the classification and nomenclature of disease. A few, however, seem genuinely to be new diseases, the most obvious examples being Aids, Legionnaire's Disease, and possibly Lyme Disease.

Diseases are grouped under the most likely reason for their decrease or increase respectively. Some, therefore, appear more than once, the most striking example being tuberculosis, whose decline can be attributed in part to immunization, in part to screening and therapy, and in part to better social conditions, although the relative importance of these reasons is debatable.

In most instances the assertion that a disorder has decreased or increased between 1950 and the 1990s can be made with certainty or at any rate a high degree of probability. But in a few instances (Alzheimer's disease and anorexia nervosa are two examples) the assertion of a change in incidence is based on little more than clinical impression.

Sources: This table is based on a wide range of sources and opinions. The editors are most grateful for the assistance and advice of: Dr Jeffrey Aronson, Dr Brian Bower, Sir Richard Doll, Dr Michael Donaghy, Dr Mark Drury, Professor J. Grimley Evans, Dr Godfrey Fowler, Dr Derek Jewell, Dr Donald Lane, Dr Stephen Lock, Dr Michael Loudon, Dr Martin Rosser, Professor Terence Ryan, and Dr Anthony Storr.

general practice. Where the work of the general practitioner in the first half of the twentieth century was dominated by infectious diseases, the work of the general practitioner at the end of the century consists more and more of dealing with the long-term care of chronic disease, health promotion, and screening for asymptomatic disease.

People often ask whether these changes and the considerable improvement in the public health are largely due to better medical care, or whether the real reason is changes in social, cultural, and economic factors. The answer, of course, is that both have played their part. There is, however, as Beeson pointed out in 1980, little doubt that medical care has played a large part: 'A patient today is likely to be treated more effectively, to be returned to normal activity more quickly, and to have a better chance of survival than fifty years ago. These advances are independent of such factors as better housing, better nutrition, or health education.'[22]

Social, cultural, and economic changes have also profoundly affected health,

[22] P. B. Beeson, 'Medical Therapy during the Last Half Century', *Medicine*, 59 (1980), 79–99.

but not always in directions which are beneficial. The gap between the rich and poor remains—some would say it is as wide as ever—and cultural changes have played a large part in the appearance of Aids, drug abuse, hepatitis, malaria, and other diseases, as well as antibiotic-resistant microbes and the re-emergence of diseases such as tuberculosis.[23] Faith in the 'wonders of modern medicine' in the early years of the NHS has been tempered by scepticism, by a recognition that infectious diseases have not been eliminated (as they were expected to be in the 1950s), and by a growing realization that changes in disease result from an intricate interaction between medico-pathological and therapeutic factors, on the one hand, and factors associated with the kinds of society in which we live, on the other.[24] This, however, should not blind us to the undoubted benefits of the therapeutic revolution to which we come next.

The therapeutic revolution

Any account of medical developments since the Second World War must include at least three topics: the understanding of basic biological structures and processes, advances in surgery scarcely dreamt of fifty years ago, and the development of new drugs. Those who entered general practice in or around 1950 can remember the bottles of ineffective but harmless medicine—expectorants, linctuses, tonics, and antacids—which were dispensed in huge quantities but which rapidly disappeared from the dispensary shelves during the 1950s and 1960s. They will also remember the dogmatism of their teachers who insisted that 'clinical experience' alone was all that was needed for judging the effectiveness of a medical or surgical procedure. The gradual acceptance of the randomized trial—described by Lock as 'one of the most important developments in medicine of all time'—has been one of the central features of the therapeutic revolution.[25]

Table 4.2 lists the effective medical remedies available in general practice before 1950. Although effective drugs were scarce commodities in the first half of this century, it is clear that the start of the therapeutic revolution cannot be pinpointed to a particular year or decade. What can be said, however, is that the rate of producing new drugs has accelerated to such an extent that it would be impossible, in the space available, to provide a table of new drugs introduced since the NHS began.

Any account of the advances in drug treatment over the last fifty years must include vaccines (Table 4.3), antibiotics, drugs for hypertension and heart disease, drugs for the treatment of psychoses, anxiety, and depression, drugs

---

[23] L. Garrett, *The Coming Plague* (Harmondsworth, 1995).

[24] A. Karlen, *Plague's Progress: A Social History of Man and Disease* (London, 1995).

[25] S. Lock, 'Medicine in the Second Half of the Twentieth Century', in I. Loudon (ed.), *Western Medicine. An Illustrated History* (Oxford, 1997), 127.

TABLE 4.2 *Effective drugs and vaccines which were available to medical practitioners before 1950*

Period	Drugs or vaccines	Used for the treatment or prevention of
Before 1900	Opium and its derivatives	Pain and sedation
	Digitalis	Heart disease
	Quinine	Malaria
	Vaccination	Smallpox
	Ether and chloroform	Anaesthesia
	Iron preparations	Anaemia
	Aspirin	Pain
	Chloral	Sedation
	Diphtheria antitoxin	Treatment of diphtheria
1900	Arsenicals (Salvarsan)	Syphilis
1910	Tetanus antitoxin	Prevention of tetanus
1920	Insulin	Diabetes
	Liver (raw liver and liver extract)	Pernicious anaemia
	BCG immunization	Prevention of tuberculosis
	Tetanus toxoid	Prevention of tetanus
1930	Ergometrine	Obstetric haemorrhage
	Vitamins B, C, and D	Beri-beri, scurvy, and rickets
	Sulphonamides	The first antibiotics, active against certain bacterial diseases
	Diphtheria vaccine	Prevention of diphtheria
1940	New antimalarials (paludrine, mepacrine, and others)	Malaria
	Vitamin B12	Pernicious anaemia
	Folic acid	Megaloblastic anaemia of pregnancy
	Streptomycin	Treatment of tuberculosis
	Antihistamines	Hay fever and other allergies
	Penicillin	Antibiotic against certain bacterial diseases

Note: By 'effective' we mean that it is likely that all of these drugs and vaccines would be so judged if subjected to a modern randomized trial.

for arthritis, epilepsy, asthma, and peptic ulcer, drugs with wide applications such as the steroids, drugs for the treatment of malignant disease, and drugs for contraception and infertility. Within each class of drugs, some were introduced many years ago, while others are new versions of established drugs, introduced because they are allegedly better in general or in special circumstances, or because of greater freedom from side effects, or because they permit

TABLE 4.3 *Routine immunization programmes with dates of introduction*

Programme	Date of introduction
Tetanus	1940s
Diphtheria	1940
BCG*	c. 1945
Pertussis (whooping cough)	1947
Poliomyelitis	1956
Influenza	1960s
Measles	1968
Rubella	1970
Hepatitis B	1985
Mumps	1989
Hepatitis A	1993
Haemophilus influenza B	1993

Note: The majority of these forms of immunization are given routinely to all babies or small children. Some are confined to special risk groups.

* BCG (Bacille Calmette-Guérin), which consisted of injecting an attenuated strain of bovine tuberculosis, was introduced between 1906 and 1921. Accidental contamination of some batches of BCG with virulent strains of tuberculosis led to what became known as the Lubeck disaster in 1931 (Lubeck is in Germany), in which many children died after receiving BCG vaccination, and held up its general acceptance for many years.

easier dosage.[26] The therapeutic revolution has been as much about producing safe well-tolerated drugs as the invention of new classes of drugs for hitherto untreatable diseases.

Thus the modern general practitioner has had to absorb an enormous volume of sophisticated and constantly changing therapeutic knowledge as part of the profound changes in the content of general practice. New therapies have meant that many disorders which were previously treated in hospitals have moved into the realm of primary care. This is a recurrent theme which we meet later in this chapter.

The massive increase in new therapies has been beneficial in most instances, but it has been accompanied by new dangers and worries about drug

[26] The ideal drug is safe, comfortable to take, should only need to be taken once or twice a day (compliance with a regime in which the drug has to be taken four times for a long period is very low), and produces favourable symptomatic improvement which can be recognized by the patient—at least initially.

interactions and side effects.[27] Ever since the thalidomide disaster, doctors have been aware of, and the public increasingly distrustful of, the dangers of side effects associated with new drugs, including addiction.[28] In October 1995, for example, the Committee on Safety of Medicines warned of an increased risk of thromboembolism with the newest generation of contraceptive pills, which were popular because they were supposedly safer than their predecessors.[29] Scare headlines in the media persuaded many women to abandon the contraceptive pill, resulting in unplanned pregnancies of which some went to term, and some were aborted. Ironically, the risk of thromboembolism associated with this type of contraceptive pill was extremely low—much lower than the risks associated with unplanned pregnancies.

Similar examples of the complex issue of risks associated with taking drugs (or eating foods) have been numerous. The therapeutic revolution is often presented in the media in black and white terms: 'breakthroughs' are good news, 'scares' are presented as disasters. There is no room for doubts, uncertainties, or nuances. General practitioners, faced more and more often by patients who see the use of drugs in such black and white terms, are well aware of the difficulty of explaining that no form of medication is totally free of risk.[30] It may, incidentally, be the absence of side effects due to the extreme dilution of medications that explains the growing popularity of homeopathic medicine.

In spite of the problems of learning about new drugs, their cost, side effects, and drug interactions, modern general practitioners and their patients are provided with a range of remedies for a wide range of disorders which were not available when the NHS began. It is, therefore, not surprising that prescribing is one of the most expensive parts of primary care, or that the proportion of NHS expenditure on the pharmaceutical services has risen from 8.4 per cent in 1950 to 11.2 per cent in 1995 (see Table C1). Further, the annual number of prescriptions per head of population has risen from 4.5 in 1949 to 8.9 in 1994 (see Table C5), with the largest increase occurring in prescriptions for the elderly (see Table C6).

Until the reforms of the 1990s (since when fundholding general practitioners have been required to meet the cost of prescriptions from their

---

[27] An example of drug interactions is when a general practitioner prescribes a drug for a patient who is already on anticoagulant therapy, but is unaware that the newly prescribed drug interferes with the anticoagulant, resulting in internal bleeding. There are many such interactions of which the general practitioner has to be constantly aware.

[28] Thalidomide was introduced in the 1950s as a very safe sleeping tablet at a time when there were many over-doses and deaths from the barbiturates. It then became used for treating sickness of pregnancy. Only after it had been used for some time was it recognized in 1961 that thalidomide given in early pregnancy led to gross deformities (phocomelia—partial or complete absence of limbs).

[29] Contraceptive pills containing gestodene and desogestrel.

[30] Weatherall has said: 'the half-magical faith in medicines, and ignorance about how they work, blinds most people to the fact that drugs are like knives, dangerous when mishandled, and that only very feeble drugs, like very blunt knives, can be used with impunity in unskilled hands' (M. Weatherall, *In Search of a Cure: A History of Pharmaceutical Discovery* (Oxford, 1990), 274).

budgets[31]) general practitioners were free to prescribe as much as they chose. Governments, aware of extremely wide variations in the prescribing habits of general practitioners, have worked hard to curb costs.[32] Certainly there were cases of over-prescribing (and some of under-prescribing), but the increases in cost have been an inevitable consequence of the therapeutic revolution, and increased cost has occurred throughout the world. It is worth noting that the number of prescriptions per person and total expenditure on drugs is lower in the UK than it is in many other countries (see Fig. C3).

It is obvious that the rapid increase in medical knowledge since the NHS began, and the changes in medical care associated with the therapeutic revolution, have led to profound changes in hospital care as well as general practice. What we have hinted at, but which may be less obvious, is the changes which have occurred in the relationship between the hospital service (or secondary care) and general practice (or primary care). This is our next subject.

The hospital and the general practitioner

Under the NHS, everyone has to be registered with a general practitioner, and, if they require specialist care, they cannot go directly to a specialist; they have to be referred by their general practitioner. This well-known fact is the principle (or system) of referral, and is often referred to as the 'gatekeeping' role of the general practitioner.[33] Registration, as we know it in the NHS, began in 1911 with the introduction of the National Health Insurance Act of 1911 (services were introduced in July 1912). This provided medical care for workers under a certain wage level, and registration was necessary because general practitioners were paid on a capitation system.[34] By 1938 NHI covered 43 per cent of the population and ensured that, when the NHS was introduced, the capitation system would continue.

The principle of referral dates back even further, to the second half of the nineteenth century, when vast numbers of the poor—and some of the not so

---

[31] In fact non-fundholders have 'indicative prescribing budgets' but neither type of general practitioner, at the time of writing, has to adhere strictly to a budget; both can overspend. This, however, may be altered.

[32] In 1958 a senior and respected Edinburgh general practitioner admitted to an average monthly drug cost per patient of 10d. An equally respected general practitioner was spending 3s. 6d. a month, when others were spending 5s. a month and one Glasgow practitioner 10s. a month (C. Webster, *The Health Services since the War*, ii. *Government and Health Care: The National Health Service, 1958–1979* (London: HMSO, 1996), 14).

[33] There are a few exceptions, such as admission to accident and emergency departments, and a few 'open-access' clinics at hospitals, such as clinics for sexually transmitted diseases.

[34] A capitation system means that general practitioners are paid a certain fee per annum for every patient who registers with them, as opposed to a salaried system, or a 'fee-for-service' system, when general practitioners are paid a fee for every consultation.

poor—began to go in droves to the casualty departments of hospitals.[35] General practitioners, who suffered large financial losses as a consequence, demanded the right to determine who should be seen at a hospital in order to protect their incomes. It was a long time before the principle of referral was accepted by the whole of the medical profession as an ethical rule.[36] But the two systems, registration and the principle of referral, were more or less firmly in place by the time the NHS began. The result, as Stevens pointed out, was that 'The physician and the surgeon retained the hospital, but the general practitioner retained the patient.'[37] Although everyone in the UK takes this system of medical care for granted, it operates in only a few Western countries such as Denmark and the Netherlands. In France, Germany, or the USA, for example, patients are not formally registered with a general practitioner and they can, and do, shop around as they choose between generalists and specialists (see Chapter 11).[38]

In this section, therefore, we look at the system of referral, how it has changed since the NHS was introduced, and whether it is a sensible way of delivering medical care. Apart from a brief section on cottage hospitals, we will not deal with in-patient admissions, nor the vexed question of patients trying to use accident and emergency departments as a source of primary care for non-urgent conditions. Instead we will concentrate on outpatients.

Referral to outpatients

At the beginning of the NHS, outpatient departments betrayed their eighteenth-century origins. Most were dingy, dark, overcrowded, lacking in privacy, and ill equipped, with entrances round the corner or at the back of the hospital like servants' entrances to the big country houses on which the early voluntary hospitals were modelled. Waiting times were long and consultants usually disliked outpatient clinics compared with ward rounds. In their seminal study of outpatients in 1968, Forsyth and Logan noted that most hospitals faced with an emergency in-patient admission would stretch their facilities even to the point of putting up extra beds. 'And yet the same hospital doctors can be quite inflexible in their approach to out-patient departments.'[39]

[35] At the London Hospital in Whitechapel, for instance, the annual number of *new* outpatient attendances in 1800 was approximately 1,000, or about three or four a day excluding Sundays. By 1870 this had risen to 52,000 and by 1911 to the astonishing number of 221,000 a year, or over 600 a day. See I. Loudon, 'The Historical Importance of Outpatients', *British Medical Journal* (1978), i. 974–7.

[36] In 1910, when the principle had been recognized for at least two decades, the percentage of outpatients who had been referred by general practitioners as opposed to going directly to the hospitals was 6.0% in Charing Cross Hospital, 2.6% in Guy's Hospital, and 2.4% at the London Hospital (ibid.).

[37] R. Stevens, *Medical Practice in Modern England, the Impact of Specialization and State Medicine* (New Haven, Conn., 1966), 33.

[38] See I. Loudon and R. Stevens, 'Primary Care and the Hospital', in J. Fry (ed.), *Primary Care* (London, 1980), 139–75.

[39] G. Forsyth and R. F. Logan, *Gateway or Dividing Line? A Study of Hospital Out-Patients in the 1960s* (London, 1968), 120. They also remarked: 'The [outpatient] system was carried over into the National

If any part of the hospital service cried out for reform in 1948, it was the outpatient departments. The gap between the ideal and the reality was recognized by Sir James Spence in 1953 when he wrote: 'Above all the out-patient department should offer a true consultation on the lines of private practice—just the consultant with the patient and his own doctor', to which he added: 'If many suburban general practitioners today have ill-equipped and unsuitable surgeries it is partly because they have copied what they saw as students in the out-patient departments of their teaching hospitals.'[40] Ideally, the NHS should have begun by creating new, spacious, and well equipped outpatient departments as the central feature of hospitals. The cost would have been fully justified, for the number of outpatients was, and still is, enormous.[41]

Between 1953 and 1993, when the total population in the UK rose, in round figures, from 50 million to 58 million, total outpatient attendances rose from 46 million a year to 65 million (see Table 4.4). A rise of 67 per cent in new outpatient attendances is not surprising. The more general practitioners there are, and the more specialists and special clinics, the more referrals there will be; and Table 4.4 shows that, relative to the population, the number of general practitioners rose between 1953 and 1993 by 33 per cent, and hospital staff by 206 per cent.[42]

But there is more to change than just numbers. In the early years of the NHS, hospital staff, who frequently distrusted the abilities of general practitioners, tended to see patients repeatedly at follow-up clinics. Once a patient had been sent to hospital, there was little willingness to share responsibility for patients between primary and secondary care.[43] That was the ethos in the early years of the NHS. Gradually, however, there was a new spirit of cooperation, symbolized by the introduction of the concept of shared care. Shared care is especially important for the management of chronic disease, when, for example, an outpatient consultation may be used to plan long-term care, but all or most of the subsequent care remains in the hands of the general practitioner. One of the results, as Table 4.5 shows, is that, while new outpatient attendances have risen by 67 per cent, follow-up attendances have stayed at virtually the same level.

Health Service because the National Health Service is a political artefact. . . . In a democratic system we like to think that the framework of our institutions is determined by the community in the community's interest, rather than factions. This is probably naive in an age of pressure-group politics' (p. 127). Attitudes of hospital staff to outpatients are also mentioned in I. Loudon, *The Demand for Hospital Care: In-Patient Care: Alternatives and Delays* (Oxford: United Oxford Hospitals, 1970).

[40] Sir J. Spence, 'Function of the Hospital Out-Patient Department', *Lancet* (1953), i. 275.

[41] I. Loudon, 'A Question of Numbers', *Lancet* (1976), i. 736.

[42] The comparable figure for admissions to the wards (counted as deaths and discharges) were, in round figures for the UK, 4.2 million in 1953 and 9.5 million in 1993.

[43] An investigation at the Radcliffe Infirmary, Oxford, in 1970 found that, when in-patients were discharged, they were, regardless of necessity, routinely provided with an outpatient follow-up appointment by the ward sister or house officer. No patient was referred straight back to his or her general practitioner (Loudon, *The Demand for Hospital Care*).

TABLE 4.4 *Changes in outpatient attendances at NHS hospitals, and changes in general practitioners and whole-time hospital medical and dental staff, UK, 1953 and 1993*

Outpatient attendances and medical staff	Number		Rate per 1,000 population		% change in rate (1953–93)
	1953	1993	1953	1993	
Total outpatient attendances	46,721*	63,670*	923	1,098	19
New outpatient attendances	11,629*	24,884*	256	429	67
Follow-up outpatient attendances	35,092*	38,786*	667	669	0.3
General practitioners	20,162	30,130	0.039	0.052	33
Hospital medical and dental staff†	15,474	55,254	0.031	0.095	206

* Thousands.

† Whole-time equivalents, excluding locums and general practitioners participating in hospital staff funds, but including all junior hospital medical staff.

Source: Office of Health Economics, *Compendium of Health Statistics* (9th edn, 1995).

Other important changes have taken place. An increasing number of outpatient consultations occur in the premises of general practitioners, such as health centres and community hospitals, and an increasing number of clinics, wholly or largely run by general practitioners, have been established in general practitioners' premises. In short, there have been major shifts in the provision of continuing medical care away from the hospitals to primary care, with much closer cooperation between hospital staff and general practitioners.

What do we know of the nature of referrals? On the whole, reasons for referral are straightforward and consistent. A study of 18,754 referrals in 1989 showed that 35 per cent were referred for treatment or operation, 28 per cent to establish the diagnosis, and 14 per cent for advice on management and referral back.[44] The clinics with the largest number of referrals in the 1980s were general surgery and urology, gynaecology, ear, nose, and throat surgery, general medicine, trauma and orthopaedics, and ophthalmology, in that order.[45]

That much we know, and might have guessed. What is much more surprising is the enormous variation between individual general practitioners, and this

[44] Other reasons were: for a specialist to take over management (9%), for a specified investigation (7%), to reassure the general practitioner (2%), and to reassure the patient or the patient's family (2%). A. Coulter, 'Auditing referrals', in M. Roland and A. Coulter (eds.), *Hospital Referrals* (Oxford, 1992), 150–62.

[45] A. Coulter, A. Noone, and M. Goldacre, 'General Practitioners' Referrals to Specialist Out-Patient Clinics, part 1', *British Medical Journal* (1989), ii. 304–6, table 1, p. 305.

TABLE 4.5 *Pathology reports and radiology units of treatment provided by the NHS, England and Wales, 1959–1974*

Facility	1959	1965	1969	1974
Clinical pathology				
Total pathology reports (thousands)	17,279	28,560	38,792	51,802
Pathology reports requested by general practitioners as a percentage of total reports	5.8	8.9	11.3	12.9
Approximate number of requests from general practitioners (thousands)	1,006	2,532	4,962	6,690
Radiology				
Radiology—total units of treatment (thousands)	21,127	27,704	33,882	225,706*
Number referred by general practitioners as a percentage of total	9.0	10.4	11.0	9.9

* Unit values revised in 1973.

Source: Office of Health Economics, *Compendium of Health Statistics* (8th edn., 1977), table 3.12.

is something the reader should bear in mind throughout this chapter. In almost every respect there is a much wider variation between individual general practitioners and practices than there is between hospitals, and this applies to methods and standards of care. For example, Wilkin found in 1987 that amongst a group of 200 general practitioners in Greater Manchester:

Consultation rates varied from less than two per patient per year to more than five, prescribing rates varied from 50 per 100 consultations to more than 90, investigation rates from less than one per 100 consultations to more than fifteen, *referral rates from less than three per 100 consultations to more than 17.*[46]

Many other investigations have shown similar variations in referral rates. Some variation may be a statistical anomaly due to small samples, but this accounts for only a small part of the differences.[47] What is striking is the failure to account for such wide variation. Many possible factors have been investigated such as different types and rates of morbidity in different regions, the age of the general practitioner, whether the general practitioner has had extensive postgraduate hospital experience, size of partnership, type of practice premises, and whether there was a link between rates of referral to outpatients and rates of ordering hospital investigations. No clear answers have emerged.

[46] D. Wilkin, 'Patterns of Referral: Explaining Variation', in Roland and Coulter (eds.), *Hospital Referrals*, 75–92, at 76 (emphasis added). See also D. C. Morrell, H. G. Gage, and N. A. Robinson, 'Referral to Hospital by General Practitioners', *Journal of the Royal College of General Practitioners*, 21 (1971), 77–85.
[47] M. Roland, 'Measuring Referral Rates', in Roland and Coulter (eds.), *Hospital Referrals*, 62–75.

One doctor may consistently refer less than five out of every 100 patients to hospital, while another in an adjoining practice, or even a partner of the first, serving the same type of population, refers more than twelve or fifteen out of every 100 consultations. Even if they work in the same health centre, it is probable that neither is aware that they occupy the opposite extremes of a distribution curve of referral. Referral rates cannot predict what kind of differences we would expect to find between these two doctors; nor can we say which is providing the better service. Are those with very low rates using their skills to the full and avoiding unnecessary referrals? Or are they failing to refer numerous patients who would profit from hospital care? Are others with high referral rates more adept at identifying patients who would profit from specialist care, or are they unloading as many problems as they can out of inherent laziness?[48]

No one has yet been able to answer such seemingly simple questions. But they do suggest that rates of referral are determined not only (as we might like to assume) by agreed clinical guidelines, but also by personal characteristics of the general practitioner. There is, as yet, no estimate of what is the 'right' rate of referral, or even if such a rate could be defined. Indeed, it could be argued that the problem of wide variation in outpatient referral may not be a problem at all, but simply an example of the variation in techniques used by different general practitioners in their daily work.

Another aspect of referral to hospitals provides a particularly vivid illustration of the changes that have taken place between general practice and hospital care: the question of the access of general practitioners to laboratory and radiological investigations.

Open access to laboratory and radiological investigations

During the rapid expansion of hospital services in the early years of the NHS (see Tables D2 and D7),[49] two of the most rapidly expanding specialities were clinical pathology and radiology. During the first decade of the NHS the number of investigations in radiology rose from 7.8 million to 21 million, and in clinical pathology from 11.5 million to 17.25 million.[50] All medical schools instilled the vital importance of investigations for the practice of modern scientific medicine. Yet, when their students entered general practice during

---

[48] Forsyth and Logan remarked in 1968 that, ever since NHI was introduced in 1911, British general practitioners 'were often glad to send patients off to out-patient departments. It cost them nothing' (Forsyth and Logan, *Gateway or Dividing Line?*, 5).

[49] Between 1949 and 1959 the number of consultants in England and Wales had increased by about 60% compared with a 21% increase in general practitioners (G. E. Godber, 'Trends in Specialisation and their Effect on the Practice of Medicine', *British Medical Journal* (1961), ii. 843–7).

[50] Ibid. 845. The most notable increase in clinical pathology was in biochemical pathology, which led to the need to train chemists 'for the new sub-specialty of chemical pathology. . . . The all purpose pathologist of twenty years ago has been replaced by the group of consultants each taking charge of a section of the work.'

the early years of the NHS, they found that they were denied access to such investigations. If they wanted an investigation to be carried out, they often had to refer their patient to a consultant at a hospital. It was, as the Chief Medical Officer George Godber remarked in 1961, absurd that

The student sees his teachers carrying out diagnosis and treatment with the assistance of a battery of scientific investigations . . . When he is a house officer he orders such investigations on behalf of his chief . . . If this man then goes on to be a registrar, he often reaches at least the primary diagnosis and the initiation of treatment on the basis of the results reported. If this man then goes into general practice it is absurd to prevent him from having similar aids to diagnosis and the control of treatment . . . If [general practitioners] are prevented from using them, they have little chance to practise medicine with a full understanding of the benefits that their patients could have from such aids.[51]

'Open access' to radiology and laboratory medicine had been adopted as the policy of the BMA as early as 1946.[52] But the extent to which it was granted was patchy, and usually it was confined to chest X-rays and simple laboratory tests. The first survey into open-access facilities (sponsored by the Nuffield Provincial Hospitals Trust) was carried out in 1961 by Macaulay.[53] He found that teaching hospitals in large conurbations were much more reluctant to grant open access—even to their own graduates practising in the vicinity—than hospitals in smaller provincial towns, a feature confirmed by other surveys. Amongst the London teaching hospitals in the early 1960s, only University College Hospital and St Mary's Hospital granted open access. Fearing that they would be swamped with demands, investigations were restricted and both hospitals took care not to publicize the service.[54] Provincial medical schools were more willing to provide open access, and the most willing of all were the non-teaching district general hospitals.

Radiologists were always more reluctant to provide a direct service to general practitioners than clinical pathologists,[55] and Macaulay remarked on the paradox that the investigatory facilities for general practitioners were worst

[51] Ibid. 846.

[52] P. L. Cook, 'Experiences in the First Year of an "Open Door" X-ray Department', *British Medical Journal* (1966), ii. 351–4.

[53] H. M. C. Macaulay, 'Diagnostic facilities for General Practitioners', *Lancet* (1962), i. 791–3.

[54] St Thomas's Hospital refused to provide open access until it was pointed out that general practitioners might well send all their in- and outpatients to another London hospital which did provide open access. St Thomas's promptly opened its laboratories and radiology departments to general practitioners (Professor David Morrell, personal communication).

[55] Macaulay, 'Diagnostic facilities'; Forsyth and Logan, *Gateway or Dividing Line?*; W. J. Mair *et al.*, 'Use of Radiological Services by General Practitioners', *British Medical Journal* (1974), ii. 88–94, R. H. Green, 'General Practitioners and Open-Access Pathology Services', *Journal of the Royal College of General Practitioners*, 23 (1973), 316–25. A possible reason for the greater reluctance was that pathology tests were carried out by technicians who could slot general practitioners' requests relatively easily into their routine, and who in any case were not in a position to object to 'outside' work. All X-rays, however, had to be read by consultant radiologists, who often felt they had enough work, dealing with the demands of their hospital.

where the resources were best—in the large hospitals.[56] However, things got better during the 1960s. The Middlesex Hospital in London introduced open access in February 1961,[57] Guy's Hospital in 1964,[58] and Sheffield in April 1965.[59] Forsyth and Logan found in 1968 that most practices had access to the full range of clinical pathology, but access to radiology was patchy.[60]

The power to provide or deny open access to general practitioners lay entirely in the hands of the hospitals. Denial was often based on the belief in hospitals that, if a patient needed investigation, then the case must be beyond the scope of the average general practitioner, or that the average general practitioner would be incapable of interpreting the results of tests. Further, radiologists and laboratories feared that they would be swamped with unnecessary and inappropriate requests. All these fears proved groundless and open access was granted in most areas by the mid-1970s.[61] But as late as 1971 there were still a few radiological departments which refused to provide open access at all, or refused to undertake contrast media radiology for general practitioners.[62]

Surveys showed, in fact, that general practitioners who used radiology and pathological investigations to support (or refute) a provisional diagnosis, or for assistance in the surveillance of chronic illness or for certain types of screening, did so responsibly, with discrimination and outstanding benefit in terms of clinical care.[63] In the 1960s the average number of X-ray examinations required by general practitioners was 50 per year per 1,000 patients, varying from 29 to 151.[64] Rates subsequently increased rapidly, as shown in Table 4.5, page 107.

Once again, as with referrals to outpatients, there was wide and bewildering variation in rates of investigation. Attempts to correlate high (or low) rates

[56] Macaulay, 'Diagnostic facilities'.

[57] Cook, 'Experiences'.

[58] J. A. D. Anderson, 'Requests for X-Ray Examinations from General Practitioners and Hospital Outpatients', Lancet (1968), ii. 97–8.

[59] A. H. Clarke and D. F. Rickards, 'Economics of Open Access to Diagnostic Services', Lancet (1965), ii. 336–7.

[60] Forsyth and Logan, Gateway or Dividing Line?, 39–41.

[61] Green, 'General Practitioners and Open-Access Pathology Services'.

[62] D. Irvine and M. Jeffreys, 'B. M. A. Planning Unit Survey of General Practice 1969', British Medical Journal (1971), ii. 535–43. Contrast media radiology means such X-ray examinations as barium meal or barium enemas for investigating disorders of the stomach and colon, and intravenous pyelography (IVP) for disorders of the kidneys or bladder.

[63] Editorial, 'Investigations in General Practice', Journal of the Royal College of General Practitioners, 23 (1973), 302–4; Green, 'General Practitioners and Open-Access Pathology Services'; and J. Inch, 'The General Practitioner's Use of Radiology', Journal of the Royal Society of Medicine, 72 (1979), 88–94. One way of judging the quality of requests for investigation from general practitioners, but not necessarily a way that would be easy to defend, was to compare the number of positive results revealed by the investigations ordered by general practitioners with those ordered from outpatient clinics. Almost invariably the general-practitioner requests yielded the higher proportion of positives.

[64] G. E. Godber, 'Trends in Specialisation and their Effect on the Practice of Medicine', British Medical Journal (1961), ii. 843–7; Editorial, 'Investigations in General Practice'.

with some defined characteristic—age, partnership size, postgraduate experience, type of practice, and so on—failed to provide an answer.[65] But on one
point there was total consistency. A majority of requests for hospital investigations came from a minority of general practitioners. In one instance, three-
quarters of requests for investigations came from one-quarter of all general
practitioners.[66] In another it was shown that many who used the facilities of
pathology and radiology departments used them for only a small and restricted
number of investigations.[67]

Winning the battle for open access and allowing general practitioners to
make use of the rapid advances in diagnostic technology played a part in
the renaissance of general practice which occurred in the 1970s. It allowed
young general practitioners to absorb the special features of primary care
but at the same time to practise clinical medicine at a high standard. But the
issue is not dead. When new investigations are introduced (CAT scans and
echocardiography are examples), requests from general practitioners for open
access are often resisted with the very same arguments that were heard in the
1960s.

One further point of importance should be mentioned here. Since the late
1960s, many practices have invested in the means by which they can undertake
investigations in health centres and surgeries. These include electrocardiogra-
phy, peak-flow meters for respiratory function, audiometry, various bood investigations such as haemoglobin and blood sugar, bacterial culture of infected
urine, occult blood in the stools, and in some practices doppler-flow measure-
ments for peripheral vascular disease, sigmoidoscopy, and ultrasonography. At
the beginning of this chapter we cited the description in the Collings Report
of the 'excellent' general practitioner he had met who had introduced a few
simple means of investigation into his surgery—and the fact that his colleagues
thought he was crazy to do so, because he would bankrupt himself. These
changes, outlined above, are due to new technologies, new aspirations, new
confidence in general practice, and new ways of payment of expenses which
have made them possible.

Outpatient referral and the use of radiological and laboratory facilities
provide a broad picture of the changes which have taken place in the interface
between primary and secondary care. We now turn to three specific examples.
In the first (midwifery), care has tended to move away from general practice to
hospital care; in the other two examples (diabetes and the care of the dying),
there has been movement in the other direction.

---

[65] Editorial, 'Investigations in General Practice'; Forsyth and Logan, *Gateway or Dividing Line?*,
39–41; Green, 'General Practitioners and Open-Access Pathology Services'; B. B. Wallace *et al.*, 'Unrestricted Access by General Practitioners to a Department of Diagnostic Radiology', *Journal of the Royal
College of General Practitioners*, 23 (1973), 337–43.
[66] J. S. A. Ashley, 'Demand for Laboratory Services', *British Medical Bulletin*, 30 (1974), 234–6.
[67] D. Mechanic, 'General Practice in England and Wales', *Medical Care*, 6 (1968), 245–61, table 4,
p. 255.

Midwifery

In the past, it was an article of faith in general practice that midwifery was the basis for building your practice; if you delivered the babies, the families would become loyal patients for life.[68] As a Somerset physician remarked in 1844: 'The successful practice of midwifery . . . at the outset of life, as surely establishes a professional man's reputation as the contrary retards his progress'; without midwifery 'it is vain to expect employment in the country and not very easy in the metropolis'.[69] Furthermore, until this century, hospital obstetricians and maternity beds in hospitals were so few that midwifery was essentially a part of general practice, undertaken in competition with midwives.

By the 1930s, however, midwifery in general practice began to decline, partly because of greater competition by well-trained midwives, partly because general practitioners believed that fees for midwifery were too low, and partly because of the foundation of the (Royal) College of Obstetricians and Gynaecologists (RCOG) in 1929 and the growth of hospital obstetrics—although initially the College knew that the backbone of British midwifery would have to be home deliveries by midwives and general practitioners simply because there were not enough obstetricians, let alone maternity beds, to cover the country as a whole.[70] Radical changes occurred in the Second World War, when the remarkably efficient Emergency Maternity Service led to a rapid increase in the number of women who were delivered in hospital.[71] By the end of the war, women were demanding hospital delivery, and home deliveries were beginning to be seen as unsafe and old-fashioned.

Thus the decline in home deliveries by general practitioners had begun before the NHS began. In 1953 Hadfield found that about one-third of general practitioners disliked midwifery and did none or as little as possible; one-third 'are not very attracted' but felt they had to do it; and one-third were keen and did as much as possible.[72] By 1950 about half of total deliveries (as opposed to about one-third in the mid-1930s) took place in consultant maternity units. The

---

[68] I. Loudon, 'Obstetrics and the General Practitioner', *British Medical Journal*, 300 (1990), 703–7.

[69] Jonathan Toogood, 'The Practice of Midwifery, with Remarks', *Provincial Medical and Surgical Journal*, 7 (1844), 103–8. For a general discussion of the role of the general practitioner in midwifery in the nineteenth century, see I. Loudon, *Death in Childbirth: An International Study of Maternal Care and Maternal Mortality, 1800–1950* (Oxford, 1992), 182–7.

[70] Moreover, the distribution of obstetricians and maternity facilities was extraordinarily patchy. For example, in the early 1930s there was not a single trained obstetrician/gynaecologist in the county of Gloucestershire, where a general practitioner who encountered a hair-raising obstetric complication had little choice but to deal with it himself as best he could, or call in another general practitioner. Lancashire, on the other hand, was exceptionally well supplied with obstetricians and maternity beds (Loudon, *Death in Childbirth*, 206–33).

[71] S. Ferguson and H. Fitzgerald, *History of the Second World War: Studies in the Social Services* (London, 1954). During the Second World War many consultant obstetricians from London and other large cities were posted on war service to the provinces. They were shocked by the low standard of maternal care in many parts of the country and were fortified in their determination to do what they could to raise standards and abolish home deliveries.

[72] Hadfield, 'A Field Survey of General Practice, 1951–52', 683–706.

great migration of childbirth from home to hospital was well under way, as the number of specialist obstetricians increased, more maternity beds were provided, and there was a striking reduction in the length of stay in hospital.[73]

From the late 1930s to the 1990s, three trends have occurred simultaneously. Home deliveries have declined steeply (see Fig. 4.1), maternal mortality has fallen far more steeply and continuously than anyone had imagined possible in the 1940s (see Fig. B2), and perinatal mortality has fallen as well.[74] Obstetricians were convinced that the profound falls in maternal and perinatal mortality were due to the fall in home deliveries and the decline in general-practitioner involvement in delivering babies. To them, it was solid proof that all women should be delivered in hospitals, including normal deliveries, because no one can be sure that a delivery is normal until it has taken place. The Standing Maternity and Midwifery Advisory Committee said in 1980: 'We think that sufficient facilities should be provided for 100% hospital delivery. The greater safety of hospital confinement for mother and child justifies this objective.'[75] Thus, by the 1980s, home deliveries by general practitioners in the UK had become rare, with the exception of general-practice deliveries in GP maternity units, which deserve a separate section.

GP maternity units

By the 1980s, between 6 per cent and 9 per cent of all deliveries took place in about 300 GP maternity units in England and Wales (see Table D9).[76] In the Oxford region, for example, there were formal links between most of the GP maternity units in market-town cottage/community hospitals and an integrated GP maternity unit within the consultant maternity department in the city of Oxford.[77]

[73] In the 1950s most maternity patients were kept in hospital for ten to fourteen days after delivery. By the 1980s some maternity hospitals were following a policy of admitting a woman in labour, and, if the delivery was normal, sending her home under the care of a district midwife on the day of delivery or the next day.

[74] Maternal mortality is the number of maternal deaths per 1,000, 10,000, or 100,000 births. Perinatal mortality is the number of stillbirths added to the number of infant deaths in the first week of life, per 1,000 births. Maternal and perinatal mortality are the yardsticks by which the effectiveness of maternal care can be measured.

[75] Standing Maternity and Midwifery Advisory Committee (Chairman, Sir John Peel), *Domiciliary Midwifery and Maternity Bed Needs* (London: HMSO, 1980). This view prevailed in most Western countries, with the notable exception of the Netherlands, where there has always been and still is a large number of home deliveries; and the records as far as the decline in maternal and perinatal mortality are concerned have been as good as in the UK.

[76] These assertions are based on L. F. P. Smith and D. Jewell, 'Contribution of General Practitioners to Hospital Care in Maternity Units in England and Wales', *British Medical Journal*, 302 (1991), 13–16. They estimated about 6% of all deliveries took place in GP maternity units. Dr Michael Bull, however, using a method based on the fees paid to general practitioners for maternity services, believes the true figure may be close to 9% (M. Bull, personal communication), and M. Bull, 'Ten Years' Experience in a General Practitioner Unit', *Journal of the Royal College of General Practitioners*, 30 (1980), 208–15.

[77] This unit was first established in 1966 in the Churchill Hospital, and since 1972 in the new maternity department in the John Radcliffe Hospital.

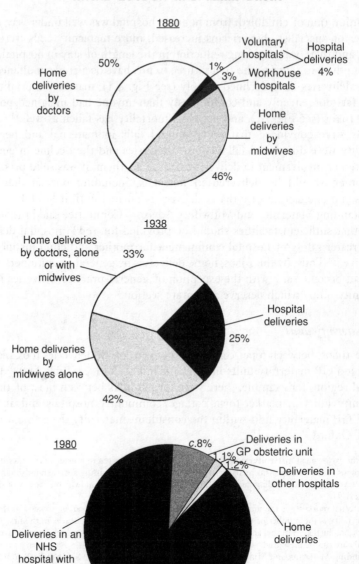

Fɪɢ. 4.1 The distribution of deliveries, England and Wales, 1880, 1938, and 1980

Sources: For 1880 and 1938: I. Loudon, *Death in Childbirth: An International Study of Maternal Mortality and Maternal Care, 1800–1950* (Oxford, 1992). For 1980, see text.

By the 1980s the Oxford City GP unit was used by over seventy general practitioners. Bookings for delivery rose from 600 a year in 1967 to a peak of over 1,000 in 1988, but declined to slightly less than 700 in 1995.[78] The delivery of mothers in this and other GP units was (and still is in 1995) undertaken by community midwives and general practitioners. On average, general practitioners attended two out of every three deliveries, thus providing continuity of care by the primary-care team from early pregnancy to the post-natal period.

With the decline in home deliveries, GP maternity units have allowed a minority of general practitioners to deliver enough patients to maintain a proper level of skill in intra-partum care. The majority of general practitioners, however, do not undertake intra-partum care, but continue to play a large part in antenatal and post-natal care.

Antenatal and post-natal care and the primary-care team

Before the NHS, antenatal care was split between general practitioners, local-authority clinics, and maternity hospitals, often with little communication between the three. In the 1950s the antenatal care of patients booked for hospital delivery was often carried out entirely by the hospital in grossly overcrowded clinics, and local-authority antenatal clinics faded away.

Then, from the 1950s and 1960s, general practitioners became increasingly involved in antenatal care, not least because midwifery was one of the earliest parts of general practice to attract payment on a fee-for-service basis. By the 1980s it was common for the general practitioner and the community midwife to undertake joint antenatal clinics in a surgery or health centre, while maintaining close connections with the hospital in which the mother was due to be delivered. The importance of such arrangements has been that the primary-care team can contribute vital knowledge about the patient's background, past medical history, and general state of physical, mental, and social health. A much better organized and comprehensive system of antenatal care in collaboration with maternity hospitals is another example of the reality of shared care between the primary and secondary sectors.

By the late 1980s it seemed likely that home deliveries would soon disappear completely, apart from general practitioners with access to GP maternity units. By 1995-6, however, there were tentative signs of a possible return to home deliveries.

[78] A minority of women booked for a GP delivery were transferred to the consultant unit if there was some anticipated or actual complication which made transfer necessary. Out of the 1,000 bookings in 1988, actual deliveries in the GP unit amounted to about 800 (Oxford GP Maternity Unit Annual Report for 1995). I am most grateful to Dr Michael Bull for data on the Oxford City GP maternity unit.

A future for home deliveries?

It should be emphasized that during the early years of the NHS, when too few consultant maternity beds were available, large numbers of women were disappointed at being turned down for a hospital delivery; only a very small minority chose to be delivered at home when they could be delivered in hospital. By the late 1970s, or early 1980s, however, when maternal and perinatal mortality had fallen to very low levels, maternal satisfaction began to be the major issue. A minority of women (and it is uncertain how large that minority is) and a number of midwives deplored the alleged inhumanity and lack of 'homeliness' of hospital deliveries, where, they said, women were subjected to unnecessary interference in labour, excessive induction-for-convenience, and intrusive 'high-tech.' techniques such as continuous foetal monitoring. Hospitals, they said, represented authoritarianism and insensitivity to the needs of women in labour, while home deliveries, which were 'low-tech.', homely, and friendly, were a safe way of providing a form of maternal care which allowed mothers to have a feeling of power over the conduct of their labour.

It should be said that this perceived dichotomy between hospital and home deliveries, thus presented, may be false. It is not the place of delivery that matters; it is the conduct and attitudes of midwives and doctors, wherever they work. Many of the wishes expressed by the supporters of birth at home—especially continuity of care and control over their labour—can be met in GP maternity units. Still, the dichotomy, true or false, has become deeply embedded in a vocal section of the population and arouses very strong feelings.

Obstetricians view a return to home deliveries with dismay, saying the risk to mothers and babies is unacceptable. But is there greater risk in home deliveries of selected low-risk cases? Four papers were published on home deliveries in the *British Medical Journal* of 23 November 1996; two from England, one from the Netherlands, and one from Switzerland.[79] All provided convincing evidence that there was no increased risk to mothers or babies amongst carefully selected cases of mothers delivered at home, compared with a matched group of mothers delivered in hospital. 'Carefully selected' is the important phrase, for one of the papers showed a considerably increased risk in *unplanned* home deliveries.

---

[79] Home Birth Study Steering Group, 'Prospective Regional Study of Planned Home Births', *British Medical Journal*, 313 (1996), 1302–6; Northern Region Perinatal Mortality Survey Coordinating Group, 'Collaborative Survey of Perinatal Loss in Planned and Unplanned Home Births', ibid. 1306–9; T. A. Weigers, M. J. N. C. Keirse, J. van der Zee, and G. A. H. Berghs, 'Outcome of Planned Home and Planned Hospital Births in Low Risk Pregnancies: Prospective Study in Midwifery Practices in the Netherlands', ibid. 1309–13; U. Ackermann-Liebrich *et al.*, 'Home versus Hospital Deliveries: Follow-Up Study of Matched Pairs for Procedures and Outcome', ibid. 1313–18. These had been preceded by many other publications, especially those by Marjorie Tew, claiming to confirm the safety of home deliveries, and most importantly by the report: Department of Health, *Changing Childbirth: Report of the Expert Maternity Group* (London: HMSO, 1993), which recommended greater independence for midwives and a possible increase in the number of home births.

If one accepts the evidence of these and other publications which claim that home delivery can be as safe as hospital delivery for certain low-risk cases, it has been estimated that up to 10 per cent of all births in Britain could in theory take place safely at home. Those who supported home deliveries, however, often found that general practitioners were 'unsupportive' and unwilling to attend.[80] This is not surprising. If we assume, for the sake of argument, that, in 1995, 10 per cent of total deliveries took place at home, that all general practitioners were supportive, and that in practice they were called by the community midwife to about one-third of deliveries, they would on average have attended *less than* one delivery a year, or, if they attended all deliveries, 2.3 deliveries per year. From this it is clear that, if there is to be a return to home births, it may have to be undertaken by independent community midwives, as in the very successful system which operates in the Netherlands. With such a low level of continuing practical experience, general practitioners could not expect to be involved in intra-partum care.

Diabetes and diabetic clinics

There have been many changes in the long-term management of chronic diseases such as arthritis, hypertension, heart disease, and so on. We have chosen diabetes simply as one example of how the changes have affected primary care.

Before the discovery of insulin in 1922, the treatment of diabetes had relied on strict diet. It was depressing. At best it slightly postponed the death of the patient from diabetic coma. The introduction of insulin therapy produced a surge of clinical enthusiasm and resulted in the formation of specialist diabetic clinics. One of these was established in Edinburgh Royal Infirmary in 1924. Three months after it opened thirty patients were attending weekly. By 1953 there were 141 diabetic clinics in the UK seeing 200,000 patients, and by 1971 between 400 and 500 clinics seeing most of the 500,000 diabetic patients at least once and usually at regular intervals. It became apparent that outpatient care for all diabetics was unrealistic, that it was geared to the detection and treatment of complications rather than their prevention. The key to the future was patient education.[81]

Through the growth of hospital diabetic clinics, there was little chance for general practitioners to learn how to manage the disease. Although the prevailing attitude in the early decades of the NHS was that only hospital doctors had the skills to monitor insulin therapy, in reality diabetic clinics were

[80] Home Birth Study Steering Group, 'Prospective Regional Study of Planned Home Births'.

[81] In the 1990s there are something over half a million diabetics in the UK; 20% of diabetics are classified as type I and are dependent on regular injections of insulin; 75% are type II, or non-insulin-dependent diabetics, whose disease is controlled by diet alone or the addition of blood-sugar-lowering tablets; 5% are of other types.

staffed by junior hospital doctors on short-term contracts. Anyhow, many non-insulin-dependent diabetics were already being looked after by their general practitioners. The idea that diabetes should be managed only in hospital clinics soon became untenable.[82] Unsurprisingly, simply discharging patients back to their general practitioner led to a deterioration in standards of care. Hayes and Harries speculated that the main reasons for this were the lack of an automatic recall system and ready access to laboratory, dietetic, ophthalmic, and chiropody services.[83] Structured care is a prerequisite of high-quality care.

In recognition of this, Dr Malins, a consultant physician specializing in diabetes in Birmingham, and general practitioners working as clinical assistants with him, developed a system of taking the clinics into surgeries where, on one day each year, they would see all the diabetic patients with their own general practitioner.[84] Russell, a single-handed GP also working with Malins, developed a mini-clinic run by practice staff alone, and Singh, in a study of this system, found no difference from standards of hospital care.[85]

An alternative to this approach, which overcame the paradox of general practitioners becoming specialists, was a community-care service, developed in Poole by R. D. Hill.[86] An educational programme for primary-care teams was combined with improved support from laboratory services, mutually agreed guidelines, and a patient-held record. Patients overwhelmingly preferred the care of their general practitioners, who, in spite of increased workloads, were satisfied with the scheme. From these sorts of initiative, most care of diabetics is, in the 1990s, undertaken in general practice. Structured care is the key to managing this development without sacrificing standards. There must be a register of diabetics, protected time, a practice nurse with experience of diabetic care, a protocol for management, and the means to audit it.

Not all diabetic physicians were happy with the growth of diabetic clinics in general practice. Because such clinics attracted extra payment, the writer of

---

[82] As soon as he qualified in medicine in 1951, one of the very first tasks of one of the authors of this chapter (IL) was to see all the 'follow-up' diabetic patients at the Radcliffe Infirmary, Oxford, diabetic clinic, at the rate of about one every two or three minutes for three hours. His task was to adjust their dose of insulin and arrange for the next attendance at the clinic. Aware of his own gross inexperience, he suggested that most could be looked after more safely by their general practitioners. This suggestion was rejected because the diabetic physician believed that he alone was responsible for all the care of all the diabetics in the region.

[83] T. M. Hayes and J. Harries, 'Randomised Controlled Trial of Routine Hospital Care versus General Practice for Type II Diabetics', British Medical Journal, 289 (1984), 728–31.

[84] J. M. Malins and J. M. Stuart, 'Diabetic Clinic in a General Practice 1971', British Medical Journal (1971), iv. 161.

[85] P. A. Thorn and R. G. Russell, 'Diabetic Clinics Today and Tomorrow: Mini-clinics in General Practice', British Medical Journal (1973), ii. 534–6. B. M. Singh and M. R. Holland, 'Metabolic Control of Diabetes in General Practice Clinics: Comparison with a Hospital Clinic', British Medical Journal, 289 (1984), 726–8.

[86] R. Hill, 'Community Services for Diabetics in the Poole Area', British Medical Journal, (1976), i. 1137–9.

an editorial in the journal *Diabetic Medicine* in 1991 detected 'a growing under-current of criticism of diabetes care in general practice from amongst my specialist colleagues', who suggested that general practitioners 'are only interested in [diabetes care] because of a dubious financial opportunity'.[87] As the writer pointed out, however, hospital care was inadequate. Little more than half the population of diabetics attended hospital clinics and 5 per cent of those were lost to follow-up each year. Whatever the motives and interests of general practitioners, many practices had, by the 1990s, set up systems of structured care which have at their core registers, recall systems, and a multidisciplinary approach. There are innate advantages for the patient. Care is available nearer to home, in familiar surroundings, and by staff who know the patients and are able to meet the key requirement for patient education.

There could scarcely be a better example of the profound changes that have occurred in general practice in the management of a chronic disease which, as a consequence of those changes, has moved from almost total hospital care to shared care. These changes have depended on the transfer of skills, resources, and the ability (largely as a result of computerization) to monitor a specific section of the practice population; and the initiatives that have led to such a change came from consultants as well as general practitioners.

Care of the dying in general practice

Until quite recently, doctors and nurses have spent much more time, energy, and thought on the beginning of life, than the end. Care of the dying is a part of general practice which has received very little attention from historians, probably because at first sight such care seemed to belong to hospitals rather than primary care. Thus, a number of surveys from the 1950s to the present have shown that on average about two-thirds of patients die in hospital, one-third at home.[88] Further, general practitioners can, on average, expect to be involved with only two patients a year dying from cancer at home, while four of their patients die of cancer in hospitals or hospices.

There are, however, several reasons for looking in some detail at what is variously called terminal or palliative care, not least because it illustrates once again the shift from secondary to primary care. The statistics cited above are only part of the picture. General practitioners are, and always have been, involved in terminal care to a much greater extent than the statistics imply. Cartwright, for example, showed in 1973 that general practitioners provided nearly all the

---

[87] S. Walford, 'Primary Care Teams and the Treatment of Diabetes', *Diabetic Medicine*, 8 (1991), 307–8.

[88] A survey of deaths in England and Wales in 1956 showed that two-thirds occurred in hospital and only a third at home, and another survey of 130,000 deaths in 1982 showed 59% and 7% died in hospitals and hospices respectively and 33% at home (H. L. G. Hughes, *Peace at Last* (London, 1960); see also B. Lunt and R. Hillier, 'Terminal Care: Present Services and Future Priorities', *British Medical Journal*, 283 (1981), 595–7.

care to about three out of every ten people in the last year of their lives, and usually looked after the other seven before they were admitted to hospital.[89] The need for effective terminal care has increased, and will continue to increase as fewer people die suddenly of acute diseases in youth or middle age and more die slowly of malignant disease—largely, of course, because of the ageing population (see Tables B1–B5). Further, terminal care is not confined to cancer. A survey of general practitioners' views in the Thames Valley in 1993 concluded that about thirteen patients per practice per year who did not have cancer could be considered as candidates for continuing terminal care, most of whom were suffering from cardiovascular disease, stroke, and chronic pulmonary disease.[90] Of course, people still die suddenly and unexpectedly—mostly from heart attacks—but for most of us death will be the end of a process of dying which is stretched out over weeks or months. If and when that occurs, we will seldom have been so dependent on the skills and sympathy of our primary-care team.

1960 and before

The concept of terminal care as a branch of medicine which requires special training and skills was virtually unknown before 1960. Most doctors felt threatened by the prospect of death and reluctant to acknowledge their failures to cure. As a psychiatrist once observed, dying seemed to be regarded in hospital as a form of deviant behaviour, where it was often the practice to remove the 'hopeless' case to a side ward as a grim indication of his journey to the mortuary, and it was rare for patients to be told they had cancer. In his book *An Introduction to General Practice*, published in 1953, Craddock expressed the belief that patients should not be told that they have cancer.[91] Sir Heneage Ogilvie reported he had only ever told three patients, two of whom 'lost all heart and rapidly sank'.[92] Aitken-Swann and Easson suggested in 1959 that the reluctance to tell patients with cancer the diagnosis reinforced the perception that any type of cancer was synonymous with a sentence of death.[93] Cicely Saunders showed in the same year that, in spite of the fact that most had not been told openly by their doctors, most dying patients entering the hospice already knew of their predicament. In hospital and general practice, doctors lied to patients with terminal cancer, but usually told the truth to the relatives. It seldom seemed to occur to anybody that this imposed impossible strains on the patient and the family.

[89] A. Cartwright, L. Hockey, and J. L. Anderson, *Life before Death* (London, 1973).

[90] I. M. Wilson, J. S. Bunting, R. N. Curnow, and J. Knock, 'The Need for an Extension of In-Patient Palliative Care Facilities for Non-Cancer Patients in the Thames Valley', *Palliative Medicine*, 9/1 (1995), 13–18.

[91] D. Craddock, *An Introduction to General Practice* (London, 1953).

[92] H. Ogilvie 'Biopsy in Malignant Disease', *Practitioner*, 166 (1951), 488.

[93] J. Aitken-Swann and E. C. Easson, 'Reactions of Cancer Patients on Being Told their Diagnosis', *British Medical Journal* (1959), i. 779–83.

Lack of openness was often combined with inadequate pain relief, partly through pharmacological ignorance, and partly through a ridiculous fear of addiction. In 1962, J. R. Caldwell, a general practitioner in Sussex, recalls being 'roundly berated' by his consultant when, as a house physician, he prescribed morphine for a patient dying of gastric cancer, with the words, 'I do not want him given morphine—he might well become an addict.' The patient died a few hours later.[94] It is clear that, as long as a policy of secrecy prevailed, however sympathetic the doctors and nurses might be, it was impossible to devise an efficient form of terminal care. Only gradually was the need for greater openness accepted. Seale found that, whereas 29 per cent of patients in 1969 knew they had cancer, by 1987 the figure was 73 per cent.[95]

Unfortunately, we know very little about the care of the dying in general practice before the 1960s, except that it was shrouded in silence. Few talked about it, wrote about it, or were taught anything about it as students. Probably the district nurse played a larger part than the general practitioner in some areas,[96] while general practitioners varied widely in the way they dealt with the dying. They did what they felt should be done on the basis of no training other than what they might pick up from their senior partners or other general practitioners. All this was altered by the introduction of the hospice movement.

Terminal care since the 1960s and the hospice movement

With new attitudes to the medical care of the dying, it was a recognition of the gap in care between the community, where general practitioners lacked resources and skills, and the inability of hospitals to meet the needs of the dying, that produced the hospice movement. This was introduced almost single-handedly by Dame Cicely Saunders, who founded St Christopher's, the first modern hospice, in 1967.[97] Her aim was to combine the skills of hospital medicine with the atmosphere of a home, in a way which shifted the emphasis of treatment from disease to patient. This patient-centred approach was in tune with developments in primary care, and many of the medical staff of the

[94] J. R. Caldwell, 'The Management of Inoperable Disease in General Practice', *Journal of the Royal College of General Practitioners*, 8 (1964), 23–48. That this form of crass insensitivity by hospital doctors still occasionally occurs in 1996 can be seen in a memorable 'Personal View' by 'Staff Nurse Jones', entitled 'Dear Doctor', *British Medical Journal*, 313 (1996), 888.

[95] C. Seale, 'Communication and Awareness about Death: A Study of a Random Sample of Dying People', *Social Science and Medicine*, 32 (1991), 943–52.

[96] The importance of home nursing in the care of patients with cancer had been highlighted by Wilkes in 1965, who found that district nurses, who visited 63% of patients dying at home, played a central role in terminal care (E. Wilkes, 'Terminal Cancer at Home', *Lancet* (1965), i. 799–801).

[97] Mother Mary Akenhead, 'a saintly nun of the last century', founded the order of the Irish Sisters of Charity, and first coined the phrase hospice as applied to 'Our Lady's Hospice for the Dying'. In 1902 five peripatetic nuns from the Irish lodge founded St Joseph's Hospice in Hackney with thirty beds for 'the dying poor'. Dame Cicely Saunders arrived there in 1952, and stayed until 1959. She started a building fund for St Christopher's in 1964, which opened in 1967. She was first a nurse, then an almoner/social worker, and then qualified in medicine.

hospice were recruited from the ranks of general practitioners. Perhaps her greatest achievement was to break the veil of silence and encourage openness, to show that terminal care required new attitudes, special skills, and sometimes special equipment. She showed it was a branch of medical care which could, and must, be taught.

Because the expansion of the hospice movement was dependent largely on the charitable and voluntary sectors rather than the NHS, its development was uncoordinated and based on local demand and enthusiasm. In 1980 a survey found seventy-two variations on the theme of hospice.[98] By 1983 there were ninety-three services listed by the British Hospice Information centre, of which less than half were in the NHS. Fifty-eight of these were in-patient units, thirty-two home-care teams, and eight hospital support teams. Funding had been taken over by the NHS in only half of the 1,730 hospice beds that existed in 1984, and there were marked regional variations. Access to a hospice bed was more a matter of the accident of geography than a result of planning.

The very success of the hospice movement, however, created its own problems. By the 1980s it was seen that in-patient care in hospices was not, and probably never would (or should) be, the complete solution to the provision of terminal care. Because many, possibly most people would prefer to die at home, such a solution would mean that hospices would undermine their own objective of patient-centred care. Primary-care teams would lose any skills they had in the treatment of the dying. It was, therefore, proposed to slow down the development of in-patient facilities in favour of home-care teams, improved training, and an integrated service with coordination between general practice, hospitals, and the hospice movement.[99]

Although it was restricted at first to a few areas, from the 1970s care began to be shared between hospice-based community teams and primary care, through the provision of what were called 'outreach services'. As early as 1969 St Christopher's Hospice developed a specialist domiciliary nursing service, and this was expanded by the MacMillan nursing scheme, which, from 1975, provided nurses with special skills to support primary-care teams looking after terminally ill patients with cancer at home.[100]

Thus the hospice stepped into the gap between the general practitioner and the hospital, and specialist home-care services were developed in recognition of the wishes of patients.[101] This has allowed treatment to be tailored to the individual patient, who could receive terminal care in the hospice, at home, or intermittently in both places, as a result of integrated teamwork. In

---

[98] Lunt and Hillier, 'Terminal Care'.

[99] National Terminal Care Working Group, 1980, 'Report of the Working Group on Terminal Care', *Journal of the Royal College of General Practitioners*, 30 (1980), 466–71.

[100] By 1994, 1,200 MacMillan nurses were in post. In 1996 there were also 6,000 nurses in post funded by the Marie Curie Foundation.

[101] Cartwright, Hockey, and Anderson, *Life before Death*.

some regions, the team providing outreach services for the dying includes not only nurses and doctors but social workers and others skilled in providing administrative and voluntary support. Higginson found that patients and relatives rated such workers more highly than general practitioners and community nurses, who in turn were rated more highly than hospital doctors and nurses.[102]

The introduction of these measures has been accompanied by much more effective pain relief. In the early days of the NHS various mixtures of drugs were used with little evaluation of their effectiveness.[103] In 1976 Twycross demonstrated that, as analgesics, morphine and diamorphine (heroin) were as effective as each other and that the addition of cocaine had no additive analgesic effect.[104] A combination of clinical work based on a firm pharmacological background acquired through the experience of hospices has led to a more rational and analytical approach to symptom control.[105]

It is, of course, true of terminal care, as it is of all aspects of clinical care in general practice, that the extent to which changes have been adopted varies between regions, and within regions between individual practitioners. Nevertheless, the means available to general practitioners in the 1990s for providing better care for the dying is a major, if often unrealized, aspect of change in primary care during the life of the NHS. Terminal care may be a small component of primary care as a whole, but, as many will realize in the last weeks of their lives, it is a component of great importance, shamefully neglected in hospitals and general practice in the early years of the NHS.

Specialization in general practice

With the growth of large partnerships, primary-care teams, and clinics within general practice (such as diabetic clinics, described above), there has been a tendency towards a certain degree of specialization in general practice. General practitioners often develop a special interest in some aspect of medicine, and those who do usually find it intellectually stimulating and satisfying. So, why not develop a system in which one partner specializes in hypertension, another in diabetes, a third, perhaps, in geriatrics, and so on? These would not replace

[102] I. Higginson, A. Wade, and M. McCarthy, 'Palliative Care: Views of Patients and their Families', *British Medical Journal*, 301 (1990), 277–81.

[103] A very popular mixture, consisting of morphia, cocaine, chloroform water, and alcohol, known as the 'Brompton cocktail', was invented by the Brompton Hospital in 1952 and was still being used in the 1970s.

[104] R. G. Twycross, 'Management of Pain in Malignant Disease', *British Medical Journal* (1976), i. 1198.

[105] For example, the portable syringe driver (a method of administering drugs by continuous infusion under the skin that allows patients to remain mobile) was found to have had a dramatic impact on numbers of patients who were referred to St Mary's Hospice, Birmingham, increasing the number of patients able to die at home from 30% to 55% between 1981 and 1986. Syringe drivers are now widely available in general practice.

hospital specialists, but they might raise the expertise, standards of knowledge, and clinical care within a practice. If such a tendency was taken to an extreme, however, partnerships would in effect become polyclinics, in which patients would be directed not necessarily to the doctor of their choice, but rather to one specializing in their complaint.

To many patients, an increase in specialization and the development of something close to a polyclinic-style of primary care would be a retrograde step. Experience has shown that within any large partnership there are some patients (usually a minority) who are happy to see any doctor for any disorder. Most of these are young people, a trace impatient perhaps, for whom the main thing is to see a doctor as soon as possible. Other patients may know, and be happy to see, any one of two or even three partners, having met them before and felt confidence in them. A substantial number, however—and this has been shown to be especially true of the elderly—are strictly 'one-doctor' patients, who insist as far as possible on seeing 'their own doctor', in whom, alone, they feel that they have total confidence. For these in particular, a difficulty arises if, for instance, they develop diabetes and are told they should not see their personal doctor, but must go to the partner who is responsible for the diabetic clinic and who aims to see every diabetic patient within the practice. Not only does the patient find this disturbing, but it can be argued that, if one partner is the diabetic 'specialist' of the practice, the others will lose their skills in managing that disease; and the same, of course, applies to any other specialized clinics within general practice.

This may sound like a trivial day-to-day clinical problem, scarcely worth mentioning, and which in practice can usually be solved by the patient's personal doctor calling in a partner with a special interest when the occasion arises. But it serves to remind those who favour increased specialization in general practice, and see it as one of the ways in which primary care should develop, that the development by general practitioners of areas of special interest has much merit, provided it is recognized that the development of special interests must not diminish the generalist role of all the partners.

Cottage and community hospitals

Before this chapter ends, there is one feature of general practice which must be mentioned briefly: the story of the cottage hospitals.[106] When Albert Napper opened the first one in Cranley Village in 1859, his idea was admirably simple. Apart from the difficulties of transport and distance (thirty-five miles to the nearest main hospital in the case of Cranley), rural patients often dreaded being sent to large voluntary hospitals where they found themselves amongst

---

[106] The sources used in this section are the excellent history of cottage hospitals by M. Emrys-Roberts, *The Cottage Hospitals 1859–1990* (Motcombe, Dorset, 1991), and Burdett's series of *The Hospital Annual and Year Book of Philanthropy* (London, various years in the late nineteenth century).

strangers in a large ward, far from their family, friends, and their own familiar doctor. Napper therefore proposed erecting a small village hospital of three or four beds, where the rural sick could be treated by their own doctor and a local matron in residence, which was designed deliberately to look reassuringly like a workman's cottage.

It was an astonishingly successful idea, welcomed by local general practitioners, by patients, and by the local gentry and others who provided the means whereby cottage hospitals sprang up all over the country. Almost all were rural, but with the expansion of towns many later found themselves enveloped by the suburbs. By 1870 eighty had been founded in places as far apart as Lanark and Fife in Scotland and market towns in southern England.

From the start they stood apart from the county hospitals and infirmaries. They were staffed by local general practitioners, all of whom had the right to admit and treat their patients in these hospitals. Soon, a new generation of rural general practitioners was designing cottage hospitals as miniature versions of the hospitals in which they had been trained. They increased in size, many having twenty or more beds, and soon had operating theatres, labour wards, and sometimes small laboratories and (later) X-ray departments.

Although they served a useful purpose in rural general practice, they had often acquired a mixed reputation in the years preceding the NHS. It was said that they concentrated too much on surgery, with some general practitioners undertaking operations for which their training was inadequate. They did, however, provide nursing care for medical cases, and were often active in providing midwifery of a high standard. Further, even before the NHS began, cottage hospitals often provided the means whereby local consultants could hold clinics in various specialities and meet the local general practitioners. When the NHS was introduced, one of the priorities was to provide specialist care of high quality all over the country instead of just in the large towns and cities. Many patients who, previously, would have been admitted to a cottage hospital were now admitted to a district general hospital. To an increasing extent cottage hospitals were left to look after the elderly with chronic disorders, patients who lived alone and needed hospital care (but not specialist care) for 'social reasons', and convalescent patients.

In 1948 there were 2,800 cottage hospitals in Britain. They came under the administration of local hospital boards and had to compete for resources. Some were closed for financial reasons, and by 1965 the number had dropped to 2,500. More would have been closed but for the uproar caused by the local inhabitants when a cottage hospital was threatened with closure. What was really missing, however, was a clear policy on cottage hospitals. Where did they fit into the provision of hospital care?

There was something of a breakthrough in 1972 when the Oxford Regional Hospital Board took the cottage hospitals of the Oxford Region under its wing and renamed them as community hospitals.[107] The change in name was justified by recognizing that community hospitals were not a 'peripheralization of secondary services' but an extension of 'primary care'. Until then, some hospital consultants (especially geriatricians) felt that all hospital beds, cottage/community hospitals included, 'belonged' to consultants. The Oxford Regional Hospital Board put community hospitals firmly back into general-practice territory, and proceeded to build a modern and very well-equipped community hospital in Wallingford (Oxfordshire) in which there were seventeen general practitioner beds, seventeen maternity beds, and thirty-eight beds for long-stay patients.

This hospital, which opened in 1973, became the experimental ground for new ideas and played a large part in preventing what otherwise might have been a policy of mass closure. A few have been closed since 1973. Most are still active, and some new community hospitals have been opened. At the time of writing their future is still uncertain. Because most people live in towns and cities, cottage and community hospitals have always served only a small part of the total population. But for that small part they have been since the 1870s, and continue to be, a far from negligible part of the provision of primary care.

Conclusion

When people discuss changes in primary care, they usually single out features described in other chapters in this book: changes in practice organization, practice premises, the growth of the primary-care team, and concepts of illness. These are the outstanding features which are usually invoked to explain why general practitioners in the last quarter of the twentieth century have developed a new sense of identity and self-confidence. Oddly, few stress the considerable changes that have occurred in clinical aspects of general practice, which have been the subject of our chapter.

We hope we have demonstrated the nature of change in clinical care and clinical standards, but there is a risk that our account will be seen as too triumphalist or 'whiggish' in tone. Perhaps we should emphasize again, as we have already, several times, that there always has been and still is very wide variation in general practice. Many of the changes we have described are partly or wholly confined to 'innovative' practices which have welcomed, and often created, change. There are other practices which have resisted change and in which standards are still low. And there is another point which must be made.

In seeking explanations for change, we have stressed the impact of the therapeutic revolution, of access to diagnostic technology, and the growth of

---

[107] The people most responsible for the new look at the cottage hospitals were Dame Rosemary Rue, Regional Medical Officer to the Oxford Region, and Dr (later Professor) A. E. Bennett.

the concept of shared care between the primary and secondary sectors of the NHS. But that is not the whole story. One cannot exaggerate the extent to which the factors which have brought about changes are closely interlocked, or that changes in clinical care have been dependent on changes described in other chapters. Without much better education and learning for general practitioners, without better premises, without raised self-esteem and self-confidence, even, perhaps, without computers, changes in clinical care could not have taken place to the extent to which they have. Conversely, without the marked improvements in the standards of clinical care since the NHS began, even in the grandest, most modern, and well-equipped practice premises with the most comprehensive primary-care team, general practice could not command the respect of the profession as a whole, or of the patients it serves.

5

General Practitioners and the Other Caring Professions

MARGOT JEFFERYS

This chapter charts, and tries to account for, the changes in the first fifty years of the NHS which, little by little, transformed the typical size, orientation, and occupational composition of the units providing health services outside the hospitals; and in doing so affected the customary attitudes to one or another of the various occupational groups involved in the enterprise.

The post-war settlement which saw the formation of the NHS in the UK is rightly regarded as constituting a historical watershed. It reflected the radical determination of the electorate to eliminate many of the negative, class-ridden, provisions of the inter-war years, and to lay the basis for a fairer distribution of the benefits of the burgeoning capacity to prevent much ill health, and deal effectively with the major scourges of infectious illness.[1]

Some contemporary as well as later social-policy analysts, however, rightly emphasized the perpetuation in the post-war welfare-state provision of pre-war structures of authority and the division of labour, which was nowhere more apparent than in the non-hospital health and welfare sector. This meant that self-employed, and usually single-handed, male general medical practitioners continued to be the sole source of medical advice and treatment provided on an ambulatory basis. Local-authority departments, directly or through voluntary societies, continued to provide eligible applicants, with or without payment, with relevant support services such as home nursing, domiciliary midwifery, home helps, and meals on wheels. For this purpose they continued to employ staff directly, or contracted to provide such services through voluntary societies.

Unlike general practitioners, who formed a section of a long-recognized venerable and overwhelmingly male profession, the majority of those providing these services were women, whose status as professionals was by no means always established or respected by the long-established professions. They had various nursing or social-work backgrounds and qualifications, and were grouped together in units under the control of the Medical Officer of Health. He, of course, had a medical qualification, and his post might also be combined

---

[1] T. McKeown, *The Role of Medicine: Dream, Mirage or Nemesis?* (London, 1976).

with leadership of the authority's Welfare Department, and, by arrangement with the Education Department, of the School Health Service.

In this chapter, therefore, it is relevant to consider at the outset the mutual expectations and beliefs which all occupational groups involved in the community-based health service were likely to have inherited from their predecessors when the NHS was introduced. That complex legacy has been a persistent influence, ever since, in the lives and expectations of all the practitioners in the various professions, who were called upon to adapt their customary work patterns and assumptions in the interest of increasing the effectiveness and efficiency of the nation's health and welfare measures. So, this chapter begins with a review of the arrangements for delivering non-hospital-based care as they had evolved during the inter-war years.

Before the National Health Service

General practitioners as independent professionals

Some of the contributors to this history of general practice under the NHS may remember the general practitioner with whom they (or their parents on their behalf) registered in 1948. My own memory, although flawed, stretches back further than that. These personal reflections may give those who have only experienced services since the advent of the NHS the flavour of the provision which it replaced, at least for those who were expected to pay for their medical services.

My family lived for most of the inter-war years in a small town within commuting distance of London. Our family doctor lived in an elegant house in the High Street. As private, paying, patients (my father was a professional man with a medium income), we consulted him there. We went in through the front door and waited to see him in a well-furnished sitting room. My mother did not hesitate to ask him to visit us at home if she thought that we were not well enough to walk the half mile to his surgery. I believe that his other paying patients did likewise.

Our doctor also had panel patients. They were mainly working-class men, entitled to consult him by virtue of their compulsory NHI payments.[2] They used a side entrance to his house, and waited to see him on benches along a passageway. In the early 1930s, because the town grew and his practice expanded, he took on a medically qualified assistant (not a partner), and a dispenser. He also rented a lock-up shop nearby where panel but not private patients were seen.

The wives and children of panel patients were not entitled to free advice or treatment from him or to medication. Our doctor, like many of his fellow

[2] R. W. Harris, *National Health Insurance 1911 to 1946* (London, 1957).

general practitioners, may well have been reluctant to charge or to collect outstanding debts from the poorest who may have consulted them. Some may have
used fees derived from their private practice to underwrite losses and salve their
social consciences.

Our doctor employed no nurse or receptionist. His wife was criticized by
some of his private patients for her alleged reluctance to play the socially
expected role of receptionist or of chaperone for her husband's female patients.
His daughter, when she left school, was praised for her willingness to
undertake these unremunerated tasks as well as other 'good works'—such as
Girl Guide troop leader.

Our doctor, on occasion, undertook surgical procedures such as adenoidec-
tomies, which were then believed to be prophylactically sound. I and my two
sisters had our tonsils removed in our dining room, temporarily transformed
into an operating theatre. I was then 9 years old. He engaged a London
Hospital-trained nurse to assist during the surgery and to keep an eye on us in
the following twenty-four hours.[3] He also occasionally undertook emergency
operations. For example, when I was 19, he removed my appendix in a local
private nursing home in which he and another locally based doctor had a
financial interest.

I believe this type of general practice was fairly typical of those in towns
where the doctor could count on a reasonable number of paying patients as
well as a modest number of panel patients. Perhaps it was most likely to
be found in the commuter belts surrounding major cities, particularly in
the Home Counties. Such areas attracted growing numbers of professional
and business-class men with increasing social aspirations. Elsewhere, in
more solidly working-class areas or in towns built during the nineteenth-
century expansion in the manufacturing and extractive industries, general
practitioners were as likely to be male and single-handed. They were, perhaps,
more likely, however, to have their surgeries in lock-up shops rather than in
their own homes.

To return to my own recollections, so heavily tinged with the prevailing
social-class divide, I am sure that our doctor would not have provided his panel
patients or their families with emergency or prophylactic surgery. Those
requiring emergency treatment were most likely to receive it in a voluntary
hospital, and their capacity to contribute to its cost would have been assessed
by a hospital almoner. Older people, likely to develop chronic debilitating
illness, would be considered candidates for beds in erstwhile poor-law
infirmaries, which by 1929 had been taken over by the health or welfare departments of local authorities.[4] School-age children, on the other hand, were likely
to have their tonsils and adenoids removed with the rest of their classmates
when they reached a certain age, as a matter of routine policy.[5]

---

[3] Nurses trained at the London Hospital (now the Royal London Hospital) were particularly prized
and added prestige to the standing of family doctors who secured the use of their services.

[4] M. Bruce, *The Coming of the Welfare State* (London, 1961; rev. edn., 1968).

[5] Personal memory (told to author in 1927 by a newly recruited 15-year-old housemaid).

Midwives, health visitors, and home nurses

It should not be inferred, however, that working-class women and children were even less likely than their middle-class counterparts to receive community or domiciliary-based health-care services. On the contrary, as the target of social reformers and legislators who had been alerted to the poor state of health of the population, they, rather than the affluent middle class, were likely to be the recipients of a good deal of health surveillance and advice. Working-class women in particular, as mothers and child-rearers, were likely to be the main recipients of charitable enterprise as well as civic responsibility.

Expectant mothers of all social classes were likely to be delivered in their own homes. Better-off women were likely to ask their family doctor to arrange the delivery. He would either undertake it himself or recommend another doctor to attend. He might make a private arrangement with a registered midwife. Working-class mothers, however, were likely to be delivered by a salaried midwife, employed by a voluntary association or by the local author-ity, without the attendance of a medically qualified doctor except when a com-plication arose. The expectation was that the majority would not be able to meet most if any of the cost.

In some areas expectant mothers might be encouraged to attend a maternity and infant welfare clinic. After delivery, they were expected to attend such clinics regularly for advice on child nutrition and care, as well as on hygiene in the home, from a health visitor. At the clinic, the mother might be given vitamin supplements free of charge as well as simple remedies for respiratory or diges-tive symptoms. Regular weighing of the infant at such a clinic would indicate whether her offspring was making satisfactory progress and also became the talisman by which her maternal capacity would be judged. However, not only failure of the infant to gain weight in the expected fashion, but even the failure of the mother to attend regularly, might serve as an indicator that the home in question needed to be watched—for health visitors also had child-protection duties to perform.[6]

It was not altogether surprising, therefore, that, as local-authority services became more ubiquitous and more used, some family doctors should feel that potential paying patients were seduced into using the free clinics instead of consulting them. The health visitor was nearly always a single childless woman who, given the surplus of females in the child-bearing age group compared with males, had low expectations of marriage and family-rearing during her own lifetime career. Because of this, and also because her duties were as much to do with maintaining social order as with helping individuals, she was apt to be treated with suspicion, if not hostility, by the public as well as by other professionals whose income or authority she might inadvertently challenge.

The picture I have painted of my own memories of the community-based health services available in my locality, supplemented by observations and my

---

[6] G. F. McCleary, *Early History of the Infant Welfare Movement* (London, 1933).

historical reading, suggests a set of diverse arrangements embedded in a highly class-divided and class-conscious society. The middle classes expected their private doctors to provide them with services, including minor surgery and some which verged on major, and to secure the ancillary nursing help required to undertake it. Most of them did not avidly seek out routine health-maintenance advice or procedures. Working-class men with an acute illness expected advice and medicine from their panel doctor, free of charge. Their wives and children were not entitled to such services free, but many doctors might waive notional fees for humanitarian reasons. The local authority, however, had the power or obligation to provide a range of domiciliary-based preventive, remedial, and supportive services to classes of individuals who were unlikely to be able to afford them.

Thus, before the NHS, the community-based health services reflected two distinct approaches to the provision of services. One affirmed the responsibility of the state for securing the health of its citizenry. The other—given certain safeguards against abuse by its practitioners, and compulsory insurance to which state and employers should contribute for those too poor to pay private medical fees—asserted that the market mechanism was both the time-honoured and the most feasible way of dealing with medical care. The result was that the personnel of the two community-based health services had not only quite different sex and occupational compositions, but inevitably different objectives, motivations, and assumptions about their relationship with their clients or patients and their accountability to others.

Those in charge of the development of local-authority responsibility for providing health-visiting, school-health, and district-nursing services were aware that they had to tread warily to avoid damaging general practitioners' professional and pecuniary sensitivities. General practitioners were finding themselves increasingly excluded by their more successful specializing peers from hospital-based practice, and hence from honorary but potentially lucrative and highly valued consultancy status. They were also dissatisfied with the degree of control they had had to accept in the past from local authorities, trades unions, and friendly societies, in order to sustain their incomes in a highly competitive market.[7] They were apt, therefore, to be resentful and suspicious of the activities of local and central government, particularly if they saw them as a threat to their clinical freedom and to their already shrinking share of the private market for medical advice and treatment.

As a consequence, to placate the politically powerful medical profession, demarcation lines were laid down in the relevant enabling Acts of Parliament which confined the health workers employed by the local authority or voluntary societies to purely advisory roles. If the health workers in these services found someone in need of medical attention, they had a duty to refer the person to the family doctor. Similarly, the district nurses were called upon to consult

---

[7] F. Honigsbaum, *The Division in British Medicine* (London, 1979).

and report to their patients' personal doctors (if they had them) in any situation where they judged a medical opinion was required.

Despite the tacitly or explicitly negotiated demarcation lines, however, some general practitioners undoubtedly felt that the expanding numbers of doctors, nurses, and other health-related workers employed in local-authority clinics and other services were providing their patients—actual or putative—with advice and treatment which otherwise would have come to the doctor's surgery. It is not possible to estimate how frequent such complaints were, or how justified. But the correspondence columns of the medical journals suggest that many general practitioners—particularly those practising in impoverished working-class areas—habitually had little contact with, but nevertheless harboured grave suspicions about, the activities of the local-authority Medical Officers of Health and their growing armies of nurses, health visitors, and other health-related ancillary staff.

Doctors sometimes alleged that poorer mothers were the unwilling recipients of overly intrusive surveillance and rigid advice on the care of their newborn babies, forced on them by health visitors. No doubt such accusations were sometimes justified. They also suggested that mothers were seduced with offers of free milk, other gifts, and simple remedies to take their sick children to local-authority clinics rather than consult an aspiring 'family' doctor.

In addition to the expansion in the numbers of local-authority and/or voluntary society-employed staff in nursing, midwifery, and child-health services, the inter-war period also witnessed a growth in the numbers concerned with containing or treating society's deviants, by which was meant those who threatened public order by either their criminal or their bizarre behaviour. Although the causes of what was seen as an escalating problem was a matter of professional and lay dispute, it was being increasingly acknowledged, first, that a policy of wholesale incarceration could not by itself provide a satisfactory solution, and, secondly, that deviancy could not be entirely accounted for by original sin or inherent wickedness. In many of its forms deviancy came to be seen as more closely related to disease, and therefore intrinsically a matter for medical rather than judicial or penal intervention.

Despite this secular shift in the explanation of deviancy, the treatment of mental illness or cognitive disorders in the early twentieth century still held a peripheral place in medicine as a whole, and family doctors for the most part rejected the notion that the management of deviancy was part of general practice. Moreover, the standing of those members of the medical profession who accepted posts in the burgeoning mental-hospital programme of the late nineteenth century was not high. The few who entered the field were apt to acquire by proxy the low status of their patients or charges. Given the state of knowledge about the causes and treatment of the major manifestations of mental illness, as well as the absence of effective pharmaceutical remedies, the medical task appeared to be confined to vigilance and command of the army of

controllers drawn from less exalted ranks in society, rather than clinical interventions. Until the post-Second World War years, general practitioners were
only too ready to hold themselves aloof from dealing with such economically
and socially unrewarding patients. As a result they had only limited contacts
with, or understanding of, the work of the new army of minimally trained
welfare officers, often drawn in mid-life from the ranks of retired police, the
armed forces, and other authoritarian and bureaucratic bodies.

Increasing occupational complexity

There are several observations on the picture I have painted of pre-NHS
general practice, and its typical relationships with other health personnel
working in the same locality, which are relevant to the theme of this chapter.
First, nearly all the general practitioners who were in practice before the
Second World War and who joined the NHS in 1948 had at best only intermittent experience of any kind of continuous working relationship with other
kinds of health workers. The few exceptions were likely to be those men who
had married nurses. The pre-1948 legacy which most general practitioners
brought with them into the NHS was most frequently founded on an almost
total lack of experience of working with other health and social-service personnel who might be serving the same community. This was combined with a
good deal of prejudice and suspicion, fuelled by possibly exaggerated fears of
a competitive invasion, an undermining of their independence, and a lowering
of their incomes.

   At the same time, the inter-war and the war years had seen a substantial
growth in a community-based labour force, composed of a perplexing diversity of new occupational groups, whose task it was to service or police the
nascent welfare state. The members of this force were drawn in the main from
social-class groups occupying a lower position in the social hierarchy than
doctors, and were overwhelmingly women. As such, they were beginning to
present the mostly male general practitioners, who were operating as private
contractors in what was in effect a cottage industry, with unprecedented problems. They felt their standing, compared with that of hospital consultants, was
declining. It was not surprising, therefore, that they sought to maintain the
comparatively high social and professional status which they held in the
network of extra-hospital health and welfare services.

Community-based services under
the National Health Service

The settlement negotiated by the Labour Government to secure cooperation
between various branches of the medical profession and local government in
the nascent NHS made little initial impact on the habitual mutual relationships

of the various occupational groups providing community-based health and welfare services. Although the Act included a provision (part III, section 21) enabling local-authority Health Departments to establish health centres where general practitioners would work in the same building as the authority's own health workers, the clause represented virtually all that was left of the 1920 Council on Medical and Allied Services' never-implemented recommendations.[8] The latter had envisaged a network of local centres staffed by doctors and other health personnel to serve a gamut of preventive, curative, and supportive health purposes.

In a modified form, health centres had been a plank in the Socialist Medical Association's proposals for post-war UK. In the event, the Labour Government's failure to introduce health centres was essentially pragmatic and political rather than ideological, and hardly any use was made of this statutory provision until the mid-1960s. Local authorities, overwhelmed by the need to tackle high housing priorities, and preoccupied with developing a raft of welfare and child-care services, had neither the means, the time, nor the incentive to encourage the development of health centres.

The continued isolation of general practitioners

It is probable, moreover, that if there had been plans to build health centres, they would have been resisted by most general practitioners. The latter, partly as a result of the NHS provisions negotiated with the professional body representing hospital consultants, saw themselves as effectively excluded from the hospitals and hence condemned to an inferior status within the medical hierarchy. Faced by onslaughts from many sides on their professional competence, they retreated into a defiant, ultimately isolating, defensiveness, laying particular stress on their independence. With the exception of a few notable individuals with vision—who were responsible ultimately both for rescuing the sector from its despondency and paranoia and providing it with renewed confidence in its own unique role[9]—general practitioners were still prone to regard with suspicion, if not hostility, doctors, nurses, and other health and welfare staff employed by local authorities.

Domiciliary midwives

The 1950s were also difficult years for other community-based health-care workers. Domiciliary midwives who, prior to the NHS, had been largely unsupervised and responsible for the majority of home deliveries, were having to yield ground to hospital obstetric departments. Their hospital-based peers had

---

[8] *Interim Report of the Consultative Council on Medical and Allied Services*, Cmd. 693 (The Dawson Report; London: HMSO, 1920).

[9] J. Fry, J. H. Hunt, and R. J. F. H. Pinsent (eds.), *A History of the Royal College of General Practitioners: The First 25 Years* (Lancaster, 1983).

the advantage of back-up from specialist obstetricians who were persuading expectant mothers that hospital-based delivery was almost always safer than delivery at home. Increasing proportions of pregnant women, with rising expectations of effective pain control during childbirth and of a successful outcome in terms of their own and their offspring's health, were, when given the choice, opting for hospital delivery. This tendency was reinforced by the post-war housing difficulties experienced by many young newlyweds, who were often separated from the help of their families.

Moreover, domiciliary midwives still faced, as they had for many years, competition on their own doorstep from general practitioners. Virtually all expectant mothers were now registered with general practitioners from whom they were entitled to seek antenatal care and delivery, if their general practitioner was on the list to provide obstetric services. Not all general practitioners made themselves available for this purpose, but when they did, they received a fee-for-service payment, on top of the standard *per capita* payment for a registered patient. Some midwives, rather than welcoming this provision, resented the financial incentive offered to those general practitioners, whose part in providing maternal care was often little more than token. Further, because they usually delivered far more babies a year than general practitioners, midwives could also argue that their own expertise was greater than that of the general practitioner, and some midwives found it difficult to share the rewarding emotional relationship with the mother and her family which follows a successful delivery.

For domiciliary midwives, therefore, as well as for general practitioners, the administrative provisions which could bring them together were not necessarily the most conducive to allay mutual suspicions and prejudices or encourage interprofessional openness and cooperation.

Health visitors

Health visitors received many accolades for the role they had played during the war years in improving the nutrition of women and children, and in encouraging higher standards of hygiene and child management, despite the privations and disruptions of the war. They were credited with being the agents of the reduction in the incidence and severity of gastrointestinal and respiratory infections in infants and the consequent improvement in infant mortality rates.

Oblique public recognition of the importance attached to their work was contained in the National Health Service Act of 1946. Health visitors were required to visit all mothers who had given birth and were living in the district assigned to them by the local authority's Medical Officer of Health, as soon as possible after they were discharged from hospital or from the care of a domiciliary midwife. The Act gave the health visitors the power to insist, if necessary, on entry to the home in order to examine the infant.

Despite these statutory endorsements of the value of their work, and the suggestion that they should be responsible for the health of the whole family, health visitors were not without their critics. In particular, the adequacy of their training to perform child protection duties was successfully challenged in 1947, and led to the passage in the following year of the Children Act, which required local authorities to establish departments headed by Children's Officers who possessed social-work or social-welfare qualifications. Their responsibility was directly to the Home Office, not through the Medical Officer of Health to the Ministry of Health.

An emergent élite section of social workers—university-trained psychiatric social workers—had begun to enter local-authority services through the child-guidance clinics established by most local education departments. They were particularly critical of the suitability of health visitors' nursing background and training as preparation for dealing with the kind of psychiatric disturbances which underlay most forms of child neglect or abuse.

Under these circumstances the Ministry of Health set up a departmental working party in 1953, under the chairmanship of Sir Wilson Jameson, to consider the proper role of health visiting in the future and its training requirements. It reported in 1956, but its work was in many ways disappointing. It did not seize the opportunity to undertake a detailed study of health visitors' work in different urban and rural settings, or of their relationships with other health and social-service workers in cognate fields. Nor did this working party look at the reception by, and their impact on, their clientele.[10]

While endorsing the received wisdom of the time which held that health visitors constituted a fine body of workers whose backgrounds in nursing, midwifery, and an academically sponsored health-visitor training (concerned with the environmental threats to the health of the family) which needed only modest changes, the working party's report failed to convince doubters in the broader social welfare and health fields. It considered the possible advantages and drawbacks of relating health visitors' duties to families on a general practitioner's list, rather than to those residing in a given geographical district, but came down against wholesale adoption of such a proposal.

As a result, many of the misgivings, and much of the scepticism about claims to health visitors' effectiveness, remained. Unless health visitors happened to be also the district nurse and district midwife—as happened sometimes in rural areas, where all three roles might be combined in one individual—they continued to work largely in isolation from other health workers. Moreover, they were still likely to meet hostility, indifference, or misrepresentation from many

[10] W. Jameson, *An Inquiry into Health Visiting: Report of a Working Party on the Field of Work, Training and Recruitment of Health Visitors* (London: HMSO, 1956).

general practitioners, who were perhaps feeling equally unsure at the time about their own role and their standing with their medical peers.

District nurses

In the early years of the NHS, the relationship between general practitioners and district nurses was also unclear. The nurses' work had become more concentrated on older people, often housebound if not bedridden. Their work consisted mainly of visiting chronically ill patients discharged from hospital, and patients referred by general practitioners to the local-authority Health Department for continuing injections, dressings, or other forms of medication and treatment.

The intention was that district nurses would inform general practitioners of any changes in their patients' health status. In a study of interprofessional relationships and roles in Buckinghamshire in the early 1960s, however, nurses sometimes communicated by pinning a report to a patient's nightdress, if they were confident that the doctor would visit. Others felt that the proper channel was through the district nurses' office with whom the hospital or general practitioner had first made the request for their service. Personal contact between the two health workers providing the hands-on service was rare.[11]

District nurses valued the independence which the nature of their work allowed them. Many were critical of, and somewhat cynical about, the dedication of some general practitioners. They were wary of suggestions that they should work only with patients attached to particular practices—an idea which was then beginning to be seriously considered for them as well as for health visitors.

Social workers

Yet another kind of worry affecting the efficiency of the arrangements for health care outside hospitals began to surface in the first post-war decade. It was concerned with the plethora of staff, with various skills and nomenclatures, who had been employed by single-interest voluntary societies to help sufferers with a continuing handicap. Their work was, at that time, taken over or subsidized by local authorities. This meant that families with two or more difficulties could be recipients of regular visits from workers unaware of each other's concern and possibly giving families conflicting advice.

The problem in the early post-war years was whether the occupational groups who provided *intermittent* support such as care in acute illness, maternity care, or advice on child health had the training and incentive also to

[11] M. Jefferys, *An Anatomy of Social Welfare Services* (London, 1967), chs. VII, IX, and XX.

serve those with *continuing* handicaps such as sensory deficits or learning difficulties.

In the first half of the twentieth century, there were voluntary societies concerned with those who were born with, or acquired in early life, an irreversible condition such as a mental or physical handicap. These societies had recruited and trained people in ways of lightening the economic and communication burdens, as well as the social stigma carried by sufferers and their families. When the responsibility of providing such services was clearly recognized as falling on the state, the pragmatic solution adopted by most local authorities was either to subsidize existing voluntary societies to continue to provide the services, or to absorb their staff into their own health or welfare departments. Some supporters of particular single-concern societies were worried about the possible loss of independence, flexibility, and capacity to initiate improvements, which had been the hallmarks and justification for continuing voluntary rather than statutory provision. Many, however, recognized the increasing difficulties of fund-raising and recruiting supporters, and were reconciled to being absorbed by health and welfare departments.

The result was that local-authority Health and Welfare Departments, as well as Education and Housing Departments, combined or severally, contained a motley collection of variously named workers in the 1940s and 1950s. Most of them were women with interests focused on meeting the overt needs of people with specific handicaps or disabilities. To these were added the officers who had been responsible for poor relief under the Poor Law until its final demise in 1948, and for guardianship orders under the Board of Control, who were mostly men.

In the immediate post-war years the Carnegie Trust asked an academic lecturer—Eileen Younghusband—to report on the qualifications and background of those involved in social-work intervention.[12] Her second, and fuller report contained detailed recommendations for the future.[13] In 1955 she was appointed to chair a working party set up by the Ministry of Health to inquire into 'the proper field of work and the recruitment and training of social workers at all levels in the local authorities' health and welfare services under the National Health and National Assistance Acts, and in particular whether there is a place for a general purpose social worker with an in-service training as a basic grade'.[14] The working party's report in 1958 recommended the setting-up of a training council to establish and oversee training courses to which people who had some practical in-post experience could be admitted, and given the opportunity to up-grade their status. Those who possessed Master's degrees were likely to qualify for leadership positions in training, and in the planning and organization of social-work units in local government

---

[12] E. L. Younghusband, *Report on the Employment and Training of Social Workers* (Edinburgh, 1947).
[13] E. L. Younghusband, *Social Work in Britain* (Edinburgh, 1951).
[14] E. L. Younghusband, *Report of the Working Party on Social Workers in the Local Authority Health and Welfare Services* (London: HMSO, 1959).

and elsewhere. These recommendations were implemented in 1963, together with the simultaneous establishment of a Council for the Training of Health Visitors.[15]

There was a wider aim: that of providing a basically trained general purpose social worker who was capable of coping with the psychosocial needs of all those requiring personal counselling, rather than medical supervision or care related specifically to an underlying physical or mental condition. This was not immediately welcomed by the voluntary single-interest societies and their staff, or by the medical specialists who had frequently built up close cooperative relationships with dedicated and experienced workers.

The activities of the powerful lobby wanting to increase the power and status of social workers in community-based services did not, however, take off on a grand scale until the mid-1960s, and they were not successful until the early 1970s.[16] When the legislation embodying their objectives was enacted, like many others in history if for different reasons, their victory at the expense of Medical Officers of Health turned out to be somewhat pyrrhic.[17]

The period of crucial transition: the 1960s

With hindsight it is not difficult for the historian of health and social-service institutions to suggest why the 1960s was a crucial period in the development of the welfare state in the UK. Enough time had passed to judge whether the projected aims of greater equity in access to resources had been furthered, and if so at what cost, and with what unforeseen consequences. In so far as the welfare state was judged by its supporters to have fallen short of achieving its aims, the reasons had to be sought and remedies undertaken. Those who felt it had not been able to guarantee that every crisis in health or social security would be met were able to argue that society's commitment could theoretically be unlimited, and that priorities had to be established and adhered to. In view of the rise in public expectations, however, as well as changes in the ratio of older dependants to workers, the burden on the workers could become unbearable unless there was continued growth in *per capita* gross national product. The sceptics, on the other hand, could argue that the 'nanny state' had diminished personal incentive to earn, because people did not retain the fruits of their own enterprise. In the sceptic's view, the costs of monopolistic state provision had been excessive and had contributed to the decline in the nation's economic prosperity and threatened its viability.

[15] *Health Visitor and Social Work Training Act* (London: HMSO, 1962).

[16] *Report of the Committee on Local Authority and Allied Personal Social Services*, Cmnd. 3703 (The Seebohm Report; London, 1968); Local Authority Social Services Act (1970); National Health Service Reorganization Act (1973).

[17] M. Jefferys suggested this in 'The Transition from Public Health to Community Medicine: The Evolution and Execution of a Policy for Occupational Transformation', *Bulletin of the Social History of Medicine*, 39 (1986), 47–63.

Concurrently, noticeable and disturbing changes were occurring in the relationships between members of different generations, between men and women in and outside the family, between employers and employees, and between teachers and the taught. They brought into question all kinds of time-honoured assumptions about the legitimacy of the hierarchical social order, which had been largely reinstated in the immediate post-war world. These changes in social climate were not themselves due to the introduction of the welfare state. They were also occurring elsewhere in the world. They arose from the effects of the phenomenal increase in productivity brought about by the rapid application of scientific knowledge and technology. This increase affected the production and distribution of goods, transport, and communication, which, in turn, affected the expectations and opinions of virtually everyone in their multiple roles of producers and consumers.

The professions providing community-based health and personal social services became increasingly aware in the 1960s of the ways in which their own circumstances had changed relative to those of other sections of society with which they were in contact. General practitioners, for example, believed that their contribution to society's well-being had been taken too much for granted, undervalued, and hence undermined over the years. While their specialist colleagues in hospital continued to attract public esteem as miracle men, and to obtain an increasing proportion of the limited resources available for health services, general practitioners felt that their existing contracts condemned them to second-class status within the profession. At the same time they found that their patients seemed better-off, more demanding, and less likely to accept their services uncritically and gratefully; this was particularly true of young women.

Nurses, midwives, and health visitors had not been able to secure settlements with government bodies which rewarded them adequately for their professional work. Recruitment to their ranks from school leavers was proving more difficult, given the competition from private industry for secretarial staff. And wastage from their ranks occurred as disparities in career earnings became more apparent. Some of their leaders believed that the difficulties they faced sprang from the lack of academic standing of its training courses. Some blamed the willingness with which this group—nurses, midwives, and health visitors—had meekly accepted their limitations to innovate, to undertake clinical procedures, or to make decisions in situations where their judgement and competence might well be greater than that of medically qualified personnel. Because the great majority of nurses, midwives, and health visitors was female, it was assumed that most were not oriented towards a lifelong career, and that most would not occupy the position of being heads of family households. On these grounds it was argued that their pay was justifiably less than that of male employees with comparable abilities.

Many community nurses, midwives, and health visitors were unhappy about becoming members of primary-health-care teams, where their work would be with the patients of a practice rather than the residents of a specific district. They feared losing the relative freedom of working unsupervised in exchange for what they believed might be unwelcome subordination to medical practitioners. Although they had not been accustomed to be consulted about strategic deployments and had little personal incentive to change, some of their leaders appeared to favour such radically different arrangements for primary health care in the future.

Turning now to general practitioners, although there were signs of reviving confidence in a new, distinct role for personal doctors—based on the acknowledgment that their unique long-term relationship with patients could be used for therapeutic purposes[18]—it was at about this time that the prevailing gloom among the main body of general practitioners led to threats of resignation from the NHS (see Chapter 9). Fortunately, in political and administrative circles it was becoming recognized that the proper use of family doctoring, rather than increasing reliance on hospital-based specialists, carried few health risks and might reduce the disturbingly escalating costs of the NHS.

The return in 1964 of a Labour Government more robustly committed than its predecessor to maintaining the main pillars of the welfare state marked a turning point for general practice. The appointment by the Wilson Government of a Minister who was transparently concerned with improving health-service provision began a shift in government's relations with primary-care doctors which had to be achieved if the system instituted in 1948 was to continue to work. The Minister, Kenneth Robinson, saw the necessity of negotiating a satisfactory contract with general practitioners which would help to restore their self-esteem *vis-à-vis* their hospital colleagues. The Family Doctor Charter provided general practitioners with facilities, including the possibility of working closely with other health workers employed by local health departments. It rewarded them financially if they took steps to improve their practice premises. And now, at last, the widespread development of local authority-owned health centres was actively promoted. The Charter also encouraged general practitioners to form groups of two or more partners, and recompensed them if they attended approved continuing education or refresher courses.[19]

The revised contracts which followed the Charter were probably the single most important factor in making general practice one of the most popular choices for aspiring and able medical graduates. They changed the shape of primary care. Previously, it was the single-handed or two-doctor partnership with separate units of health visitors, district nurses, and midwives which had characterized a divided primary-health-care sector. Following the Charter, the old pattern was replaced through the 1970s by multi-professional primary-health-care teams, working together in a health centre or practice-owned premises. These teams consisted of a mixture of independent contractors (the

[18] M. Balint, *The Doctor, his Patient and the Illness* (London, 1957).
[19] *The Family Doctors' Charter* (London: HMSO, 1966).

general practitioners), employees partly subsidized by grants (typically secretaries and receptionists), and attached personnel provided at first by local government and later by the Health Authority (nurses, midwives, and health visitors, for example).

It only remains to say that the professionalizing zeal of an élite band of university-trained social workers, closely associated with the new administration, was rewarded in 1965 when the Government was persuaded to set up a Committee under Frederick Seebohm of the Joseph Rowntree Foundation to consider the future organization of community-based personal social services. Its report in 1968 recommended the setting-up of local-authority Social Services Departments which would be responsible for all the personal social services then provided, directly or indirectly, by the existing authorities' Health, Welfare, Children's, Housing, and Education Departments. Medical and psychiatric social workers in the hospital sector were also to be brought under the aegis of the new departments. The nursing, midwifery, and health-visiting workers now became employees of the Community Services of the NHS rather than of the local authority.

There were at least two important effects of these measures for the developing primary-health-care units, almost all based in group general practices. One was to draw an even clearer administrative distinction between health and social-welfare-oriented personnel than had previously existed. The other was to reduce the pressure on the primary-health-care teams to include social workers.[20]

In the mid-1960s a few self-critical but professionally confident general practitioners were open-minded enough to agree to attach a social worker on an experimental basis to their already expanding, multi-occupational practice teams.[21] There were some, however, who had been wary of claims made by non-medically qualified people to new and relevant knowledge of human behaviour and pathology. All too often these new occupational groups appeared to want to complement if not replace what they described as a basically flawed, unidimensional medical model.[22] Placing academically trained social workers in the team who might challenge the doctors' views of the nature of general practice to an extent which other attached workers were unlikely to do could be threatening to general practitioners. A social-work presence might be a divisive rather than a cohesive influence on the work of the team. However, the main preoccupation of the leaders of social work was controlling personal social services in the public sector. And this was not seen by many general practitioners as a handicap to their own leadership in primary health care.

---

[20] M. D. Warren, *The Genesis of the Faculty of Community Medicine* (Canterbury, 1996); J. Lewis, *What Price Community Medicine?* (Brighton, 1986).

[21] E. M. Goldberg and J. E. Neill, *Social Work in General Practice* (London, 1972).

[22] J. Huntington, *Social Work and General Medical Practice: Collaboration or Conflict?* (London, 1981).

The growth of teamwork in primary care

The seeds of change affecting the different occupational groups in the primary-health-care sector were sown in the 1960s when social and cultural upheavals were affecting every sector of society. The harvest was reaped in the next decade when general practitioners became more clearly committed to working with other community-based health workers than seemed possible in the early 1960s. The resulting pattern of primary care, consisting as it did of a mixture of independent contractors and salaried public-sector employees, came to be regarded as bearing the hallmark of a typical 'British' compromise, which, if it worked, would do so against the odds. It preserved the jealously guarded if somewhat fictitious independent contractor status of the general practitioners. But it provided enough economic and professional incentives to make it worthwhile for them to cooperate with public-sector salaried health and management personnel in order to increase the effectiveness and efficiency of their work. However, it excluded for some time to come the possibility of more radical changes in direction and focus.

It was, therefore, at this period in the second half of the twentieth century— from the late 1960s through the 1970s—rather than at the end of the Second World War or at the foundation of the NHS that the most significant shift took place in the relationships between the groups involved in providing domiciliary-based health care. Other influences, however, were also at work.

First, there was growing confidence amongst workers in primary care in their skill, their knowledge, and their contribution to the NHS. This confidence was boosted by increasing public scepticism about the capacity of specialist medicine by itself to solve all the problems of health and sickness. Science, it was widely felt, needed to be infused with understanding and sympathy and not mere technical competence. It was also clear to those involved in primary care that the guardians of the public purse were now committed to policies for strengthening community-based health services. Government saw primary care as a way of staunching the incessant haemorrhaging of scarce resources into costly hospital-based innovations which benefited relatively few at the expense of attaining a higher quality of life for many.

The reasons why these changes occurred at this period rather than earlier were also due to widespread changes in the general cultural climate during the 1960s which we described above. The behaviour expected of participants in any health-related interaction depended on the assumption that those engaged in them knew the unwritten rules for their part in them. By the end of the 1960s, however, those who on any of these counts could have expected to show deference to the doctor a decade previously were no longer persuaded that it was necessary or appropriate for them to do so.

It would be an error to conclude, however, that the unwritten rules which had governed interprofessional behaviour during the earlier years of the century, and which had been scarcely affected by the advent of the NHS itself, disappeared overnight. Nor did changes in the unwritten rules occur without resentment by those in superior positions in the social hierarchy when they began to work more closely with others in more subordinate positions. Conventional attitudes died hard. The walls of Jericho did not tumble down at once. Time-honoured assumptions about who should carry responsibility and authority for decisions persisted, even when challenged by the possibility of modifying tasks to reduce unnecessary duplication and authorization without risk to patients. General practitioners felt vindicated in their claim that their work was vital to the success of the NHS; but they had to adapt to becoming members of a substantial unit which included managers, secretaries, receptionists, and other health workers, some of whom were their employees and some employees of the Area (later District) Health Authority.

Although most of those who came together were anxious to make the new arrangements a success, many recognized that they had to adapt to using the new structures for the benefit of patients and clients while retaining their own sense of self-worth. Most professional groups felt that it was possible to lose as well as gain from the changes. Sharing responsibilities involved, at the least, mutual acceptance of new rules for sharing and exchanging information, maintaining confidentiality, and securing the consent of their patients for new ways of providing consultation and treatment in the surgery or at home. Further, they had to develop ways of settling differences of opinion quickly and amicably. And they had to ensure that the wider aim of promoting interprofessional education on a national if not international scale, for the benefit of future generations, was furthered by encouraging all the health-care occupational groups to play a positive part in its development.[23]

The 1990s and beyond

The first decisive steps to creating a viable primary-health-care system based on interprofessional understanding and mutual confidence began in the late 1960s and early 1970s. It has not broken down since. Yet it has not fulfilled all the high hopes which accompanied its initial promotion. Technological and fiscal pressures, together with changes in the nature of the issues confronting health and social-policy decision-makers at all levels, continue to mean constantly but erratically shifting goalposts and attempts to recreate a level playing field. The great, unanswered question at the end of the twentieth century is whether there is a satisfactory way of ultimately bringing together community health and social-welfare carers, in order to pursue common objectives in the British/European context in the new millennium.

[23] M. Jefferys, 'Primary Health Care', in P. Owens, J. Carrier, and J. Horder (eds.), *Interprofessional Issues in Community Health Care* (London, 1994), 185–201.

6

Research in General Practice:
Perspectives and Themes

JOHN HOWIE

Research is the process of critical thinking or organized enquiry. In medicine, it has interfaces with education, with clinical practice, with management, and with politics. During the first half-century of the NHS, research has had a lower profile in the evolution of general practice than it has in many of the other disciplines of clinical medicine, but its contribution has been a growing one. This chapter presents one view of its development. It is inevitably a personal view. It is a view written from the disciplinary perspective of general practice. It is also a view written by someone whose personal experiences belong to the second half of the period rather than to the first.[1]

The medicine of the pre-NHS era was relatively unsophisticated technically and undeveloped theoretically. General practice was fundamentally an activity carried out by single doctors or in small partnerships, and there did not appear to be any great need for general practitioners to embrace the culture of research or to develop the skills required to undertake it. In the first decades of the century, James Mackenzie made his reputation as a general-practitioner researcher at the interface with his other expertise in cardiology. He predicted that, if general practice was to develop and survive, it would need its own research institutions, and in 1919 he founded the Institute of Clinical Research in St Andrews.[2] Unfortunately, by then he had severe angina and he retired from active research shortly before his death in 1925. William Pickles, the other doyen of general-practice research, developed the skills of an epidemiologist as he traced the spread of infectious disease around his practice in Aysgarth.[3]

In the early years of the NHS, general practice continued as before, with little evidence to suggest that research influenced either its structure or its practice. It took the observations in 1950 of a visitor from abroad, J. S. Collings,

---

[1] Older readers of my first draft wanted more about the early years of the NHS, but my plans to carry out a living history approach and to interview early researchers personally were limited by lack of time. In general I have referred by name only to researchers of the earlier years of the period. Their work is easier to put in context than is that of contemporary researchers whose work will be more easily valued in future years.

[2] R. Macnair Wilson, *The Beloved Physician* (London, 1926).

[3] J. Pemberton, *Will Pickles of Wensleydale: The Life of a Country Doctor* (London, 1970).

to disturb its academic neglect and the existing combination of complacency and inertia to which both profession and government had contributed.[4] The major political landmarks of the founding of the College of General Practitioners in 1952, the development of vocational training, the evolution of departments of general practice, and the contract reforms in 1966 and 1990 are described elsewhere in this book (see Introduction and Chapter 9).[5] These institutions and events have both shaped and been influenced by the research interests and contributions which this chapter describes.

At least five distinct contributions to research in or about general practice can be described. There are good reasons for putting the contribution of the (Royal) College of General Practitioners first on the list. The College provided the first organized forum for general practitioners interested in research to share experiences, to learn from each other, to recognize challenges, and to plan to meet the needs and opportunities they saw available to them. The history of the evolution of research in the College in its early years has been vividly described first in its 1983 history of 'The First 25 Years' and more recently by Pereira Gray in his review of the 'First Forty Years'.[6] (Pereira Gray's pen portraits of individuals and the context in which they worked could only be repeated here rather than improved on, and I have drawn heavily on his work in the early part of this chapter.) Pereira Gray drew a hypothetical boundary between the early leading role of the College in research in general practice and the subsequent transfer of both activity and leadership in research to the university departments around the mid-1970s. The contribution of the university departments thus becomes the second major intra-professional influence worthy of separate description. A third influence spanning the period is the smaller but interesting and independent constituency of single-handed researchers, of whom Fry, Marsh, and Tudor Hart stand out, all having made major contributions from different and often distinctively personal starting points.

The other two research perspectives are rather arbitrarily drawn from outside the professional confines of general practice and general practitioners. The first perspective is disciplinary, including the often very different contributions of the disciplines within the social sciences, and from public health, epidemiology, and specialist medicine. The second perspective is institutional, and covers the influence of the institutions which support, purchase, or commission research; these include the Medical Research Council (MRC), the variously titled bodies which distribute government funding for research

---

[4] J. S. Collings, 'General Practice in England Today: A Reconnaissance', *Lancet* (1950), i. 555–85.

[5] For the foundation of the College, see J. H. Hunt, 'The Foundation of a College', *Journal of the Royal College of General Practitioners*, 23 (1973), 5–20.

[6] J. Fry, J. H. Hunt, and R. J. F. H. Pinsent (eds.), *A History of the Royal College of General Practitioners: The First 25 Years* (Lancaster, 1983), 131–7; D. J. Pereira Gray (ed.), *Forty Years On: The Story of the First Forty Years of the Royal College of General Practitioners* (London, 1992), 45–63. See also Pereira Gray, 'History of the Royal College of General Practitioners—the First 40 Years', *British Journal of General Practice*, 42 (1992), 29–35.

and development, the research charities, and the pharmaceutical industry (which has played a smaller role in general-practice research than in specialist research).

Five perspectives

The Royal College of General Practitioners

The foundation of the College was a response to the devaluation of general practice and the demoralization of general practitioners during the early NHS years. It was to be expected that those who had had the vision and commitment to lead change should underpin their political activity by promoting education and research. Given the almost total absence of a literature of general practice, it was not surprising that education was at first based on replicating hospital knowledge and skills in the community. From there priority was rightly given to using the experiences of the founder members and their many supportive colleagues to create a new language for the discipline. In due course the criteria of an independent discipline were defined as a unique body of knowledge, specific clinical skills, the ability to support research, and the possession of a philosophy; and the case was made for recognizing that general practice satisfied these criteria.[7]

Over time the academic activities of the College have contributed to all these qualifying criteria and the accounts of the early events in the academic development of the discipline are splendidly chronicled in the history of 'The First 25 Years' (where Pinsent and Watson wrote the chapter on research) and in 'Forty Years On' (where Pereira Gray interprets the same events in an informed and sympathetic way but with a longer view of the past).[8]

The authors of the first of these commentaries refer to their own early steps as 'amateur'. Although in some ways true, this is also unfair, in that they understate their own achievements. Their critical analyses of the world they worked in had to rely on methods drawn from epidemiology and hospital medicine, which were not always easily transferable to the medicine of general practice, and their work had to be done in their own time and without supporting infrastructure. The early story is of remarkable endeavour by individuals, whose memorial may be their willingness to attribute their activities to a concept (the College) which represented their cause (general practice), rather than to claim credit for what they contributed personally. This 'institutionalization' of research provided the basis of many of the early successes that were centred on the College, but also of some of the later weakness in its faculties or periph-

---

[7] I. R. McWhinney, 'General Practice as an Academic Discipline', *Lancet* (1966), i. 419–23; I. M. Richardson, 'The Value of a University Department of General Practice', *British Medical Journal*, iv. (1975), 740–2.

[8] Fry, Hunt, and Pinsent (eds.), *History*; Pereira Gray (ed.), *Forty Years On*.

ery. The original Research Committee (set up within four months of the founding of the College) met in Bath, midway between the homes of its members (Abercrombie and Hunt in London, Watson in Surrey, French in Kidsgrove, and McConaghey in Dartmouth). The Committee developed two strategies for promoting research growth which seemed logical and complementary—central research units and peripheral networks.

The first units were Watson's Epidemic Observation Unit at Peaslake in Surrey, and Pinsent's Records and Statistical Unit in Birmingham—which later became the Birmingham Research Unit under Crombie's direction. The Manchester Research Unit became the focus for administering the Oral Contraceptive Study, conceived by Kuenssberg and masterminded by Kay, which eventually involved more than 1,000 general practices.[9] Although the Manchester Research Unit's creation was ten years or more behind the earlier units, the gap was almost imperceptible within the central Research Committee, where the 'small-group' ethos had been preserved by an inbuilt stable core membership. The addition of subsequent units (the Research Support Unit in Dundee and the Cardiovascular Research Unit in Leigh) and the permanent committee-member status of Unit Directors ensured continuity, but limited diversity. The Research Committee focused mostly on major national collaborative epidemiological work, initiated by or coordinated in units: for example, the National Morbidity Studies, the Oral Contraceptive Study, and the infectious-diseases surveillance programmes. There was less emphasis on the place of philosophy in research in the discipline generally or about how doctors worked and related to patients. The Research Committee and its members established effective networks with the College's institutional counterparts (the MRC, the Public Health Laboratory Service (PHLS), the Department of Health) but were less effective in forming links with their periphery—the research committees of faculties.

It is probably fair to say that the concept of faculty research committees has been less successful than was hoped. Research is an activity led by individuals with their own ideas, and few researchers wanted committees either to change their ideas or to take them over. The idea that local committees would recruit doctors for national studies or increase the base for individual practice studies rarely proved to work on the ground, and the only faculty research committees which prospered were those where strongly motivated individuals were happy to take on the entrepreneurial role. In time, the university departments were to provide the kind of role that faculty research committees had been intended to have, and they arrived on the scene at the wrong time for the development of research as a peripherally devolved College activity.

The most public successes of research run by the College have been the National Morbidity Studies (latterly run from Birmingham), which have

[9] C. R. Kay, 'The Happiness Pill?', *Journal of the Royal College of General Practitioners*, 30 (1980), 9–19.

sketched the clinical and operational outlines of the discipline; the work on infectious-disease surveillance (pioneered by Hope-Simpson and later by Watson and Williams), and the Oral Contraceptive Study (based in Manchester).[10] Fostering the development of what has become the most frequently cited journal concerned with general practice has been an equally important contribution.[11]

Despite these important achievements, general practitioners as a whole have not adopted the culture of research into their daily activities. Too many of them feel the output of their journal lacks relevance and reality. And, despite two appeals, the Scientific Foundation Board—the College's closest equivalent to a funding body—has too little recurrent income to do more than 'pump-prime' (which it nevertheless has done successfully).[12]

Two issues reflect inherent dilemmas which the College did not resolve in its early years. The loss of unit leaders through premature death or retirement faced it with uncertainty over whether to close units or to appoint new leaders. The reluctance to close units out of loyalty to previous ideas, or to individuals, led to previously successful enterprises drifting away from their intended purpose and eventually being disowned, with loss of morale to the College's research effort generally. Had the College recognized more explicitly the importance of individuals as against committees in promoting the cause of research, it would almost certainly have proved easier to change course to reflect the change in needs over time. The College is, of course, not alone in having found problems of succession in units a difficult issue to deal with. The Department of Health required to commission the Williams Report to relieve itself of outdated investments and the MRC has developed the ruthless but probably sensible policy of normally closing its own units when a leader retires.[13] Had the College or general practice had better access to 'programme' funding during its first two decades, it is likely that its use would have prevented this problem arising.

The second dilemma coincided with the move to Europeanism which the College's central research leaders adopted in the early 1980s. At the same time,

[10] Everyone concerned with the early years of general-practice research pays particular homage to the work of Edgar Hope-Simpson. He travelled on his rounds armed with throat swabs which he made use of at every opportunity. He has published a very large number of epidemiological papers; he was the first to show on epidemiological grounds that herpes zoster and chickenpox were due to the same virus; and his book *The Transmission of Epidemic Influenza* (New York, 1992) is a major and highly original contribution to the understanding of the spread of viral diseases. Ian Watson and W. O. Williams took over his mantle in later years. I learnt of their reputations from my own father (Director of the PHLS 1962–72), whose respect for their work (never easily earned) was impressed on me during my own early researches on respiratory infection in general practice.

[11] D. Pereira Gray et al., 'The Discipline and Literature of General Practice', British Journal of General Practice, 47 (1997), 139–43.

[12] The Scientific Foundation Board has some £75,000 to disburse annually (1997 prices) which it does in sums of up to £10,000 per project. During the last five years, over 50% of funded projects have produced publications in peer-reviewed journals.

[13] P. O. Williams, Review of the Role of DH Funded Research Units: Strategies for Long-Term Funding of Research and Development (Department of Health, March 1992).

the expansion of university departments of general practice reduced their own role in research in the UK. Early College research had generally been descriptive rather than analytic, with both numerators and denominators often being defined in necessarily simplistic terms. Instead of addressing these methodological challenges at home (which would have included greater acceptance of the role of non-medical scientists), the College attempted to repeat what had succeeded previously in the UK in the wider setting of Europe. At this time it is difficult to identify any significant conceptual gain which has followed the move to international comparative studies of only marginally adequate design, although the political networking involved may well be regarded as a compensating bonus.[14]

Recent years have seen the Research Division of the College actively promote the case for training fellowships and local networks of research practices. Both initiatives have come at a propitious time, and may prosper in the new (1996) climate of the 'primary-care-led NHS' and the recognition in the Culyer Report on NHS R&D that primary-care research requires a strengthened infrastructure.[15]

The university departments

The history of the development of university departments is described in Chapter 7, and has been documented in two RCGP documents and in the Mackenzie Report.[16] The foundations of the first department (in Edinburgh) were laid at the introduction of the NHS in 1948, when F. A. E. Crew (a Professor of Public Health and Social Medicine) took over a dispensary practice, and appointed a senior lecturer (Richard Scott—later appointed the first Professor of General Practice in the world in 1963) to manage the practice, design teaching, and create a body of community-related research. As happened in all early practice-based academic departments, the service load seriously eroded

---

[14] College researchers played major roles in founding and developing the European General Practice Research Workshop (EGPRW) and the Societas Internationalis Medicinae Generalis (SIMG). Both groups helped bring together those interested in developing service, teaching, and research throughout Europe at a time when general practice in Europe was less developed than it was in the UK.

[15] The Culyer Report (*Supporting Research and Development in the NHS* (London: HMSO, 1994)) describes proposals to create a single funding stream for all NHS-supported R&D. A specific section is devoted to the problems which have affected R&D in primary and community care.

[16] C. M. Harris, *General Practice Teaching of Undergraduates in British Medical Schools* (Reports from General Practice No. XI; London, 1969); P. S. Byrne, 'University Departments of General Practice and the Undergraduate Teaching of General Practice in the United Kingdom in 1972', *Journal of the Royal College of General Practitioners*, 23, suppl. 1 (1973). The Mackenzie Report (J. G. R. Howie, D. R. Hannay, and J. S. K. Stevenson, *General Practice in the Medical Schools of the United Kingdom* (University of Edinburgh, 1986)) was written to reinvigorate negotiations with the NHS for infrastructure support for departments of general practice equivalent to Service Increment for Teaching (SIFT) and Additional Cost of Teaching (ACT) (see n. 35). The negotiations started in December 1981 and were concluded in 1992, but became becalmed in their early stages because of failure to persuade either the Department of Health or the Department of Education to take responsibility for the exclusion of academic general practice from equitable funding either by the NHS or through medical schools.

research opportunity. Relatively little was published in the early years, although studies on case mix, social problems, and the health of children (including studies of otitis media and urinary infection) were carefully designed and carried out. Teaching practices (in Manchester and at St Thomas's Hospital in London) were forerunners of later practice-based departments, but the first attempt at a non-practice-based department came in Aberdeen, where Richardson (appointed a Reader in 1968 and Professor in 1970) laid the foundations of a research-based department, with better opportunities to carry out research than existed where service commitments had to take priority. Richardson's background (like Scott's) was in public health and based on elegant epidemiology. His early work (on the geographical distribution of patients on practice lists in Aberdeen) was used by health-service planners to develop the Aberdeen health-centre strategy—but few doctors acted on its findings.[17] His subsequent series of three time studies (of general practitioners, district nurses, and health visitors) used the strict principles of epidemiology, borrowed techniques from other disciplines (time study and participant observation), and were carried out by salaried researchers from different disciplines. By the mid-1970s, as the College's own attempts to foster local research activities and networks were beginning to mark time, the rapidly increasing number of university departments of general practice were organizing studies which involved local practices, and were managed locally by people with (at least some) protected time. These people were also bringing new disciplinary skills and perspectives to old problems and questions.

Three major contextual issues (one arising within general practice and two from without) had significant influences on the evolution of research in university departments. The first was the after-waves of the Balint movement which had so substantially influenced the philosophy of general practice in the late 1960s and early 1970s (see Chapter 3). At about the time when 'College research' was focusing on the design and interpretation of one national and two major regional morbidity and workload studies, Shepherd, an academic psychologist leading an epidemiological research unit, had noted that interpretations of the prevalence of psychological illness at general-practice consultations ranged from 5 to 50 per cent. The Balint movement (whose bible was the seminal *The Doctor, his Patient and the Illness*), and its articulate and influential proponents, however, settled on an interpretation of consultations that made 50 per cent seem a minimum figure.[18] The first 'academic' general publication from the College (*The Future General Practitioner*) was written by a strong team of the College's 'thinkers' of the day, several of whom had been directly influenced by Balint.[19] It set out a philosophical lead for general practice that determined the direction of postgraduate education thereafter. Harris

---

[17] I. M. Richardson and I. Dingwall-Fordyce, 'Patient Geography in General Practice', *Lancet* (1968), ii. 1290–3.

[18] M. Balint, *The Doctor, his Patient, and the Illness* (London, 1957).

[19] RCGP, *The Future General Practitioner: Learning and Teaching* (London: RCGP, 1972).

and Marinker (and their equally influential Balint-trained colleague, Freeling) became professors, as did Byrne—and Horder, later in his career on a 'visiting' basis—ensuring that, whatever direction university departments' research would take in the future, it would not be simplistically organic or quantitative in its orientation.

The second influence was the completely inadequate infrastructure base of many of the single-discipline early university departments, and the unrealistic expectations that medical schools had of them. Medical school leaders appeared to expect that these small groups of academic staff could introduce innovation in medical education, have a clinical role, represent their discipline politically and managerially in the university setting, and carry out research. General practice was seen as a facility for extending hospital research rather than for developing new perspectives. But too few of the early academic staff had the research experience or methodological skills (or both) to provide convincing and rigorous research. In the suddenly harsh funding realities of higher education in the early 1980s, general practice was threatened as an academic discipline just when it had appeared to be prospering, and the need to increase the professionalism and the relevance of its research became a major priority.

The third influence was the advent in 1986 of the first (to date) of four national assessments of the quality of research in higher-education institutions. On the surface, the first two of these were not immediately relevant to general practice, but the third (in 1992) identified 'general practice' as a major part of a constituency of 'community-based clinical subjects', and this continued into the 1996 review.[20] By the later part of the 1980s it was already clear that general-practice departments with a lower commitment to developing a research portfolio which had depth and quality in at least some areas would be hard pressed to maintain their standing within medical schools—and, by implication, the level of their staffing.

At the start of this section I referred to the organizational split between departments of general practice based on NHS practices and those which were free-standing. There has been a further structural debate over the degree to which departments should be based within or be independent from departments of public health or epidemiology. In reality, most departments have had close links (for example, at St Thomas's Hospital between Holland and Morrell[21]), although some have been more formal than others. Over time, as general practice worked to establish its own disciplinary identity, the majority of departments became academically independent. However, as the term

---

[20] This constituency included general practice, public health and epidemiology, and psychiatry. Assessments were made of the achievements of the constituency as a whole. In general a single-subject submission was associated with higher ratings than when all three subjects were declared together.

[21] W. W. Holland and D. C. Morrell, 'A Marriage of Convenience', *British Journal of Medical Education*, 6 (1972), 121–4.

'general practice' again becomes a statement of locus, with the discipline becoming 'primary care', a further change in title and structure is already taking place.

It will never be easy to conclude which organizational models have provided the better platform for research, and I have decided against trying to quantify or comment on the significance of the substantial literature which staff of departments of general practice have generated over five decades. However, in the later part of this chapter I will refer to the outcome of the 1996 'research-assessment exercise' and make some general observations about the research agendas which different departments have followed.

The personal researchers

The first parts of this review of the history of general-practice research have been presented from an institutional rather than a personal point of view. This approach plays down the essential individuality of research and researchers (including those whose work has been centred within the institutions), and it fails to recognize the vision and persistence of many of the individuals who have epitomized 'research' over the five decades of the NHS. Some notable researchers need separate mention to give balance to this narrative. Although Pickles's *Epidemiology in a Country Practice* was published in 1939, and strictly precedes the remit of this chapter, his meticulous mapping of infectious disease was to underpin much later College research and paralleled the work of Hope-Simpson, also one of the early individual researchers of the period.[22] Watts, too, made his reputation as an individual researcher (on psychiatric illness) before becoming involved in the College structure in the same way as Hope-Simpson did.[23]

Although Keith Hodgkin probably presented the more balanced of the early major outlines of general practice morbidity and its presentation,[24] John Fry undoubtedly became the best-known single-practice general-practice researcher of the 1960s and 1970s. His work from his own practice led to the publication of *The Catarrhal Child* and *Profiles of Disease*, which are enduring examples of simple but elegant description of the natural history of common illnesses in the community, and rightly ensure his place in the history of general-practice research.[25] His later output based on his own workload and on the prevalences of disease in his own practice, however, lacked variety in approach and method and reflected the inevitable difficulties single researchers generally face in adapting to changing needs and opportunities over longer periods of time.

---

[22] W. N. Pickles, *Epidemiology in Country Practice* (London, 1939; republished 1984); on Hope-Simpson, see n. 10.

[23] C. A. H. Watts and B. M. Watts, *Psychiatry in General Practice* (London, 1952).

[24] K. Hodgkin, *Towards earlier diagnosis* (Edinburgh, 1963).

[25] J. Fry, *The Catarrhal Child* (London, 1961); *Profiles of Disease* (Edinburgh, 1966).

Geoffrey Marsh and Julian Tudor Hart have been the two other most notable single-practice researchers of the last two decades. Marsh, working in Cleveland, first described team-working in his large group practice, and advocated the unpopular case for larger lists in general practice (as indeed John Fry had also done).[26] He also tackled a variety of clinical issues including childhood illness and obstetric care. Tudor Hart, in a declining Welsh mining community, brought his epidemiological expertise (learned through association with the MRC) to the longitudinal study of cardiovascular disease in his local community, generalizing from his work to the wider issues of the politics of disadvantage—as, indeed, Marsh had done too.[27] All these individual researchers have also been involved in College activities and, in more recent times, might well have made formal links with university departments too. Their legacy is the demonstration of the central importance of having values and beliefs to add to the key ingredients of curiosity and ordered thinking when conducting good general-practice research.

Selecting a few examples of outstanding researchers emphasizes the potential of single-practice research but inevitably underplays valuable work undertaken and reported by others over many years. Their contributions are found in the pages first of the *Research Newsletter*, and later in the *Journal of the Royal College of General Practitioners*, now renamed the *British Journal of General Practice*.

Boundary disciplines

General practice has clinical interfaces with self-care, community care, and secondary care. Research also has connections with the social sciences, with specialist medicine, and with public health. Social scientists, specialists, and epidemiologists have had interests in researching both *about* primary care/general practice from their own perspectives, and researching *in* primary care/general practice, with or without collaboration from general practitioners. These contributions have been important in different ways and this part of the chapter tries to sense the nature of them.

As already referred to earlier in this chapter, the disciplines of public health and epidemiology have provided major support for the researchers of general practice. Senior and influential people in the disciplines (including Godber and Acheson who were English Chief Medical Officers and Brotherston who was a Scottish Chief Medical Officer) facilitated the evolution of general-practice research at both College and university-department level. Many fruitful partnerships helped underpin the early departments of general practice.

[26] G. Marsh and P. Kaim-Caudle, *Team Care in General Practice* (London, 1976).
[27] J. Tudor Hart, 'The Management of High Blood Pressure in General Practice: Butterworth Gold Medal Essay, 1974', *Journal of the Royal College of General Practitioners*, 25 (1975), 160–92; 'The Inverse Care Law', *Lancet* (1971), i. 405–12; G. N. Marsh, 'Clinical Medicine and the Health Divide', *Journal of the Royal College of General Practitioners*, 38 (1988) 5–9.

Epidemiological skills and cooperation have made possible the series of four National Morbidity Studies.[28] And individual researchers in general practice have also had close links with public-health expertise (for example, Pickles with Pemberton, and Tudor Hart with the MRC). Not unnaturally, epidemiologists have researched independently within primary care (Holland, for example, in the field of chronic respiratory illness), and their work has contributed significantly to the literature of general practice.

While public-health research has generally been both 'in' and 'about' general practice, the involvement of *specialist medicine* in research in general practice has, not surprisingly, been almost entirely 'in' rather than 'about' general practice. The availability of College research networks, and of general-practice departments, has tempted respiratory physicians, cardiovascular physicians, gastroenterologists, psychiatrists, orthopaedic surgeons, and many others to try to recruit patients from general practice to extend studies of their own design. Inherently such projects generally lack interest for general practitioners, and many involve adherence to protocols which are so detailed that few patients can be found who satisfy their entry criteria. In addition, few doctors have time to apply them to those patients who are eligible. The MRC— whose role in general-practice research is referred to again in the next section—succeeded in getting round these problems in 1973 when it created its General Practice Research Framework (GPRF) to facilitate their outstandingly successful study of 'mild hypertension'. It has worked hard to repeat this success in other clinical areas, of which osteoporosis is (in 1997) a current example.[29] The pharmaceutical industry has also, for many of the reasons described above, had less support from general practice for its surveillance and testing requirements than might have been expected, although many individual practitioners do contribute to their studies. Despite these observations, specialist research has made notable contributions to general-practice thinking, the work of Shepherd and of Goldberg in the field of psychiatry being particularly good examples.

The contribution from the various *social and behavioural* science disciplines to research both in and about primary care/general practice has been a more positive story. Disciplines such as sociology, psychology, and anthropology have provided the main focus for the study of health and illness in populations and the perceptions and behaviours of people, professionals, and institutions. Jefferys and Cartwright were amongst the first to form close research links with general practice. Both originally worked at the London School of Hygiene and Tropical Medicine. Cartwright moved to Edinburgh to work with Brotherston

[28] OPCS (A. McCormick, D. Fleming, and J. Charlton), *Morbidity Statistics from General Practice: Fourth National Study 1991–1992* (London; HMSO, 1995).

[29] The GPRF is a network of over 900 practices throughout the UK covering over 10% of the UK population; each practice has a part-time trained research nurse who is responsible for day-to-day management of projects. Medical Research Council Working Party, 'MRC Trial of Treatment of Mild Hypertension: Principal Results', *British Medical Journal*, 291 (1985), 97–104.

(and was closely associated with the new department of general practice there), and then became Director of the Institute for Social Studies in Medical Care. Her important contributions to general-practice literature include *Patients and their Doctors, General Practice Revisited,* and *Medicine Takers, Prescribers and Hoarders.*[30] Margot Jefferys moved to Bedford College, where she wrote *Rethinking General Practice* and other contributions to the developing literature of general practice.[31] (Both Cartwright and Jefferys were elected honorary fellows of the RCGP in 1988.)

A range of other social scientists have made important contributions to general practice (including Tuckett in his much-referenced book *Meetings between Experts*), and the social science literature on general practice has been heavily influential in developing the future of education and practice in the community.[32] Some of the literature has, however, been less happily received. Honigsbaum's 1972 critique of 'quality in general practice', with its emphasis on the division in British medicine between general practice and hospital medicine, had an impact similar to that of the Collings Report, and generated a large volume of hostile correspondence causing the College to distance itself from automatic association with the papers published in its Journal.[33]

The funding institutions

Research both 'in' and 'about' general practice has been influenced by attitudes towards it from the nation's major research-funding institutions. The research-funding charities (some of which are 'general' charities, such as Nuffield, Wolfson, Leverhulme, Wellcome, and King's Fund; and others of which are more specific, such as the Mental Health Foundation and the Imperial Cancer Research Fund (ICRF)) have supported research both through project grants and through research-training fellowships. The pharmaceutical industry, as well as funding drug trials, has also supported research through major endowments (the Pfizer Chair of General Practice in Dundee; the Eli Lilly National Audit Centre in Leicester), and the sponsorship of conferences and travel.

However, the two bodies with the most influential roles have been the MRC and the Health Departments of the UK. The MRC has always emphasized that it wishes to support general-practice or primary-care research proposals,

---

[30] A. Cartwright, *Patients and their Doctors* (London, 1967); A. Cartwright and R. Anderson, *General Practice Revisited: A Second Study of Patients and their Doctors* (London, 1981); K. Dunnell and A. Cartwright, *Medicine Takers, Prescribers and Hoarders* (London, 1972).

[31] M. Jefferys and H. Sachs, *Rethinking General Practice* (London, 1983).

[32] D. A. Tuckett, M. Boulton, C. Olson, and A. Williams, *Meetings between Experts: An Approach to Sharing Ideas in Medicine Consultations* (London, 1986).

[33] F. Honigsbaum, 'Quality in General Practice', *Journal of the Royal College of General Practitioners,* 22 (1972), 429–51. Press statement from the RCGP, 'Quality in General Practice', *Journal of the Royal College of General Practitioners,* 22 (1972), 705 (followed by 16 'letters to the editor' on pp. 708–17).

but the competitive and sometimes apparently inappropriately critical nature of its peer-review system has discouraged applications. The appointment of a Professor of General Practice (Roland) as Chair of its Health Services Research Committee in 1994 confirmed that it recognized the ability of the top researchers in the discipline and the value of the generalist vision. The contribution which MRC made to the Oral Contraceptive Study signalled its wish to support research 'in' general practice, and the creation of its GPRF in 1973 was a major attempt to put in place a mechanism for gaining access to general-practice populations for epidemiological study. The GPRF attracted a degree of ambivalence from both the College and the university departments of general practice, who saw it as a competitor supporting research 'in' rather than 'about' general practice. This became a particularly sensitive issue during the early 1990s, when the Department of Health created its new Directorate of Research and Development for the NHS and began to identify the pool of existing resources available to support general-practice and primary-care research. Once again, the MRC moved to resolve the tensions by appointing a senior general practice academic (Stott) to chair the GPRF and by promoting a 'topic review' of primary care/general practice research. The review had a strong general-practitioner input and has produced a significant and well-argued report.[34]

The role of government in the development of general-practice research is referred to last because of its all-embracing importance. Throughout the time of the NHS, government has supported general practice as a locus for research and encouraged the development of research skills in general practitioners. Links between successive Chief Medical Officers and principal Medical Officers connected with general-practice services, on the one hand, and College and academic leaders, on the other, have been consistently warm and supportive. It has, however, not been easy to translate this goodwill into the financial and contractual measures needed by the general-practice research community to empower and sustain its evolution. Early in the period, the Department of Health supported the multidisciplinary Health Services Research Unit, linked to the Department of General Practice at St Thomas's Hospital Medical School, and provided similar support in Manchester, Birmingham, and Oxford. Early Health Department support to the College and its units was also valuable, but generally at 'project'-support level.

However, the general reluctance of government to support 'programmes' of research in general practice, or to enable the NHS to support the infrastructure of research in departments of general practice, has been a fundamental barrier to progress which has disadvantaged general-practice research in relation to research in all other clinical disciplines. The first serious attempts in 1974 to examine resource allocation in the NHS (the Resource Allocation Working Party (RAWP) in England and Scottish Health Authorities Resource

---

[34] MRC, *Topic Review of Primary Health Care Research* (London, 1997).

Equalization (SHARE) in Scotland) identified the very substantial excess costs which the NHS had historically incurred in supporting academic medicine in the NHS.[35] Moves in the early 1980s from the academic general-practice community to obtain a share of this support for education and research in general practice were hindered by the prevailing ambivalence of the general-practice community towards its academic wing. Equally important was the absence of support from the hospital-based medical specialisms who saw support for equal academic opportunity for general practice as a threat to their own resourcing. The Culyer inquiry into R&D in the NHS commented on the need for infrastructure and access to project- and programme-funding for general-practice research; *SIFT into the Future* emphasized the overlapping and related issues of the infrastructure needed for teaching.[36] There is, in 1997, optimism that the rhetoric of the 'primary care led NHS' will be translated into a shift of funds from specialist to generalist medicine at least for teaching, and possibly (or probably) for research as well.

The history of the Health Department's relationship with general-practice research has one more strand. In 1975 the Department established an NHS-funded research unit within the Department of General Practice in Manchester, with Byrne as its part-time director. Metcalfe succeeded Byrne in 1978 and began a series of researches into equality (or inequality) in primary care, in response to the findings of the Black Report.[37] The Centre for Primary Care Research (CPCR), as it was subsequently titled, continued on rolling funding through the 1980s, developing substantial primary-care-research expertise through its mix of medical and social science staffing. Without doubt, CPCR's ability to develop and deliver its own research programme was handicapped by its contractual obligation to respond to Health Department's requests for 'quick and dirty' short-term projects. In 1992 it was faced with withdrawal of its core funding as part of the general NHS R&D move to rationalize (and

[35] The RAWP of the NHS in England and Wales and the parallel SHARE working party in Scotland identified large cost differences between teaching and district general hospitals. Excluding London hospitals, three-quarters of the difference was designated as due to the excess costs of teaching clinical medical students and labelled Service Increment for Teaching (SIFT) in England and Wales, and Additional Cost of Teaching (ACT) in Scotland. At 1975–6 prices this equalled £8,372/clinical student, a sum which rose to over £40,000/clinical student by 1990. General-practice teaching and research were excluded from receiving this substantial subsidy (which helped provide NHS-financed junior medical and nursing staff for other clinical academic departments). Negotiating with the NHS for a share of this pool or for an equivalent source of support for general practice began in 1981, but it took until 1992 to achieve success through a pool £2.3m. of 'tasked money' in England and Wales and a per capita sum of £1,000/graduating clinical student in Scotland.

[36] *Supporting Research and Development in the NHS* (The Culyer Report); *SIFT into the Future* was published in May 1995 by the NHS Executive. The document was subtitled 'future arrangements for allocating funds and contracting for NHS service support and facilities for teaching undergraduate medical students' and has enabled the temporary 'tasked money' (see n. 35) to be put on a more secure and equitable longer-term footing.

[37] D. Black, J. N. Morris, C. Smith, and P. Townsend, *Inequalities in Health—The Black Report* (England, 1982). The Black Report, *Report of a Research Working Group on Inequalities in Health*, was first published by HMSO in 1980. See also D. Black, 'Deprivation and Health (the Chadwick lecture)', *Journal of the Royal College of Physicians of London*, 30 (1996), 466–71.

generally reduce) its commitment to medium-size research units. At the same time and as a wholly new venture in R&D support, Peckham (the Director of NHS R&D) announced his vision of a major dedicated primary-care R&D centre with £1.5m. core funding per year for ten years, to be sited in an English university or universities. After a competitive tendering process, the contract was awarded to a consortium from Manchester, Salford, and York universities with Wilkin and Roland leading from Manchester, and Popay and Maynard from Salford and York respectively.

Creation of such a powerful unit has caused anxiety amongst other researchers that the creation of a strong centre will be at the cost of opportunity to other university departments and to individual practice-based researchers.

Two themes

In this attempt to trace the history of general-practice research since the beginning of the NHS, I have taken a descriptive approach, exploring five perspectives of research in general practice which, although perhaps somewhat arbitrarily chosen and not always discrete, help tease out real differences in emphasis and approach. To complete the chapter, I will try to draw together a number of themes which have run through it.

A chapter on research might be expected to examine either the topics covered by researchers, or the disciplinary base of the researchers, or the methods they have used. The natural history and management of illnesses and diseases would be expected to have been the major interests of clinicians and epidemiologists. Early clinical research in general practice did begin with a focus on infectious disease and its epidemiology, but much less has been attempted in the clinical area in recent years than might have been expected and perhaps hoped. The major emphasis throughout the period has been on operational research, with the College investing heavily in its early years, and both clinical academics and social scientists developing substantial portfolios in later years. Variability in doctor behaviour has been the single theme that has provided the best opportunities, and social scientists, epidemiologists, and general practitioners have researched extensively on activities such as prescribing, referral, the use of time, and clinical decision-making (see Chapter 4). The failure of research to explain more than small proportions of the variation in any of these key activities indicates that this problem (if indeed variation *is* a problem) is not yet worked through.

Issues of discipline and method could also be the basis of a synthesis. Doctors have undertaken extensive studies on how they work, mainly using quantitative survey methods which have served to show the extent of problems. But they have rarely explored their nature adequately. Social scientists have used similar methods, but have also used more qualitative approaches which offer different ways of thinking and are often able to suggest causal pathways between associations. The sharing of disciplinary understandings and methodological approaches offers great opportunity for social scientists and doctors (not all of whom will be general practitioners) to explore the beliefs and expectations of patients, and of professionals, and to understand how relations between them are formed and can be used to improve care. The coming-together of different professions in departments of general practice has been an important part of the general-practice-research story of the 1980s and 1990s. So also has been the titling, or retitling, of some of these departments as departments of primary care. The re-creation of larger intra- and inter-professional groupings which include general practice, public health, and other health workers and scientists raises two issues which will become more relevant as the 'primary-care-led' NHS of the 1990 reforms develops.

Culture, infrastructure, and training

In 1988 the Chief Scientist at the Scottish Home and Health Department commissioned an enquiry into why so few applications for centrally funded research came from general practice and why so few of these proved supportable. The cross-disciplinary working group which was appointed drew three general conclusions which mirror the issues which have faced general-practice research over the half-century covered by this review.[38]

The Report noted that, unlike in medicine generally, the *culture* of general practice was not based on a tradition of research. Indeed many general practitioners chose general practice to escape from collecting data for research which was carried out by their seniors and seemed of doubtful use. At times the 'culture' of general practice has in fact appeared anti-intellectual, with those who work on behalf of the College or in departments of general practice being seen as having opted out of 'real' general practice. It is a weak defence that research output (oral and written) has on occasions been insensitive or hostile to the difficulties faced by those working full time in patient care.

The second issue was the absence of *infrastructure* support for those engaging in research in general practice. At one level, infrastructure support allows time to think, plan, and carry out research. At another level, it provides technical and clerical support. And at another level, it provides access to the statistical and other disciplinary expertise that is central to successful research carried out by other clinicians. College policy statements,[39] policy statements

---

[38] Chief Scientists' Organization, *Report of the Working Group on Research in Health Care in the Community* (The Howie Report; Edinburgh: Chief Scientists' Organization, Scottish Home and Health Department, Oct. 1988).

[39] Conference of Academic Organizations in General Practice, *Research and General Practice* (London: RCGP, 1994), Conference of Academic Organizations in General Practice, *Developing Primary Care—the Academic Contribution* (London: RCGP, 1996).

on behalf of university departments,[40] the House of Lords Select Committee on Medical R&D,[41] and the Culyer Report on R&D in the NHS have all accepted the urgency of addressing this problem.[42] Recent negotiations give some reason for optimism that a solution will be found.

The absence of a tradition, or of opportunities for relevant research *training*, was the third issue identified by the working group. Various research-fellowship schemes have had some success in the last decade and the College (in particular) and the Health Departments and other funding institutions (for example, MRC and ICRF) are committed to increasing the opportunities for these. New initiatives to develop higher professional training for general practitioners generally will not only provide training and experience in research, but also help to raise the research culture and improve infrastructure at the same time.

Theory, rigour, and cohesion

This leads to the final theme in this section. Medicine generally has built its academic base on the biological sciences which underpin its various clinical specialisms. Clinical medicine is the activity which attempts to integrate these sciences, but it has no obvious uniting theory. General practice is also an applied science, but—as well as lacking any obvious unifying theory—it is based on a tradition of accepting uncertainty and a pragmatic approach to decision-making.[43] The term 'theory' frightens people, but a theory is no more than (and no less than) an attempt to unite available knowledge and understanding by a formula of words, or by a schematic representation or explanatory model. A satisfactory theory not only explains the present but will also predict what is not yet known. Research is most useful when it either reflects or tests an existing or proposed theory, or provides new information which can then, or in the future, add to a theory.

Any review of general-practice research and its literature will confirm that only a minority of published work has been theoretically based, or has proposed or rigorously tested hypotheses. On the other hand, social scientists generally approach research from a theoretical basis, and the increasingly apparent

---

[40] Howie *et al.*, *General Practice in the Medical Schools*.

[41] House of Lords Select Committee and Science Technology, *Medical Research and the NHS Reforms, Third Report* (London: HMSO, 1995), 28–9, 112–14.

[42] *Supporting Research and Development in the NHS* (The Culyer Report).

[43] Kuhn has suggested that scientific disciplines undergo a periodic 'paradigm-shift' when the existing theory which governs their researches no longer helps provide useful answers to questions posed. For example, Newton's thinking revolutionized research in physics, but Einstein's theory of quantum mechanics was required to allow later developments in the field. Although Kuhn excluded medicine from his theory, others—most notably McWhinney—have argued that general practice has contributed to a paradigm shift in medicine by emphasizing patient-centredness as against disease-centredness in clinical reasoning. Researches in general practice between 1948 and 1998 have certainly moved in this direction: T. S. Kuhn, *The Structure of Scientific Revolutions* (Chicago, 1962); I. R. McWhinney, 'Changing Models: The Impact of Kuhn's Theory on Medicine', *Family Practice* (1983) i. 3–8.

benefits to general-practice research of working with social scientists flows from this. It is interesting that one of the other major influences on general-practice research during the NHS years should have been the relatively non-quantitative contribution of the Balint movement, which was itself based on a psychoanalytical interpretation of the doctor–patient–illness interrelationship. Stott and Davis proposed a different kind of model to analyse the content of consultations.[44] Donabedian presented another to help systematic analysis of the relationships between 'structure', 'process', and 'outcome' of clinical care.[45] Howie has produced a more recent model which brings these 'theories' together, placing 'values' and 'context' (of different styles of consulting behaviour) between 'content' and 'outcome'.[46] General-practitioner researchers have been aware for some time of the value of drawing from social-science theory. Crombie's earliest work drew on anthropological interests. Since then, Armstrong and Helman have made significant contributions from similar multidisciplinary perspectives.[47]

The corollary to the importance of a theoretical approach to research is to apply rigour to planning, carrying out, and interpreting the research. If general-practice research has tended to be atheoretical, so also has the work sometimes seemed to lack rigour. Numerator data have often been subjective rather than objective, denominators have been imprecisely described, and correlations and associations within data sets have been analysed too simplistically. However, the problem of the sufficiency of 'rigour' should lessen as the general standard of research improves and as journals become more selective in what they publish.

The results of the 1996 Research Assessment Exercise (RAE) have been published.[48] 'General-practice' research fell within the area of 'community-based clinical subjects'. Ratings were based on assessments of the quality of submitted output (mainly peer-reviewed research reports) and on judgements about the 'strength of the research environment' which were formed from reading the research plans of the institutions against the background of the number and proportion of staff declared to be 'research active'. Comparisons with the 1992 RAE ratings are complicated by the fact that a number of institutions were new entrants in 1996, and others either did not declare 'general practice' as an identifiable component, or created a new grouping (such as 'health-services research') which encompassed their general-practice researchers.

[44] N. C. H. Stott and R. H. Davis, 'The Exceptional Potential in Each Primary Care Consultation', *Journal of the Royal College of General Practitioners*, 29 (1979), 201–5.

[45] A. Donabedian, *A Guide to Medical Care Administration, ii. Medical Care Appraisal Quality and Utilization* (New York, 1969).

[46] J. G. R. Howie, 'Addressing the Credibility Gap in General Practice Research: Better Theory; More Feeling; Less Strategy', *British Journal of General Practice*, 46 (Aug. 1996), 479–81.

[47] D. Armstrong, *An Outline of Sociology as Applied to Medicine* (Bristol, 1980); C. Helman, *Culture, Health and Illness* (Bristol, 1984).

[48] The Higher Education Funding Councils (HEFCs), *1996 Research Assessment Exercise: The Outcome* (Bristol: *Higher Education Funding Council for England*, Dec. 1996).

Some general observations can, however, be made. First, even the larger general-practice-research groups are small alongside the major research teams of longer-established research disciplines. Secondly, it requires at least a decade to build a cohesive programme of theoretically based research. Thirdly, in a department with low critical mass, it takes only a short time to lose the momentum of a strong team if key members move elsewhere. Finally, higher ratings were generally given to groups with a portfolio of research which was developing or based on theory and likely to produce results which would be generalized, rather than to groups carrying out studies with a primarily local 'health-service-research' application.

Summary

Over the fifty years since 1948, research 'in' and 'about' general practice has increased in volume (from virtually nothing), and also in scope and in quality. This chapter has reviewed the substantial changes which have taken place from the perspectives of different individual, institutional, and professional groupings. It has finally tried to reconstruct what has taken place, identifying two themes which have seemed to recur and be of more importance throughout the period.

The many different groups which are interested in general practice or primary-care research share a policy commitment to increasing the understanding of the nature of general-practice care and improving its delivery. Not surprisingly, the strategies which different groups have evolved to achieve the same ends have rarely pointed in the same direction at the same time. Thus progress has sometimes seemed slow. It appears that two sets of issues have been and still are more important than others. The first is a cluster relating to matters about the 'workforce'—culture, infrastructure, and training. The second cluster is about the nature of the research undertaken and can be summarized as issues of 'quality'—the theoretical underpinning of the work, its cohesiveness, and its rigour.

The NHS has intentions to address the 'workforce' issues; HEFC (university) priorities are to promote 'quality' by committing resources more narrowly rather than more widely. There is a risk that the evolution of research in general practice may be endangered if a choice has to be made between increasing the capacity and capability of the workforce, on the one hand, or increasing the quality of what the workforce does, on the other hand. The interpretation of history which this review presents is that both issues need to be addressed simultaneously: to do either without the other would be to risk losing the ground which has been so painstakingly gained over many years.

7

Undergraduate Medical Education and General Practice

DAVID HANNAY

At the beginning of the eighteenth century there were broadly three groups of people providing medical care in the UK. These were physicians, whose distinguishing mark was the possession of a university degree in medicine (usually an MD). They saw themselves as a learned profession, and as such they never dispensed medicines (which had the mark of a trade) or undertook manual activities of a surgical kind. Then there were the surgeons, who were essentially craftsmen. And finally there were apothecaries, whose main activity was dispensing medicines from prescriptions written by physicians, but who were, from about 1700, beginning to go out to visit and treat the sick in their own homes and thus to resemble in many ways the general practitioner of the future.

The two most striking changes in medical practice during the eighteenth century, both dating from about the 1740s, were these. With the growth of the voluntary hospitals, the power and status of surgeons rose until, by 1800, they were in their own words 'On a par with the physicians', and able to found their own college, the Royal College of Surgeons in London. The other was the transformation of the apothecary into the surgeon–apothecary—or, to give him his full title, the 'surgeon–apothecary and man-midwife'. As that title suggests, and as they announced with pride, they were the only practitioners who could deal with all the medical occasions that might arise in their area, because they practised physic, surgery, pharmacy, and midwifery.

In all but name, the surgeon–apothecaries were the general practitioners, and medical registers published in the late eighteenth century showed that they far outstripped in number the physicians, the 'pure surgeons' (who limited their activities largely to surgical cases and had a hospital appointment), and the old-fashioned pure apothecaries who still existed in small numbers in cities such as London.

The main component of education for the surgeon–apothecaries was apprenticeship, but increasingly towards the end of the eighteenth century they attended courses on various subjects at the voluntary hospitals and at private medical schools. For the finest medical education in Britain, they went to Scotland, especially Edinburgh and Glasgow.

The term 'general practitioner' begins to appear around 1810, and was widely recognized by the 1820s. In 1815 the Apothecaries Act was introduced. By law, all surgeon–apothecaries/general practitioners had to take the examination and acquire the Licence of the Society of Apothecaries (LSA). Candidates were required to show that they had served an apprenticeship, and attended a year of formal teaching at hospitals. They also had to sit a written examination, and were the first members of any profession to have to do so. Later the apprenticeship died out, but the time allocated to hospital training increased.

This was the state of medical education by the time the Medical Act of 1858 was introduced. It was an Act whose primary purpose was to set up a Council to monitor standards of medical education, and not only, as sometimes imagined, to monitor the ethical behaviour of qualified doctors and strike the sinners off the medical register.

From 1858 it was possible for the first time to draw a clear and unequivocal line between the qualified and *registered* medical practitioner, and the unqualified quack. Incidentally, from the time of the Apothecaries Act in 1815, it was the habit of future general practitioners (but it was *not* a legal requirement) to take the Membership of the Royal College of Surgeons (MRCS). Almost every general practitioner between 1815 and the 1850s did so, mainly because there was more kudos attached to a surgical qualification. Indeed, many referred to themselves as 'surgeons' or 'surgeon–general practitioners'. The dual qualification, MRCS LSA, was the hallmark of the general practitioner, and it was known colloquially as the 'College and Hall'. Thus, by the latter half of the nineteenth century, general practitioners had emerged as a distinct group, derived from an amalgamation of the surgeons and apothecaries. Although the general-practitioner surgeon was quite distinct from the pure surgeon with a hospital appointment, much of surgery (especially in the provinces) was done by general practitioners, which is why we still use the term 'a doctor's surgery'.

The three principles of general practice that have evolved since the eighteenth century are as follows:

1. *non-specialization*: general practitioners saw themselves as generalists; they built up a practice of patients and later became known as 'family doctors';
2. *referral to secondary care*: general practitioners gradually became 'gate-keepers', with the responsibility of referring patients to hospitals for specialist care;
3. *list of registered patients*: general practitioners acquired a list of patients and were paid capitation fees.

The first principle dates from around the 1740s, when apothecaries became surgeon–apothecaries and were recognized as generalists who could practise medicine, surgery, pharmacy, and midwifery. Thus the 'surgeon–apothecary and man-midwife' was the direct precursor of today's general practitioner or family doctor.

The second principle—the gatekeeper role—was introduced in the late nineteenth century but only gradually accepted (see Chapter 4). The gate-keeper function originated from the time when general practitioners found themselves competing with the outpatient departments of charitable hospitals established in the growing industrial cities of Britain. If patients could be seen free of charge in a hospital outpatient department, however crowded, then they were less likely to pay fees to see a general practitioner. Through the gradual acceptance of the principle of referral, the general practitioners kept their patients, while the specialists retained all hospital privileges and also totally dominated medical education.

The third principle of general practice—namely, the registration of patients with a particular general practitioner, who is responsible for providing medical care and is paid for each patient by a capitation fee—began with the Lloyd George National Insurance Act of 1911 (which was introduced in July 1912, but the medical benefit part was implemented only in January 1913). This Act allowed working people below a certain level of income (and it included working women as well as men) to obtain free medical care by applying to one of the 'panel' (or list) of general practitioners who agreed to accept NHI patients: hence the terms 'panel doctors' and 'panel patients'. NHI was a health-care system modelled on a German scheme of health insurance for workers. As such it excluded non-working women and children and the retired, who had to pay for care from a general practitioner.

As far as general practice was concerned, the introduction of the NHS was essentially an extension of the NHI system to the whole of the population in 1948. At that time, general practitioners were mainly single-handed, with few staff, and comparatively large lists of patients in order to maintain their income, almost all of which was paid by capitation fees.

University departments of general practice

There was little or no formal teaching of general practice in most medical schools at the start of the NHS. Those who went into general practice were considered to be less able or to have fallen off the specialist ladder. Some form of attachment scheme was the earliest method of teaching, as in Edinburgh, where Richard Scott was appointed in 1948, and at St Mary's, where, in addition, six annual lectures on general practice had been given since 1935.[1] During the 1950s several medical schools made arrangements for attachments, but in only three was the attachment compulsory and for two of

[1] G. O. Barber, 'Education in General Practice', *British Medical Journal* (1952), ii. 490–1.

these the attachment was for one day only.[2] Subsequent surveys showed an increasing number of attachment schemes and elective periods during the 1960s, usually optional, with occasional lectures or with general practitioners involved in topic teaching.[3] Pressure for change often came from medical students;[4] for instance, in Glasgow the request for general-practice teaching was made by final-year students three years before there was a department of general practice.[5]

The first Chair of General Practice was established in Edinburgh in 1963, by which time only eight medical schools offered all medical students some experience of general practice.[6] In 1967 the GMC recommended that all medical schools should have 'growing points' for general-practice teaching.[7] This was supported by the undergraduate education committee of the Royal College of General Practitioners and by the Todd Report in 1968,[8] which suggested that general practitioners involved in teaching undergraduates should be offered senior academic appointments. These developments reflected the renaissance of general practice with the Family Doctor Charter in 1966. In 1972 there were eleven departments of general practice with six chairs, and all students had some general-practice teaching in twenty-two schools.[9] By 1986 all medical schools in the UK had departments of general practice, of which eighteen had chairs, and all students were being taught general practice.[10] Ten years later every medical school had established a chair of general practice (Table 7.1).

The early departments tended to be 'practice based', with the department responsible for running an NHS practice. There were five such departments, which were more generously funded with more staff than subsequent 'practice-linked' departments, where academic clinical staff worked in different service practices.

Some schools attempted to establish departments by engaging doctors who were partners in a practice on a sessional basis, but this created conflicts of

[2] G. O. Barber, 'The Teaching of General Practice by General Practitioners', *British Medical Journal* (1953), ii. 36–8.
[3] C. M. Harris, *General Practice Teaching of Undergraduates in British Medical Schools* (Reports from General Practice, No. XI: London: RCGP, 1969).
[4] H. G. Sturzaken and M. Hoskisson, *Report on Medical Education: Suggestions for the Future* (British Medical Students' Association, 1965).
[5] D. R. Hannay and J. R. Strang, 'Medical Students and General Practice', *Update* (1972), 899–903.
[6] P. S. Byrne, *University Departments of General Practice and the Undergraduate Teaching of General Practice in the United Kingdom in 1972*, Supplement No. 1, Vol. 23 (Royal College of General Practitioners, 1973).
[7] GMC, *Recommendations as to Basic Medical Education* (London: GMC, 1967).
[8] *Report of the Royal Commission on Medical Education* (Cmnd 3569 The Todd Report; London: HMSO 1968).
[9] Byrne, *University Departments*. See note 6.
[10] R. C. Fraser and M. E. Preston-Whyte, *The Contribution of Academic General Practice to Undergraduate Medical Education* (Occasional Paper No. 42, London: RCGP, 1988).

TABLE 7.1 *Development of university departments of general practice, 1968–1996*

	1968	1972	1988	1996
Number of undergraduate medical schools studied	27	29	25	29
Departments of general practice or equivalent	5	11	25	29
Chairs in general practice	1	6	18	28
All students taught in general practice	12	22	25	29

Sources: 1968: C. M. Harris, General Practice Teaching of Undergraduates in British Medical Schools (Reports from General Practice, No. XI; London: RCGP, 1969); 1972: P. S. Byrne, University Departments of General Practice and the Undergraduate Teaching of General Practice in the United Kingdom in 1972 (Supplement, No. 1, Vol. 23, Royal College of General Practitioners, 1973); 1988: R. C. Fraser and M. E. Preston-Whyte, The Contribution of Academic General Practice to Undergradute Medical Education (Occasional Paper No. 42; London: RCGP, 1988); 1996: D. R. Hannay and P. D. Campion, 'University Departments of General Practice: A Changing Scene', *British Journal of General Practice* (1996), 46, 35–6.

time and academic role.[11] The Association of University Teachers of General Practice was formed in 1974, and two years later had eighty members. This number more than doubled in the next ten years. In 1991 the name changed to the Association of University Departments of General Practice and the membership broadened, so that by 1994 there were 354 members, of whom 39 were professors, 146 full-time, and 179 part-time staff. This rapid increase had been partly due to additional funding for departments of general practice from Regional Health Authorities, and most departments had non-clinical members, reflecting the widening remit of teaching and research, especially in relation to behavioural science.

Although departments of general practice were eventually established in all medical schools, they were comparatively small in relation to the expanding demands of teaching and research. This was a reflection of two problems, the first being the historic split between the undergraduate and postgraduate sides of general practice, and the second being the lack of reasonably secure funding arrangements. There is no other clinical discipline with such an organizational divide between undergraduate university departments and postgraduate training.[12] In North America, for instance, the majority of family-medicine residences are run by university departments of general practice, which are also responsible for undergraduate teaching. The reasons for this contrast are both historical and political. When pressure was building up for vocational training

[11] J. G. R. Howie, D. R. Hannay, and J. S. K. Stevenson, *General Practice in the Medical Schools of the United Kingdom* (The Mackenzie Report; Edinburgh, 1986).
[12] D. R. Hannay, 'Undergraduate and Postgraduate Medical Education: Bridging the Divide', *British Journal of General Practice* (1994), 44, 487–8.

in the 1950s and 1960s, it was easier to achieve this on the education budget in North America and on the health-service budget in the UK. This was partly because in North America it was felt that fees attracted by family doctors would help to pay for university departments involved in postgraduate training, whereas in the UK a separate postgraduate organization had been set up with health-service funding, and, when pressure mounted for undergraduate teaching in general practice following the Todd Report,[13] small university departments were established, depending upon local circumstances. Each was the result of bargains struck by 'founding fathers' with relevant university and health-service support. By and large universities got their departments of general practice cheaply on the back of service agreements. There were no proper funding arrangements, such as those available to other clinical disciplines from Service Increments for Teaching (SIFT) payments. At the same time, postgraduate advisers and course organizers were developing vocational training with little formal contact with undergraduate teaching or research. Much was achieved from these shaky foundations, but more appropriate funding was required in view of the proposed shift of medical education to the community.[14] There was also a growing recognition of the need to bring the undergraduate and postgraduate sides together, which had so far only been achieved in one centre by the formation of a Centre for General Practice at Dundee.[15]

Most departments emerged from under the umbrella of Social or Public Health Medicine. This is still the most likely combination in medical schools where there is no autonomous department of general practice, as indicated in Table 7.2. This shows the results of a survey of all thirty-two heads of department, both undergraduate and postgraduate, in the UK and Eire.[16] Autonomous departments were defined as those for which the head of department was directly answerable to the dean and medical faculty, with responsibility for departmental budgets and staff. However, the concept of autonomous departments is now becoming problematic with the move towards larger groupings in medical schools for multidisciplinary collaboration in teaching and research, driven by the research and teaching assessment exercises.

Perhaps the optimum solution would be Institutes of General Practice and Primary Care which combined the undergraduate and postgraduate sides of general practice, as part of larger groupings which recognized the multidisciplinary nature of primary care.

---

[13] Report of the Royal Commission on Medical Education (The Todd Report). See note 8.

[14] GMC, Tomorrow's Doctors—Recommendations on Undergraduate Medical Education (London: GMC, 1993).

[15] J. Bain, R. Scott, and D. Snadden, 'Integrating Undergraduate and Postgraduate Education in General Practice: Experience in Tayside', British Medical Journal (1995), 310, 1577–9.

[16] D. R. Hannay and P. D. Campion, 'University Departments of General Practice: A Changing Scene', British Journal of General Practice (1996), 46, 35–6.

TABLE 7.2 *Arrangement of thirty-two departments of general practice in 1995*

Autonomous	13
Autonomous but:	
in larger groupings for research	3
within school of health sciences	3
within department of medicine	2
within school of clinical medicine	1
Combined with public-health medicine	4
Part of postgraduate medical school	2
Integrated undergraduate postgraduate department	1
Part of division with public health, child health, and psychiatry	1
Unit in department of clinical pharmacology and therapeutics	1
Unit in institute of public health	1

Source: D. R. Hannay and P. D. Campion, 'University Departments of General Practice: A Changing Scene', *British Journal of General Practice* (1996), 46, 35–6.

Concepts and methods

General practice is the largest branch of the medical profession, but practising a craft and being a profession is not the same as a scientific discipline, which implies the development of a unique body of knowledge that is recognized as such and which can be researched and taught. Pereira Gray considered that general practice emerged as a discipline in its own right only during the 1960s,[17] and it was during this time that it began to make an impact on medical schools. Richardson argued that the criteria for a university medical discipline were in four areas. First, the subject should encompass a substantial and distinct area of clinical practice; secondly, there should be distinctive skills and techniques of problem management; thirdly, there should be a recognizable philosophy, as exemplified by the focus on the whole person rather than the disease entity; and, finally, there should be active research involving critical analysis and experimental thinking.[18]

Given that these could be amply demonstrated by general practice, then the discipline had an important contribution to make to medical schools as a whole. These contributions included the teaching of common illnesses which are not seen in hospital, and the positive philosophy of caring for patients in the community, which implies an understanding of epidemiology and the natural history of disease, in the context of the whole patient and his or her

[17] D. Pereira Gray, 'The Emergence of the Disciplines of General Practice, its Literature, and the Contribution of the College Journal: McConaghey Memorial Lecture 1988', *Journal of the Royal College of General Practitioners* (1989), 39, 228–33.
[18] I. M. Richardson, 'The Value of a University Department of General Practice', *British Medical Journal* (1975), iv. 740–2.

family.[19] The role of general practice in a medical school has been conceptualized to include the following:

1. emphasizing person-orientation and communication skills,
2. providing general-practitioner role models;
3. anchoring theory to patients and the community;
4. teaching specific skills of general practice;
5. presenting an appropriate vehicle for a problem-solving curriculum;
6. building bridges between future general practitioners and specialists;
7. exposing students to primary care.[20]

Another way of looking at the role of general practice in a medical school is to see it as performing an integrating function to re-create the teaching of general medicine as a whole discipline. The issue is one of education as well as training—the latter being about specific tasks whereas the former concerns the development of intellectual and moral capacities to cope with the unknown.[21] The integrating function of general practice was highlighted by an analysis of the educational objectives for a basic medical education, as identified by the GMC in 1980. It was considered that at least sixteen of these objectives could not be achieved at any reasonable level without using the resources of general practice.[22] The overall objective of undergraduate education is to produce basic doctors able to assume the responsibilities of a pre-registration house officer. Undergraduate teaching is not, therefore, primarily vocational, and exposure to general practice is as important for those who are not going to be general practitioners as for those who are.

Over the last fifty years there has been growing concern about the inappropriate factual overload in medical education based on traditional specialities.[23] These concerns were endorsed by the GMC in *Tomorrow's Doctors*, which recommended a reduction in the amount of factual information, more active learning, an emphasis on attitudes and communication skills, an integrated core curriculum with special study modules, and more community-based teaching.[24] Clearly general practice was in a key position to provide this kind of teaching, and representatives from university departments have been involved in planning revised curricula in the light of these recommendations, which imply a considerable increase in teaching in the context of general practice.[25] One

[19] Byrne, *University Departments*. See note 6.
[20] B. K. E. Hennen, *General Practice in the Newcastle Undergraduate Curriculum* (University of Newcastle, New South Wales, 1982).
[21] M. Marinker, 'Changing Patterns in General Practice Education', in G. Teeling Smith (ed.), *Health Education in General Practice* (London: Office of Health Economics, 1985).
[22] J. Wright, *Undergraduate Medical Education in General Practice* (Report of Working Group of the Association of Teachers in General Practice; 1984).
[23] A. Towle, *Critical Thinking: The Future of Undergraduate Medical Education* (London: King's Fund Centre, 1991).
[24] GMC, *Tomorrow's Doctors—Recommendations on Undergraduate Medical Education*. See note 4.
[25] R. Jones and C. Drinkwater, *Primary Care Departments and the New Curriculum* (Newcastle upon Tyne: Department of Primary Health Care, 1992).

medical school has started an experimental community-based clinical course in which students spend most of the time in general practice, with clearly defined objectives and key conditions.[26]

Such teaching brings its own perspectives—for instance, on clinical problem-solving, which differs in emphasis from the inductive reasoning of hospital specialists. This is not appropriate in much of primary care, where the most likely solutions have to be considered and tested by hypothetico-deductive reasoning.[27] Other special considerations in general practice are the use of time, the effect of prevalence on the predictive value of tests, and the psychological and social contexts of symptoms and signs in terms of the life situations of patients and their families. These considerations bring a fresh perspective to clinical medicine, which complements traditional experience in hospital specialities where only a minority of clinical contacts take place.

General practice has also developed its own methods of teaching such as computer-assisted learning,[28] the use of role playing and simulated patients,[29] and audio and videotape recordings,[30] especially for communication skills.[31] Teaching in general practice usually involves one-to-one attachments to a general practitioner tutor, with an emphasis on written course material with clear objectives. Course booklets have ranged from mini-textbooks of general practice to increasingly briefer outlines, as more literature and references have become available. Log diaries and recording booklets have also been developed as a means of guiding experience and as a basis for small group tutorials.[32]

These approaches have lent themselves to the overall educational philosophy and methods originating from McMaster,[33] with its emphasis on self-directed problem-based learning in small groups. Such methods are particularly appropriate for general practice, which has meant that the discipline has often been in the forefront of innovations and changing attitudes towards undergraduate medical education.[34]

[26] N. Oswald et al., 'Long-Term Community-Based Attachments: The Cambridge Course', Medical Education (1995), 29, 72–6.

[27] H. S. Barrows and P. J. Feltovich, 'The Clinical Reasoning Process', Medical Education (1987), 21, 86–91; E. J. M. Campbell, 'The Diagnosing Mind', Lancet (1987), i. 849–51.

[28] T. S. Murray et al., 'Computer-Assisted Learning in Undergraduate Medical Teaching', Lancet (1976), i. 474–6.

[29] D. R. Hannay, 'Teaching Interviewing with Simulated Patients', Medical Education (1980), 14, 246–8.

[30] B. R. McAvoy, 'Teaching Clinical Skills to Medical Students: The Use of Simulated Patients and Videotaping in General Practice', Medical Education (1988), 22, 193–9.

[31] D. R. Hannay, 'Teaching Interviewing with Videotape and Peer Assessment', Update (June 1980), 1439–46.

[32] T. S. Murray, J. H. Barber, and D. R. Hannay, 'Introduction of Recording Booklets in General Practice Teaching', Medical Education (1977), 11, 192–6.

[33] D. R. Hannay, 'Educational Methods at McMaster University, Canada', Journal of the Royal College of General Practitioners (1980), 30, 430–2.

[34] T. Usherwood, 'Student-Directed Problem-Based Learning in General Practice and Public Health Medicine', Medical Education (1991), 25, 421–9.

Content

A recent survey of community-based teaching for medical undergraduates emphasized that general practice is only a part, although an important part of such teaching, which may be community oriented, agency based, general-practice based, or specialist.[35] Community-oriented teaching may be led by GP tutors, or by others such as epidemiologists or behavioural scientists. Agency-based teaching might involve the social services or voluntary agencies. General-practice-based teaching may be using practice patients as a resource for teaching clinical skills, or may focus on the discipline of general practice. Specialist teaching implies teaching clinical specialities such as paediatrics and psychiatry outside rather than traditionally within hospitals. Whether organized by departments of general practice or not, the location of much of this teaching will be in a general-practice setting.

The general-practice components of such community-based teaching for undergraduates have been identified as four main models.[36] First, early clinical contact in the preclinical years; secondly, teaching clinical skills in the context of general practice; thirdly, practice attachments for clinical students; and, fourthly, electives in general practice. To these could be added a fifth—namely, specialist teaching in this setting by other disciplines. Departments of general practice in most medical schools would typically now have an input into both the preclinical and clinical years, although the distinction between these two parts of the curriculum is being eroded by more integrated teaching, of which general practice is a part.[37]

Early clinical contact helps to integrate basic sciences with an experience of patients. Broadly, it either involves interviewing members of the public who may or may not be ill, or it takes the form of a family attachment where students follow a family member who is expecting a baby or has a chronic or life-threatening illness. The aim of these attachments is to give students practical experience of such things as family dynamics and illness behaviour. The interviews may be part of a course on communication skills or doctor–patient relationships.[38] Family attachments may involve following up patients who have been discharged from hospital or may focus on the behavioural aspects of family interactions with the arrival of a new baby.[39] Many of these early clin-

[35] P. McCrory, F. Lefford, and F. Perrin, *Medical Undergraduate Community-Based Teaching: A Survey for ASME on Current and Proposed Teaching in the Community and in General Practice in UK Universities* (Association for the Study of Medical Education, occasional publication No. 3; Dundee, 1991).

[36] R. Higgs and R. Jones, 'The Impacts of Increased General Practice Teaching in the Undergraduate Medical Curriculum', *Education for General Practice* (1995), 6, 218–25.

[37] G. C. Metcalfe *et al.*, 'Teaching Primary Medical Care in Southampton: The First Decade', *Lancet* (1983), i. 697–9; R. C. Fraser and B. R. McAvoy, 'Teaching Medical Students at Leicester: The General Practice Approach', *Medical Teacher* (1988), 10/2, 209–17.

[38] D. Armstrong *et al.*, 'Teaching Communication Skills to Preclinical Medical Students: A General Practice Based Approach', *Medical Education* (1979), 13, 82–5.

[39] N. J. Fox, J. Joesbury, and D. R. Hannay, 'Family Attachments and Medical Sociology: A Valuable Partnership for Learning', *Medical Education* (1991), 25, 155–9.

ical contacts are part of multidisciplinary courses which have been developed for first- and second-year medical students. Examples would be the Health and Society course in Sheffield (Behavioural science, Evidence-based medicine, Ethics); Human Development, Behaviour, and Ageing in Newcastle (Community medicine, Child health, Psychiatry); Foundations of Community Clinical Practice in Aberdeen (Interpersonal skills, Ethics, Problem solving, Population medicine); and Man and Society in Leicester (Provision and delivery of care, Health and disease in populations, Health, illness and the individual).[40] Such courses are continually evolving, but depend crucially on the input of general practitioners from university departments.

Clinical skills are increasingly being taught in the context of general practice, partly because that is where most clinical contacts take place and partly because of the high turnover of specialized hospital beds. Initially the focus may have been on teaching communication skills, often in the context of an introductory clinical course,[41] or it may have been on the presentation of problems in primary care.[42] However, there are now medical firms based in the community, as at King's College Medical School, with an emphasis on skills development, with assessment and feedback.[43] At Cambridge there is an experimental course where most of the clinical years are spent in general practice.[44]

Practice attachments for fourth- and fifth-year students have been the core of general-practice teaching. These are traditional apprenticeship arrangements based on a one-to-one attachment with opportunities for students to sit in with a general practitioner, go on house calls, see patients on their own, and gain experience of the organization of general practice and the roles of other members of the primary-health-care team. Many involve attachments to more than one practice to give experience of different settings such as inner-city and semi-rural practice. Most are problem-based and student-centred with an emphasis on learning from experience and reflective practice. Course books have become increasingly sophisticated, with educational objectives, often supplemented by small-group tutorials and self-directed learning tasks, such as assignments, projects, log books, and diaries. Table 7.3 shows the content areas for the final-year module in general practice at Sheffield. These content areas are the basis for small-group tutorials based on self-directed learning, with student presentations backed up by resource material.

[40] Fraser and McAvoy, 'Teaching Medical Students at Leicester'. See note 37.

[41] W. G. Irwin and J. S. Perrott, 'Systematic Use of Closed-Circuit Television in a General Practice Teaching Unit', *Journal of the Royal College of General Practitioners* (1981), 31, 557–60; H. E. Joesbury, N. D. S. Bax, and D. R. Hannay, 'Communication Skills and Clinical Methods: A New Introductory Course', *Medical Education* (1990), 24, 433–7.

[42] T. S. Murray, J. H. Barber, and D. R. Hannay, 'Using the First Consultation in Acute Illness for Teaching Third Year Medical Students', *Journal of the Royal College of General Practitioners* (1976), 26, 687–90.

[43] M. Seabrook, P. Booton, and T. Evans, *Widening the Horizons of Medical Education: Innovation in Medical Education Project* (London: King's Fund, 1994).

[44] Oswald, 'The Cambridge Course'. See note 26.

TABLE 7.3 *Content areas of general practice* (for self-directed learning in small groups)

A	Characteristics of General Practice
B	Primary-Care Team
C	Clinical Method
D	Anticipatory Care
E	Referral
F	Common Problems
G	Prescribing
H	Medical Records
I	Terminal Care
J	Counselling
K	Ethics
L	Comparative Primary Care
M	Alternative Medicine
N	Sexual Issues

Electives in general practice, usually for final-year students, have been available for many years and usually involve a residential attachment for up to four weeks, living either in a general practitioner's home or in local hospital accommodation. This is an optional opportunity to gain experience at first-hand without the pressures of assignments or assessments, although most medical schools require some report from students. Electives help to place undergraduate teaching in perspective and may provide valuable pointers to future career decisions.

Specialist teaching in the community mainly involves the specialities of paediatrics, psychiatry, and obstetrics, which increasingly require the context of general practice because of the shift of patient care from hospitals to the community outside. Thus, teaching paediatrics may aim to demonstrate the early presentation and variety of childhood ailments, and the effects of chronic illness or handicap on a family.[45] Teaching may also involve more than one speciality and provide horizontal integration for related clinical subjects such as community medicine, general practice, geriatric medicine, and mental health.[46] Community-based research projects drawing on the skills of public-health medicine are also a form of specialist teaching within general practice, and, like the preclinical and clinical courses mentioned above, require extensive collaboration by university departments of general practice.

It is important for the discipline to be clear about its own educational objec-

[45] T. S. Murray *et al.*, 'Medical Undergraduate Teaching of Paediatrics in the Community', *Medical Education* (1977), 11, 129–32.
[46] R. W. Stout and W. G. Irwin, 'Integrated Medical Student Teaching', *Medical Education* (1982), 16, 143–6.

tives, because the potential breadth of teaching could overwhelm university departments, with comparatively small numbers of academic staff trying to cope with increasing demands for community-based experience. Educational objectives help, rather than hinder, collaborative teaching, and also clarify those topics which are not specific to general practice such as 'ethics' and 'palliative care', but have been omitted from elsewhere in the curriculum. These have tended to be taken up by departments of general practice, which as a result have sometimes been viewed as either the 'dustbin' or the 'conscience' of a medical school.

Assessment

The requirements for a registrable qualification were defined in terms of proficiency in medicine, surgery, and obstetrics, until the Medical Act of 1978, which broadened the definition to what was sufficient 'to undertake safely pre-registration appointments'. Not only was factual knowledge required, but also the understanding of principles, the ability to think logically, to express clearly, and to be clinically competent. The contribution of general practice towards basic medical education was fundamental,[47] but assessment tended to be incorporated in other disciplines. A survey in 1988 identified four departments involved with formal assessments in the preclinical years (mainly in the form of essays as part of integrated examinations), of which only two were university degree examinations with an external examiner; in the clinical years twelve departments had formal assessments in the fourth year, of which four were part of the final MB; and thirteen departments had formal assessments in the fifth year, of which six were part of the final MB.[48] A survey of twenty-one medical schools in 1996 found that in only six were general practitioners making significant contributions as examiners to the final examinations.[49]

Although the distinctive contribution of general practice has often not been reflected in final examinations, the teaching has been assessed in a variety of ways, both formative and summative. Written examinations have included Modified Essay Questions and Multiple Choice Questions, as well as traditional essays and short notes. In addition, recording booklets,[50] profiles of student projects,[51] and computer-assisted learning[52] have been developed, as

[47] Wright, *Undergraduate Medical Education*. See note 22.

[48] Fraser and Preston-Whyte, *The Contribution of Academic General Practice*. See note 10.

[49] J. Bain, personal communication (1996).

[50] T. S. Murray, J. H. Barber, and D. R. Hannay, 'Use of Recording Booklets to Evaluate Teaching in General Practice', *Medical Education* (1979), 13, 359–62.

[51] T. Usherwood and D. R. Hannay, 'Profile-based Assessment of Student Project Reports', *Medical Teacher* (1992), 14, 2/3, 189–96.

[52] T. S. Murray, J. H. Barber, and D. R. Hannay, 'Computer-Assisted Learning as a Means of Self-Assessment', *Update* (Sept. 1976), 532–4.

well as a number of ways of assessing communication skills.[53] These latter assessments emphasize specific competencies as well as formative feedback.[54] There has been a shift from norm-referenced written examinations (in which ranking depends on the distribution of marks of other candidates) to the criterion-referenced assessment of competence (in which ranking depends on achieving specified criteria). One method developed for assessing competencies is the Objective Structured Clinical Examination, in which students pass through a number of stations at which specific tasks are performed and marked.[55]

Two examples from departments of general practice illustrate the range of assessments being used in the clinical years. Both courses lasted for five weeks full time, one for fourth-year students and the other for fifth-year students. Both depended on students being attached on an individual basis to practices, with teaching for one day a week in the department. In the fourth-year course there were formative assessments (assessment with feedback to facilitate learning) by clinical teachers, and a summative assessment (assessment to ascertain achievement of learning objectives) which was part of the final examination. The formative assessments with feedback were made at the midpoint and end of the attachments in the following areas: interviewing/history-taking; physical examination; problem solving/patient management; behaviour/relationship with patients; anticipatory care. The summative assessment consisted of a two-hour written paper on patient management problems and a half-hour problem-solving oral with two examiners. Both parts comprised 50 per cent of the marks, with practice reports and group project work taken into account for borderline candidates.[56]

The assessment for the fifth-year course in another school was also part of the final examination, but depended on continuous assessment during the five weeks. This exempted the student from a formal written examination equivalent to those in medicine and surgery. Exemption is based on five assessments, which included two written assignments, one a medical audit project and the other a description of a critical incident, both arising from the practice attachments. The other three assessments were of clinical competence in the practice, of contributions to small group work, and of interviewing skills. The course depended on the principles of self-directed, experience-based learning, with explicit assessment criteria. Clinical competence was defined in terms of history-taking, physical examination, explanation to patients, management plans, and writing prescriptions and referral letters, together with the assess-

[53] R. C. Fraser, R. K. McKinley, and H. Mulholland, 'Consultation Competence in General Practice: Establishing the Validity of Prioritised Criteria in the Leicester Assessment Package', *British Journal of General Practice* (1994), 44, 109–13.

[54] M. Challis, T. Usherwood, and H. Joesbury, 'Assessing Specified Competencies in Medical Undergraduate Training', *Competence and Assessment* (1993), 22, 6–9.

[55] R. M. Harden and F. A. Gleeson, 'Assessment of Clinical Competence Using an Objective Structure Clinical Examination (OSCE)', *Medical Education* (1979), 13, 41–54.

[56] Fraser and McEvoy. 'Teaching Medical Students at Leicester'. See note 37.

ment and management of common presenting complaints. Small-group work was assessed by general-practitioner tutors acting as facilitators rather than experts, with students presenting topics themselves and so taking responsibility for their own and the group's learning (see Table 7.3). Communication skills were assessed by audiotape feedback of consultations with patients in the practice, again with specified performance criteria. Continuous assessment in this way was not an easy option, being time-consuming for all concerned, but students found it rewarding, and only a few failed to pass at the time and have to sit the written exemption examination.[57]

Role of service general practitioners

From the earliest voluntary attachments and electives to the present courses which are formal parts of the curriculum, the role of service general practitioners has been crucial. At a time when university departments were vestigial or non-existent, general practitioners were introducing students to the practice of medicine outside hospitals, where half of them would eventually work and where the great majority of patient contacts took place. This was done on the basis of goodwill or token payments, which increasingly failed to compensate for the time required when general-practice teaching became a compulsory part of the curriculum. A variety of *ad hoc* arrangements were made by medical schools, but there was no overall mechanism for compensating general practitioners for taking students, as there was in teaching hospitals. These received considerable sums from the National Health Service via SIFT in England and Wales, or ACT, the equivalent in Scotland, which were intended to reflect the difference in costs between 'teaching' and 'district' hospitals.[58]

The 1990 contract for general practitioners attempted to redress this anomaly by incorporating sessional payments for undergraduate teaching as claims which could be made to the new FHSAs. However, at about £12 a session, this did not compensate for the increasing amount of time required of general practitioners for teaching, especially when they were under pressure from other aspects of the health-service reforms such as health promotion and fundholding. In 1996 these sessional payments were transferred to SIFT, although each health authority was left to decide its own level of payment for the new teaching contracts. A reasonable estimate for the excess costs of teaching students, based on target net remuneration and locum costs at that time, would be £100 a session if no patients were being seen, £50 if the consultation rate was reduced by half because of a student present, and £25 for minimal supervision while the doctor continued to see patients.

---

[57] Usherwood, 'Student-Directed Problem-Based Learning'. See note 34.
[58] Howie, Hannay, and Stevenson, *General Practice in the Medical Schools of the United Kingdom* (The Mackenzie Report). See note 11.

These estimates were a far cry from the original honoraria given to general practitioners and considerably more than the initial payments in the new contract. However, they did not take into account other members of the primary-care team who provided a valuable resource for attached medical students, nor the extra facilities required for students such as additional consulting rooms. The advent of teaching contracts implied more quality control of teaching, but at least there was a shift of resources from secondary to primary care, where medical education will increasingly take place. Already 4,000 or more students a year have placements in general practice,[59] where, often for the first time, students are in close contact on a one-to-one basis with an experienced doctor, who can pick up those problems of confidence and personality which are so important for the personal relationships of medical practice. Such individual contact may be impossible in teaching hospitals or elsewhere in the course, and it is appropriate that the vital contribution of general practitioners to undergraduate teaching is beginning to be recognized.

The future

We live in times of rapid change, some of it due to technical advances, such as information technology and cell biology, and some of it socio-political, such as the new public management where change is part of the culture. It is, therefore, important that medical education should prepare students not only to handle change but also to question it. Stability has its place—for instance, when children are growing up, students are qualifying, and doctor–patient relationships are developing. General practice is about continuing relationships for patients, but also increasingly for students with the shift towards community-based medical education. This may take a number of forms, such as community placements, outreach clinics, and primary-care centres, as well as general-practice attachments or student attachments to a patient or a family.[60] The teaching methods used will include planned or guided learning as well as opportunistic learning from clinical encounters.

In most of these developments, general practice will play a crucial part both as a locus for teaching and as access to patients. However, there is a need to be clearer about the different models and expectations of general practice as a discipline, which in turns depends upon an underlying philosophy or value system. Toon identified three main models influencing general practice— namely, a biomedical model based on scientific medicine, a humanist model concerned with human relationships such as the Balint movement, and a preventive or public-health model emphasizing anticipatory care.[61] To these were added two other concepts of general practice; first, general practice as a busi-

[59] Howie, Hannay, and Stevenson; Bain, personal communication. See notes 11 and 49.
[60] Seabrook, Booton, and Evans, *Widening the Horizons of Medical Education*. See note 43.
[61] P. Toon, *What is Good General Practice?* (Occasional Paper 65; London: RCGP, 1994).

ness with patients as customers, and, secondly, general practitioners as family doctors. All these models have underlying assumptions which influence how we define good general practice, and have implications for medical education.[62] For instance, a biomedical model implies an objective view of factual information which can be taught didactically and assessed through traditional examinations. A humanist model, on the other hand, would emphasize the subjective nature of experience, best expressed in small group teaching and assessed through projects and portfolios. An anticipatory care model might emphasize the acquisition of skills through training in practice attachments, with assessment of competencies. In short, the changing complexity of general practice in the modern world requires teasing out underlying assumptions, not only to make teaching and assessment more appropriate, but also to give students perspectives to make sense of their professional lives.

It is likely that present university departments of general practice, primarily concerned with undergraduate teaching, will become part of larger units for the purposes of collaboration in teaching and research.[63] It is also likely that the move to draw the undergraduate and postgraduate sides of general practice together will continue.[64] In many ways postgraduate training and continuing medical education in general practice have been in the forefront of educational methods in medicine, but there is a need for more coordination with undergraduate departments, especially as the same people are often involved with both. The other reason for drawing the two sides together is to provide a career structure for academic general practice,[65] with similar opportunities for research training as for hospital doctors, as well as to provide professional development in educational methods, management, and public health.[66] Centres or institutes of general practice, integrated in this way, would be in a strong position to build upon what has already been achieved and to lead undergraduate medical education into the twenty-first century.

[62] N. J. Mathers and S. Rowland, 'General Practice—a Post-Modern Speciality', *British Journal of General Practice*, 47 (1997), 177–9.

[63] Hannay and Campion, 'University Departments of General Practice'. See note 16.

[64] Bain, Scott, and Snadden, 'Integrating Undergraduate and Postgraduate Education.' See note 15.

[65] R. Fraser *et al.*, *A Career Structure for Academic General Practice* (Final Report of a Working Party of the Association of University Departments of General Practice, 1993).

[66] D. R. Hannay, 'Primary Care and Public Health', *British Medical Journal* (1993), 307, 516–17.

8

Postgraduate Training
and Continuing Education

DENIS PEREIRA GRAY

In this chapter 'postgraduate' is defined as the period in a doctor's career after graduation (qualification) and so includes the pre-registration year. Medical education is conventionally divided into four parts:

- Undergraduate education comprising the student years and culminating in qualification as a doctor (see Chapter 7).
- The pre-registration year (which was only introduced in 1952 after the Goodenough Report of 1944).[1] Doctors at this stage work under provisional registration with the GMC.
- Post-registration—i.e. fully registered doctors undertaking vocational training, ending in a qualification for independent practice.
- Continuing education for established doctors throughout their career in practice.

Education in General Practice after the Second World War

When the Second World War ended in 1945, general practice had to adjust not only to a new set of attitudes and expectations in society, but to an entirely new system of organization in the form of a new NHS. This was enacted in Parliament in 1946, and introduced on 5 July 1948. In the UK it was believed to be the leading health-care system in the world.

The general-practitioner service was built mainly around single-handed practitioners who were usually male and had no training for their job. They were not required to have done any postgraduate training. Although many had voluntarily done some hospital work, many had done none at all. They often had no nurse, no secretaries, and no receptionist with whom to work: health visitors and midwives were separate and virtually competitors. Many worked alone from their own homes or shops, often supported only by their wives.[2] Their work was almost entirely reactive. They waited for their patients

---

[1] Goodenough Committee, *Report of the Interdepartmental Committee on Medical Schools, Ministry of Health and Department of Health for Scotland* (London, 1944).

[2] S. Hadfield, 'The State of General Practice Today', *British Medical Journal* (1956), ii. 58; P. Bartrip, *Themselves Writ Large: The British Medical Association 1832–1966* (London, 1996).

to ask for advice and then they saw them quickly, virtually always the same day, in their surgeries or often in the patients' homes.

All postgraduate training, postgraduate examinations, and qualifications were exclusively the preserve of specialist organizations which were controlled by the then three medical Royal Colleges in England and three in Scotland (mainly for physicians or surgeons). General practice was not seen as a discipline. It failed all of McWhinney's four tests.[3] Crucially, it had no literature, no scientific journal, no chair in any university, and no academic organization. Thus it had no academic voice of its own. Essentially, the structure of the medical profession remained a hierarchy as it had been since the nineteenth century. This was illustrated by the professional qualifications in medicine: general practitioners occupied the lowest tier, licentiate (LRCP), the specialists the middle tier, membership (MRCP), and the leaders of the profession were usually fellows (FRCP).

The history of general-practice postgraduate education can be considered in three phases: from 1946 to 1961 the establishment of general practice as a discipline, from 1962 to 1981 the introduction of vocational training for general practice, and from 1983 to 1997 the development of continuing education for established principals.

These phases each lasted on average about seventeen years and in each there was a pattern of current educational provision and development which charted the future framework of practice and education.

The establishment of a discipline, 1946–1961

The major educational event during this period was the establishment of the College of General Practitioners in 1952. Such were the pressures on the visionary founders that this College had to be founded in secret and in the teeth of opposition from all three of the then existing medical Royal Colleges,[4] the Royal Society of Medicine, and professional leaders like Lord Horder.[5] The significance of the College was, first, that it provided a new mechanism through which interested general practitioners could communicate with each other, and, secondly, that it at once became and continued to be the voice for academic general practice. The crucial change in this period was the gradual acceptance of general medical practice as a discipline in its own right, as opposed

[3] I. R. McWhinney, 'General Practice as an Academic Discipline', *Lancet* (1966), i. 419.

[4] Sir R. Brain, Letter on behalf of the Presidents of the then three medical Royal Colleges to Dr John Hunt, 1951 (quoted in full in D. Pereira Gray (ed.), *Forty Years On: The Story of the First Forty Years of the Royal College of General Practitioners* (London, 1992), 28).

[5] J. Hunt, 'The Foundation of a College: James Mackenzie Lecture 1972', *Journal of the Royal College of General Practitioners*, 23 (1973), 5–31; J. Fry, J. Hunt, and R. J. F. H. Pinsent (eds.), *A History of the Royal College of General Practitioners: The First 25 Years* (Lancaster, 1983), 91; D. Pereira Gray, 'History of the Royal College of General Practitioners—the First 40 Years', *British Journal of General Practice*, 42 (1992), 29–35.

to being a field in which medicine from a number of other specialities was practised at a more superficial level.

This change took the whole of this period to achieve. The evidence was set out in the 1988 McConaghey Memorial Lecture.[6] It consisted of the establishment of an academic journal for general practice (and recognition of it as a general-practice journal for the first time by the National Library of Medicine in the USA through *Index Medicus*); the appearance of two clinical books in a single year on general practice written entirely by general practitioners;[7] and finally the more formal status given to the College of General Practitioners by the Board of Trade.[8] All these changes, which governed how general practitioners saw themselves, and later how others viewed them, occurred in 1961, which can therefore be taken as the historical point when general practice became a discipline.

Becoming a discipline was a necessary precursor for future educational developments. The characteristics of a discipline were defined in 1966 by McWhinney, probably the world's leading theorist in general practice, and the next phase in the development of general practice can be summarized by the systematic achievement of each of the four features he described: defining the field of practice, publishing a scientifically based body of knowledge, pursuing an active research programme, and offering a rigorous training programme.

The pre-registration year, which was introduced in 1952 following the recommendations of the Goodenough Committee (1944), provided a compulsory six months' experience in hospital in both medicine and surgery. It was, by definition, post-qualification training, but not yet full post-registration training. This reform did, however, help to break the rigid thinking associated with the concept of the 'safe doctor' which had dogged general practice since the 1880s. It was the first official step towards accepting that, as far as career general practitioners were concerned, the basic qualifications in medicine, such as the LRCP, MRCS, or MB B.Chir., were only a step to further training and were not an end in themselves.

At the start of the period, specific postgraduate education was minimal. When the original trainee scheme was introduced into general practice in 1948, trainees were called, significantly, trainee *assistants* (my italics) because the system was seen essentially as an apprenticeship. Selection of trainers lay in the hands of local medical committees, rather than academic or educational institutions, and there were no objective standards for appointment, no training in teaching methods, and no real monitoring. Systematic vocational

[6] D. Pereira Gray, 'The Emergence of the Discipline of General Practice, its Literature, and the Contribution of the College Journal: McConaghey Memorial Lecture 1988', *Journal of the Royal College of General Practitioners*, 39 (1989), 228–33.

[7] M. B. Clyne, *Night Calls—A Study in General Practice* (London, 1961); J. Fry, *The Catarrhal Child* (London, 1961).

[8] D. Pereira Gray, 'The Emergence of the Discipline'.

training did not exist, and many saw no need for it. Only when general practice was seen as a discipline in its own right did it become clear that there was a need for specific vocational training, and responsibility for this initiative fell almost entirely on the College of General Practitioners, which was nine years old in 1961.

The introduction of vocational training, 1962–1981

There were six stages in the development of vocational training for general practice in the form of requirements which had to be achieved. These were: first, to conceptualize the idea and to campaign for it; secondly, to establish working models; thirdly, to develop an assessment of its end point; fourthly, to define its content; fifthly, to establish new institutions which could implement and monitor it, backed by law, and, lastly, to enforce it.

The need for a formal period of training for those doctors who were planning a career in general practice was first identified by the BMA in the two Cohen BMA Reports.[9] However, there was no further significant action until after the College of General Practitioners was founded in 1952, when the new College faced an interesting problem in priorities. Undergraduate education in general practice was rare, ineffective, and ill organized; at the same time, there was no vocational training and arrangements for continuing education were unsatisfactory. Where should the College start?

It started by working on all three fronts. It surveyed undergraduate education, publishing a national survey in the *British Medical Journal*, and required a declaration of participation in continuing medical education in its application forms for membership.[10] By 1961, however, it decided that the main educational priority was to be the development of vocational training for general practice. This would not have been an easy decision, for there was only one national model to follow, the majority of the profession did not support the idea, the mechanisms had not been worked out, and it was bound to be expensive.[11]

Within a small College an even smaller number of people became involved in this new activity. Ekke Kuenssberg (Edinburgh), Annis Gillie and John Horder (London), George Swift (Winchester), John McKnight (Northern Ireland), Pat Byrne (Manchester), and Bill Hylton (Somerset) were the main leaders. The first three were strategic thinkers, two of whom later became Chairmen of the Council. John McKnight was an efficient organizer dissem-

---

[9] *The Training of a Doctor: Report of the Medical Curriculum Committee of the BMA* (The First Cohen BMA Report; London, 1948). *General Practice and the Training of the General Practitioner* (The Second Cohen BMA Report; London: BMA, 1950).

[10] College of General Practitioners, 'The Teaching of General Practice by General Practitioners', *British Medical Journal* (1953), ii. 36–8.

[11] J. P. Horder, 'The General Practitioner in Yugoslavia, Czechoslovakia and Israel: Special Vocational Training', *Lancet* (1965), ii. 123–5.

inating information from the College. Bill Hylton, Pat Byrne, and John Horder all in turn chaired the Education Committee, the latter two becoming Presidents of the College. A second wave of support from members came later and these included Donald Irvine (Northumberland), Marshall Marinker and Paul Freeling (London), Conrad Harris (Manchester), and John Stevens and Ian Tait (Aldeburgh).

The early mid-1960s was a critical time in medical politics and in the educational world (see Chapter 9). The original general-practitioner contract which had started with the NHS in 1948 had come to the end of its life. Doctors were paid simply on the basis of capitation fees, so all the incentives were to minimize costs. In particular, general practitioners with better than average premises paid all the costs themselves, as well as the whole of the salaries of any receptionists or nurses they employed. As late as the 1960s, their average professional expenses, recorded in practice accounts, were as low as £254 per year. A crisis arose and 18,000 general practitioners signed undated letters of resignation from the NHS. Peace was negotiated in 1965 through a new contract which was to last for fourteen years.

While the crisis over pay and expenses was being resolved, the educational crisis was worked out, with much less publicity but with longer lasting and far-reaching effects. Two unfavourable factors were operating against the College. The climate in the profession was not supportive, because many specialists considered that the age of generalism was over and that an era of specialism had arrived. This culminated in Sir Arthur Thompson's much quoted lecture 'Is General Practice Outmoded?'[12]

Meanwhile young doctors were simply voting with their feet. Emigration to the English-speaking countries, mainly in the Commonwealth, was dramatic. In the early 1960s as many as one in three of all new general practitioners left general practice in the UK. As they went, they often said: 'This is not the medicine for which we have been trained.' They were quite right, but it did not occur to them to blame the training instead of the job. So great were the difficulties that the government established a Royal Commission on Medical Education under the Chairmanship of Lord Todd. This gave the new College its first major chance to give evidence at national level about education for and in general practice. One member of the Royal Commission was a general practitioner, J. N. M. Parry from Wales, who was for some years a member of the College Council.

The recommendations of the General Medical Council, 1967

While the Royal Commission was deliberating, the GMC published one of its *Recommendations as to Basic Medical Education*.[13] Although somewhat overshadowed by the Royal Commission on Medical Education at the time, and in

---

[12] Sir Arthur Thompson, Royal Society of Health, 70th Health Congress, Eastbourne (1963).
[13] GMC, *Recommendations as to Basic Medical Education* (London, 1967).

subsequent analysis, this document was of historic importance and radical in its conclusions. It reviewed the role of the undergraduate curriculum in all British medical schools. It quietly but firmly concluded that the role of undergraduate education was to offer a broad set of principles and understanding of humankind and disease, in preparation for specific postgraduate education for all doctors in their chosen branch of medicine. This effectively downgraded the importance of the qualifying degree in medicine, setting it as an intermediate step rather than the end point of medical education. It was of critical importance that the GMC was making it clear that it expected postgraduate training programmes for general practice as well as in specialist practice. Lord Cohen, who had produced the BMA reports of 1948 and 1950, now delivered the principle as GMC policy. In doing so, the GMC confirmed the emergence of general practice as a discipline and gave a strong lead to the Royal Commission, which was deliberating at that time.

In 1967 the College of General Practitioners was awarded its Royal Charter, and became the fourth Royal Medical College in seniority in England after the Royal College of Physicians of London (founded in 1518), the Royal College of Surgeons of England (founded in 1800),[14] and the Royal College of Obstetricians and Gynaecologists (founded in 1929). The effect of the Royal Charter was to recognize and therefore to encourage the College at this critical time.

The report of the Royal Commission on Medical Education, 1968

The College prepared the case for vocational training, deploying its leading thinkers on the task. For the first time it started to publish its ideas under its own imprint, the first publication being *Special Vocational Training for General Practice.*[15] This was the first Report from General Practice from the College, and it initiated a series of College statements which have continued ever since, numbering twenty-seven by the end of 1996.

The next year the College published *Evidence of the College to the Royal Commission on Medical Education.*[16] The College was invited to attend for oral evidence and to answer questions. The subsequent interview lived for years in the minds of several Commissioners. The brunt of the challenge fell to Dr John Horder, who defended the idea of general practice as a discipline in its own right and hence the need for specific training in preparation for it. A historic watershed had arrived and a major question confronted the Royal Commission. Was general practice viable? This question represented a hidden agenda.

[14] The Royal College of Surgeons was first founded as the Royal College of Surgeons of London in 1800. It changed its name to the Royal College of Surgeons of England with its second charter in 1843.

[15] College of General Practitioners, *Special Vocational Training for General Practice: Report from General Practice No. 1* (1965).

[16] College of General Practitioners, *Evidence of the College to the Royal Commission on Medical Education: Report from General Practice No. 5* (London: HMSO, 1966).

If general practice was not viable, there was no point in designing elaborate and expensive plans for what was easily the largest branch of the medical profession. Specialist outreach systems or polyclinics might be an alternative. On the other hand, if general practice was viable, there were far-reaching implications for a training programme both for it and for other branches of medicine. This was a central issue for the Royal Commission, and it was against this background that the College's evidence suddenly became critical. Its proposals were clear and simple, but radical: 'such a service [general practice] can only survive if those who work in it have as rigorous a training, as satisfactory working conditions and as good opportunities as those who work in the specialist service.'[17]

In April 1968 the Royal Commission on Medical Education reported.[18] Its conclusion on general practice was virtually a complete endorsement of the evidence of the College of General Practitioners. General practice was accepted as a speciality, and the Royal Commission advised a formal post-graduate training programme of five years, broadly equivalent to speciality training. The case had been made satisfactorily and won in the most important arena of the time.

As the campaign continued, however, the next step was to obtain legislation and support from the government. The College published its sixth Report from General Practice, *The Implementation of Vocational Training*.[19] College activists continued to use eponymous lectures as a vehicle for getting its message across—notably in Irvine's William Pickles Lecture, in which he used the words 'general practice is no longer prepared to be the dustbin of medicine!'[20] General practice was systematically seeking to achieve systems of education after basic qualification analogous to specialist medicine.

The first working model of vocational training had come from the north of Scotland and was developed in Inverness in 1952.[21] There was an important early College publication entitled 'Memorandum for the Guidance of Train-ers' developed in the Midlands and published by the College.[22] The idea of a half-day release was imported from Yugoslavia and was developed in Canterbury in 1964.[23] In the decades 1965–85 vocational training schemes of

[17] College of General Practitioners, p. v.

[18] *Report of the Royal Commission on Medical Education*, Cmnd. 3569 (The Todd Report; London: HMSO, 1968).

[19] Royal College of General Practitioners, *The Implementation of Vocational Training: Report from General Practice No. 6* (London: HMSO, 1967).

[20] D. H. Irvine, 'The Quiet Revolution? William Pickles Lecture', *Journal of the Royal College of General Practitioners*, 25 (1975), 399–407.

[21] A. R. Adams *et al.*, 'A Postgraduate Training Scheme in Scotland', *British Medical Journal* (1954), ii. *suppl.*, pp. 71–2.

[22] College of General Practitioners, 'Memorandum for the Guidance of Trainers', *Journal of the College of General Practitioners*, 2/1 (1959), *suppl.*

[23] College of General Practitioners, 'A Prototype Training Course for General Practice', *Journal of the College of General Practitioners*, 9 (1965), 318–19; J. P. Horder and G. Swift, 'The History of Vocational Training for General Practice', *Journal of the Royal College of General Practitioners*, 29 (1979), 24–32.

many kinds developed all over the UK. Judged only by their publications, the better known and more influential arose in Ipswich,[24] Exeter,[25] the Midlands,[26] Northumberland,[27] Oxford,[28] and Wessex.[29]

In 1972 Donald Irvine's publication of *Teaching Practices*, the College's Report from General Practice No. 15, set out the characteristics of those practices selected as trainers in the northern region, in which Irvine was now a Regional Adviser in General Practice. Training in general practice was about to change the following year towards a university-based system, but Irvine's report was the first definitive description at that time of the characteristics of trainers and their practices across an NHS region.[30]

Meanwhile, there was one area in which the College was quite free to operate on its own account. What should be the criteria for entry to membership? After much debate and strong opposition from some of the founding fathers, it was decided to introduce a requirement that, from 1965, entry to membership would be by passing the Membership of the Royal College of General Practitioners (MRCGP (MCGP until 1967)) examination. Although at first only a handful of doctors took this examination, numbers built up so that by 1986 there were 2,001 candidates in the year.[31]

The introduction of the MRCGP changed general-practice education. Courses sprang up not only for trainees, but also for principals; and the topics assessed became *de facto* topics for education. When, some years later, the College altered the MRCGP to include a critical reading paper; this, too, stimulated education and courses on this skill. Wakeford and Southgate showed that trainee reading of original papers was increased by this change in the nature of the examination.[32]

Behind the battle over the establishment of the MRCGP were two themes: first, a further attempt to develop general practice as a discipline, by examining its own body of knowledge and skills, and, secondly, a deliberate attempt to introduce an end-point assessment of the new vocational training which the College was determined to introduce. The place of the MRCGP as this end point was publicly ratified by the Council of the College later, but was clearly in the minds of the proponents of the MRCGP at the time.

[24] J. Stevens, 'Vocational Training for General Practice: A Theoretical Model for an Educational Analysis: Report of an Upjohn Travelling Fellowship for the Royal College of General Practitioners' (unpublished, 1969).

[25] D. J. Pereira Gray, *A System of Training for General Practice* (Occasional Paper 4; London, 1977).

[26] College of General Practitioners, *Outlines of General Practice* (London, 1958).

[27] D. Irvine, *Teaching Practices* (Report from General Practice No. 15; London, 1972).

[28] Oxford Region Course Organizers and Regional Advisers Group, *Priority Objectives for General Practice Vocational Training* (Occasional Paper 30; London, 1985; 2nd edn., 1988).

[29] British Postgraduate Medical Federation (BPMF), *Final Report on an Experiment on Training for General Practice by the University of London Committee for Postgraduate Medical Education in the Wessex Region* (London, 1966).

[30] Irvine, *Teaching Practices*.

[31] Royal College of General Practitioners, 'Appendix 8', in *RCGP Members' Reference Book 1996* (London, 1996); R. Moore, *The MRCGP Examination* (Exeter, 1994).

[32] R. Wakeford and L. Southgate, 'Postgraduate Medical Education: Modifying Trainees' Study Approaches by Changing the Examination', *Teaching and Learning in Medicine*, 4 (1992), 210–13.

As early as the 1950s, reports had appeared delineating the content of general practice and essentially showing why it was different from hospital medicine.[33] In the late 1960s and early 1970s, the RCGP tackled the outstanding issue of the content of general practice. This had to be defined, if it was to be taught systematically to the next generation. It would, of course, have been more logical in theory to have defined the content first, and then introduced an assessment for learning it. However, in the real world of national organizations strict logic is not always possible and progress has to be made as and when opportunities arise.

The MRCGP came in 1965 partly for reasons of status, but the College realized the need for the content of general practice to be much better defined. The best known output of this work came with the publication of the first book from the College entitled *The Future General Practitioner: Learning and Teaching*.[34] It was written by a working party in which the College deployed six of its leading theorists, and was chaired by John Horder, who wrote the first chapter on health and disease. The party included Patrick Byrne, who wrote the chapter on the consultation; Paul Freeling, who wrote the chapter on human development; Conrad Harris, who took the chapter on human behaviour; Marshall Marinker, who wrote on medicine and society; and Donald Irvine, who wrote the chapter on practice organization.

In every way this book broke new ground. First, it put learning before teaching in the title, symbolically reshaping much of medical education. Secondly, it was the first textbook to be couched in educational objectives, thus placing a new emphasis on what the learner was expected to learn. Thirdly, it encapsulated a new understanding of the nature of general medical practice in which the whole of what most doctors had previously conceived of as medicine was placed in but one of five sections. Fourthly, it was written entirely by working general practitioners, and was the first book to be commissioned and written entirely from within the College. For the first time the content of general medical practice had been comprehensively defined.

The response to the book was mixed. Churchill Livingstone, which had published most of the early books from general practice as well as the College's *Journal* and was known as the leading publishing house for general practice, turned the book down. Most general practitioners barely understood its significance, and even the Council of the College was uncertain. However, it was published by the *British Medical Journal* and has become a classic, still in print and still selling steadily, twenty-five years later.

Meanwhile, general-practitioner leaders continued to use academic lectures

[33] C. A. H. Watts and B. M. Watts, *Psychiatry in General Practice* (London, 1952). J. Horder and E. Horder, 'Illness in General Practice', *Practitioner*, 173 (1954), 177–87; M. Balint, *The Doctor, his Patient and the Illness* (London, 1957); W. P. D. Logan and A. A. Cushion, *Morbidity Statistics from General Practice* (London, 1958), i and ii; K. Hodgkin, *Towards Earlier Diagnosis* (Edinburgh, 1963); J. H. Hunt, 'The Renaissance of General Practice: The Lloyd Roberts Lecture', *Journal of the Royal College of General Practitioners*, 22 (1972), suppl. no. 4.

[34] RCGP, *The Future General Practitioner: Learning and Teaching* (London, 1972).

as a means of clarifying key issues. Horder's 1977 lecture on the general practitioner–specialist relationship effectively illuminated not just that relationship (different but equal) but also some of the content of general practice at that time.[35] Huygen's *Family Medicine: The Medical Life History of Families* was a classic being published in English by Dutch publishers.[36]

The organization of vocational training, 1972

In 1972 the Department of Health and Social Security and the Welsh Office released Health Circular HM (72)75, which authorized regional hospital boards to fund general practitioners part-time, to be called regional advisers in general practice, at the rate of one per region.[37] Most regions did this through local medical schools and their postgraduate departments headed by the medical postgraduate deans. A few, such as East Anglia, employed the Regional Adviser in General Practice directly. These arrangements followed the successful pilot by Dr George Swift in the Wessex region.[38] They proved to be an effective method of implementing vocational training for general practice.

In 1973 responsibility for the selection of trainers moved into the hands of universities with the newly appointed regional advisers in general practice as principal officers. Regional advisers were soon supported by general-practitioner course organizers, who ran local training schemes and were paid as trainers by the DHSS. These changes greatly strengthened the hand of the new but small College of General Practitioners, since many of the new regional advisers were also active members of the College. Indeed between 1979 and 1998—for all but two and a half years—no fewer than six Chairmen of the Council of the College would be Regional or Deputy Regional Advisers.[39] Regional advisers in general practice were successful in constructing a national system of vocational training across the UK involving up to 2,000 trainees per year in a relatively short time. On the other hand, this development, which has never occurred before or since in any other branch of medicine, divided academic general practice into two parallel and sometimes competing strands. It was to be twenty-one years before serious attempts were made to reunite academic general practice.[40]

[35] J. P. Horder, 'Physicians and Family Doctors', *Journal of the Royal College of General Practitioners*, 27 (1977), 391–6. Also published in the *Journal of the Royal College of Physicians*, 11/4 (1977), 311–22.

[36] F. J. A. Huygen, *Family Medicine: The Medical Life History of Families* (Nijmegen, 1978; London, 1990).

[37] Department of Health and Social Security and Welsh Office, 'Appointment of Regional Advisers in General Practice', Circular HM (72)75 (London, 1972).

[38] BPMF, *Final Report on an Experiment on Training*; Editorial, 'Postgraduate Advisers in General Practice', *Journal of the Royal College of General Practitioners*, 22 (1972), 426–7.

[39] D. J. Pereira Gray (ed.), *Forty Years On* (London, 1992).

[40] D. J. Pereira Gray, 'Two Sides of the Coin', *Postgraduate Education for General Practice*, 4 (1993), 85–8; J. Allen, A. Wilson, R. Fraser, *et al.*, 'The Academic Base for General Practice: The Case for

One important implication of mandatory training (training backed by force of law) was the need to establish the means for overseeing it. This was different from the needs of the medical specialities, where the relevant training was only indirectly required by statute, through Royal College nominees on consultant appointment committees, and where the Royal Colleges themselves supervised postgraduate education. The RCGP was only just over twenty years old and the BMA committee, the GMSC, had been a powerful medico-political body since it was introduced in 1913. The GMSC refused to accept the role of the new College as analogous to the role of the specialist colleges, even though its expertise and influence were obviously necessary.

The solution, said to have been devised by Ekke Kuenssberg, was the establishment of a new national body, called the Joint Committee on Postgraduate Training for General Practice (JCPTGP), with two parent organizations, the RCGP and the GMSC, each electing six members and a trainee (registrar).[41] These two bodies would also appoint a Joint Honorary Secretary, and would nominate the Chairman alternately. Agreed membership included representatives from the Joint Consultants Committee, medical postgraduate deans, regional advisers in general practice, clinical tutors, and the armed services, together with three junior doctors, two of whom were trainees.[42]

The Joint Committee was established in 1975 under the Chairmanship of John Lawson, immediate past Chairman of the Council of the RCGP. It soon developed a major influence on general-practice education, first through a series of regional inspections, which always included a session alone with the trainees, and, secondly, through written guidance or recommendations, which, in effect, set down a whole set of new and higher standards for both general-practitioner trainers[43] and later for hospital posts.[44]

General practice, alone amongst the branches of medicine, sought parliamentary regulation. This occurred because it had relatively few of its practitioners with an appropriate professional qualification—that is, the MRCGP. The College and the university departments of general practice were then too weak to introduce a system comparable with specialist practice, which was based on the (specialist) medical Royal Colleges.[45] Parliament passed the National Health Service Vocational Training Act in 1976 with a requirement which specified three years of mandatory training for general practice from a date to be specified in Regulations. The law was consolidated in the National Health Service Act 1977. In December 1979, the Regulations under the Act

Change', British Medical Journal, 307 (1993), 719–22; A. Rashid, J. Allen, W. Styles, et al., 'Careers in General Practice: Problems, Constraints, Opportunities', British Medical Journal, 309 (1994), 1270–2.

[41] In the mid-1990s, the term 'registrar' (in general practice) was substituted for the old term 'trainee'.

[42] JCPTGP, 'Annual Report', in RCGP Members Reference Book 1995 (London, 1995).

[43] JCPTGP, Criteria for the Selection of Trainers in General Practice (London, 1976).

[44] JCPTGP, Guidelines on the Selection of Posts in Hospital and Community Medicine (London, 1980).

[45] D. J. Pereira Gray, 'Why compulsory training?', in Training for General Practice (Plymouth, 1982), ch. 17.

were duly laid in Parliament and set out a phased introduction of compulsory training, which was extended from one to three years by 1982. Vocational training, as defined, had to include a minimum of twelve months in an approved training general practice and two years in selected hospital posts. So-called 'prescribed experience' included posts in accident and emergency, geriatrics, medicine, paediatrics, psychiatry, obstetrics, gynaecology, and surgery. Arrangements were made to allow the JCPTGP to judge whether other experience and training could be regarded as suitable for the issue of a certificate of equivalent experience.

The effect of the new law was that general practitioners could only be appointed as principals allowed to undertake unsupervised general medical practice in the NHS if they presented to the appropriate authority a certificate from the JCPTGP. After 1 January 1995 certificates from competent authorities in the EU countries were also accepted. In December 1994, the Vocational Training Regulations (Statutory Instrument No. 3,130) were altered by Parliament to give the Joint Committee much greater powers, including a new duty to 'supervise' vocational training and status as a 'Competent Authority' in Europe.[46]

Thus, after thirty-five years of effort, the postgraduate educational system in general practice had achieved the following: defined standards for the appointment and reappointment of trainers, open application by all NHS general practitioners and selection against regionally agreed standards, compulsory attendance at a course for general-practitioner teachers before appointment as a trainer, and limited tenure of teaching status with automatic review at least every five (usually every three) years. It had also achieved payment of the trainers (implying recognition that these were professional posts), and protected teaching time for trainee and trainer each week. All this amounts to establishing the position of trainer as a privilege which has to be earned rather than a right associated with any particular service appointment.[47] Even in 1997, no other branch of medicine had yet achieved this.

Recent developments

Despite the relative success of the MRCGP examination (the number of candidates had increased to 2,001 by 1986), general practice was left in the early 1990s with a problem of quality. The MRCGP was voluntary and some doctors either declined to take it, or took it and failed. Yet most obtained a JCPTGP certificate and went on to enter unsupervised practice as a principal in the NHS. There was no objective standard of entry.

[46] Statutory Instrument No. 3130, *The Vocational Training Regulations for General Medical Practice (European Requirements) Regulations 1994* (London, 1994).

[47] D. J. Pereira Gray, 'Selecting General Practitioner Trainers', *British Medical Journal*, 288 (1984), 195–8.

The RCGP first drew substantial attention to this in its widely quoted report *Quality in General Practice*, which pointed out that: 'Since 1981, for example, of over 7,000 applications for prescribed experience considered by the JCPTGP, less than 0.2 per cent have been refused.'[48] In 1990, the Chairmen of the JCPTGP, the RCGP, and the GMSC took legal advice and published the so-called 'three-chairmen letter'. This stated that the satisfactory completion of vocational training did not mean time served but that 'the trainee has achieved a satisfactory level of *competence*' (my italics).[49] By the early 1990s this had emerged as the main issue, following a working party established by the JCPTGP under the Chairmanship of Donald Irvine. The working party concluded that the highest priority was to introduce an objective assessment, independent of the training practice, for all doctors completing vocational training.

The JCPTGP consulted widely, and eventually, in May 1993, under the Chairmanship of Idris Humphreys, promulgated a new policy of summative, or end-point, assessment of vocational training to be introduced by January 1996.[50] This defined six components, all of which were to be required: factual knowledge, problem-solving skills, consulting skills, clinical skills, writing skills, and a satisfactory trainer's report.

These developments tested the national organizations of general practice and their policies and degree of influence. Between 1990 and 1996 three key factors now influenced events. First, the GMSC declined to accept the MRCGP; in effect, it demanded another form of assessment. Secondly, the RCGP made no leadership move and did not seek to establish the MRCGP as the end-point assessment, as had been recommended by both the Royal Commission on the NHS[51] and the National Association of Health Authorities and NHS Trusts.[52] Thirdly, the postgraduate wing of general practice, through the regional advisers in general practice, set about developing a completely new assessment system. Professor Stuart Murray's team in the west of Scotland led the way,[53] and important development work was also done in Oxford.[54] This new assessment was designed, unlike the MRCGP, to test *minimum* competence.

[48] RCGP, *Quality in General Practice: Policy Statement 2* (London, 1985), para. 28.

[49] D. Irvine, D. Pereira Gray, and I. Bogle, 'The Meaning of Satisfactory Completion', correspondence, *British Journal of General Practice*, 40 (1990), 434 (emphasis added).

[50] JCPTGP, *Report of the Working Party on Assessment* (London, 1993).

[51] Royal Commission on the NHS, Chairman Sir Alec Merrison, *Report*, Cmnd. 7615 (London, 1979).

[52] National Association of Health Authorities and NHS Trusts, *Partners in Learning* (London, 1994).

[53] L. M. Campbell, J. G. R. Howie, and T. S. Murray, 'The use of Videotaped Consultations in Summative Assessment of Trainees in General Practice', *British Journal of General Practice*, 45 (1995), 137–41; J. R. M. Lough, J. McKay, and T. S. Murray, 'Audit and Summative Assessment: A Criterion Referenced Marking Schedule', *British Journal of General Practice*, 45 (1995), 607–9.

[54] N. Johnson, J. Hasler, J. Roby, *et al.*, 'Consensus Minimum Standards for Use in a Trainer's Report for Summative Assessment in General Practice', *British Journal of General Practice*, 46 (1996), 140–4; N. Johnson, J. Hasler, J. Toby, *et al.*, 'Content of a Trainer's Report for Summative Assessment in General Practice: Views of Trainers', *British Journal of General Practice*, 46 (1996), 135–9.

Having examined the evidence on this new system, which consisted principally of articles published in the peer-reviewed literature (for example, the *British Journal of General Practice* and *Medical Education*), the JCPTGP debated at length the implementation of its assessment policy. At a special meeting of eighteen general-practitioner leaders, including ten general practitioners holding national chairmanships and three registrars, a professional consensus was forged. Finally, in November 1995, the JCPTGP, Chairman Denis Pereira Gray, followed up its August 1995 decision and resolved unanimously that summative assessment of vocational training should be 'professionally expected' with effect from 4 September 1996.

The Conference of Postgraduate Advisers in General Practice, chaired by Professor Stuart Murray, and the Committee of Regional Advisers in England, chaired by Jacky Hayden, set up a committee to organize a national system to be chaired by John Hasler. It developed a four-part modular system, which was published and operated in every NHS region.[55] Factual knowledge and problem-solving were to be tested in a multiple-choice test, consulting skills by video recording, and writing skills through description of an audit in general practice. The trainer's report was extended, standardized, and codified, after seeking the views of over 1,000 trainers. The whole summative assessment system was offered free of charge to registrars, funded from NHS regional postgraduate educational budgets.

In the autumn of 1996, the general-practice branch of the profession maintained its unity. The six chairmen of the RCGP, the JCPTGP, the GMSC, the UK Conference of Regional Advisers, CRAGPIE, and the Heads of University Departments of General Practice all signed a letter to the Secretary of State for Health asking for a meeting to discuss mandatory summative assessment. In December 1996 the government finally responded to the profession's successive requests, and the Secretary of State for Health (1996) in *Primary Care: Delivering the Future* committed the government 'to require GPs to meet minimum standards as a condition of GP vocational training. Summative assessment, which has already been introduced on a voluntary basis, will be mandatory by September 1997.'[56]

Events in the years 1994–7 altered the relationship between medicine and the state. In December 1994, regulations were laid before Parliament which were approved and took effect from 1 January 1995. Three main changes then occurred. First, the UK complied with the European Medical Directive Title IV, 93/16/EEC.[57] Secondly, the JCPTGP was appointed by government as the Competent Authority for General Practice in Europe (the second after the GMC). Thirdly, arrangements were made for doctors with defined experience of working in general practice in the UK , but without vocational training, to

---

[55] D. B. Percy, *Summative Assessment: General Practice Training* (Winchester, 1996).

[56] Secretary of State for Health, *Primary Care: Delivering the Future* (London, 1996), para. 3.9.

[57] European Council [Medical] Directive Title IV, 93/16/EEC of 5 April 1993, *Official Journal of the European Committees*, 36 (1993).

continue to work as locums and assistants (but not as principals in the UK) through so-called 'acquired rights'. Finally, and for the long term, the most important change was the introduction of the words 'shall supervise' with reference to vocational training into the JCPTGP's duties and powers.

Soon afterwards, in 1995, the government laid Regulations to propose a new 'Specialist Medical Order' and to establish a new Specialist Training Authority (STA) of the Medical Royal Colleges. This came into effect in 1996 and assumed responsibility for issuing certificates of completion of specialist training, which in turn led to the establishment of a specialist register, with a corresponding entry in the *Medical Register*. The effect of these parliamentary regulations, coming at the mid-point of the 1990s, was to increase considerably the influence of government, through the Department of Health, in medical education for both generalist and specialist practice, particularly at the postgraduate training stage.

Continuing education for established principals

The term most used in the period 1946–96 was Continuing Medical Education (CME), often shortened simply to continuing education, when the medical context was clear. This is the term used in this chapter. Later on other terms came into use including Continuing Professional Development (CPD).

The story of continuing education is one of increasing variety of provision, increasing involvement of general practitioners, both as learners and as teachers, progressive decentralization of the site of the learning, and movement of learning time from private into working hours. It was further characterized by a radical change in attitudes to it by professional associations, by general practitioners themselves, by the NHS at all levels, and by the public.

Acceptance of the need for regular continuing education throughout a lifetime in practice grew slowly, and was a 'top-down' policy. It was encouraged in 1952 when the new College of General Practitioners included a commitment to undertake continuing education in its requirements for membership. Although this was not measured, it represented a statement of faith that good professional practice depended on keeping up to date. More formal steps came from the Conference organized by the Nuffield Provincial Hospitals Trust in 1961, which led to local postgraduate medical centres being established;[58] from the GMC in 1967, through its guidelines indicating that the basic medical qualification would no longer be enough in general practice; from the Royal Commission on Medical Education in 1968; from the State through Section 63 of the Public Health Services Act; and from the State (i.e. the Department of Health) in the 1990 contract for general practitioners.

[58] Nuffield Provincial Hospitals Trust, 'Conference on Postgraduate Medical Education', *British Medical Journal* (1962), ii. 466–7.

Once the new College was founded, it quickly introduced events like the annual James Mackenzie Lectures, which, with one exception, were given by general practitioners. From then on, general practitioners started to play a progressively increasing part in their own continuing education. The 1974 Nuffield Course for general-practitioner educationalists, directed by Paul Freeling, stimulated interest in educational theory, especially the optimum conditions for adult learning, and the theory and practice of learning in interactive small groups.[59] General practitioners were now the teachers.

These statements and policies were increasingly influenced by developments in medical science, reports in the media, and the rise of consumerism through patient groups and societies, like the British Diabetic Association. In this way, new ideas spread quickly through members and sometimes ahead of their professional advisers. At the same time, the public came to understand that it was necessary for doctors to keep up to date. Finally, the rapid rise in litigation in the 1990s acted as a further spur. One interpretation of these events is that general-practice education was gradually being brought into line with specialist thinking and practice.

Hospital-based education

A major issue throughout the first two-thirds of the twentieth century was the need for continuing education at all. The nineteenth century had been dominated by the idea of the 'safe doctor'. Following the Medical Act of 1886, the dual qualification of MRCS and LRCP, provided by the two medical Colleges (the RCP and the RCS), was taken by many general practitioners. The assumption was that doctors were given a bolus of knowledge in medical schools that would last them a professional lifetime. They were judged safe at the point of qualification and thought to be safe thereafter, although this was never considered appropriate for specialists. The FRCS England was introduced in 1843 and the MRCP in 1859. It was generally believed that there was no need for higher qualifications for general practice.

Thus medical education was sharply divided between specialist medicine, in which higher qualifications had existed for over 100 years, and general practice, in which academic standards were based simply on the basic medical qualifying examination. As a result, virtually all continuing education for principals consisted of specialists talking to and teaching general practitioners.[60] Only exceptionally was a general practitioner the lecturer. The content was predominantly to do with the management of disease, with little or no discussion on psychological aspects, but a little about practice organization was included. The lecture was the dominant teaching method. Small-group

---

[59] Editorial, 'The Nuffield Experiment', *Journal of the Royal College of General Practitioners*, 25 (1975), 547–8; P. Freeling and S. Barry, *In-Service Training* (Windsor, 1982).

[60] See, e.g., the contents of a course described in College of General Practitioners, *Annual Report* (London, 1954).

discussions hardly ever occurred. Discussion was rare apart from time for a few questions at the end of the lecture. There were no educational organizations specifically for general practitioners, or any specified place or centre of learning. Much education had perforce to take place in hospitals, often in the library or boardroom, thus symbolizing that the hospital was the focal point of knowledge and learning.

One of the main achievements of the NHS in 1948 was the appointment of well-trained specialists as consultants in district hospitals around the UK. Within a few years there was a reasonably well-balanced consultant service within reach of all the main population centres. Teaching developed in step, so that, as more consultants were appointed, more education for general practitioners began to occur in local hospitals.

Education outside hospitals

The pharmaceutical industry quickly grasped the fact that general practitioners were the principal prescribers in the new NHS. For forty years their drug costs represented about 10 per cent of the budget of the whole NHS (see Table C1). The industry therefore sent representatives to visit every general practitioner who would see them, and in the early days most did. The industry also offered, as it still does, educational meetings at which speakers, usually a consultant, would talk, often after a meal, about some new treatment.

In many parts of the country, local medical societies, some of which had been formed as early as the eighteenth century, organized meetings, many of which were educational, and many of which still continue in the 1990s. However, their influence and importance declined steadily during this period. Professional sources were also important. For example, the local divisions of the BMA played a major role in bringing doctors together across all specialities, especially in rural areas. Many organized local educational events which general practitioners attended. These, however, were typically organized outside the working day, because general practitioners never considered engaging locums to cover them for educational reasons. Meetings were usually held in the evenings and often on Sunday mornings,[61] and were almost the only source of postgraduate medical education before 1950.

In the same way, as the new College of General Practitioners grew, its educational meetings increased in number and size. By the 1960s College meetings were occurring in most faculties, and at least one annual event such as a faculty symposium was common. For the first time lead speakers started to be from general practice itself and local general practitioners increasingly had chances to meet nationally known general-practitioner figures. One educational development was an audio-visual service started in 1957 by two RCGP

---

[61] See, e.g., the contents of a course described in College of General Practitioners.

members, John and Valerie Graves.[62] Run first from their home in Essex, it eventually became the largest service of its kind in the country, was influential in bringing tape recordings and slides to local groups of general practitioners, and later spread beyond general practice to other health professions. Of importance, after Section 63 was introduced in 1968, was the formal approval of these group sessions in the 1970s at a time when most general-practice education was specialist led.

University departments of general practice developed slowly (see Chapter 7). As they were relatively poorly resourced, their main priorities were to establish themselves and to gain access to the undergraduate medical curriculum. Later, they began to organize teaching for established practitioners within the medical school, and gradually overtook both the local medical societies and the RCGP as educational providers.

Regional advisers in general practice and local general-practitioner tutors

The job description of regional advisers in general practice included, from the start, continuing education for established general practitioners as well as vocational training.[63] At first, however, the regional advisers were busy setting up the new national scheme for vocational training. They first entered the field of continuing education on a large scale through the general-practitioner trainers they had appointed. Attendance at a general-practitioner teachers/trainers' course was a compulsory requirement before approval as a trainer, and in this, general practice was ahead of specialist medicine.

Since there were soon to be as many as 2,000 trainers—between 10 per cent and 15 per cent of all general practitioners—a substantial number of such courses, most of one week's duration, sprang up in the period 1975 to 1985, so that there was soon at least one in each of the then twenty-one regions in the NHS (counting the Scottish Health Boards, Wales, and Northern Ireland). These courses were particularly influenced by the Nuffield Course.[64] Their influence was far greater than the acquisition of teaching and learning skills, in that they were defining the discipline of general practice for the first time and clarifying the content which had to be learnt. The book *The Future General Practitioner:—Learning and Teaching* was especially influential in this respect.

Since general practitioners were being taught to become teachers themselves in their own practices, there was a need to model teaching on these courses.[65] The success of *Doctors Talking to Patients* by Byrne and Long brought

[62] G. Swift, 'Postgraduate Education and Training', in J. Fry, J. Hunt, and R. J. F. H. Pinsent (eds.), *A History of the Royal College of General Practitioners: The First 25 Years* (Lancaster, 1983), 91.

[63] Department of Health and Social Security and Welsh Office, 'Appointment of Regional Advisers'.

[64] Freeling and Barry, *In Service Training*; Editorial, 'The Nuffield Experiment'.

[65] J. Freeman and P. S. Byrne, *The Assessment of Vocational Training for General Practice: Report from General Practice No. 17* (London, 1976).

tape-recording into use for consultation analysis,[66] and video-recording followed, once the equipment and techniques became available. Teaching and learning focused early on real consultations examined as random or problem cases, and interactive small-group teaching was used a great deal as a teaching method, so that issues of adult learning surfaced and remained on the educational agenda.[67]

The success of general-practitioner course organizers was replicated through various forms of general-practitioner tutor being introduced by regional advisers in general practice and medical postgraduate deans during the 1980s. They were usually based on postgraduate medical centres and sometimes, as in the south-west, were appointed as university clinical tutors as well. In the 1990s, following the success of the Association of Course Organizers, a National Association of General Practitioner Tutors was formed. When they were first set up in the 1960s, postgraduate medical centres did not cover the country. However, by 1992 general practitioners in the NHS were attending an average of forty-nine hours of approved continuing education per year and as much as two-thirds of this was taking place in local postgraduate medical centres.[68]

Meanwhile, stimulated in particular by the group-practice allowance of the 1966 Family Doctors' Charter, payable when three or more practitioners worked together, group practice was continuing to develop. Partnership size rose progressively throughout the period and by 1996 the commonest size was four partners (see Fig. D1). Thus the combination of trainees arriving under the new Vocational Training Regulations, and rising number of partners stimulated by the 1966 Charter, created the new possibility of significant *intra*-practice learning. Partners, of course, naturally sought each other's advice informally, but protected time was now demanded for vocational training, following a lead from the JCPTGP in its *Criteria for the Selection of Trainers in General Practice*. Within practices, developments included shared teaching of trainees and the establishment of practice libraries and teaching slides, and practice case discussions.[69] The development of medical audit, following initiatives in 1979, also led to a new emphasis on protocols and more working together in partnerships and teams within practices.

Developments in the last twenty years

The first master's degree programme for general practitioners was introduced at the University of Glasgow in 1983, followed by Leeds and then Exeter in

[66] P. S. Byrne and B. E. L. Long, *Doctors Talking to Patients* (London, 1976).

[67] D. Pereira Gray, *A System of Training*; Freeling and Barry, *In-Service Training*.

[68] F. Difford and R. C. W. Hughes, 'General Practitioner Attendance at Courses Accredited for the Postgraduate Educational Allowance', *British Journal of General Practice*, 42 (1992), 290–3.

[69] M. Hammond, *The Practice Library* (Exeter, 1988).

1986. They then spread rapidly.[70] At the time of writing there were ten universities offering M.Sc. courses for general practitioners.[71]

By 1987 the then Secretary of State for Health, Mr John Moore, was making speeches about the importance of putting a microcomputer on every general practitioner's desk,[72] and soon, stimulated by the 1982 'Micros for GPs' scheme led by the Department of Health,[73] the great majority had done so.[74] By 1996, over 90 per cent of general practices were computerized. UK general practice was ahead of most other countries in the world in adopting the computer and also ahead of UK specialist practice.

The educational potential of easy access in the practice to real clinical information about groups of patients opened new and exciting possibilities for learning within the practice. The Birmingham Research Unit of the RCGP had for years promulgated ways of using practice data for audit using the term 'practice activity analyses'. In addition, new techniques such as 'significant event auditing' focused new attention on learning from clinical experience in the practice itself.[75]

Distance learning, introduced in 1988 in Scotland by the Centre for Medical Education at the University of Dundee, emerged as a new and powerful mechanism for continuing education in general practice.[76] The Centre, led by Professor Ronald Harden, awarded from 1992 both a diploma and a master's degree in medical education (M.Ed.). Three of the first six M.Eds. from Dundee were awarded to general practitioners and, at December 1996, thirty-two general practitioners were enrolled for masters or diplomas in medical education.[77] These proved of particular interest to trainers, course organizers, and tutors.

Before 1989, Fellows of the RCGP were appointed by a committee solely on the basis of reputation and achievements. In 1989, the RCGP introduced a quality assurance programme as the new route to Fellowship of the College.[78] This was based entirely on the care of patients and consisted of a published set of operationally measurable standards of care for patients. It was open to every member of the College of five years' standing. By December 1996, 107 doctors had achieved this[79] and about half a million patients were being

[70] J. I. Koppel and R. G. Pietroni, *Higher Professional Education Courses in the United Kingdom* (Occasional Paper 51; Exeter, 1991); L. F. P. Smith, 'Higher Professional Training in General Practice: Provision of Masters' Degree Courses in the UK in 1993', *British Medical Journal*, 308 (1994), 1679–82.

[71] RCGP, *RCGP Members' Reference Book* (London, 1996).

[72] J. Moore, Secretary of State for Health and Social Security, Speech (unpublished, 1987).

[73] *General Practice Computing: Evaluation of the 'Micros for GPs' scheme: Final Report* (The Singer Report; London, 1985).

[74] NHS Management Executive, *GP Computing—1991 Survey* (London, 1992).

[75] M. A. L. Pringle, C. Bradley, C. M. Carmichael, H. Wallis, and A. Moore, *Significant Event Auditing* (Occasional Paper 70; Exeter, 1995).

[76] 'Distance learning' simply means learning in which the teacher and the taught are not face to face. Correspondence courses, the Open University, and learning from the Internet are three examples.

[77] R. Harden, personal communication (1996).

[78] RCGP, *Fellowship by Assessment* (Occasional Paper 50; London, 1990; 2nd edn., 1995).

[79] RCGP Fellowship by Assessment Group, personal communication (1996).

cared for in NHS practices in which at least one partner had attained this qualification.

By defining an important end point or educational outcome, this new route to Fellowship provided a new logic for continuing education, which was soon recognized by regional advisers for the postgraduate educational allowance, who awarded hours of recognized attandance at postgraduate courses for both preparation and the assessment visit.

This development was stimulated by the 1990 general-practitioner contract, which offered financial inducements for health promotion and the care of certain diseases such as asthma and diabetes. Intra-practice work and learning were now linked with remuneration. At the same time, medical audit was considered to be essential in branches of medical practice in the NHS.

The new contract, imposed upon general practitioners without the agreement of the GMSC, has had the effect of bringing continuing education into the NHS terms and conditions of service, but without it being made compulsory. Instead, £2,025 of the then £34,680 target net remuneration for general medical practitioners in the NHS in 1990[80] was withheld from the pay of general practitioners unless they demonstrated attendance at educational events approved for the purpose by a regional adviser in general practice.

The content of continuing education was divided into disease management, service management, and health promotion. Certain proportions in each category were to be required over a period of years. This arrangement had the effect of increasing substantially the proportion of practitioners complying, but it was much resented. A minority of practitioners complied mainly by attending free events such as pharmaceutical industry meetings; others continued exactly as before.

The Academic Plan for General Practice was approved by the Council of the RCGP in December 1989 and published the following year.[81] It called for at least twelve places in each health service region to be made available for open competition for young general practitioners to develop their skills in research. In the years 1990–6 a small number of research bursaries, grants, or research training fellowships began to become available to general practitioners. These were mainly financed by the NHS either at regional level or more locally from some progressive family health-service authorities or health authorities. Thus for the first time some general practitioners with an interest in research began to develop this through continuing education. This was first implemented in Scotland in 1996 through the Scottish Council for Postgradu-

[80] Review Body on Doctors' and Dentists' Remuneration, *Twentieth Report*, Cm. 937 (The Wilkins Report; London, 1990), 46, 48.

[81] RCGP, 'An Academic Plan for General Practice', in *A College Plan—Priorities for the Future* (Occasional Paper 49; London, 1990).

ate Education.[82] In 1993 a system known as portfolio-based learning and mentoring[83] was the basis of a paper published by an RCGP working party, chaired by Roger Pietroni.[84] It proved to be popular, leading to an interest in adult learning techniques and experiments with mentoring in general practice.[85]

Thus the decade 1983–93 was characterized by the development of diplomas, degrees, and professional qualifications tailored specially for general practice/primary care. These formed new educational outcomes in terms of competence and offered new incentives to general practitioners. One estimate was that by the end of 1996 about 150 UK general practitioners were involved in working for one or other of these further university-based qualifications and eighty-five had notified their intention to take Fellowship by Assessment. These developments marked the arrival of both assessment in continuing professional development and the concept of career progression within general practice. It suggests that at that time about 1 per cent of NHS general practitioners were actively involved in what can be described as formal academically based continuing education.

The explosive development of the Internet occurred in 1995 and 1996. It started to impinge on general-practice education in 1996, especially after 'Medline' became available free of special charges on the Web.[86] Suddenly, even single-handed practices could, at affordable cost, find and download information, including articles published in the world's international peer-reviewed literature, straight into the practice itself.

The final decentralization of general-practice education also followed from information technology. Clinicians need information most of all when they are consulting with patients and access to information in the consulting room makes it especially valuable. Computerized education started with simple prompts, such as reminding a doctor that a particular patient was allergic to penicillin. In 1995 the *British National Formulary* became available on the computer, and is now quickly accessible whilst prescribing.[87] More sophisticated support systems, such as a programe called Prodigy, are currently being tested in NHS general practices at the time of writing.[88]

[82] G. Buckley, Chief Executive of Scottish Council for Postgraduate Education, personal communication (1996); Scottish Council for Postgraduate Medical Education, *Strategic Plan* (Edinburgh, 1996).

[83] A mentor in this context is usually a senior and more experienced colleague whose job is not simply to be a teacher, or even a guide, but a facilitator and something of a friend, a colleague, as well as a tutor. In 'portfolio-learning' learners are encouraged to identify their educational needs and to build up a 'portfolio' of papers. The papers can be presented as evidence for an external assessor of what has been learnt.

[84] RCGP, *Portfolio-Based Learning in General Practice* (Occasional Paper 63; Exeter, 1993).

[85] R. Freeman, 'Information in Mentoring Must Remain Confidential', *British Medical Journal*, 314 (1997), 149.

[86] M. Pullen, 'Free "Medline" on the Web', *British Medical Journal*, 313 (1996), 1068.

[87] BMA and British Pharmaceutical Society, *British National Formulary* (London, 1996).

[88] I. Purvis, *Prodigy Interim Report* (Newcastle upon Tyne: Sowerby Unit for Primary Care Informatics, University of Newcastle upon Tyne, 1996).

Conclusion

To summarize, continuing medical education has been transformed in the fifty years 1946–96. It has had to adapt to the changing role of general practice and the changing arrangements in practices and major changes in the NHS itself. It has become an integral part of the general practitioner's life and is no longer seen as an optional activity. Over 90 per cent of all practitioners obtain eligibility for the PGEA, which indicates an attendance of at least 30 hours per year.[89] In some parts of the UK, such as Northern Ireland, as few as six out of 996 general-practitioner principals failed to receive the allowance.[90]

The content has become much more complex, and more general-practice specific, reflecting the emergence of general practice as a discipline in its own right. Education and continuing learning have moved progressively away from weekends and into the working day. Approaches such as significant event auditing and building up portfolios of learning and mentoring, are felt to be appropriate.

Educational attainments, appropriate for, and specific to, general practice have been developed, especially master's courses and the RCGP's quality-assurance programme through Fellowship by Assessment. At the end of 1996, more practitioners were working for higher university degrees and/or Fellowship by Assessment than ever before.

Continuing education has been progressively decentralized, first from the teaching hospitals, then to district hospitals, then to local groups of colleagues. It has now entered the practice itself, which seems set to become a 'learning organization' as well as a service organization.[91] Methods of communication have extended from the interactive small group in the 1970s to sophisticated electronic methods which allow practitioners to learn in their own practices from the Internet. The most recent decentralization is the input of education, on a computer and in the consulting room, during consultations with patients.

---

[89] Department of Health NHS Executive, *General Medical Services Statistics England and Wales* (Leeds, 1995), 5.
[90] A. McKnight and T. Bradley, 'How do General Practitioners Qualify for their PGEA?', *British Journal of General Practice*, 46 (1996), 679–80.
[91] J. Burgoyne, 'Creating a Learning Organization', *Journal of the Royal Society of Arts*, 140 (1992), 321–2.

9

The General Practitioner
and Professional Organizations

MICHAEL DRURY

The professional organizations representing general practitioners were almost universally opposed to the National Health Service Bill when it first appeared in March 1946. It was, of course, the product of nearly fifty years of debate and, although the various doctors' organizations all spoke of the necessity of establishing a universal network of services, they were deeply troubled by many of the proposed provisions. As far as general practice was concerned, some extension of the National Insurance Act, introduced by Lloyd George in 1911, was acceptable, for, although it initially covered only about one-sixth of the workforce and those only in high risk of cyclical unemployment, by the middle of the 1940s 21 million people were covered by its provisions and two-thirds of general practitioners were participating in the 'panel' system.

In early 1944, faced with the certainty that some form of national service would be established, a powerful grouping from the organizations representing doctors and afterwards called, more in hope than anticipation, 'The Negotiating Committee' had been set up under the chairmanship of Dr Guy Dain, a Birmingham general practitioner who was Chairman of Council of the British Medical Association.[1] This group included the main bodies representing general practitioners—the BMA, the Society of Apothecaries, and the medical Royal Colleges, all of whom had general practitioners as members or licenciates. It published in 1946 a list of seven 'principles' whose acceptance they regarded as essential if they were to cooperate with the government.[2] Some of these related more to hospital medicine, but there were four of particular relevance to the general practitioner. These were the rejection of a whole-time salaried service, the rejection of direction of labour, the right of every registered medical practitioner to participate in the service, and the right to adequate representation in the administration of the service. The view of the BMA Council was that every one of these four principles had been

---

[1] Dr Guy Dain (later Sir Harry), the son of a draper, was in practice in Birmingham for nearly fifty years. He was a member of the GMC, 1934–61, and was Chairman of the Council of the BMA, 1943–9. He had the gift of presenting complex matters in a straightforward and understandable way, thereby getting to the root of the problem quickly.

[2] Editorial, 'British Medical Association and the National Health Service: The Principles of the Profession', *British Medical Journal* (1946), i. 468.

breached by the provisions set out in the 1946 Bill, but it was the threat of the imposition of a whole-time salaried service which was the real *casus belli*. An editorial in the *British Medical Journal* said 'Except for a small minority of doctors grouped around a party political flag, by far the greater part of the profession is rigidly opposed to a whole time medical service.'[3] A subsidiary, but only a little smaller cause of anger, was the proposal to abolish the sale of goodwill of practices. It had been the custom to establish this as a price to be paid by all new incumbents to practice prior to the introduction of the NHS, but was seen by many, including Bevan, as being tantamount to the buying and selling of patients.[4] It was anathema to them and a key feature of the Bill was that it should be abolished. When it came to the crunch, however, it was the amount to be paid in compensation rather than the principle involved which angered general practitioners, and many older doctors complained that they had been robbed.

The passions aroused were enormous. A leading article in the *British Medical Journal* spelt out the future of the general practitioner as one where he[8]

will work in a Health Centre owned by the Local Health Authority and be paid, to begin with, partly by salary. He will be unable to start practice or change practice, except by permission of a central committee under the direction of the Minister at the Ministry of Health. Owning nothing except the right to work under direction— presumably not even the tools of his craft—and inspired by the prospect of controlled security, what kind of effort will the future general practitioner put forth? Will the kind of regulated service contemplated give the right setting and stimulus to the Jenners, Hunters, Budds, Snows and James Mackenzies of the future?[5]

The correspondence columns of the *British Medical Journal* were filled with angry letters, some referring to 'National Socialism' and others questioning whether this was not what we had fought against for the previous five years?[6]

The National Health Service Bill became law on 6 November 1946, but in a plebiscite of all doctors held by the BMA 55 per cent voted against any further discussion with the government. That was a narrow majority but sufficient to warn the Minister that his scheme was under threat. After a flurry

---

[3] Editorial, 'The Bill in the Commons', *British Medical Journal* (1946), i. 725–6.

[4] Aneurin Bevan (1897–1960) was Minister of Health with the responsibility of drafting and introducing the National Health Service Act. He was the son of a Welsh miner and spent some time as a miner himself before entering local politics. Largely self-educated, he became Member of Parliament for Ebbw Vale and remained as such until his death in 1960. He was a heavily built man crowned by a thatch of black hair streaked with grey. A passionate speaker, he had an attractive stammer that he used to good effect and could charm even those who were most violently opposed to his ideas. Perhaps his most daring ideas were the nationalization of all hospitals and his abolition of the sale of general practices.

[5] Editorial, 'The Health Service Bill', *British Medical Journal* (1946), i. 489–91.

[6] A former secretary of the BMA, Dr Cox, wrote to the *British Medical Journal* saying 'it looks to me like the first step, and a big one, towards National Socialism as practised in Germany. The medical service there was early put under the dictatorship of a "medical Führer". This Bill will establish the Minister of Health in that capacity.'

of alarm when the Presidents of the Royal Colleges appeared to have broken ranks by writing to the Minister seeking clarification of some important points, without consulting the other members of the Negotiating Committee—an action which damaged relationships between consultants and general practitioners for some years—discussions with Mr Bevan began. Concessions to the consultants were quickly made on the matter of private practice, but the sticking point of the whole-time salaried service remained unresolved. A second plebiscite was held and this time the result was unequivocal—84 per cent of the profession voted, and of these 90 per cent voted against entering the service in its present form.

Bevan made a number of important modifications to the published proposals. Two of these proved decisive in lessening the opposition of general practitioners to entering the service. These were the undertaking, first, to prohibit a whole-time salaried service being introduced by regulation, thus requiring additional legislation before introducing such a measure, and, secondly, to agree to further discussions about the method of remuneration of general practitioners. Opposition to the Bill amongst general practitioners weakened. In a third plebiscite there was a sufficiently high number of general practitioners who wished to join the NHS to suggest to those who did not that, if the latter refused to join, they would lose the bulk of their patients to those who had decided to join. There was a widespread feeling amongst the general practitioners of the time that they could not trust each other enough for the troops to stand firm. In the event only five weeks before the introduction of the service the doctors agreed to take part. Of the 21,000 general practitioners, 20,500 joined and between 95 and 98 per cent of the population registered. It was last-ditch stuff and, as Nicholas Timmins wrote, 'Like Waterloo, however, it had been a damned close thing.'[7]

It was soon apparent that most people, including the government, had completely underestimated the demand. The initial and widespread euphoria (in Edlington, south Yorkshire, a brass band had paraded to the surgery on the appointed day to be met by the Union Flag and a free drink from the doctor) gave way to a recognition of the size of unmet need.[8] Doctors were often shocked by the amount of long-standing chronic illness and serious pathology uncovered by the introduction of the NHS. In the first six months 75 million prescriptions were issued and Bevan himself was admitting 'I shudder to think of the ceaseless cascade of medicine which is pouring down British throats at the present time.'[9] Equally shocking to the general practitioners, however, was the smallness of the first quarterly cheque they received. These two issues, workload and remuneration, became the paramount features in the

---

[7] N. Timmins, *The Five Giants* (London, 1996).
[8] *Independent*, 5 July 1988.
[9] C. Webster, *The Health Services since the War*, i. *Problems of Health Care: The National Health Service before 1957* (London: HMSO, 1988), 145.

activities of the organizations representing general practitioners over the next few years.

Securing proper representation of all general practitioners has always been difficult. Not all general practitioners are members of the BMA, and there has always been some resentment within the Association of the advantages gained by those 'outside' doctors who do not contribute to the costs, but reap the benefits. The governing body of the BMA is the representative body, consisting of some 600 members and elected about half on a geographical basis and half on a basis of the branch of medicine concerned, but not, of course, involving those doctors who are not members of the BMA. It is normally called together at the annual representative meeting and can take 'binding decisions' of the Association by a two-thirds majority. Below this is a Council of about fifty-four members, drawn from the various committees and the representative body, which is, in effect, the executive committee of the representative body.

In 1913, soon after health insurance was first established by the National Insurance Act, the BMA called together a meeting of representatives of local medical and panel committees which had been set up by law to administer the Lloyd George scheme. This became the Insurance Acts Committee of the BMA and represented all doctors taking part in the scheme thereby with the curious result that it represented members of the BMA and non-members. In 1949 this became the General Medical Services Committee. At the same time a comparable committee representing hospital specialists in the NHS, the Central Consultants and Specialists Committee, was formed. The relationship of these two committees to the BMA has always presented some constitutional problems and been reviewed a number of times, but they now have 'delegated authority' and this device seems to have served reasonably well for a number of years.

During the various disputes with government it was argued that if the BMA became a trade union, it would have more power. A device for obtaining these additional powers was adopted in 1949 by establishing a British Medical Guild, with similar membership to the British Medical Association Council, and two other trusts, the General Medical Services Defence Trust and one representing the specialists, to cover the separate 'crafts'.

The medical Royal Colleges, although primarily concerned with education and standards rather than pay and conditions of service, became much more involved in the 1940s with medical politics; hence the conflicts which periodically arose. Since that time they have exercised a role as important policy-making bodies. With the establishment of the two 'craft' committees described above some of this tension disappeared, although there are always areas of overlap.

The NHS had only been in place for a few months when the topic of remuneration became a matter of dispute between general practitioners and the government. It has been a recurring issue during the next fifty years. When the pay of general practitioners entering the service was first calculated, it was done on the basis of average incomes pertaining to 1939. To this a 'betterment factor' was added by the government to take account of alterations in the value of money and changes which had taken place in the income of other professionals. The figure settled on was one of 20 per cent. A leader in the *British Medical Journal* claimed that 'doctors have been grossly overworked and some of them have been on the brink of a financial disaster'.[10] The dispute about pay rumbled on in an increasingly bitter atmosphere until 1952, when the Minister of Health, Mr Macleod, referred the matter to an 'independent arbitrator', and Mr Justice Danckwerts was appointed. In the event the result was a surprising vindication of the BMA's case and a betterment factor of 85 per cent was applied to the 1948 figure and of 100 per cent to the year 1950/1.

There were two quick results of this; first, that many practices were able to afford to take on new partners, thus helping to allay the problems of overwork, and, secondly, that never since has the government of the day attempted to solve the pay issue by the use of independent arbitration. A variety of solutions have emerged over the years to the thorny question of general practitioners' pay, each put forward at the end of a period of disquiet and dispute. In 1957 a Royal Commission on doctors' and dentists' remuneration was set up under the chairmanship of Sir Harry Pilkington.[11] It was projected that it would conclude its work within one year, but in the event it took three years before the report was published.[12] The most important feature of its conclusions was that an independent Review Body was established to advise the Prime Minister on a regular basis and this became the central feature of pay negotiations over the next forty years.

Any illusions that this would prove to be a mechanism whose conclusions were acceptable to both sides was soon dispelled. The problem was not only that the earnings of the average practitioner proved less than satisfactory; the method of payment had a built-in disincentive to any doctor seeking to improve the quality of his work.

There were a number of ways in which general practitioners could be paid. A straight salary had been rejected by the profession, as it was believed that it opened the door to too much governmental control. Payment of a fee, a 'capitation fee', had been the method of payment in the old NI system. It was at least tried and tested, but too much reliance on this method might encourage some doctors to take on too many patients in some areas. Payment for individual tasks performed, such as a course of immunizations for a child, was a

---

[10] Leading Article, 'Finance and the NHS', *British Medical Journal* (1949), i. 314–31.

[11] Sir Harry (later Lord) Pilkington chaired the Doctors' and Dentists' Review Body during the troubled years of 1957–60. He was a Director of the Bank of England and had worked his way up the family's glass business. An enthusiastic rose-grower in his retirement, he would surprise old employees by turning up with a pair of secateurs without warning and pruning their roses.

[12] Editorial, 'The Royal Commission Report', *British Medical Journal* (1960), i. 556–7; see also suppl., pp. 63–78.

new feature of payment under the NHS. This was at any rate acceptable in those areas where a 100 per cent target was desirable, such as preventive medicine, but again had the danger of tempting doctors to do more than was necessary or wise for patients. In 1948 the capitation fee was the major element of pay and to this was added a payment averaged out to cover practice expenses. It was a complex system and had the effect that, the lower the actual expenses incurred by a doctor, the greater would be the difference, and hence 'profit', between the average reimbursement and the real expenditure. This meant that those who spent money on staff, premises, or equipment, ended up out of pocket and those who had large lists of patients, spent little, and did little for them were best rewarded. In any case, the general practitioners were tired of being regarded as the poor relations of the medical profession and in 1963 the BMA passed a motion at its annual representative meeting requesting urgent action to upgrade the financial status of family doctors.

Initially the BMA was worried by the militancy of some of its members, but a new breakaway body, the General Practitioners' Association, which overnight had secured 7,000 members, had no such qualms. Spurred on by the Association, when the recommendations of the Review Body had proved so unacceptable to them, both in terms of total sums and distribution, the doctors exploded. The British Medical Guild found itself holding 18,000 undated resignations of general practitioners from the NHS, to be used if negotiations with the Minister of Health, Mr Kenneth Robinson, failed.[13] The case for a substantial rise in remuneration was heightened by the steady emigration of dissatisfied doctors, including general practitioners, to Australia, New Zealand, and North America, coupled with poor recruitment of new graduates to practice.[14] The Medical Practitioners Union, a tiny but more serious organization, prepared a charter for family doctors; and when this rocketed their membership upwards, the BMA cited substantial parts of this as the basis for its negotiations.

The negotiations with Mr Robinson succeeded in that a 'price' for a radically new contract, which became known as the Family Doctor Charter (although not initially so-called) because of its favourable terms, was agreed (as had been the National Insurance Bill of 1911 for the same reason). The structure of the contract held sway for the next twenty-five years. There were directly claimable reimbursements for those employing certain categories of staff or improving their premises and the contribution made by item of service payments, limited to areas of preventive medicine, was greatly increased. Thus the proportion of payment by capitation was reduced. The size of the award, however, introduced a concept new to the doctors—a phased award—part to

[13] Kenneth Robinson was the son of a general practitioner and a protégé of Aneurin Bevan. He had been a hospital board member since 1950 and his first act as Minister was to abolish prescription charges. He was regarded by doctors, and by politicians, as the doctor's friend.

[14] In 1962 Dr John Searle had alarmed the profession and angered the Minister of Health, Mr Enoch Powell, when he said that a quarter of the annual output of the medical schools was lost each year to emigration.

take effect at once and part delayed. This was to be a feature of several subsequent awards, when the national interest has been held up by the government of the day as the justification for phasing.

The Royal College of General Practitioners

Anxieties about the quality of care provided by general practice surfaced almost as soon as the NHS began. Many practices were ill organized and inefficient, with few if any supporting staff. General practice had fought against a salaried service only to see its hospital colleagues enjoying its fruits— supporting services, sickness and study leave, holidays with pay, enhanced pensions, and special payments for perceived merit. Practices were mainly housed in the private dwelling of the doctor or at best an annexe built alongside. Health centres did not exist, apart from one or two experiments, and general practitioners had been excluded from working in the larger hospitals and from using diagnostic and other facilities in virtually all hospitals (see Chapter 4). The discipline was not regarded as a speciality. There was no Royal College to champion its cause. Many specialist colleagues thought, and said, that the general practitioner was of lesser intellectual calibre. They were able to be more openly disparaging than they had been before the NHS, as they no longer relied on general practitioners for most of their income.

In the middle of the nineteenth century there had been a serious attempt to found a College of General Practitioners.[15] It had failed partly because of misguided actions by its protagonists and partly because of the attitudes of both the Royal College of Physicians and the Royal College of Surgeons. In fact the physicians took very little interest in it and, even if they did not strongly oppose it, their support was half-hearted. They were secure in their belief of their inherent superiority. The surgeons, on the other hand, appeared to have been won round, but at the last minute withdrew their support. The sticking point was that many general practitioners were already members of the Royal College of Surgeons, membership of this College (MRCS) being a basic qualifying diploma, and these general practitioners liked to call themselves 'physician and surgeon'. The Royal College of Surgeons had to do everything to erect an iron curtain between itself and mere general practitioners—hence the rejection.[16]

At about the same time, the idea of one all-embracing College of Medicine for all practitioners was mooted but dismissed, as there was no basis for agreement between the existing colleges. For nearly 100 years the idea lay dormant, but, when resurrected in 1945, proposals for a combined Academy of Medicine were once again scuppered by conflict between the existing Royal

---

[15] A National Association of General Practitioners in Medicine, Surgery and Midwifery was founded in 1845 when about 1,200 practitioners attended an inaugural meeting. *Lancet* (1845), i. 127.

[16] I. Loudon, *Medical Care and the General Practitioner, 1750–1850* (Oxford, 1986), 282–96.

Colleges. Sir Robert Platt, himself a past President of the Royal College of Physicians, said: 'Surgeons, I suspect, see themselves in a setting of glamour conquering disease by bold strokes of sheer technical skill. Physicians quietly remind us that they were educated gentlemen centuries ago when surgeons and apothecaries were tradesmen. They see themselves as the traditional thinkers of the profession.'[17]

During the next seven years many individuals spoke or wrote about the concept of a new college. The BMA was criticized for the lack of support to general practice in some letters, saying such things as 'the interests of general practitioners had never been so mismanaged or neglected as in recent years', and others stressed the need for a new organization to represent academic interests.[18] The notion of an independent college for general practitioners gained even more urgency when the Interdepartmental Committee on Medical Schools reported in 1944.[19] Amongst other proposals, it recommended full-time professorial units in medicine, surgery, and obstetrics and gynaecology, and one year of pre-registration hospital work after qualification before the doctor could work alone. It also recommended that the award of all postgraduate medical diplomas other than those in public health, clinical pathology, bacteriology, and tropical medicine (which would remain with the universities) should be undertaken solely by the Royal Colleges. It was an added affront to general practitioners to feel that their education and their standards would continue to lie in the hands of doctors from other disciplines.

In 1950 two publications increased the drive towards the establishment of a college. The BMA published the report of the Cohen Committee set up by the Association, on *General Practice and the Training of the General Practitioner.*[20] This was generally helpful to the notion that general practice was a discrete discipline in medicine, particularly as only a third of the members of this committee were general practitioners. A three-year training period for new entrants was proposed, including one year as a trainee assistant. However, it also revealed the underlying, and patronizing, sentiments in comments such as 'it is suggested that he', the general practitioner, 'should read each week at

---

[17] R. Platt, *Doctor and Patient* (London: Nuffield Provinical Hospital Trust, 1970), 3.

[18] P. K. Murphy, letter entitled 'Royal College of General Practitioners', *British Medical Journal* (1949), i, suppl., p. 124; G. Ralston, 'FFGP (Anticipatory), A Faculty of General Practice?', *Lancet* (1949), i. 372; T. B. Layton, 'A Faculty of General Practice', *Lancet* (1949), i. 415.

[19] Ministry of Health, *Report of the Interdepartmental Committee on Medical Schools* (The Goodenough Report; London: HMSO, 1944).

[20] *General Practice and the Training of the General Practitioner* (The Second Cohen BMA Report; London. BMA, 1950); summarized in *British Medical Journal* (1950), i. 1251–5. Henry Cohen (1900–77) was the brilliant son of Russian émigré parents. He won a scholarship to Oxford to read Law, but transferred to medicine at Liverpool, where he qualified with first-class honours and a distinction in every subject, followed two years later by an MD with special merit. He became Professor of Medicine at Liverpool at the age of 34 and remained there until he had a coronary thrombosis in 1952. Unusually, he followed doctors' advice to the letter and gave up clinical work, but he became a household name to general practitioners as chairman of nearly every important committee available. His advice to the Ministry helped to keep it in touch with medicine. He organized the polio immunization scheme and was a brilliant speaker, who must have addressed nearly every medical society in Britain.

least one article which might be designated "high brow", and endeavour to understand its message and significance'. Other proposals, such as the one to encourage the appointment of general practitioners working part-time in hospital as clinical assistants 'to keep them in touch', revealed the ambivalence of the committee, for some saw their role as signalling the natural and evolutionary disappearance of general practitioners from an enlarged hospital service, whilst others visualized it as an essential support to maintain hospital services.[21]

The second publication was more momentous. The editor of the *Lancet*, Sir Theodore Fox, was a long-time champion of general practice and he encouraged and published a long article entitled 'General Practice in England Today: A Reconnaissance', by an Australian research fellow from Harvard, Dr J. S. Collings (see Chapter 4).[22] Collings described his survey, involving 104 doctors from fifty-five practices, as a 'grim analysis of the present position and future prospects' and concluded: 'Few skilled craftsmen, be they plumbers, butchers or motor mechanics, would be prepared to work under such conditions or with equipment as bad.'[23] It was a damning condemnation of practice in its present form and identified the amount general practitioners were paid and the manner of their payment as the twin root causes of the problem.

The picture painted was so dire that critics accused Collings of ignoring much that was good in practice and of biased selection. Partly to combat this, the BMA appointed its own committee under Dr C. W. Walker of Cambridge 'To review the present position of general practice, its difficulties and its trends'.[24] The secretary of this committee, Dr Stephen Hadfield, an assistant secretary of the Association, was invited to make a new survey, this time involving about 200 practices selected at random. His report, 'Field Survey of General Practice 1951–52', was published in September 1953.[25] It painted a more rosy picture of the position, but even this could be no more encouraging than to conclude that 'Ninety-two per cent of practitioners seen at work were adequate or something better.'[26] There was no doubt in many people's minds that the very existence of general practice was in the melting pot. There were, of course, examples of solid achievement to be found in practices at that time and Dr Stephen Taylor was commissioned by the Nuffield Provincial Hospitals Trust to conduct a non-statistical survey to see how their example could be generally applied. The resulting report was published as a book which became, for a number of years, the 'bible' for those seeking to improve their work.[27]

A number of individual general practitioners believed that salvation would

[21] Ibid. 1255.
[22] J. S. Collings, 'General Practice in England Today: A Reconnaissance', *Lancet* (1950), i. 555–85.
[23] Ibid. 557.
[24] S. Hadfield, 'Field Survey of General Practice 1951–52', *British Medical Journal* (1953), ii. 683.
[25] Ibid. 683–706.
[26] Ibid. 705.
[27] S. Taylor, *Good General Practice* (London, 1954).

not come until general practice had its own College and set its own standards based on reliable facts and were actively pursuing this notion in the early 1950s—Geoffrey Barber, Fraser Rose, Talbot Rogers, and John Hunt in particular. John Hunt wrote of the series of happy chances and hard work that led to the formation of the College.[28] Others who were influential included Sir Wilson Jameson, an ex-Chief Medical Officer at the Department of Health who was about to become Master of the Worshipful Society of Apothecaries, and the Rt. Hon. Henry Willink, Master of Magdalene College, Cambridge, who had been Minister of Health from 1943 to 1945. In 1951 John Hunt and Fraser Rose wrote a letter which appeared in the *British Medical Journal* asking 'for evidence upon the subject of a possible College of General Practitioners' from its readers.[29] This seems to have been the catalyst. The time had clearly come and there was much support within the letter columns and elsewhere. An editorial in the *Lancet*, commenting upon the Danckwerts award, said 'General practice, no less than the specialities, needs a leavening of exceptionally able men and women; and exceptional ability often needs to be attracted by exceptional reward. In this light the formation of a College should not be long delayed.'[30] However, editorials in the *Manchester Guardian* of 27 June 1952, and *The Times* on the following day, were much more sceptical.

Attempts were made to secure the active support of the three existing colleges, physicians, surgeons, and obstetricians and gynaecologists. They gave some support to the idea of a Joint Faculty, but this was seen as a device by the older colleges to retain control over general practice. They were more concerned about the possible dilution of their authority than about general practice as a discipline, and it became apparent, after Willink had lunched privately with the three Presidents, that they would neither support an independent college nor produce a viable alternative. This might have been expected, for twenty-three years earlier when the obstetricians and gynaecologists had been seeking to form a College, the physicians and surgeons had jointly taken them to court in an attempt to prevent it. Many senior members of these Colleges were personally abusive and John Hunt describes how he met a senior Fellow of the Royal College of Surgeons in Wimpole Street who said 'It's absolute nonsense, you might as well found a college of ingrowing toe-nails!'[31] It is true to say, however, that, once the initial battles had been fought and won, the new College was accepted and cooperation was developed in many fields. Later, the Conference of Medical Royal Colleges,

---

[28] John Hunt, later Lord Hunt of Fawley, was a general practitioner in private practice in London with many influential people as patients. He was a big man in many respects and an avalanche of honours came his way. His practice was hardly typical and he had a succession of lady drivers to take him on his visits whilst he sat in the back dictating his notes. An indefatigable worker, he would sit at breakfast with two telephones to hand, one for incoming calls and one to make outgoing calls. See J. Fry, J. H. Hunt, R. J. F. H. Pinsent (eds.), *A History of the Royal College of General Practitioners: The First 25 years* (Lancaster, 1983).

[29] *British Medical Journal* (1951), ii. 908.

[30] Editorial, *Lancet* (1952), i. 1147.

[31] Fry *et al.* (eds.), *A History of the Royal College of General Practitioners*, 19–20.

renamed the Academy of Medical Royal Colleges in 1996, was established. It is a body consisting of the Presidents of all Colleges that meets at intervals of every few months. It was eventually agreed that, by virtue of numbers, the RCGP should have two representatives on this body; the other specialist colleges have one each.

There was enough support within the profession and from notable figures outside to set up a Steering Committee, and to follow this in less than nine months by the signing, on 15 November 1952, of a Memorandum and Articles of Association establishing an incorporated body, with the title of College of General Practitioners. Applications for foundation membership of the new College opened on 1 January 1953 and within two weeks 1,000 had joined. By the end of six months the number had risen to 2,000 and the exercise was obviously viable.

The purpose of the College was, from the time it was founded, to be academic. This was important, not only because there was no academic body concerned with general practice, but also to avoid conflict with the BMA. This latter objective was aided by the establishment of a liaison committee with the GMSC which exists to the present date. In spite of this, the relationship between the two bodies has not always been straightforward. Specialists were also occasionally involved in a similar difficulty of relationship, but they had an advantage that general practice did not possess, in that virtually every specialist belongs to an appropriate College. To begin with, the mandate of the College covered only some 10 per cent of general practitioners. It only reached more than 50 per cent by 1990. The GMSC, by its structure, was mandated by 100 per cent of general practitioners; and when difficult issues arose that straddled the borders between the standards of practice and the cost of practice, such as, for example, incentives for house calls, there were those who did not tire of reminding the College of its limited mandate.

Mostly the relationship worked well, and the joint approach achieved many notable gains, particularly in the area of further education, where a Joint Committee on Postgraduate Training was established in 1975 with officers rotating between the two parent bodies. At times the division of relationships became painful, notably when battles between government and the profession were at their height such as in 1965 and 1990. There were those who suggested that the government was not averse to exploiting differences.

From the start, the founders of the College were determined that it should not become a London-dominated organization. Regional faculties were set up throughout the British Isles to deal with local affairs, and from these the majority of the representatives of the Council of the College were appointed. The new College set about its tasks with energy and enthusiasm, covering four areas: education, research, ethics, and the structure and standards of practice. The first three of these were also the fields in which the colleges of specialists were concerned. The last area was different, for only general practitioners had to provide the wherewithal to carry out their clinical activities by virtue of their status as independent contractors.

In research it was very much a matter of gathering in those individual general practitioners who were already researching, and slowly developing the methodology required, which was different from much other research. Many ethical issues required a different perspective, and others arose with changes in medical care. It was in the fields of education and, to a lesser extent practice organization, that the greater gains for the discipline were to be made in the short term.

Initially it was thought that the best way to attack the educational deficit of new entrants to general practice was at the undergraduate end; but in the 1950s and 1960s this was a dismal failure, partly because of the innate conservatism of the medical schools, but perhaps more importantly because the discipline was unable to articulate the reasons for a presence. For a clinical department to be seen to have as a major target recruitment to its branch of medicine was the kiss of death as far as other departments were concerned. Until it could be demonstrated that the discipline had an essential contribution to make, without which all newly qualified doctors would be deficient in some way, its presence was unacceptable. So in the 1960s the emphasis changed to the immediate post-qualification period. The establishment for general practice of a programme of specific postgraduate training prior to entry became the priority. This was a subject upon whose importance both the GMSC and the College agreed, though, whilst the College would have preferred to insist that it became a requirement for entry, the GMSC, conscious of the potential for antipathy amongst some sections of practice, was more cautious. In 1965 a report on vocational training was published, and, after this, evidence to the Royal Commission advanced the case both for mandatory postgraduate training and for undergraduate departments.[32]

The practice organization activities of the College were handicapped from the start by the contract of the general practitioners, which effectively penalized those who invested in staff and equipment. But it was clear, as Collings had pointed out in his report, that this was one of the major barriers to quality care.[33] Premises, equipment, systems, and staff all needed attention, and the nature of the various problems required exploring first. The health centre, fully equipped and catering for a group of health-care workers, had been one of the objectives of Aneurin Bevan at the start. It remained unfulfilled for more than twenty-five years. But a steady improvement of the structure of practices began with the College and gained impetus when the new contract, the Family Doctor Charter, was introduced in 1966. The College early on established a Practice Equipment and Premises Committee. At first the only body of knowledge it had to rely on was Stephen Taylor's book.[34]

[32] College of General Practitioners, *Special Vocational Training for General Practice: Reports from General Practice No. 1* (London, 1965).

[33] Collings, 'General Practice in England Today'.

[34] The Nuffield Provincial Hospitals Trust invited Dr Stephen Taylor to do a non-statistical survey of 'good' practices in 1952 and write a report. This was published as Taylor, *Good General Practice*, which became the standard work of reference for some ten years.

The doctors had generally done badly in financial terms in the 1950s, but better in the 1960s. During the 1970s they again lost ground, as was recognized by the report of the Review Body in 1972. At the same time the NHS was again under scrutiny. There was a major problem in that the government funded the Service, but control lay with the medical authorities, who resented central interference. In effect the piper was unable to call the tune. The result was the 1974 reorganization of the NHS, which was introduced by Keith Joseph following a Consultation Document in 1971 and a White Paper published in 1972. Its origins lay far back in the split that Aneurin Bevan had established between hospital, general practice, and social services. There was a need to move towards some degree of unity. Existing health authorities were modified or abolished and boundaries redrawn.

These changes should have resulted in far better liaison and cooperation between general practice, the hospital service, and the local authority. In the event bureaucracy mushroomed, and, as Timmins wrote, 'in time hospital porters were to demand (unsuccessfully) that there should be district, area, and regional porters to run the service, while civil servants became locked in theological debate about whether or not there should be a district remedial gymnast'.[35] The end result was a dismal failure, compounded by the speed at which it was attempted. Any hopes of benefit to general practice were sacrificed by the doctors' determination to keep their Family Practitioner Committees ring fenced. General practitioners had recognized the danger of the acute hospital service raiding the community service budget too often in the past for them to invite a Trojan Horse into their midst.

The era following the reforms was to some extent a time of relative tranquillity in practice. The spotlight had shifted to the hospital services. The consultants felt themselves squeezed by the general practitioners' new contract. Bitter battles broke out about private patients, an area of medicine from which most general practitioners had been forced to withdraw in 1949, whilst strikes amongst ancillary workers became commonplace. The key event for general practice at this time was the Medical Act of 1978, which reconstituted the GMC.

The General Medical Council

In the middle of the nineteenth century, at a time when qualified practitioners perceived the profession to be overcrowded, there was great resentment amongst these doctors that their educational investment was devalued by competition from unqualified practitioners. The establishment of a council to regulate medical education and entry to the profession, and thus remove this

---

[35] Timmins, *The Five Giants*, 295–6. 'A Biography of the Welfare State', in which the attempts to combat the five evils of Want, Disease, Ignorance, Squalor, and Idleness between 1946 and 1996 by successive governments are chronicled.

problem, was the principal reason for the Medical Act of 1858. The Council so set up consisted of twenty-four members, eighteen representatives of the Royal Colleges and the universities, and six persons nominated by the Queen on the advice of the Privy Council. There was always a possibility that general practitioners could be members, but when it was established, there were none.

Over the course of the next ninety years medical education was standardized by the Council, standards of intra-professional conduct were established, leading to a national system of medical ethics; and disciplinary procedures were set up. During the same period the membership expanded, some elected members were introduced, and a lay person was nominated, so that, by the time of the introduction of the NHS, the Council had expanded to 42, of whom 38 were medical and 7 of these elected. Further expansion resulted from the Medical Act of 1950 leading to a Council consisting of 50 members, 28 of whom were appointed by the Royal Colleges and universities, 5 nominated by the Crown, and 11 elected. To these were added 3 lay members and 3 dentists. Democracy was making a slow entrance to the Council but still no women were included.[36]

The power of the Council, and thus much of the control of the profession, rested in the hands of the specialist medical Royal Colleges and very much in the hands of the President. This monopolistic system remained unchallenged until the 1960s, when a number of issues came to a head. The historical discontent of general practitioners with their relative exclusion from the Council had never been satisfied. Elected members remained in the minority, so their voice was bound to be relatively weak. The unease in the consultant ranks grew with the recommendations of the 1968 Todd Report on medical education, which had included a suggestion of specialist registers. This not only threatened the authority of the Royal Colleges, but was also viewed by general practitioners as continuing their role as second-class citizens. Regional consultants, who also felt excluded from the corridors of power filled with representatives of London medical schools and London-based consultants, sought a greater say in matters. But most of all, the junior hospital doctors of the time felt disenfranchised and alienated from the whole system.

The GMC had its own problems. It was financed by a fee paid by a doctor when admitted to the register, but this was proving inadequate to fund the increased responsibilities of the Council. There were also problems associated with the rigidity of the disciplinary procedures, the control of 'sick' doctors, and the registration of overseas doctors. The Council promoted a Bill in 1969 to give them powers to levy an annual retention fee and to deal with their other problems. It was the issue of the retention fee that crystallized opposition. General practitioners were soon in the forefront of those demanding that

[36] The 1957 Act set up the General Dental Council and removed the GMC's direct responsibility for dental surgeons.

elected members should be in the majority and the battle cry was to be 'no taxation without representation'.

The Bill received Royal Assent on 25 July 1969, and one might have expected resistance to subside from that point on. But in fact it stiffened. Publications aimed at general practitioners, including particularly *Pulse* and *World Medicine*, became increasingly critical, and in January 1970 a postal survey showed 11,540 doctors opposed to the annual levy and only 466 in favour.[37] The BMA had been less than firm on this point. A Special Representative meeting agreed to the levy, but only on condition that elected members were in the majority on the Council, and elected members were adequately represented on the GMC committees. A review of the structure and functions took place.

A number of enquiries were set up, but before these could resolve the situation, the issue of doctors who were refusing to pay the annual levy on the grounds that they had already subscribed for life at entry arose. The GMC voted to strike off these doctors. Until this point the government, having given the profession the right of self-governance, avoided involvement. But, faced with the prospect of a significant number of doctors being erased, it set up an independent committee of enquiry in 1972.[38] Much of the matter discussed and concluded by the Merrison Committee related to the structure of the Council, or to the whole profession, but two issues were of particular importance to general practice. First, the Committee advised that there should be three stages of medical education—undergraduate training, graduate clinical training, and specialist training. These should all be carefully defined and coordinated by the regulating body, but the end product for all doctors should be independent practice as a specialist including the *speciality* of general practice. This meant that at last there was a degree of equivalence between the general practitioner and specialist colleagues.

The second issue arose from the enlarged Council. There were to be defined constituencies throughout the UK and elected members were to have an overall majority. The Merrison Committee had included ninety-five recommendations on education and registration. The Labour Government introduced a very short Bill in the House of Lords which omitted all the recommendations on education and registration. This could have been a disaster, but the influence of John Hunt, ennobled as the first general-practice peer in 1973, was decisive as he amended, lobbied, and persuaded until all the key recommendations had been reintroduced. In 1976, twenty-seven of the forty-six members were appointed by universities and Royal Colleges, and eleven were elected, of

---

[37] Between 1955 and 1996 a number of publications arose aimed at the general-practice market and appearing some weekly and others at fortnightly or monthly intervals. The great majority of these, *Pulse* and *World Medicine* included, were funded by advertising largely from the pharmaceutical industry.

[38] The Committee, chaired by Sir Alec Merrison, Vice-Chancellor of Bristol University, had seven medical members and quickly reaffirmed professional self-regulation.

whom five were general practitioners. By 1989 the size of the Council had risen to 102, of whom fifty-four were elected. General practice had risen to be the largest speciality represented, although still not in numerical proportion to the number in the UK. Several of the more important committees had general practitioners as chairmen and in 1995 Sir Donald Irvine became the first general practitioner to hold office as President.[39] Most important of all, the GMC now had real power over the educational process, and the role of general practice at all stages of education was secure.

It was extraordinary that the 1974 reorganization of the NHS should have failed so dismally that by 1976 there were calls for yet another reorganization, but it was not until 1983 that the second reorganization was complete. The effect of all these changes upon the management of practices can be best seen by recalling briefly the history of this administration.

The administration of general practice

The NHS missed a golden opportunity in 1948 to integrate health care in hospital and the community. A completely separate administration was set for each branch of the Service, and the general-practice element was to have its contracts managed by Executive Councils. General practitioners, as we have seen, were so concerned about professional autonomy in 1948 that they considered it essential not to be employees of the state, but to enter into independent contract with the NHS; and for them this was represented by Executive Councils. These were the successors to the Insurance Committees, which had been set up under the National Insurance Act of Lloyd George in 1911 to administer 'contracts' with participating general practitioners. They were acceptable, for they were known and understood and had few powers to influence general practitioners; their limitations were well known. Consultants had become employees of the state in 1948 but even here they had successfully resisted local control of their contracts until 1990. There were 134 of these Councils in England and Wales and they corresponded approximately to the larger local authorities. But they were not in any way administratively connected with these. In 1974 they became Family Practitioner Committees, and their boundaries were then largely coterminous with the boundaries of the Area Health Authorities. Thus there was some encouragement for joint working at last, although these alterations in name led to little change in their own relatively narrow administrative remit. When the tier of Area Health Authorities was abolished in 1982, joint work became even more difficult, for they did not match the District Health Authorities at all.

Of the ninety Family Practitioner Committees in England, sixty related to

---

[39] Sir Donald Irvine was a general practitioner in Ashington, Nothumberland, who became, first, Honorary Secretary, and then Chairman of the Council of the Royal College of General Practitioners. He was a member of the Merrison Committee on Medical Education.

one or two districts, seventeen to three, seven to four, and six to five or more. In 1985 the Family Practitioner Committees became health authorities in their own right, and were renamed Family Health Service Authorities in 1990. From this point on, their responsibilities were greatly extended to include managing and planning for improvements in the service. They also extended their roles in monitoring performance and in adjudicating and resolving conflicts between doctors and patients.

The quality of management in the NHS had been a recurring cause of complaint. In 1982 Roy Griffiths, managing director of Sainsbury's, was invited to report on this.[40] Critics saw this as an attempt to secure privatization of the Service, but Griffiths was, at heart, very much a supporter of the NHS. He had been a 'Bevin Boy' down the mines during the war, had won a scholarship to Oxford, and then had worked for several commercial organizations before coming to Sainsbury's.

He and his colleagues reported within six months and the essence of their conclusions was that at no level of the NHS was a decision the responsibility of a single person—all decisions were dependent on a group, a committee, or a board.[41] They recommended that managers should replace administrators, doctors should run budgets, and treatments should be evaluated to determine whether they were cost effective. These were simple ideas, but revolutionary to health care. Griffiths wrote: 'If Florence Nightingale were carrying her lamp through the corridors of the National Health Service today she would certainly be looking for the person in charge.'[42] There was initial opposition from doctors and nurses, but it soon evaporated when it was realized that such simple measures could result in a clarity of purpose and loss of ambiguity which had not existed before. The recommendations were carried out almost to the letter. The effect upon the administration of general practice was as profound as upon other areas of the NHS and the administrators of the Family Practitioner Committees became the managers of the FHSAs.

The sharp division of responsibility between health care and social care was another problem area established by Aneurin Bevan in 1948. Some hospital patients would be better cared for in the community whilst some patients nursed in the community needed hospital care. Moving them across the boundaries was always difficult and often impossible. Griffiths's second report addressed this issue.[43] It was firmly stated that most people with long-term illness would prefer to be treated in their own homes. Voluntary organizations were seen to be important contributors to this care and Health Authorities were allowed to extend joint funding arrangements to voluntary organizations as well

[40] R. Griffiths. *Report of the NHS Management Inquiry* (London: DHSS, 1983).

[41] *NHS Management Inquiry Report* (London, The Griffiths Report; HMSO, 1983). This inquiry was set up by the Secretary of State to advise him privately. Originally it was not intended to publish it, but this decision was received so badly that it was eventually published in the form of a letter in October 1983.

[42] *NHS Management Inquiry Report*, 12.

[43] R. Griffiths, *Community Care: Agenda for Action* (London: HMSO, 1988).

as to local authorities. However, primary care was also seen as a cheaper option, and in the result sometimes led to inadequate provision and to the premature discharge of patients from long-term in-patient care to ill-prepared community care.

Arguably the most radical changes of all since 1948 to the care provided by general practitioners came at the very end of the period at which we are looking. They were probably driven chiefly by financial considerations rather than considerations of quality of care. They were also introduced with a haste that alarmed supporters and critics alike. Appetite for health care appears to be insatiable and the solution adopted by the government was to subject the NHS to market discipline where competition between the providers of care would lead to more efficiency whilst giving the consumer more choice. Four White Papers spelt out the fact that the bureaucratic organization of the NHS was about to be disbanded.[44]

Key proposals of the papers, which would have powerful effects upon primary care, were the introduction of practice budgets for large practices who wished to purchase a selected range of health care for their patients, and 'indicative prescribing amounts' for general practitioners to control prescribing costs. There were also major changes in the role and composition of the Family Practitioner Committees (FPCs), renamed Family Health Service Authorities (FHSAs), and an insistence that clinical audit be introduced. Professional opinion was largely hostile and even some supporters of the changes were worried by the timetable for change. Nevertheless the Bill received Royal Assent in June 1990. Prior to this Bill, hospital consultants had traditionally had more power in determining expenditure priorities. From 1990 on, some general practitioners with their own budgets acquired the capability of affecting hospital provision. Thus there was a significant shift in the balance of power within the medical profession for the first time in fifty years.

The second White Paper was concerned with community-care proposals. In general this was more welcomed and the time scale of introduction was more carefully paced. The third White Paper was an answer to those who said that successive reforms had been concerned with structure and process, but rarely with outcome. It took five major causes of premature death or avoidable mortality and set targets for improvement. Whilst this had been going on, negotiations for a new general-practice contract were being thrashed out between the profession's negotiators and the government. The negotiations were protracted and, at times, bitter, but agreement was eventually reached in August 1989, only for it to be rejected by the membership.

Despite this, the Secretary of State decided to impose the contract and it

[44] *Working for Patients*, Cm. 555 (London: HMSO, 1989); *Caring for People: Community Care in the Next Decade and Beyond*, Cm. 849 (London: HMSO, 1989); *The Health of the Nation: A Strategy for Health in England*, Cm. 1986 (London: HMSO, 1992); *Community Care in the Next Decade and Beyond*, Cm. 849 (London: HMSO, 1992).

came into effect on 1 April 1990. The general practitioners' contract is complex. It includes payments for a variety of features, but the essential difference with the new contract was that it was sensitive to work done. If high-coverage levels were achieved for items such as cervical cancer screening, childhood immunization, and health-promotion sessions, income would be considerably increased.

Fundholding is a more radical change. Essentially the concept was that certain practices, initially the largest but gradually extending until, by 1996, 50 per cent of practices were included, would have budgets from which they could purchase a limited range of in-patient, outpatient, and diagnostic services, and pay for the cost of staff employed and the pharmaceuticals prescribed for their registered patients. It was argued that this would give general practitioners an incentive to offer patients a wider choice of hospitals, and make hospitals and consultants look upon general practitioners as persons whose confidence must be gained because the choice would be made by general practitioners.

Since the start of this scheme a variety of developments have occurred. The variety of practices allowed to become fundholders now includes smaller groups. Loose alliances of practices, known as multifunds, have begun offering economies of scale when purchasing services, and new methods of purchasing have developed, including an experiment in total fundholding by all the practices in one town, Bromsgrove. There is no doubt that these schemes have brought hospitals and general practitioners together in a way that no other development since 1949 has succeeded in doing. They have encouraged a search for cost effectiveness, and for new and more flexible ranges of services within the practices participating. Unease remains about the administrative burdens within these practices and about the inequity in service provision between fundholding practices and those outside the scheme. Over the next few years there are likely to be further changes, but the concepts behind splitting the roles of purchasers of services from those of providers of services are likely to remain.

This Bill, and the new contract accompanying it, divided general practice sharply between those who saw the final product as one giving power in exchange for a guarantee of higher quality service, and those who saw it as providing a two-tier service, with a large increase in administration for no clinical gain to patients. There is some truth in both arguments and some modification has already taken place. But in other areas the jury is still out.

10

General Practice, its Patients, and the Public

IAN TAIT and SUSANNA GRAHAM-JONES

General practice has been seen as the approachable familiar face of medicine; it has enjoyed a remarkable degree of popularity. Surveys of public opinion carried out over the years have confirmed this, and reveal a consistent picture of what the public want from their general practitioners. They want a doctor who knows them, listens to them, understands them, and explains things to them. This chapter will examine the relationship of general practice with its patients and the public in the last fifty years.

When Ann Cartwright carried out her study for her book *Patients and their Doctors* in 1964 she found that the vast majority of the patients questioned felt that their doctor was a good listener, good about not hurrying them, and good at explaining things.[1] Such a rosy view of general practice seems to contrast with reports and studies of general practice which described examples of poor hurried work. Such discrepancies suggest that the wish for these pastoral qualities in their general practitioners may at times have induced patients to believe in their presence, even when the reality was very different. In Cartwright's second study, undertaken in 1977, she noted, with approval, that more patients 'were willing to criticise their doctors and to question what he did or said'.[2] Nevertheless she still reported high levels of general satisfaction, with 91 per cent of patients being satisfied with the care they received from their own doctor. Recently, in a survey carried out by *Which?* magazine in 1995 entitled 'What makes a good GP', the respondents' first requirement was still 'a doctor who listens and explains'.[3]

General practice has diversified and doctors are now seen as members of an extended team. In this process the traditional personal intimacy between patients and their doctors has been weakened; patients may now claim allegiance to a named group practice rather than to an individual doctor. The ability to provide an increasing range of powerful drugs, free or for a relatively small prescription charge, has been another important factor in the relationship between general practice and their patients. For some decades both

---

[1] A. Cartwright, *Patients and their Doctors* (London, 1967); the figures were 93%, 88%, and 75% respectively.

[2] A. Cartwright and R. Anderson, *General Practice Revisited: A Second Study of Patients and Their Doctors* (London, 1981).

[3] Consumers' Association, 'What makes a good GP?', *Which?* 18 (June 1995).

doctors and patients tended to think of these new drugs as 'magic bullets' promising trouble-free cures for all ills. The huge cost and the potential dangers of many of them has led to a much more guarded attitude to their use on the part of patients and doctors. The power of doctors was greatly enhanced by these drugs, but so was the potential for disagreement and mistrust in their relationship with patients.

Another historical trend is the change in cultural attitudes towards authority. This has influenced both doctors and the public. Paternalistic advice-giving, which was such a marked feature of the traditional image of the medical practitioner, has been put in question. Doctors as well as patients appear to have accepted the need for a more equal relationship in which responsibility for decisions is shared. Some general practitioners have sought to limit the expectations of patients, inviting them to see their doctor more akin to a 'plumber than a father figure', as McCormick expressed it.[4] In the years under review the public has become much better informed about health matters. This mass education has come primarily through the media and the popular press, and not directly from doctors. Not all the publicity has been accurate and responsible, but deliberate efforts to educate the lay public about health matters have been made by consumer groups, by the Health Education Authority, and indeed by schoolteachers. Some patients nowadays know rather more about their disease than their doctor does.

The government has always been an important third party in the relationship between general practice and its public. For much of the life of the NHS general practice has been notably free of external controls over the way in which the individual practitioners organized their work. In recent years, however, the government has become a much more intrusive partner. Underlying many of the recent changes is a political and social philosophy that sees the exercise of more consumer power as desirable in the relationship between the profession and the public. Market forces were accepted by the Conservative Government as an appropriate dynamic for change within medicine. This new ethos is another factor influencing the doctor–patient relationship.

Overview

In what follows we have divided our history into three parts. First, the years 1946–70, between the introduction of the NHS and the reforms associated with the Family Doctor Charter.[5] This was a time when general practice struggled to cope with the new demands of the NHS, aspiring to equitable provision across the UK, with health services infrastructure which had remained unchanged since the 1920s.

[4] J. McCormick, *The Doctor: Father Figure or Plumber?* (London, 1979).
[5] BMA, *A Charter for the Family Doctor Service* (London, 1965).

The second period (1971–85) was one in which the support given by the Charter led to the development of larger partnerships. Purpose-built premises permitted the employment or attachment of ancillary staff, practice nurses, and other professional colleagues. Morale in general practice was relatively high; vocational training for general practice was introduced and developed largely through initiatives arising within general practice itself. Standards of performance were defined, and the fantasy that there was no such thing as a bad doctor had to be abandoned by the public as well as the profession.

Finally we consider recent changes from 1985 to 1996, when the gap between what medicine could achieve and what the NHS could afford was thrown into sharp relief. The escalating costs of secondary health care meant that reform of the NHS as a whole was essential. The radical changes enacted by Conservative Governments under Margaret Thatcher and John Major have been discussed in earlier chapters, along with the new contract imposed on general practice, and the introduction of fundholding. These changes have had a mixed reception from both doctors and patients. Whilst publicizing the rights of the consumer, the administration of the health service depends on the gatekeeper function of the general practitioner in the NHS to contain costs. This is founded on the trust placed in the doctor by the patient, which in turn is based on a public perception that the role of the doctor is that of advocacy for individual patients.

In the attempt to contain NHS costs, general practitioners are required under the 1990 contract to take responsibility for preventive health care. Screening programmes are being implemented by primary-care workers whom patients know and trust. If cost-effective uptake of preventive care can be achieved in this way, such programmes are expected to limit the cost to the nation of curative and palliative care for heart disease and cancers.

The turmoil in general practice in the 1990s, including a catastrophic drop in recruitment to the speciality, is directly related to the formidable agenda facing today's general practitioners. They and their colleagues in primary-care teams have the task of reconciling two sets of conflicting values and priorities; those of the advocate of the individual patient, and those of the public-health physician.

The early years, 1946–1970

Many of the administrative and professional structures of the NHS were already in place before the appointed day, and the professional and social standing of the general practitioner in the mid-twentieth century was determined by many factors in the social history of the UK.[6] Attitudes and styles of behaviour, both for doctors and patients, changed only slowly under the NHS. For

---

[6] R. Hodgkinson, *The Origins of the National Health Service* (London, 1967).

most general practitioners, the change was equivalent to the extension of existing NI arrangements to cover the whole population. The overriding issue was the establishment of a new relationship with the public in which fees played no part. Doctors were contracted, at least in principle, to be available to all their patients all the time. This challenge was made quite explicit by Aneurin Bevan, the Minister of Health, in 'A Message to the Medical Profession':

On July the 5th there is no reason why the whole of the doctor–patient relationship should not be freed from what most us feel should be irrelevant to it, the money factor—an aspect of practice already distasteful to many practitioners . . . The picture I have always visualised is not one of 'panel doctoring' for the less well off. . . . there is nothing of the social group or class in this; and I know you will be with me in seeing that there does not unintentionally grow up any kind of differentiation between those who use the new arrangements and those who, for any reason of their own, do not.[7]

The public took the promises of the Beveridge Report (1942) and the social values they represented to its heart. Post-war politicians had no choice but to honour the promise which the wartime Coalition Government had already endorsed. There had, however, been no research on the consequences for general practitioners. Oral histories illustrate the concerns of general practitioners in this immediate post-war period.[8] Many returning ex-service men entered general practice at this time. With their experience of a system in which fees played no part, they mostly approved of the equitable provision envisaged in the new service, even if they were suspicious of government intervention in the affairs of medicine. One doctor (RO, qualified in 1942) commented: 'I was quite keen. I always thought it was a good idea—my reasons were totally emotional. I'd no idea what was going to happen really, or how it was to evolve.' Another doctor of the same generation (JH) said, 'At the beginning of the NHS the pay wasn't awfully good but the spirit strangely enough was. One felt this was something new and you had to get on with it and make it a success. It had a lot to do with just having been through a war.' This positive attitude was not confined to what might be thought of as more privileged areas; many of the oral histories of this period have a positive, almost heroic quality. JM entered general practice in an industrial area of Durham, having served in the navy. He worked obsessively. 'Medicine was like a service, a holy grail if you will. It was something you did for mankind. It sounds grandiose now.'

For some doctors the loss of private practice was a major concern, particularly country doctors with a mixed list of private and 'panel' patients. Established doctors were surprised and somewhat hurt that so many of their old private patients elected to join the 'panel'. Long traditions and distinctions in

---

[7] A. Bevan, 'A Message to the Medical Profession', *British Medical Journal* (1948), ii. 1.

[8] M. Bevan, *The Oral History of General Practice 1935–1952* (London: Contemporary Medical Archives Centre, Wellcome Institute for the History of Medicine, 183 Euston Road). Quotations from the archive are given here with the appropriate general practitioners' initials.

the doctor–patient relationship were involved. Prior to the NHS, 'panel' patients may have received much the same medical treatment as private patients, but the manner in which it was delivered was usually very different. Private patients were visited at home or were received by appointment at the front door of the doctor's house, and welcomed by the maid or the doctor's wife.

Dr R. Green correctly anticipated the reaction of the public.

It is becoming increasingly obvious that, owing to the high compulsory National Insurance contributions and . . . income tax, most patients will feel unable to pay doctors' bills in addition, so the amount of private practice remaining will generally be very small. The vast majority of general practitioners are thus likely to be almost entirely dependent upon capitation payments for National Health Service patients.[9]

As well as the possible loss of income, doctors were concerned that ex-private patients would have unrealistic expectations of the treatment they could receive under the NHS, particularly as regards such privileges as home visiting and avoiding long waits at the doctor's surgery. DB, in a fairly prosperous country town, had a very personal private practice which constituted about half of his patients. 'The big surprise was that all the half-guinea patients, who I expected would elect to remain private patients, all joined up. So I said to them they would need to come to the surgery. But that didn't seem to put them off.' Asked if he thought that National Health had changed his attitude to patients he replied: 'Oh no I don't think so. We tried not to make any difference.'

DB's experience was the rule throughout the UK. Private general practice survived only in small pockets, and the vast majority of people of all shades of class or wealth joined the NHS. General practice under the NHS is a form of contract medicine, in which the doctor undertakes the medical care of a defined group for a fixed sum. There is in all forms of contract medicine a potential imbalance between the demands of the recipients and the response of the provider, which must be resolved if relations between the two are to be harmonious. General practitioners had extensive experience of contract medicine with the Lloyd George NHI panel. The major difference was that the doctor now had little control over his workload. Under the NHI panel the expectations of working men had been low; and they were often fearful to offend the doctor, not least because they depended on his goodwill for the care of their uninsured families. Under the NHS, however, everyone had a right to the doctor's services. In country and suburban areas a tradition of respect for the doctor continued, and consideration for his evidently busy life helped to control demand.[10] In most families of all classes, 'bothering the doctor' without good cause was frowned on.

[9] R. Green, 'The Remuneration of Doctors', *British Medical Journal* (1948), ii. 110.
[10] I. Cromarty, 'What do Patients think about during their Consultation?', *British Journal of General Practice*, 46 (1996), 525–8.

However, in some deprived areas where health services had previously been inadequate, the newly enfranchised NHS patients came across as demanding and even aggressive. The situation was aggravated by inadequate premises, and lack of organizational support. The 'pool' system of remuneration made such inadequacies very hard to change, since expenditure on such improvements was seen by the individual doctor as coming out of his personal income. Undoubtedly this led at times to poor standards of work by dispirited and fatigued doctors, and to poor relationships with patients. This was particularly likely in areas of industrial poverty and high medical demand. It was practices of this kind which were reflected in the gloomy picture of general practice painted by Collings.[11]

Most practices coped, and the defects of general practice were treated with tolerance or stoicism by both doctors and patients. Excessive workload is, however, a constant theme in the oral histories of doctors in that period. DB again:

I did work tremendously hard. I reckon I had a fourteen hour day. In the end we became a threesome, we started sharing Sundays, and that was a great help. And then eventually when the pressure was so great, I said, 'I must have a day a week' and I spent my day in bed.

MN was working in Worcester:

Time off came when there was time to have it, full stop! It was not your statutory right to have your half day. Hours of work?—I don't think we thought about it, because the job is there to be done, so you do it. That's just the way it was. I am not saying it was right.

Many general practitioners feared that they would be overwhelmed by the demands of patients who had been given open access to their services. What patients had a right to demand and what doctors had a right to refuse was always an emotive issue. JM in Bolton remembers the development of a *modus vivendi*.

In the beginning of the Health Service anyone who called could have a call there and then. There was no way in which I could say 'No'. One of the greatest things that happened somewhere about '58 or '59 was when a doctor was permitted not to go if he thought it was not necessary, if he could give advice on the telephone. I know people nowadays grumble about secretaries being dragons and not letting you see the doctor, but it all started like that. It started because the doctor was called out frivolously.

Some degree of control had to be imposed by the doctor. Some doctors with experience in the armed forces saw the 'sick parade' as an appropriate model for NHS practice. RSS (qualified 1928) said, 'I used to tell off patients, give them a ticking off. Yes. And they'd come back for more! If you are

---

[11] J. S. Collings, 'General Practice in England Today: A Reconnaissance', *Lancet* (1950), i. 555–85.

having a row with a patient, they know you're taking an interest in them.' RC described how his war experience affected his relationship with his patients in Bolton.

I came back from the war, I'd been a major, acting colonel, for a good while. . . . I think I had this attitude that patients must pull themselves together, do as they are told, and so on. I remember one chap saying to me, 'Look here doctor, you're not in the army now!' And that settled me down.

Part of the reason for doctors accepting a punitive workload was that they now had to deal with the burden of morbidity in the community which had remained unrecognized under the old system. JC, qualified in 1947 and practising in Cowley, Oxford, recalled:

Particularly at the beginning, there was a great pent up wave. . . . people who could begrudge paying money for their children's ailments turning up in droves in the surgery. You suddenly realised there was a lot more of illness about of a minor or even major nature than was hitherto thought. So there was a great rush of use of the health service in the first few years. But [after that] you didn't see children with neglected septic fingers looking like a sausage full of pus because parents would bring the child along earlier. I don't think people were abusing the health service because what came to the surgery really did merit attention. It was only many years later that people started to come along and abuse the health service demanding tranquillisers and sleeping tablets, and wasting the doctor's time.

What constituted genuine illness was and remains difficult to determine in general practice. What is clear from the oral history archive is that 'frivolous' demands were deeply resented. JR from Sheffield commented:

When the Health Service came in, the attitude came in: 'I've paid for you to come when I want you.' I always remember being sent for by a patient in the middle of the afternoon. I was hurrying up the hill because I'd got a lot of people to visit, and this woman was standing at the gate and said, 'There's no need to hurry doctor, there's no rush. I only need a prescription.'

Prescribing has always played an important part in the relationship between general practitioners and their patients. In the early nineteenth century the apothecary could charge for his medicines but not for his opinion. McQ remarked: 'This goes back to the old tie-up between their consultation and the bottle of medicine, and the 3/6d that was charged [for both]. They went together, so that when the NHS started, people expected a prescription.' MM, qualified in 1939:

The NHS enabled you to prescribe drugs which the patient would never previously have been able to afford to buy. There is nothing worse than standing on Thursday night at the foot of the kid's bed, and knowing the kid needed penicillin and knowing damn well there was no money to buy it. But the day after the NHS, you could prescribe as many bottles of penicillin as you liked. That made all the difference to doctoring.

The number of prescriptions dispensed by pharmacists rose dramatically in the first year of the NHS and has continued to do so ever since (see Tables C5 and C6). Initially the range of drugs was limited, but the pharmaceutical industry soon began to offer an ever-increasing array. Many drugs, like oral penicillins, were of great value, but there were also drugs that doctors themselves felt to be little more than expensive alternatives to their older and simpler treatments for minor conditions. The desire for a prescription was often as much the doctor's as the patient's, and there was a pressure to prescribe that was difficult to control in the new world of 'wonder drugs'. GT said 'In the days when you were dispensing yourself, you could dispense things that didn't cost very much, but when you are writing out an NHS prescription, it becomes more difficult to prescribe coloured water, and therefore you prescribe something that is going to cost more.' With the advent of the mass media, patients became better informed about available drugs.[12] Some of them made inappropriate demands. JJ, in a new town practice in the 1960s, remembers feeling discomfited when asked to prescribe amphetamines for young girls wishing to improve their figures, and the difficulty of dissuading them. The government, the profession, and the public had all been led into believing that free access to prescribed drugs would mean better health for the nation. Disasters such as the congenital defects caused by prescription of the anti-emetic thalidomide for pregnant women, and the personal and social problems linked to the prescribing of amphetamines, barbiturates, and tranquillizers became common knowledge in the late 1960s. The public began to be more critical and even fearful of prescribed drugs.

The leaven of optimism and goodwill that had prevailed through the first decades of the NHS ran out for many doctors in the 1960s. JE remembered: 'All those years trying to keep up with demands. I was like someone trying to get on a bus that was going, and you never quite get both feet on the platform at the back.' This emotional exhaustion was also recalled by JM: 'The doctor reached a point when he was so sickened by it, and he said "I can't cope with it." There was no easing of it. There was no way out of it, this constant demand of a population which was then given something for nothing.' A multitude of letters published in the supplements of the *British Medical Journal* suggested that doctors' relationships with their patients had become seriously disturbed.

From the patients' point of view, however, we have little evidence of the breakdown of relationships between doctors and patients. Ann Cartwright was involved in fieldwork for her first book during 1964–5, when the crisis in general practice which led to the threat of mass resignation and finally to the Family Doctor Charter, was at its height. Her study aimed 'to portray the relationship between patients and their general practitioners'. Part of her summary runs as follows: 'The general picture that emerges is of satisfied

---

[12] C. Lawrence, *Medicine and the Making of Modern Britain 1700–1920* (London, 1995).

and appreciative patients. Many seem to feel a definite sense of identification with their doctor. If he appears hurried or even impatient, they tend to explain this in terms of over-work and conditions under the National Health Service.'[13]

Indeed, opinion surveys of the time showed that the public held general practitioners in high esteem, placing them above headmasters, bank managers, and solicitors. During the course of her study Cartwright was struck by the reluctance of patients to criticize their doctors and by a certain discomfort at even answering questions about them. Amongst the general practitioners interviewed, work stress, lack of time, and confusion about their role were all causes of discontent. But when asked what they enjoyed about their work, 48 per cent agreed that it was 'the friendship of my patients and their respect' which counted for most.[14] The frustrations of general practice, it seems, had more to do with its organization, the conditions of work, and pay than with relationships with their patients.

The spirit of cooperation impressed R. B. Howells, Chairman of the Executive Council of Cheshire. 'Many defects in the service, or difficulties in the application of central policy to the local scene, have been remedied or overcome by the initiative and good sense of the people most intimately concerned—doctor and patient.'[15] By the mid-1960s, the NHS had won over the hearts of the British people. As Lindsey wrote: 'So much has it become a part of the British way of life, it is difficult for the average Englishman to imagine what it would be like without those services that have contributed so much to his physical and mental well-being.'[16] The Labour Government that came to power in October 1963, with Kenneth Robinson as Minister of Health, was quick to recognize the need to find a solution to the crisis in general practice, and to reach agreement with the profession. The changes in the organization and funding of general practice which were associated with the implementation of the Family Doctor Charter in 1966 have been described elsewhere in this volume. We will now consider the impact of these changes on the relationship between general practice and its patients.

The good years, 1971–1985

In the retrospective mythology of general practice, the Family Doctor Charter is seen as the beginning of a golden age. The working conditions of doctors, and their remuneration, were much improved. Morale rose, and with it the number and quality of young doctors wishing to enter general practice. A new intellectual leadership had emerged amongst general practitioners. Several members of this group were greatly influenced by Michael Balint, who used

[13] Cartwright, *Patients and their Doctors*, 9.
[14] Ibid. 39.
[15] R. Howells, quoted in A. Lindsey, *Socialised Medicine in England and Wales* (London, 1962), 229.
[16] Lindsey, *Socialised Medicine in England and Wales*, 474.

insights from psychoanalysis to study the relationships of doctors and patients within the setting of the consultation.[17] The concepts advanced by Balint became very influential in the academic life of the Royal College of General Practitioners during the next decade. Browne and Freeling wrote about Balint's concepts in an engaging, practical way,[18] and in 1972 the Royal College of General Practitioners published *The Future General Practitioner*,[16] which defined the role of the general practitioner and the range of knowledge, skills, and attitudes needed, and proposed that diagnosis should 'be composed in physical, psychological and social terms'.[19]

Vocational training for general practice was introduced and became mandatory for principals in 1975. *The Future General Practitioner* and the ideas contained in it were very influential in the development of vocational training programmes, and hence on the attitudes of doctors entering practice from 1980. Many older doctors were also influenced, particularly those who became trainers. JE, who joined his father's practice in Doncaster in 1949, recalled his experience on a trainer's course in Cambridge in the 1970s. 'They really put us through it. They would say "Well, what do you think you're achieving?" Well, you know I was made to sit down and really think.' The traditional medical model was thus challenged and redefined in the 1970s. What emerged was a picture of the consultation as an exploration to which both patient and doctor needed to contribute, and which should lead to an agreed understanding expressed in personal as well as medical terms.

Some forward-looking general practitioners also began to include other tasks besides the analysis of the 'presenting problem' in their remit—for example, anticipatory care for chronic disease, and health education. The implications of this wider role for doctors will be discussed later in this chapter.

It is easy to assume that patients benefited as much as doctors from the post-Charter rise in the self-esteem of general practitioners and their improved conditions of service. However, in terms of the things patients value most in their general practitioners, the picture was far less clear. Cartwright identified an important area of concern for patients when she noted that, between her studies of 1964 and 1977, general practitioners appeared to be 'retreating from more intimate contact with their patients'.[20] Some of the oral histories bear this out: 'I think a lot of doctors really rather chucked the sponge in', said BC, who qualified in 1946. The old 'cottage industry', as the Gillie Report described pre-Charter general practice, had been based on an intimate and continuing relationship between the doctor and patient as individuals—a relationship from which neither party could easily escape.[21] In the post-Charter

[17] M. Balint, *The Doctor, his Patient and the Illness* (London, 1957). This seminal book reported Balint's work in London with a group of general practitioners.
[18] K. Browne and P. Freeling, *The Doctor–Patient Relationship* (London, 1967).
[19] RCGP, *The Future General Practitioner: Learning and Teaching* (London: RCGP, 1972).
[20] Cartwright and Anderson, *General Practice Revisited*, 186.
[21] Central Health Services Council, Standing Medical Advisory Committee, *The Field of Work of the Family Doctor: Report of the Sub-Committee* (The Gillie Report; London: HMSO, 1963).

world, that exclusive relationship with the doctor was progressively eroded. A visit to the surgery or health centre might mean seeing whichever doctor was available, or perhaps a practice nurse instead, or a health visitor. There were gains in the range of services made available, and in some aspects of efficiency, and patients assumed their doctors were competent at their job. But Cartwright's studies confirm that they were not always happy about some of the organizational changes that came with the Charter.

Rotas with other practices for evening and weekend duties were a growing feature of general practice in the 1970s and 1980s. These rotas could weaken the sense of mutual respect and bonding between individual patients and their own doctors. Cartwright showed that more doctors were using deputizing services, especially for night work in urban areas, in spite of larger partnerships which eased the burden of on-call hours.[22] Deputizing services that involved long waits were particularly resented by patients, as were appointment systems that made it more difficult to see the doctor.[23] TMcQ recalled the changing behaviour of some patients in a northern industrial town:

A request for a visit in the late 1940s and the 1950s, and indeed into the 1960s, was often prefaced by something like 'I am sorry to disturb you, doctor.' On the other hand in the 1980s, I can remember when I was covering for another practice and they rang me, they didn't know me at all, and this was just 'can thee get the bloody doctor up here straight away'. You would never have heard that in the 1950s.

In *General Practice Revisited*, Cartwright compared her findings with those from 1964 and reported on the percentage of patients who made critical comments. In the later study there was an increased proportion of negative comments under four categories: willingness to visit (adverse comments increased from 3 per cent of respondents in 1964 to 13 per cent in 1977); hastiness (6 per cent to 14 per cent); not listening (3 per cent to 7 per cent); not explaining things fully (16 per cent to 23 per cent). Interestingly, Cartwright herself felt that these changes probably reflected a more critical attitude on the part of patients, and rising expectations of doctors, rather than a decline in standards. She found that general levels of satisfaction remained high among doctors themselves. In 1964, 52 per cent of doctors said they enjoyed their work very much and in 1977 the proportion was 55 per cent. The commonest stated cause of that satisfaction was the good relationship with their patients. And indeed, 90 per cent of patients interviewed in the 1977 study described themselves as 'satisfied' or 'very satisfied' with the care they received from their doctors. Whether these opinions still represented the 'uncritical acceptance' she had described in 1964 was less clear.[24]

Another important study of general practice and its patients that covered

[22] Cartwright and Anderson, *General Practice Revisited*, 36.
[23] D. Allen, R. Leaveyard, and B. Marks, 'Survey of Patient Satisfaction with Access to General Practitioners', *Journal of the Royal College of General Practitioners*, 38 (1988), 163–5.
[24] Cartwright and Anderson, *General Practice Revisited*, 187.

this period was carried out by Margot Jefferys and her team, who studied the move by two group practices into a brand-new health centre between 1970 and 1982.[25] She also investigated two single-handed practices in the same inner-city area. On patient satisfaction, she found considerable evidence to show that patients tend to express approval for the services they are currently receiving. Her conclusions pointed, indeed, to the considerable degree to which patients tried to adapt to what they felt their doctor expected of them. What patients most wanted, she thought, was 'an opportunity to present [their] problem in all its complexity, in the expectation that the doctor would have the knowledge, skill, and sympathy to show them how to deal with it'.[26] Their chief expressed need was for a doctor who knew them, took time, listened to them, understood and explained. Given a doctor–patient relationship of this kind, the majority of patients were tolerant about other aspects of care in general practice.

The time element was, and is, a vital component of patient satisfaction. Hull studied patients' views of the adequacy of the consultation time in relation to their perceived ability to communicate their problems to their doctors.[27] Consultation times were felt to be adequate for the presentation of physical illness, but where a significant part of the problem was felt to be psychological, less than half the patients felt they had been able to communicate as well as they would have wished. The situation was significantly worse where the doctor's mean consultation time was less than eight minutes.

In reality, the new intellectual models of consultation tasks seems to have had limited impact on the day-to-day practice of most doctors. Byrne and Long analysed 2,500 individual consultations and identified a number of 'basic styles' employed by doctors in the management of their consultations.[28] They concluded that the majority of doctors evolve a relatively static style of consulting. They felt that this style was little influenced by variation in the verbal or social skills of the patients, or in the kind of problems they presented. Few of the doctors were able to view the process of consultation in such a way that they were able to make judgements not only about 'what they were doing', but also about 'how they were doing it'.[29]

The fascination of the process of the consultation for the academic leadership in general practice, and the emphasis given to the subject in vocational training schemes, was not, seemingly, manifested by demonstrable change in consulting styles across the UK. Other constraints, particularly the brevity of the consultation, made it difficult for doctors to change long-established ways of coping. Cartwright showed that between her two studies of 1964 and 1977

---

[25] M. Jefferys and H. Sachs, *Rethinking General Practice* (London, 1983).

[26] Ibid. 302–3, 322.

[27] F. M. Hull, 'Time and the General Practitioner: The Patient's View', *Journal of the Royal College of General Practitioners*, 34 (1984), 71–5.

[28] P. S. Byrne and B. E. L. Long, *Doctors Talking to Patients* (London, 1976).

[29] Ibid. 103.

there had been no significant change in consultation rates (3.4 consultations per patient per year in 1964 and 3.6 in 1977). In the same period, consultation times became, if anything, shorter, with doctors spending less time in face-to-face contact with patients. The proportion of doctors who felt they had inadequate time to work properly rose from 20 per cent in 1964 to 27 per cent in 1977. Time pressures and the brevity of the consultation also affected patients. More than a third of patients questioned said that they worried about wasting the doctor's time, and one in eight had put off seeing the doctor because of the need to make an appointment in the last year.[30]

Despite the evident inability of general practitioners to meet the rising demands of a sophisticated public in full, this second period in our history (1971–85) was neverthless relatively harmonious. The novelty of choice may have contributed significantly. Instead of 'inheriting' their parents' single-handed family doctor, as had been the case before, patients registered with a group practice were able to consult the kind of doctor they wanted, after discussion with family and friends. Older doctors—the 'workhorses' of the early NHS days—were seeing large numbers of patients every day, with shorter consultations and high prescribing rates; the younger graduates of vocational training were more inclined to offer longer consultations and fewer prescriptions, befitting the expectations of a younger generation increasingly sceptical of drug treatments. In many practices it was possible to see a woman doctor, which many women patients and some men found they preferred.[31] By the 1980s there were also practice nurses in the larger practices who were able to see patients on a 'drop-in' basis. The demographic mix of doctors and patients during this period, and the goodwill of multidisciplinary teams of professionals, provided a wide range of therapeutic choices and a real sense of partnership and achievement in the NHS.

Cartwright had documented the emergence, in the setting of general practice, of a more discriminating public—a movement that was to gather momentum throughout the century. The 'generation gap' in post-war Britain illustrated a major shift in family life and in society at large. The emergence of significant teenage spending power, with rapid, restless change in aesthetic and cultural values, produced tension within families; the re-emergence of feminism in the UK and North America followed in the wake of the New Wave and the teenage revolution. In the flamboyant atmosphere of the 1960s, for the generation which, in Macmillan's phrase, had 'never had it so good', the old deference for authority figures such as parents, grandparents, doctors, and teachers seemed outdated and unnecessary. Doctor–patient relationships—like other relationships—became much less formal in the space of one generation. Journalists and social scientists helped to articulate the irreverent attitudes of young people and their distaste for authority. A radical

[30] Cartwright and Anderson, *General Practice Revisited*, 32.
[31] A. McPherson, 'Why Women's Health?', in A. McPherson (ed.), *Women's Problems in General Practice* (Oxford, 1993), 1–14.

critique of the medical establishment was undertaken by Ivan Illich, who argued that modern medical care was iatrogenic, in that people were becoming ever more dependent on doctors and less resourceful in looking after their own health.[32] John Berger's archetypal, solitary doctor-as-father-figure could no longer be seen as a norm.[33] The honeymoon was over; doctors, like politicians, had feet of clay.

Some doctors were better prepared for the impact of this new attitude in the consultation than others. As Johnson pointed out, deference is not always an expression of subservience; it can be used tactically by patients.[34] But the pioneers of vocational training in general practice had proposed that the doctor–patient relationship should move towards being a partnership of equals, without either the social distance or the imputation of the parent–child relationship that had characterized it in the past.[35] Greenfield took a positive view of assertive behaviour by patients, and demonstrated that it was associated with better outcomes of care.[36]

On the global stage, the Alma Ata Declaration promulgated the challenging slogan 'Health for All by the Year 2000'.[37] Primary health care was designated as the mechanism through which this vision would be fulfilled. Teams of health workers were envisaged, sharing the tasks of preventing illness, treating disease, and promoting self-care by community participation. It is reasonable to ask how far the British NHS fitted this image. As the lay public became better informed about health, were there, for example, opportunities for community participation in health care?

An early contributor in this area was the Consumers' Association, and specifically the Patients' Association, established in 1963. The Consumers' Association had been formed in London in 1961 in the wake of North American initiatives in the field of consumer rights, to encourage public awareness about consumer issues. The Association promoted good practice in advertising and fair trading—for example, ensuring accurate descriptions of and standards for household appliances. Within a few years, professional services were being looked into with a similar critical regard. The mandate adopted by the Patients' Association was that of an independent voice for patients, an advocate, to respond to and represent patients in the continuing debate about health services. There were many issues to address in the NHS, once the generally subservient attitudes to doctors were discarded; some were of concern to staff

[32] I. Illich, *Medical Nemesis: The Expropriation of Health* (London, 1975).

[33] J. Berger and J. Mohr, *A Fortunate Man* (London, 1967).

[34] M. L. Johnson, 'Patients: Receivers or Participants?', in K. Barnard and K. Lee (eds.), *Conflicts in the National Health Service* (London, 1977), 72–98.

[35] D. Pendleton, T. Schofield, P. Tate, and P. Havelock, *The Consultation: An Approach to Teaching and Learning* (Oxford, 1984); K. Fairhurst and C. May, 'Consumerism and the Consultation: The Doctor's View', *Family Practice*, 12 (1995), 389–91.

[36] S. Greenfield, S. H. Kaplan, J. E. Ware, E. M. Yano, and H. J. Frank, 'Patients' participation in Medical Care', *Journal of General Internal Medicine*, 3 (1988), 448–57.

[37] World Health Organization, *Alma Ata 1977: Primary Health Care* (Geneva: WHO, 1978).

and patients alike. As mentioned above, there were now side effects of drugs to be considered, and inefficacious or even iatrogenic treatments being recorded and talked about by a better informed and more literate public, and an ever-widening circle of fascinated doctor-watchers. Media images of doctors and nurses in the 1960s were comical, romanticized, or idealized. A generation reared on the succession of humorous 'Doctor' novels by Richard Gordon was subsequently fed a succession of medical programmes ranging from fact to fiction and soap opera, from both sides of the Atlantic. Charles Fletcher was the first 'radio doctor' for the BBC. With *Dr Finlay's Casebook*, *Dr Kildare*, and *Emergency Ward 10* on radio and television, medicine was being de-mystified as never before.

Three different ways of involving patients in the planning and evaluation of primary health care are distinguished by Pratt.[38] One is the consumerist model, represented in the early 1960s by the Patients' Association. A second model is a democratic one, with elected patient representatives engaged in dialogue with providers and managers of statutory services. Community Health Councils, set up during the 1974 reorganization of the NHS, bore some resemblance to this model. Participative development or 'community-development' approaches, when consumers are invited by providers to share in decision-making about service development, comprise a third model. We will briefly examine the extent to which each of these three approaches was adopted in the UK from the initiation of the NHS until the reforms of the 1990s.

The Patients' Association has played a limited role as a broad-based interest group with considerable expertise, a membership newsletter (*Patient Voice*), and alliances with Community Health Councils with a commitment to addressing changes in the NHS from the patients' viewpoint. It has been concerned to maintain a balance of opinion through its choice of leadership, in order to continue a productive dialogue with health professionals and with other consumer groups, such as the National Council for the Welfare of Children in Hospital, Age Concern, and the National Association for Mental Health (MIND), which focused on specific patient groups.

Self-help groups have been an important element of the consumer movement in health care. Groups such as the British Diabetic Association and the British Epilepsy Association evolved as an alliance between patients and professionals in relation to one particular disease or condition. Both these groups have contributed to developments in the care of patients with these chronic conditions, and their contributions have been duly recognized by the medical establishment. Acknowledgement of self-help groups is patchy in general practice, but no modern hospital outpatient department is complete without leaflets publicizing the activities of local branches of such groups.

Other self-help organizations are those set up in reaction to the medical establishment, by patients keen to publicize alternative views to the received

---

[38] J. Pratt, *Practitioners and Practices: A Conflict of Values?* (Oxford, 1995).

professional line. The National Childbirth Trust ran a successful campaign against unnecessary surgical intervention in childbirth in the 1970s; Rape Crisis centres were set up in several cities in the 1970s in protest against the lack of sensitive help for victims of sexual assault; and a more recent example of unresolved tension between aggrieved patients and the medical mainstream is the ME Society, which has campaigned for more attention to be paid to a fatigue syndrome entitled 'myalgic encephalitis'. The histories of self-help groups are often poignant, deriving from personal suffering of patients and carers. Their choices of alliance with or independence from health professionals make an interesting study; but their very diversity means that their influence on health policy and planning is limited. Compared to these single-issue organizations with their easily identified campaigning role and constituency, the Patients' Association with its general remit remained the smallest and most modestly funded of the consumer groups, and its voice has not been influential in general practice.[39]

Community Health Councils are statutory bodies set up alongside health authorities to represent consumer opinion; they are not truly democratic, in that their members are not elected but are nominated by voluntary organizations and health authorities. They have rights to observer status and to information from NHS authorities, and have a small budget from the health authority. Both Malcolm Johnson and Chris Ham, writing about the scope for a patients' voice in the running of the NHS, put an optimistic gloss on the potential of Community Health Councils, on the grounds that they were to have what amounted to a power of veto in relation to some of the developments envisaged at that time.[40] Their influence in primary care was limited, however; members were easily persuaded to mobilize interest to the more media-worthy stories of hospital services. Margaret Stacey was more pessimistic about the extent to which patients would be able to mobilize and act powerfully.[41] She pointed out how factors intrinsic to patienthood such as short-lived contacts with health-care institutions, illness and anxiety as well as hospital culture can hold back patient empowerment and consciousness-raising.

Patient-participation groups in primary care are an example of the third approach to consumer involvement, derived in part from community development work in developing countries. The term is used when a provider organization issues an explicit invitation to any interested consumers who wish to participate in planning or implementation of a service; sometimes the providers make such participation a condition of resource allocation. Patient participation groups in general-practice settings were first developed in

[39] C. J. Ham, 'Power, Patients and Pluralism', in Barnard and Lee (eds.), *Conflicts in the National Health Service* (London, 1977), 99–120.

[40] Johnson, 'Patients: Receivers or Participants'; Ham, 'Power, Patients and Pluralism'.

[41] M. Stacey, 'The Health Service Consumer: A Sociological Misconception', in M. Stacey (ed.), *The Sociology of the NHS: Sociological Review* (Monograph 22; Keele, 1976).

Oxfordshire in the early 1970s.[42] The earliest examples were set up to coincide with developments taking place in group practices which would be likely to affect patients directly. The aim was to promote patient involvement in decisions about service provision, as health centres and practice teams enlarged and communication channels became more elaborate. Patients were seen as potential partners in care, who would ensure that local services met local needs. The practitioners who set up such groups assumed that eligible representatives of the community would come forward as volunteers. Such patient-participation groups have been set up in a scattering of practices across Britain, but the idealistic assumptions of the pioneers have proved unfounded. It is difficult to attract and retain 'representative' patients, and groups rely on a few loyal members. Spontaneous involvement is usually related to a specific (often time-limited) issue; patients approached at random in the waiting room and asked for their views have been known to retort that running the health centre is not their responsibility.[43]

To what extent, then, were patient views used by providers in planning health services? In 1983, Cartwright expressed surprise that surveys of the acceptability of health services had not been carried out more widely and used in the planning process. 'Now that we have an NHS, a consumer movement with at least some recognition of its role in the service, and a public that is increasingly interested in and informed about health, it is surprising that surveys of acceptability are not carried out more generally.'[44] She felt that the climate had changed significantly for both patients and professionals between the 1960s and the 1980s; doctors had become more relaxed about the idea of using patients' views, and patients had become more open in expressing their criticisms and reservations.

The National Health Service reforms, 1985–1996: who calls the tune now?

In the period between 1971 and 1985, as we have seen, the Royal College of General Practitioners came of age, the new primary-health-care teams established themselves, and patients became more assertive and knowledgeable about health. The generally harmonious relationships between doctors and patients in this period were largely free of concern about the cost of the NHS; family practitioner committee budgets for general medical services were not cash-limited, and patients were referred for hospital care at the discretion of the general practitioner. Because of the trust placed in the general practitioner as gatekeeper, and public acquiescence to long waiting lists for non-urgent specialist care, the NHS was not as expensive as European or North American

[42] P. Pritchard, *Patient Participation in General Practice* (RCGP Occasional Paper 17; London, 1981).

[43] S. Graham-Jones, 'How User-Friendly is your Practice', *Practitioner*, 231 (1987), 1041–5.

[44] A. Cartwright, *Health Surveys in Practice and in Potential* (London: King's Fund, 1983), 115.

health-care systems (see Fig. C2). In the late 1970s, however, the NHS was as vulnerable as other organizations to the spiralling costs of staffing and technical innovations. Drug costs also took their toll. Margaret Thatcher's economic advisers took note of the writing on the wall. With the Griffiths Report in front of them as they emerged victorious from the 1983 general election, they prepared to confront the medical profession and remodel the NHS, insisting on the need for economic sustainability and standard-setting across districts. The devices employed to achieve this aim, such as the purchaser/provider split, the internal market, the new role for public-health physicians in health authority purchasing plans, and fundholding schemes for general practice, are described in other chapters.

In this section we look at the impact of the NHS reforms of 1990–6 on doctor–patient relationships in a population which shared the expectations of the free health service which Nye Bevan was so proud to depict to his colleagues at the Ministry of Health in 1947 as 'a great collective experiment [to be carried out] through the agency of a profession which abounds in individualism'.[45] Have there been fundamental changes in the public image of the general practitioners, or in doctor–patient relationships, as a result of the new systems for planning and delivering primary care?

Certainly, both the lay public and the medical profession were reluctant to get to grips with the Conservative Government's pronouncements about the need for cost containment and 'managed care' during the 1980s. Health economics were not part of any medical curriculum, and doctors stubbornly ignored warnings about increasing costs. The profession and its loyal public resorted to conspiracy theory as the government Green and White Papers appeared in the mid and later 1980s and the restructuring of the NHS started. The Conservatives were blamed for launching an ideological attack on the NHS, the pride of post-war socialist Britain. They counter-attacked by launching the Patient's Charter in 1991.

Despite Conservative promises of an increased voice for patients in the new NHS, consumer groups such as the Patients' Association and Community Health Councils have had little influence on health spending, owing to their lack of bargaining power in relation to government, local hospital, or primary-care administration. Chris Ham[46] cites Dahl's argument in relation to the distribution of power amongst different interest groups; that a group will have an effective voice only if it has sanctions, that is 'officials suffer . . . if they do not placate the group, its leaders, or its most vociferous members'.[47] The broad-based patients' interest groups have had little power in this coercive sense. The reforms of the 1990s have signally failed to exploit the potential of Community Health Councils in purchasing of secondary care, despite their efforts to channel information appropriately. No public consultation on rationing, of the

[45] Unpublished speech by Aneurin Bevan to the Whitley Council, January 1947.
[46] Ham, 'Power, Patients and Pluralism'.
[47] R. Dahl, *Pluralist Democracy in the United States* (Chicago, 1967), 145.

kind pioneered in Oregon in the USA, was held in the UK.[48] The 'streamlining' at the level of the health district meant that the influence of advisory bodies was actually reduced; in relation to primary care, their voice was further muted by the merging of FHSAs with health authorities in 1995–6.

Nor has the potential for patient participation been realized in primary care, despite promising beginnings. The dominance of doctors in decision-making at the practice level is as yet unchallenged. It is difficult to attract 'representative' patients into decision-making, since for most people in a community health care is ignored until illness care is needed. Patient participation groups remain sparsely scattered across the UK; few are genuinely consumer-led. Issues of participation and control have been explored, though not resolved, at the pioneering Marylebone Centre in London.[49]

The Patient's Charter represents a hybrid approach to patient involvement: a 'consumerist' exercise in target-setting for the medical profession, imposed without consultation with the profession or the public.[50] The Department of Health imposed a set of targets on NHS Trusts for delivery of health services (arbitrary limits to waiting times for elective surgery, for example). General practices were encouraged to set similar targets and display them in waiting rooms. The implication is that providers not achieving targets would be penalized. This confrontational approach was resented by many health workers already working with severely constrained resources, since the targets were often unachievable without further investment in the NHS. If targets are settled by mutual agreement, with achievable goals and accessible resources, then a robust 'boot-strap' approach to management and contracting as well as consumer involvement may indeed bring about improvements. But imposition of unachievable goals impairs the dialogue between providers and consumers and leads to a 'complaints culture'.[51] The Patient's Charter has, whilst appearing to be a pro-patient move, set doctors and practices to compete with each other openly for patient loyalty. Whilst encouraging successful practices to build up list sizes and to offer an increasing range of services, it has sown discontent and demoralization for many patients and practices in the new 'market place'.

It seems ironic that the issue of patient involvement in planning has been so neglected in the rush to reform the NHS. In primary care the divide between fundholders and non-fundholders, and the building up of local commissioning efforts by groups of non-fundholding general practitioners, has diverted attention away from the independent consumer movement. Most doctors have had little enough time in which to absorb the latest changes and discuss the

[48] R. Crawshaw, M. J. Garland, B. Hines, and C. Lopitz, 'Oregon Health Decisions: An Experiment with Informed Community Consent', *Journal of the American Medical Association*, 254 (1985), 3213–16.
[49] P. Pietroni and D. Chase, 'Partners or Partisans: Patient Participation and General Practice: The Marylebone Experiment', *British Journal of General Practice*, 43 (1993), 341–4.
[50] Department of Health, *The Patient's Charter* (London, 1991).
[51] G. Strawford, *New Complaints Procedures in General Practice* (London, 1996).

reforms with their peers, let alone with patients' representatives. There has been much resentment at the speed with which central government has changed the 'goalposts' of primary and secondary health care. Successive publications reviewing the meaning and implications of the proposed changes have been rendered out of date almost before publication. Partly because of the pace of change, the media debate about the necessity for and the handling of the NHS reforms has been a fragmented affair, rarely helpful to doctors or patients in their attempt to forge new relationships which acknowledge the realities of resource constraints.[52]

Doctor–patient relationships have been strained by anxiety about resources for health care, the politics of general practice, and the pace of change. These anxieties may indeed have generated extra consultations, contributing to the documented increase in general-practitioner workload since 1979. At the same time the public-health function of primary-care teams is being emphasized,[53] with systematic health promotion, 'life-style counselling', immunizations, and screening for heart disease and cancer overtaking the opportunistic methods employed by the previous generation of practitioners. Targets set centrally under the Health of the Nation strategy reflect government priorities. Resources have, in this case, been earmarked by the Department of Health, in the form of financial incentives for general practitioners who can provide evidence of systematic health promotion efforts; but some general practitioners are resentful at being pushed into the role of public-health functionary, especially where the evidence of benefit is scarce or where, as in the case of smoking, the government could do more by purposive legislation.

Patients are becoming habituated to preventive medicine, screening procedures, and health checks, but with mixed feelings. Attempting to marshall the public-health arguments for pertussis immunization to convince the anxious parents of 2-month-old babies is now a routine but taxing task for general practitioners, practice nurses, and health visitors, and can interfere with the relationship with the entire family. To take another example: in a population-based cancer-screening programme, attempts are made to contact non-attenders. This helps to define health needs for the planners in the practice and in the health authority, but may at the same time generate anxiety for patients who have not seen themselves as ill.[54] Tudor Hart's 'inverse care law' applies here as elsewhere in the NHS, in that resources set aside for health promotion are too often spent on the 'worried well' who need them least, rather than on high-risk non-attenders.[55] Health promotion, like other medical technologies, can have harmful effects. Research is now being funded to elucidate the negative effects of health screening on patients.[56]

---

[52] M. Konner, *The Trouble with Medicine* (London, 1993).
[53] J. C. Hasler, *The Primary Health Care Team* (London, 1994).
[54] L. J. Fallowfield, *Breast Cancer* (London, 1991).
[55] J. Tudor Hart, 'The Inverse Care Law', *Lancet* (1971), i. 405–12.
[56] J. Austoker, 'Cancer Prevention in Primary Care: Current Trends and Some Prospects for the Future—II', *British Medical Journal*, 309 (1994), 517–20.

Complementary therapies

The use of 'alternative' therapies—homeopathy, acupuncture, chiropractic, osteopathy, and herbal medicine are the most popular—has become more wide-spread in the UK. In the 1960s the uptake of alternative therapies formed part of the protest against the dominant culture of medicine which we have described. Patients were attracted to the prospect of 'natural' remedies for common illnesses, avoiding the side effects of drugs. Regardless of the efficacy of the specific remedies offered, a major underlying attraction is the generous allowance of time for each consultation. Patients are clearly willing to pay private clinic fees and take remedies which are not regarded by the medical profession as having scientific validity in order to gain access to personalized, caring therapy. It remains true that 'alternative' practitioners offer more face-to-face time in consultations than any NHS service other than formal psychotherapy.

In the last two decades there has been some collaboration between NHS and alternative practitioners, such that the term 'complementary medicine' has gained credence.[57] These initiatives have come from both sides of the divide and are now being looked at critically by purchasers. Despite willing collabo-ration in clinical settings, with acupuncture, herbal medicine, and aromather-apy coming into routine use in certain clinical settings, and a new generation of therapists willing to undertake research, there is little research funding and a dearth of large-scale, definitive studies of efficacy. Paradoxically, while the move towards 'evidence-based medicine' is under way within the NHS to rationalize therapeutic provision, the new internal market has led to a burgeoning of opportunity for unproven alternative therapies. The new contract for general practice, and moves towards voluntary acceptance of licensing for complementary practitioners, have enabled general practitioners and complementary therapists to offer services in parallel, with a mix of NHS and private provision which blurs the distinction between the two for the consumer. The offer of generous consultation times and remedies, which may be unproven in statistical terms but are generally harmless, can indeed complement the work of primary-care teams, and many patients are evidently willing to pay.

Therapeutic disasters are rare but not unknown, especially in relation to inappropriate spinal manipulation or herbal medicines. Equally, there are real dangers when severe treatable disease remains undiagnosed. But in the new mixed economy of health care it is occasionally the complementary therapist who takes the role of patient advocate in arguing for NHS services, as in the case of the patient saying, 'My chiropractor says she cannot do anything more for my back pain until you have sent me to the hospital for investigations'.

[57] E. Ernst, 'Complementary Medicine: Doing More Good than Harm?', *British Journal of General Practice*, 46 (1996), 60–1.

Necessary compromise: lest we forget

Pratt discusses the conflict of values arising from the changing and multiple roles of general practitioners and the transition to an organizational ethos which was so much accelerated by the imposition of the new contract in 1990.[58] Defining a mission statement and working to objectives are examples of new tasks which are central to business management but new to general practitioners and their colleagues in primary care. Setting priorities across a wide range of different professional and lay concerns is a tall order, involving compromise and bargaining. Successful negotiations with related groups—other practices in the area, the health authority, patient representatives—depend on finding a collective voice. The uncomfortable truth is that financial management is now the key to survival for practices as organizations. Every element of service provision must be costed in order to be included in a business plan. Increasingly, cost-effectiveness becomes an issue for debate between professionals. The doctor–patient consultation at the heart of general practice has been invaded by new elements of the doctor's agenda such as resource allocation and achievement by the practice of health promotion targets which attract remuneration. What of patient-centred medicine now; or the attractive contention that promoting patient autonomy is the basis of working for health?[59]

Referrals for specialist care in the new NHS carry great significance for patients, as do prescriptions; the stress associated with the gatekeeper role of the general practitioner is growing in proportion to public awareness of rationing of care. Each choice about medication or referral affects the patient's perception of the motives of the general practitioner. Not only must the general practitioner be able to locate information and evidence to aid decision-making; he or she must also be able to inspire the confidence of patients made suspicious by knowledge of the upheavals in the health service. Protocol-based management of common clinical problems seems a logical and arguably cost-effective development in primary care, and patients and health workers are learning fast. Nevertheless, doctors must continue to be trained to take responsibility for ignoring clinical guidelines when the need arises.

Pratt discusses the manifestations of conflict between the values of the doctor as a public-health professional, as a member of a practice committed to a set of mission statements, and as a practitioner of patient-centred care.[60] Dealing with conflict is stressful; this conflict is surely pertinent to the downward trend in recruitment to general practice. Tomorrow's doctors will need training not only in health economics, but also in management and organizational skills. General practices have been small businesses since the inception of the NHS; but the level of competition they now face has transformed their

[58] Pratt, *Practitioners and Practices*.
[59] D. Seedhouse, *Health: The Foundations for Achievement* (Chichester, 1986).
[60] Pratt, *Practitioners and Practices*.

working environment. The members of each practice are having to confront these issues and divide the workload as best they can, whilst trying to maintain the confidence of their patients. If the multiple roles envisaged for the general practitioner turn out to be incompatible, further division of labour and specialization may be possible at the practice level, such that at any one time a doctor is acting mainly as a patient advocate, or mainly as a public-health functionary in relation to health promotion, health education, or rationing of care. We do not yet know how patients will react to this. The doctor–patient relationship remains a fruitful field for both qualitative and quantitative research, but the pace of change rapidly invalidates many findings. Although it is probably still true that doctors do not make enough use of the expertise of patients in planning their care,[61] patients in the NHS have so far given no indication of the limits to their tolerance. And since 'felt needs' are in any case unlikely to be synonymous with the targets identified by public-health officials as priorities for spending on health care, those who allocate resources will not accept patient satisfaction and popular appeal as arbiters of quality of care.

Tomorrow's general practitioners will not find it any easier than today's to meet patient demands without putting pressure on available resources. In a warning shot across the bows of a Labour government-in-waiting, Bacon pointed out that the government might in the end find that the price tag of clinical freedom for the generalist was worth the expense. In his monograph he discusses the differences between 'personal doctoring' in the NHS, with the emphasis on the doctor's clinical autonomy and responsibility, and an alternative 'agency-service' model in which doctors are contracted to work to clinical policies laid down by management.[62] He notes that the consequences of the agency model, such as faster achievement of pre-set targets, must be set against the satisfaction of patients and doctors with the flexibility of the current system and the future liability of management for redress by patients if policy applied under the agency-service model is later found to be erroneous. Under these circumstances, the agency itself would be held accountable. Bacon's analysis is timely and pertinent, since one of the consistent findings in the new NHS under the Patient's Charter is the rapid increase in the volume of complaints faced by general practitioners and the concomitant increase in medical defence subscriptions.[63] This provides a salutary reminder of the strength and economy of the historic British compromise embodied in the NHS Act of 1946, and the largely healthy partnership enjoyed by patients and their general practitioners in the ensuing half-century.

[61] D. Tuckett, M. Boulton, C. Olson, et al., Meetings between Experts: An Approach to Sharing Ideas in Medical Consultation (London, 1985).

[62] A. D. Bacon, Doctors, Patients and the NHS (London, 1996).

[63] Strawford, New Complaints Procedures.

11

Developments in Other Countries

JOHN HORDER

The aim of this chapter is to place within a wider context some of the important themes discussed in earlier chapters, by examining and comparing developments in other countries over the same period of time. Major limitations govern this aim:

1. Comparisons will not include any with developing countries. In their demography, epidemiology, economic and political background, and in the extent and organization of their health services, the differences with this country are too great.

2. Even developed countries are so numerous that any attempt to consider all would be inappropriate. It is in any case unnecessary. The focus will therefore be on a small group of countries like our own in general development, but chosen because their services exhibit a wide range of similarities and contrasts during this period.

3. Comparisons are often limited because reliable information is not available or because information from one country, though reliable, is not in a form which can properly be compared with that from another.

Although the main body of the chapter will be concerned with similarities and differences, this will be preceded by tracing the development of international channels of communication and mutual influence. In 1950 these were few and little used by general practitioners. The situation today is very different.

The value of international exchange

Since the practice of medicine is first learnt within the context of national customs and arrangements, it is natural for a doctor or nurse to continue thinking in those terms. In so far as a general practitioner's particular work requires local knowledge, this habit is reinforced. But a casual meeting with a doctor doing similar work in another country is almost certain to spark interest and discussion about similarities and differences. Accompanying and observing a general practitioner in another country can be a fascinating experience; it compels the visitor to see established habits in a new light and to question whether the way in which something is done in one's own country is the only way or the best way. It can lead to a constructive exchange of ideas and to mutual benefit. This is the basic assumption which justifies the inclusion in this book of a chapter about general practice in other countries.

In the last fifty years international contacts have extended from individuals to organizations. Examples of the influence of UK general practice on other countries and of other countries on our own Service have multiplied to touch many aspects of the work discussed in earlier chapters.

The development of channels of communication

Individual and organizational links, 1950–1959

In 1950 direct exchange of experiences and ideas between general practitioners in different countries depended on individual initiatives. This contrasted at the time with the experience of doctors in most other branches of medicine. To take one example—neurology—its British journal, *Brain*, had foreign neurologists on its editorial board, a foreign readership, and articles written by foreign contributors. Aspiring neurologists in training might spend time on fellowships in the USA. The World Association of Neurologists already existed and organized international conferences. In contrast, it was rare at that date, even within this country, for a general practitioner to be invited to address his colleagues on a technical subject, contribute an article to a journal, or write a book. If direct exchange between general practitioners was initiated by them in local or national meetings, it would usually be concerned with terms of service or with money. Continuing education was available, but, whether in divisions of the BMA, in local hospitals, in medical societies, or in journals like the *Practitioner*, it usually took the form of instruction by specialists aimed at helping general practitioners to keep up to date (the 1950 volume of the *Practitioner* contained 125 main articles, of which three were by general practitioners).

A notable example of an international initiative by an individual took place between 1948 and 1950 when Joseph Collings, a doctor trained in Australia, previously working as a general practitioner in New Zealand, gained a Harvard Fellowship to study general practice in the UK. He visited a large sample of practices in England and Scotland and reported at length in the *Lancet*.[1] His report, to which reference has already been made in other chapters, was strongly critical. This report appeared at a crucial time—two years after the start of the NHS. It played a part in stimulating the foundation of the College of General Practitioners two years later.[2] No subsequent report from any

[1] J. S. Collings, 'General Practice in England Today: A Reconnaissance', *Lancet* (1950), i. 555–85.
[2] J. H. Hunt, 'The Scope and Development of General Practice in Relation to other Branches of Medicine', *Lancet* (1955), ii. 29–35.

foreign visitor has had a comparable impact on general practice in this country. But it took decades before Collings's far-sighted prescriptions were acted upon in this country or in any comparable one.

The earliest international contacts between organizations were, for the UK, with other member states of the British Commonwealth. The College of General Practitioners included in its second Council (1954) members from Eire, Australia, and New Zealand. By 1957 there were four College Faculties in Eire, five in Australia, four in New Zealand, and one in Kenya. From these beginnings Australia and New Zealand had both formed their own Colleges by 1960. During the same years visits were also interchanged between senior members of the UK and Canadian Colleges of General Practice, but, until 1964, when Dr John Hunt addressed the American Academy of Family Practice,[3] contact with doctors doing the same work in the USA depended entirely on individuals. For example, a major contribution to understanding of the American scene was made in 1960 by Dr Theodore Fox, editor of the *Lancet*, who travelled extensively in the USA before writing his report in the same journal.[4] He described the great variety of patterns of front-line practice to be found there and concluded with an impassioned plea for the preservation of continuous personal care in an increasingly specialized and fragmented medical world.

The first travelling fellowships, international conferences, and specific international organizations, 1960–1969

In 1961 the Nuffield Foundation awarded the first of a series of annual Travelling Fellowships 'to enable general medical practitioners of outstanding ability, preferably between the ages of 35 and 45, to undertake approved study overseas in some subject of importance for general practice'.[5] Between that year and 1973 a total of thirty-seven doctors were awarded these fellowships and wrote reports, many of which were published in journals. Five among them were elected from Australia, Canada, and New Zealand to visit the UK. Nuffield Travelling Fellowships became prototypes for a growing number of similar opportunities which have continued to be available, although few of them have been so generously funded.

International communication about the work of general practitioners had started in a new form in 1959 with the first of a series of initiatives by the WHO—a conference at Helsinki, entitled 'Mental Health in Public Health and General Practice', organized by the Regional Office for Europe. This was followed by a trio of Expert Committees, held at the central office in Geneva, of

---

[3] J. H. Hunt, 'Gerneral Practice in the World Today and its Academic Needs', *Lancet* (1964), ii. 29–35.
[4] T. F. Fox, 'The Personal Doctor and his Relation to the Hospital: Observations and Reflections on some American Experiments in General Practice by Groups', *Lancet* (1960), i. 743–60.
[5] Nuffield Foundation, *Fifteenth Annual Report* (London, 1960).

which the reports were circulated to all governments. The first of these (1961) was on 'The Role of Public Health Officers and General Practitioners in Mental Health Care';[6] the second (1962) on 'The Training of the General Practitioner';[7] and the third (1964) on 'General Practice'.[8] A European Regional Conference was held in Edinburgh in 1961 on 'The Training of the Doctor for his Work in the Community'.[9] It is difficult to assess the influence of these reports, since the work of the WHO at that time was thought in developed countries—wrongly—to be irrelevant to their problems. Subsequent meetings of the WHO concerned with general practice, of which there have been many, have usually been organized from one or other of the six regional offices.

Two conferences in 1962 were particularly important because they led to the formation of continuing international organizations. The English-language bias which had hitherto dominated international exchanges was altered when the Societas Internationalis Medicinae Generalis (SIMG) was formed at a conference in Salzburg, Austria. This developed out of the International College of General Practice, which had held its first annual conference in Salzburg in 1959.[10] At first predominantly Austro-German, it later involved practitioners (and organizations) from most European countries, including the UK. Central figures were Dr Robert Braun, a rural practitioner from Austria, and Dr Gottfried Heller, who practised at Klagenfurt and taught at the University of Graz. While Heller was concerned mainly with education, Braun, starting from 1944, meticulously recorded and classified the morbidity in the patients he saw throughout his career. He was later awarded a professorship in the University of Vienna.[11]

In the same year Dr Bruce Cardew, Secretary of the Medical Practitioners' Union in the UK, organized a large conference in London on behalf of the journal *Medical World*. Entitled 'Organizing Family Doctor Care', it was attended by speakers and participants from all over the world, including the WHO. This conference appears to have inspired another, held in Montreal in 1964 at the invitation of the College of General Practitioners, later of Family Physicians, of Canada. Here a liaison committee of Colleges and Academies of General Practice was formed, setting off a series of two-yearly international

[6] WHO, *The Role of Public Health Officers and General Practitioners in Mental Health Care* (Eleventh Report of the Expert Committee on Mental Health, Technical Report Series 235; Geneva, 1961).

[7] WHO, *The Training of the General Practitioner* (Eleventh Report of the Expert Committee on Professional and Technical Education of Medical and Auxiliary Personnel, Technical Report Series 257; Geneva, 1962).

[8] WHO, *General Practice* (Report of a WHO Expert Committee, Technical Report Series 267; Geneva, 1964).

[9] WHO, *Preparation of the Physician for General Practice* (Public Health Papers 20; Geneva, 1963).

[10] L. Newman, 'SIMG Societas Internationalis Medicinae Generalis' (The International Society of General Practice), in J. Fry and T. Bouchier-Hayes (eds.), *The Medical Annual 1992: The Yearbook of General Practice* (Bristol, 1992), 17–21.

[11] R. N. Braun, *Lehrbuch der arzlichen allgemeinpraxis* (Munich, 1970).

meetings which have continued ever since.[12] At the conference held in Chicago in 1970 the title World Organization of National Colleges, Academies, and Academic Associations of General Practitioners/Family Physicians was adopted (World Organization of Family Doctors after 1992). It has always been best known as WONCA. The official inauguration was in Melbourne in 1972.[13]

The objective of WONCA is

to improve the quality of life of the peoples of the world through fostering and maintaining high standards of care in general practice/family medicine, by providing a forum for exchange of knowledge and information between member organizations, by encouraging and supporting the development of academic organizations and by representing the educational, research and service activities of general practitioners/family physicians to other relevant world organizations.[14]

Its influence has gradually increased, particularly through the activity of subcommittees. Its work in classifying the illnesses dealt with by general practitioners/family physicians is so far its best-known achievement.[15]

During the subsequent decades (1970–90) both the SIMG and WONCA maintained activities in Europe which overlapped. Closer association was first considered at a meeting in Trondheim (Norway) in 1988 and an amalgamation began to take shape at a joint conference at The Hague in 1993. But it was not until 1995 that the problem was finally resolved, when a new European Society of General Practice/Family Medicine was created at Strasbourg to act as the European Region of WONCA and the successor to SIMG.[16]

All the initiatives so far described had been undertaken to exchange information about the clinical role, techniques, special training, and research development of general practitioners/family physicians. Until 1967 professional employment and remuneration were dealt with within each country independently by national organizations. The formation of the European Economic Community (EEC) under the Treaty of Rome created shared concerns between the professional groups in each country and a need for international organizations to represent their common interests. Direct representation of the interests of all doctors in the EEC with the European Commission in Brussels was now undertaken by a body entitled 'Le Comité Permanent' (Standing Committee of Doctors of the European Economic Community). However, the concerns and interests of generalists and specialists diverged in certain ways. The 'political' interests of general practitioners became in 1967 the

[12] 'Montreal Conference on General Practice', *British Medical Journal* (1964), i. 1246.
[13] E. V. Kuenssberg, 'Meeting of the Colleges of General Practice in Australia', *Journal of the Royal College of General Practitioners*, 23 (1973), 75–6.
[14] *By-laws of the World Organization of Family Doctors* (Joliment, Australia: WONCA, 1995).
[15] H. Lamberts and R. Wood, *International Classification of Primary Care* (Oxford, 1987).
[16] W. Fabb, 'WONCA Region Europe—European Society of General Practice/Family Medicine (WONCA—ESGP/FM)', *Family Practice*, 13 (1996), *WONCA News*, 22/1 (1996), pp. ii–iii.

responsibility of a new organization, the European Union of General Practitioners (Union Européenne de Médecins Omnipraticiens (UEMO)). This body has played an essential part, with the support of the Standing Committee, in helping to shape the European Community Directive on Specific Training for General Practitioners,[17] which requires a two-year period of special preparation for qualified doctors before they can apply successfully to work as a general practitioner in the social security system of any EU country. It has also published reports on their role and training in the various countries with which it is concerned.[18]

Before this Directive, general-practice qualifications obtained in one member country of the European Union (EU) were not recognized in another. Work as a general practitioner in another country is now possible, but, until very recently, there has been very little migration, doubtless because no country has been short of applicants from its own medical schools. This Directive had also received strong support from the Council of Europe, in its Resolution (77) 30.[19]

European groups for education and research, 1970–1979

The previous section has traced the progress of two important international organizations from their origins until their amalgamation in Europe in 1995. Smaller groups started independently, concerned with particular activities. Both the first Leeuwenhorst Group and the European General Practice Research Workshop started in 1974.

The Leeuwenhorst Group has focused its twice-yearly meetings on the education of general practitioners at all stages of their career. It owes its name to the place where it first came together—a conference centre in the middle of the Dutch bulb fields—during a conference organized by the Dutch College of General Practice for countries around the North Sea. Its earliest—and perhaps still its most important single achievement—was to create a definition of the role of the general practitioner which would be acceptable to doctors in the eleven countries represented in the group and which could serve as a basis for training programmes (see below).[20] This definition has stood the test of time and remains today the best-known one in most European countries, including Eastern Europe (East Germany, Hungary, and Yugoslavia had rep-

---

[17] EEC, 'European Directive on Specific Training in General Medical Practice', 86/457/EEC, *Official Journal of the European Communities* (EEC 4, no. 1, 26/26, Brussels 1986–7). (Now Consolidated Directive 93/16 EEC, ch. iv.)

[18] A long and notable contribution to this and other European organizations has been made by Dr Alan Rowe, a Suffolk general practitioner.

[19] Council of Europe, *The General Practitioner: His Training and Ways of Stimulating Interest in this Vocation* (CM/Del/Concl(77) 275, Strasbourg, 1977).

[20] Leeuwenhorst Working Party, 'The General Practitioner in Europe', A statement by the working party appointed by the second European Conference on the Teaching of General Practice, *Journal of the Royal College of General Practitioners*, 27 (1977), 117.

resentatives in the group from its start). In 1982 the members of the original group resigned in order that they could be replaced by a younger membership. The 'New Leeuwenhorst Group', similarly concerned with the development of general practice as a discipline through learning and teaching, included by 1992 members from twenty-five European countries. In that year it changed its name to the European Academy of Teachers in General Practice. At the same time it changed its constitution from a small invited group to a membership organization, open to any applicant active in teaching general practice. Throughout more than twenty years this group has provided a regular means of interchange between teachers of general practice across Europe.

The European General Practice Research Workshop, starting under the leadership of Dr Ekke Kuenssberg in the same year, aims to promote research in primary care, to initiate and coordinate multinational research projects, to exchange experiences, and, by doing so, to create a valid international base for the discipline. Like the Leeuwenhorst Group, this one also meets twice yearly in different countries and maintains its special focus. It publishes abstracts from its meetings and organizes training courses in research methods. A notable product has been *The Interface Study* (1990),[21] about the interface between primary and secondary care in European countries. The Workshop has been increasingly active in recent years. Much more recently a similar group, EQUIP, has been meeting in Europe to exchange information and ideas about quality assessment and assurance in primary care.[22]

Duing these years two particularly extensive studies of the work of general practitioners in other countries, based on personal visits of observation, were published by F. M. Hull and Dr J. W. Stephen.[23]

Further developments, 1980–1989

Much of this history of international linkages has focused on Europe or on exchanges conducted in the English language. An entirely independent development started in 1981 from Latin America—the International Centre for Family Medicine (ICFM). It aims to promote family medicine and cooperation between countries and institutions which wish to integrate this in their medical-care systems and to develop educational programmes for family doctors. It includes eleven countries (not all in Latin America—for example, Portugal and Spain) with strong support from Canada and the USA. Its special contribution is in the use of the Latin languages and in the provision of publications in Spanish. Leading figures at the start were Dr Julio Ceitlin (Argentina) and Dr Donald Rice (Canada). In 1983 this organization changed

[21] D. L. Crombie, J. van der Zee, and P. Backer, *The Interface Study* (Occasional Paper 48; London: RCGP; 1990).
[22] 'EQUIP', *European Journal of General Practice*, 1 (1995), 45–6.
[23] F. M. Hull, 'A Day with the Doctor', *Update*, 17–24 (1978–82); W. J. Stephen, *An Analysis of Primary Medical Care—An International Study* (Cambridge, 1979).

its name to the International Forum on Family Medicine for the Americas, Spain and Portugal (IFFASP).[24]

In 1984 the first international journal appeared, entitled *Family Practice* and published by the Oxford University Press. The first editor was Professor John Howie (Edinburgh) and the first editorial board had members from nine countries across the world. This journal has, from the beginning, carried a regular supplement from WONCA, with news of its activities. More recently (1995) the *European Journal of General Practice* has appeared as the organ of the European Society of General Practice/Family Medicine.

The end of the cold war, 1990

A new feature in this decade has been the opening-up of Eastern European countries to influences from the West. Before 1990, health care in Eastern Europe was for the most part based on the 'polyclinic' system in which both generalists and specialists were available to patients by direct access. These medical personnel worked in shifts, with little continuity of care. To add to the fragmentation of care, generalist doctors were also available at places of work. This system was popular with neither patients nor doctors, and all the countries behind the Iron Curtain have shown great interest in changing and strengthening their primary care. Money from national and international sources has supported mutual exchanges between doctors from Eastern and Western Europe. So far, but in a rather uncoordinated way, health care in Eastern Europe is being influenced by Western European systems and health-care policy in those countries is being reoriented towards primary care.[25]

Exchange of influence

This history of the gradual development of channels of international communication concerning general medical practice and, more recently, primary care has not considered the content of exchange—either the ways in which ideas and practice in this country have been influenced from abroad or the ways in which this country may have influenced others. A few examples must suffice at this point, but others will be implicit in the main part of the chapter, which follows and is first about ideals which are shared internationally and then about actual developments in other countries; these have increasingly been the subjects of discussion between them, as the barriers of language have been overcome.

In the early 1960s the development of a special postgraduate training for

---

[24] 'The ICFM—a brief history', *Medico de Familia*, 20 (1990), 3–4.
[25] C. Heginbotham and R. Maxwell, 'Managing the Transitions: A Western European View of Health Care Development in Eastern Europe', *European Journal of Public Health*, 1 (1991), 36–44.

general practice was influenced by what was already under way in Zagreb, Yugoslavia, initiated by Professor A. Vuletic. Several visits were made by English doctors.[26] A particular example of influence from the Netherlands is in Huygen's remarkable study of families in his practice, written in English and illustrated with his own pen drawings.[27]

The term 'nurse-practitioner' became relatively familiar in the UK in 1974 when it was shown in a well-conducted study from Canada that the work of nurse-practitioners in primary care, in isolated areas, after a two-year training, compared favourably with that of fully trained doctors.[28] There was little reason at that time to imagine that there was any role of this sort for nurses in this country, since the supply and distribution of general practitioners seemed adequate. The position has changed in the last five years. There has been growing anxiety about a sudden and serious drop in recruitment to training schemes for general practice, following the multiple reforms instituted by the government in 1989–92. A small number of nurses have now received a two-year training and are already working in this role, mainly in group practices.[29]

A fundamental example of influence from abroad is the assessment and assurance of quality, sometimes called 'performance review', sometimes 'audit'. This influence came from the USA, particularly from the work of Donabedian, who promoted the terms 'structure, process, and outcome' and their interrelationship, as a way of thinking about quality in medical care.[30] Special emphasis was put on the importance of tracing outcomes (whether these are in patients' health, in their satisfaction with the care they receive, or in the costs incurred) and on the effort to improve them through changes in the structure or the process of care. This way of thinking influenced the behaviour of innovative general practitioners in this country before any other part of the profession. It renewed interest in the concepts of effectiveness and efficiency promoted by Cochrane and has strengthened the principle of basing practice, as far as possible, on good evidence about the relative benefits and risks of alternative treatments or alternative ways of organizing services.[31]

It is difficult for an English writer to propose examples of the influence of this country on others. It is tempting to overestimate. The reality must be that it varies from country to country, depending on the extent to which a

[26] J. P. Horder, 'The General Practitioner in Yugoslavia, Czechoslovakia and Israel: 'special vocational training', Lancet (1965), ii. 123–5.

[27] F. J. A. Huygen, Family Medicine: The Medical Life History of Families (Nijmegen, 1978; London, 1990).

[28] W. O. Spitzer, D. L. Sackett, J. C. Sibley, R. S. Roberts, M. Gent, D. J. Kergin, B. C. Hackett, and A. Olynich, 'The Burlington Randomised Trial of the Nurse Practitioner', New England Journal of Medicine, 290 (1974), 251–6.

[29] A. Fawcett Henesy and P. West, 'Nurse-Practitioners: The South Thames Regional Health Authority Experience', Nursing Times, 91 (part 12) (1995), 40–51.

[30] A. Donabedian, The Definition of Quality and Approaches to its Assessment, i. 'Explorations in Quality Assessment and Monitoring' (Ann Arbor, Mich., 1980).

[31] A. L. Cochrane, Effectiveness and Efficiency: Random Reflections on Health Services (London, 1972).

particular country shares the same ideals and objectives as our own and on its nearness to achieving them.

For instance, because the characteristics of general practice and primary care in the Netherlands and Denmark most closely resemble those of the UK, influence from here might easily be assumed. The reality is more likely to be that thinking and practice were subject to the same influences and moving in the same direction about the same time in these three countries and that no one country had a dominant influence. Jan van Es, the first Dutch general practitioner to be appointed as a university professor, questioning why the role of family medicine still existed in the 1950s, given the overwhelming power of specialization, writes:

In the United Kingdom the National Health Service gave space to family medicine; in the Netherlands the health insurance system. As a consequence, both countries had patient lists in family medicine. Shielded in this way, family medicine had a chance to develop, but it was threatened nevertheless.

A post-war reform of family medicine started in the Netherlands in the first half of the 1950s. A trigger was the publication of a book in 1950: *The Family Doctor and his Patient*, by Just Buma.[32] He was a family doctor who was already trying to analyse his professional work and, building on that, to formulate what family medicine really is. I started my practice in 1949 and remember very well that he put into words what I already felt to be important. This book made a basis for the foundation of the Netherlands College of General Practitioners by a small group of enthusiastic and progressive family doctors, who had sufficient professional self-esteem to do it. They were not doctors frustrated because they were unable to get a training in one of the specialities, but genuine, inspired family doctors. The development of the Dutch College was the most decisive act in the rebirth and renewal of family medicine. We knew about similar actions in the UK and the USA. That gave us support, but did not influence the design of the Dutch College. Yours suited your educational system, ours suited the Dutch health care and social structure.

Looking at the development of family medicine in the countries around the North Sea, a key word is 'simultaneity'. It was 'in the air'. The reasons were a too rapid diversification of medicine, a loss of comprehensiveness, a growing distance between patient and specialist and a slowly increasing awareness of the rising costs of health care.

Because of this simultaneity, there were certain similarities in the development of family medicine in the countries round the North Sea. This was stimulating and supportive. I think these two words, simultaneity and similarity, cover what is wanted better than 'learning from . . .'. My conclusion is that we experienced mutual influence and inspiration.[33]

A contrasting example might be Portugal, a country in which developments in primary care have been more recent and where the channels and forms of

---

[32] J. T. Buma, *The Family Doctor and his Patient* (*De Huisarts en zijn patient*) (Amsterdam, 1950).
[33] J. van Es, personal communication (1996).

influence from this country can be traced and are acknowledged.[34] Even so other countries, notably Norway, have also been influential there.

Both language barriers and national traditions have contributed to minimizing the influence of general practice in this country on the shape of practice in France and Germany. French doctors, throughout the period covered by this volume, have been notable for their opposition to the principles of our NHS, under the banner 'médecine libérale'. This has influenced their attitude to general practice in this country, but in recent years those best informed have envied the role and status of their fellows here.

One influence, the origin of which in the UK is beyond doubt, is the work of Michael and Enid Balint, mainly at the Tavistock Clinic, London (see Chapter 3). They themselves were psychoanalysts, but they would have wished the numerous general practitioners who, from 1953 onwards, provided the patients and problems discussed in their seminar groups to share credit.[35] Their work, centred on the relationship between doctor and patient (especially on the thinking, feeling, and behaviour of the doctor), was almost entirely based on general practice. They were exceptional at that time in perceiving the importance and value of the generalist role in medicine. Their ideas, which had at first met opposition in the UK, even from general practitioners, became rapidly known in France, Germany, the Netherlands, and the USA. Their influence has since spread to many other countries, appealing especially to those doctors who give importance to the psychosocial aspects of medicine and can tolerate the difficulties of looking at their own behaviour.

It cannot be without significance that all three WHO expert committees[36] and the later Council of Europe Symposium[37] were prepared by consultants from the UK.[38]

Developments in general practice and primary care in other countries, 1950–1995

The rest of this chapter will survey similarities and differences in the development of general practice and primary care in other countries during the years covered by this volume. Comparisons with the UK will be mainly limited to a small group of developed countries—France, Germany, the Netherlands, Sweden, Denmark, Canada, and the USA, chosen because

[34] WHO, Regional Office for Europe, Primary Health Care Unit, *Draft General Practice Profile, Portugal* (Copenhagen, 1995).

[35] M. Balint, *The Doctor, his Patient and the Illness* (London, 1957).

[36] WHO, *The Role of Public Health Officers and Gerneral Practitioners in Mental Health Care; The Training of the General Practitioner; General Practice.*

[37] Council of Europe, *The General Practitioner.*

[38] The consultants were as follows: n. 36: Dr John Horder (see n. 6), Professor Richard Scott (see n. 7), and Dr John Fry (see n. 8); n. 37: Professor Marshall Marinker (see n. 19).

relatively reliable information is available in a form which permits comparisons to be made.

Before comparing realities in different countries, it is necessary to set down the ideal concepts about the role of general practitioner, as these were in fact being put forward, for the first time, on the basis of international agreement.

International ideals

Between 1961 and 1964, three expert committees associated with the head-quarters of the WHO provided the earliest definitions of the role of the general practitioner and the services he or she offers, in a form which represented the opinions of the six main regions of the Organization. Their substance can be summarized as follows. The general practitioner is a doctor with whom patients usually make their first contact and have direct access, and who accepts continuing responsibility for providing or arranging their general medical care. This care is comprehensive. It includes the prevention and treatment of any illness or injury affecting the mind or any part of the body and is not limited to patients with specific diseases or in specific age-groups. He or she offers care of the individual as a person and is someone to whom the patient has a right of continuing direct access. A large proportion of general practitioners offer this access to all members of a family.

The key words are 'first contact', 'continuing responsibility', 'comprehensive', 'personal', and 'family' care. These definitions distinguished the generalist from the specialist and provided a basis for the training of general practitioners.

Ten years later another definition was agreed by another international group, drawn from eleven European countries:

The general practitioner is a licensed medical graduate who gives personal, primary and continuing care to individuals, families and a practice population, irrespective of age, sex and illness. It is the synthesis of these functions which is unique. . . . He will include and integrate physical, psychological and social factors in his considerations about health and illness. This will be expressed in the care of his patients.[39]

Although it adds further detail, this statement does not differ in any essential from the earlier description of essentials in the three reports from Geneva.

The term 'primary care' came into use as an alternative to 'general practice' in the early 1970s to emphasize the distinction between general and specialized medical care, but also, more importantly, to allow for the increasing contribution of other health professionals to the former, nurses above all. The term gained greatly in importance when it appeared as the central theme of the Alma

---

[39] Leeuwenhorst Working Party, 'The General Practitioner in Europe'.

Ata Declaration,[40] a declaration aimed at and signed by all governments, in developing and developed countries alike. Here, however, the actual term used was 'primary health care', to imply a yet wider scene than the field in which doctors, nurses, and professions allied to medicine are active, and to involve other branches of government, such as education and housing. The report recommends that each nation devote a share of its resources to improve social, economic, educational, environmental, public health, and all other conditions affecting health; to ensure that the public has access to a basic set of health services that first and foremost emphasizes primary health care, and to ensure an adequate supply of appropriately trained physicians and other health workers to provide these services.

The Alma Ata Declaration defined primary health care as

Essential health care, based on practical, scientifically sound, socially acceptable methods and technology, made universally accessible to individuals and families in the community, through their full participation and at a cost that the community and the country can afford. It forms an integral part of both the country's health system, of which it is the central function and main focus, and of the overall social and economic development of the community.[41]

Primary health care includes at least

Education concerning prevailing health problems and the methods of preventing or controlling them; promotion of food supply and proper nutrition; an adequate supply of safe water and basic sanitation; maternal and child health care, including family planning; immunization against the major infectious diseases and prevention and control of locally endemic diseases; appropriate treatment of common diseases and injuries; provision of essential drugs.[42]

Although this list may, at first sight, appear to be relevant chiefly to less developed countries, it must be obvious that, in any country where there are general practitioners, they are likely to play a central part. But in this very broad statement there are no definitions of particular roles. Two more recent documents fill the gap. The first (1991) was published by WONCA.[43] The second (1994) was published jointly by WHO and WONCA.[44] They belong together and define the general practitioner/family physician as the doctor

---

[40] WHO, *Alma Ata 1978: Primary Health Care: Report of the International Conference on Primary Health Care, Alma Ata, USSR, 6–12 September 1978* (Geneva: WHO, 1978).

[41] Ibid. 3.

[42] Ibid. 4.

[43] WONCA, *The Role of the General Practitioner/Family Physician in Health Care Systems: A Statement from the World Organization of Colleges, Academies, and Academic Associations of General Practitioners/Family Physicians* (London: RCGP for WONCA, 1991), 2.

[44] WONCA, *Making Medical Practice and Education More Relevant to People's Needs: The Contribution of the Family Doctor*, from the joint WHO/WONCA Conference, Department of Family Medicine, University of Western Ontario, London, Ontario, Canada, 8 Nov. 1994 (London: WONCA, 1994).

who is primarily responsible for providing comprehensive health care to every individual seeking medical care, and arranging for other health service personnel to provide services when necessary. The general practitioner/family physician functions as a generalist who accepts everyone seeking care, whereas other health providers limit access to their services on the basis of age/sex and/or diagnosis . . . who cares for the individual in the context of the family, and the family in the context of the community, irrespective of race, religion, culture or social class. He is clinically competent to provide the greater part of their care, after taking into account their cultural, socio-economic and psychological background. In addition, he takes personal responsibility for providing comprehensive and continuing care for his patients.[45]

He also 'exercises his/her professional role by providing care either directly or through the services of others according to health needs and resources available within the community he/she serves'.[46] This definition was endorsed by the WHO and elaborated in 1994 in Making Medical Practice More Relevant to People's Needs: The Contribution of the Family Doctor, a joint working paper from the two organizations.[47]

All the documents from which these definitions of the general practitioner's role have been drawn emphasize the essential need for specific education and training for the generalist role, specific research, and specific resources, if the role is to be preserved and developed.

Comparing the recent statements about the role of general practitioner with those of thirty years earlier, one finds all the same essential characteristics, but with a new emphasis on the community ('The family doctor must be highly competent in patient care and must integrate individual and community health care'[48]). There is also a new theme. 'According to health resources' had not appeared in previous statements. This reflects the growing concern of all Western countries at the increasing costs of health care and the pressure to impose rationing. Most of this concern is directed at the rising cost of drugs and of complex new techniques. How far this will influence the development of primary care in the twenty-first century can only be guessed.

All these statements have been influenced by a persisting concern to preserve the role of generalist, throughout a time when medical care has been transformed by developments attributable to specialization. The broad way in which they have defined the role is compatible with its flexibility and its capacity to adjust, for example, to diminished tasks in surgical treatment and an increase in preventive tasks. Alone among them the Alma Ata Declaration points to yet broader ideals.

In 1970 the medical historian Rosemary Stevens proposed that 'the role of the generalist in medicine has been, and remains, the most important single issue in modern medicine, for the structure of the medical profession hinges on whether—and how—general practice is recognised'.[49]

[45] WONCA, *The Role of the General Practitioner/Family Physician*, 2.
[46] Ibid.
[47] WONCA, *Making Medical Practice and Education More Relevant to People's Needs.*
[48] Ibid. 3.
[49] R. Stevens, *American Medicine and the Public Interest* (Newhaven, Conn.: 1971).

The reality of general practice/primary care in other countries

First contact: Accessibility, and access to general practitioners

In all the countries selected in this chapter for comparison with the UK, the total number of physicians has increased twice as fast as the population (Fig. 11.1). General practitioners/family physicians have also increased in number relative to the population, but not proportionately (Fig. 11.2). Thus they have formed a diminishing percentage of the total, while the percentage of specialists has increased (Fig. 11.3).[50] Many patients prefer to see a woman doctor. For some women from ethnic minorities this is essential. Since 1950 the percentage of women among the medical profession has increased in all developed countries (see Table D3). Full-time general practice is not easily compatible with family responsibilities; in most developed countries in 1990 the percentage of women in general practice (around 20 per cent) was a little below the level among the whole profession.

Financial barriers scarcely exist in the countries here considered, except for the USA, where, in 1989, 16 per cent of the population had no external source (third-party coverage) of funding, with children the most affected and elderly people the least, but charitable care was available to them at hospitals.[51]

In half of the other countries charges for dentistry and/or ophthalmology, and for some pharmaceuticals, can debar the poorest members of the population from the care they need.

Distribution and coverage

In the UK in 1952, 44 per cent of NHS districts were designated as short of general practitioners. One of the most important achievements of the NHS has been the gradual elimination of such areas. In 1991 the equivalent figure was 5 per cent. Until recently, no other country has attempted a fair geographical distribution of general practitioners as an essential requirement of its health service provision, except for Denmark in 1976 and the Netherlands in 1986.[52] Success in the UK can be attributed partly to those influences and policies which maintained the supply of doctors choosing to enter this branch of medicine rather than hospital practice, and partly to the strict control of the number entering the service as specialists.

In countries with no defined general practice populations (e.g. Austria, Belgium, Germany, France, and Switzerland) there has tended to be greater

---

[50] In some countries—for example, France, Germany, and the USA—doctors trained in a speciality and, for various reasons, practising it part-time, also offer part-time primary-care services. Figs. 11.2 and 11.3 indicate only those doctors working as full-time general practitioners in France and Germany and as family physicians in the USA.

[51] National Centre for Health Studies, Health United States 1990 (Hyattsville, Md. Public Health Services, 1991).

[52] Crombie, van der Zee, and Bacter, The Interface Study.

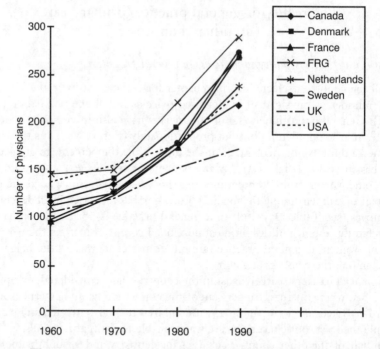

FIG. 11.1 The total number of physicians (i.e. total medically qualified personnel) per 100,000 population, various countries, 1960–1990

Sources: Various, including WHO statistics.

provision of health services in and around cities.[53] For example, the distribution has been uneven in France. In 1988, when, in round figures, the number of general practitioners relative to the population in the UK was about 1 in 1,800 (see Table D9), it was also 1 to 1,800 in France, varying between 1 to 2,350 in the north and west and 1 to 1,500 in the Parisian region, and 1 to 1,250 in Marseilles,[54] and it remained so in 1995.[55]

A strong contrast to the UK is to be seen in the USA. Although the overall physician supply increased by 60 per cent between 1970 and 1990, the number of rural and poor areas designated as 'health profession short' (2,000 in 1980), has increased. In 1988 there were 176 counties in which 700,000 people lived, with no primary care physician at all.[56]

[53] J. Gervas, M. P. Fernandez, and B. H. Starfield, 'Primary Care, Financing and Gatekeeping in Western Europe', *Family Practice*, 11 (1994), 307–17.

[54] See P. Cornillot and P. Bonamour, 'France', in I. Douglas-Wilson and G. McLachlan (eds.), *Health Service Prospects* (London: Nuffield Provincial Hospitals Trust, 1973), 55–79.

[55] *La Santé en France 96* (Paris: Ministère de Travail et des Affaires Sociales 1996).

[56] J. Fry, D. Light, J. Rodnick, and P. Orton, *Reviving Primary Care: A US–UK Comparison* (Oxford, 1995).

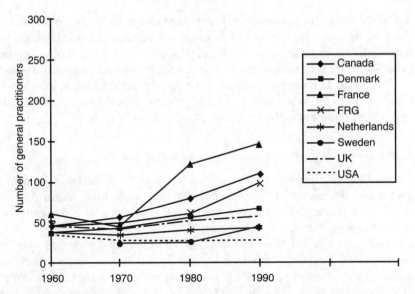

FIG. 11.2 The total number of general practitioners per 100,000 population, various countries, 1960–1992

Sources: Various, including WHO statistics.

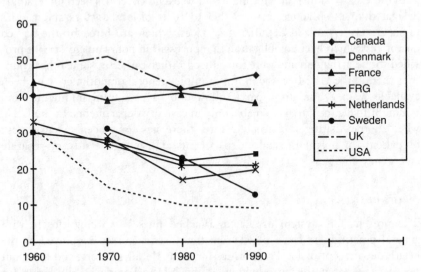

FIG. 11.3 General practitioners as a percentage of all physicians, various countries, 1960–1990

Sources: W. J. Stephen, *An Analysis of Primary Medical Care* (Cambridge, 1979); WHO, Regional Office for Europe, *Draft Profiles of General Practice* (Copenhagen, 1995); J. Fry and J. Horder, *Primary Care in an International Context* (London: Nuffield Provincial Hospitals Trust, 1994).

The contrast between the USA, France, and Germany, on the one hand, and the UK, on the other, arises first because of fundamental beliefs about the freedom of professional people to choose their own speciality and place of work (whether or not the needs of the population for health and social care are met) and, secondly, because patients also have become accustomed to freedom of choice, both in direct access to specialists or general practitioners and in multiple access to others in the same discipline.

Registration of patients, responsibility, and out-of-hours care

In the UK, registration implies the patient's right of access to a named doctor and the doctor's legal responsibility to provide care, in principle for twenty-four hours of every day of the year. It provides a basis for continuity of relationship, but the development of group practice (see below) and a diminishing number of home visits has tended to weaken the ongoing personal continuity of care for a patient with one doctor. In the contract with the social-security system patients are also registered with general practitioners in Canada, Denmark, Italy, the Netherlands, Portugal, and Spain (and, very recently, in parts of Sweden and Norway), but not in France, Germany, or the USA.[57] In the latter countries—for this reason—there is no routine passage of a lifelong case record when a patient moves to a different area and a new doctor.

In the UK, responsibility for night and weekend cover has been increasingly delegated, first to practice partners, then to 'rotas' of local doctors, and in cities to separately organized deputizing services, which are hired by the named doctor and which have an obligation to report within hours on any service provided. Such arrangements were introduced rather earlier in some other countries than in the UK. In Sweden, for example, general practitioners have been available from 8 a.m. to 5 p.m., followed by a rota until midnight; from midnight to 8 a.m., care is available only in casualty departments. In the USA, where home visiting is extremely rare, there has long been extensive use by patients of hospital casualty departments and, more recently, of separate emergency clinics.

Nurses in primary care

The present UK system of 'group-attached nurses' working closely with general practitioners has evolved from the 'district nurses' employed by the health department of local authorities for many decades before, and for about two decades after, the introduction of the NHS. Their work in caring for ill people in their homes has been paralleled in all countries of the former Commonwealth.

[57] In Germany patients register with a doctor for three months and must have permission to consult anyone else during that period only.

In most European countries, nurses working in patients' homes are employed by independent organizations. The degree to which their work must be authorized by doctors varies from country to country: in Germany, for example, always, and in the Netherlands seldom.[58] 'Practice nurses' working inside practice premises alongside the doctor are found in all the countries here included. In Sweden in 1984, 40 per cent of primary care was being provided by nurses, because there were then too few trained general practitioners.

Reference has already been made to 'nurse practitioners', a familiar feature of health care in parts of Canada, and in the USA, where there were approximately 100,000 working in 1995.[59]

Direct access to specialists

The question whether or not people have direct access for consultation with specialists is of central importance in this book. The consequences are important alike to those who use health services, those who provide them, and those who are responsible for financing them. They are particularly important for general practitioners, because the strength of their role in a health service depends very much on the extent to which they control the gateway to specialist services.

In the 1950s there were predictions in the UK that general practice would soon disappear as a result of increasing specialization; a generalist doctor was no longer possible nor even desirable. In fact, this has not happened in any country. The opposite view has prevailed. Increased specialization has made the role of the generalist more important than ever. But there are nevertheless wide differences between countries in the gate-keeping role of the general practitioner and in the degree of direct access to specialist care for patients.

In the UK, the principle of referral has remained unaltered since the NHS began. A similar pattern exists in Denmark and the Netherlands. In these three countries access to a specialist is nearly always through a general practitioner (see Table 11.1). The pattern in France is notably different. There is no shortage of 'omnipraticiens', but patients are free to consult any specialist directly. Most French people could name their general practitioner, whom they would consult in many circumstances, but most women consult gynaecologists direct and take their children to paediatricians for surveillance and immunizations. The majority of specialists work partly within hospitals and partly outside, but

---

[58] J. van der Zee, K. Kramer, A. Derksen, A. Kerkstra, and F. C. J. Stephens, 'Community Nursing in Belgium, Germany and the Netherlands', *Journal of Advanced Nursing*, 20 (1994), 791–801. See also W. G. W. Boerma, F. A. J. M. de Jong, and P. H. Mulder, *Health Care and Geeneral Practice across Europe* (Utrecht, 1993).

[59] M. O. Mundinger, 'Advanced Nursing Practice: Good Medicine for Physicians?', *New England Journal of Medicine*, 330 (1994), 211–13.

TABLE 11.1 *The accessibility of health-care systems expressed as a percentage of the medical specialities to which patients have direct access, various countries, 1985–1990*

Health-care system	Percentage of specialities to which patients have direct access
FRG	82
Sweden	74
France	65
Denmark (apart from Copenhagen)	29
The Netherlands	9
UK	0

Notes: In all the countries there were between 32 and 34 relevant medical specialities. As the table shows, in the UK none was directly accessible to patients without referral; in Germany a majority were directly accessible.

Source: based (with kind permission) on D. L. Crombie, J. van der Zee, and P. Backer, *The Interface Study* (Occasional Paper 48, London: RCGP, 1990), table 4.4.

there are also a large number who do not work in hospital at all, mixing their speciality with primary care. General practitioners are therefore not in a position to control the gateway to hospital. There is no regular system of referral from primary to secondary care and back. Communication between doctors leaves something to be desired, not least because patients have been free to consult more than one general practitioner, even on the same day. Although the system has proved uneconomic for many years, it has persisted because of strong professional adherence to the principle of 'médecine libérale'.

In Germany more than half the doctors who provide primary care have in fact been trained for work in a speciality and continue partly in that role outside hospitals (which have separate full-time staff). This was not so in 1950.[60] But since 1990 there have been proposals, driven by economic reasons, which aim to provide primary care increasingly through doctors trained more specifically for the role.[61]

In Canada patients normally consult family physicians first, but they have freedom to consult specialists without referral.

It is the USA which, as far as direct access is concerned, stands at the other end of the range from the UK. Patients are free to consult any specialist direct—and very often do so. Moreover, much of the work which would be done in the UK by general practitioners is done in the USA by doctors trained as specialists in internal medicine or in paediatrics—and even by subspecial-

[60] H. van den Bussche, 'The History and Future of Physician Manpower Development in the Federal Republic of Germany', *Health Policy*, 15 (1990), 215–31.

[61] S. Goldbeck Wood, 'General Practice Reforms Agreed in Germany', *British Medical Journal*, 312 (1996), 1560.

ists mainly working in their own speciality. This pattern of practice developed rapidly after the Second World War.[62] Some change in the opposite direction is now appearing with the advent of pre-payment plans and health-maintenance organizations, which are at present rapidly replacing fee-for-service practice.[63] Many of these plans require that patients should normally consult a doctor trained in family practice or internal medicine. The reason is economic, especially the need to control hospital admission and the use of expensive investigations.[64]

Developments in the last fifty years in Sweden (as in Finland) have been particularly interesting. Both countries created at first a predominantly specialized service, except in remote districts. Large health centres were built, staffed by specialists and equipped with beds and relatively complex technology. The policy was reversed after 1968, when control of health and social services was made the responsibility of provincial governments. A concerted effort has been made since then to train doctors specifically for primary care.[65] In 1994 registration with a named doctor was introduced by law, but the law was reversed by a new government one year later. The situation varies in this respect in different parts of Sweden.[66]

It is important to recognize that the alternatives for patients in these opposing systems do not involve a simple choice between specialist or generalist care. The choice is between direct access to specialist care, or generalist care with specialist care when needed or requested. On this question there are clearly different national prejudices, sustained by the fact that most people prefer what they know. Since 1980, however, evidence (discussed later in this chapter) has been gathered which suggests that strong primary care is associated

[62] Stevens, *American Medicine and the Public Interest.*

[63] J. Roberts, 'More US Graduates Opt for Primary Care', *British Medical Journal*, 308 (1994), 875, and S. Ramsey, 'US Graduates Lured by Primary Care', *Lancet*, 346 (1994), 1154.

[64] There has long been evidence that self-referral leads to greater ordering of unnecessary tests (H. Bakwin, 'Pseudodoxia Paediatrica', *New England Journal of Medicine*, 232 (1945), 691–7); and to unnecessary treatment—for example, to less appropriate use of tonsillectomy, with worse outcomes (N. Roos, 'Who should Do the Surgery? Tonsillectomy and Adenoidectomy in one Canadian Province', *Inquiry*, 16 (1979), 73–83).

Data on the consumption of specialist services seem to indicate that access to a specialist is more frequent when referral by a general practitioner is not required. The number of annual contacts with a specialist per person is comparatively higher in Germany (5.0), the USA (3.7), France (3.0), and Canada (2.0) than in the Netherlands (1.8), the UK (1.2), and Denmark (0.6) (S. Sandier, 'Health Services Utilization and Physician Income Trends', in *Health Care Systems in Transition* (OECD Social Policy Studies, 7; Paris 1990), 45.

An excessive number of specialists to population increases the volume of intensive, expensive, and invasive medical services and therefore the costs of health care (S. Schroeder and I. G. Sandy, 'Specialty Distribution of US Physicians: The Invisible Driver of Health Care Costs', *New England Journal of Medicine*, 328 (1993), 961–3).

[65] C. E. Rudebeck, 'General Practice and the Dialogue of Clinical Practice', *Scandinavian Journal of Primary Health Care*, suppl. 1 (1992), 9–11. See also M. Garcia Barbero and J. Goicoechia, *Health Care Delivery: Profiles and Innovations. Selected European Countries* (Copenhagen: WHO, 1977), 129–38.

[66] A. M. Lewis, 'Sweden Reforms Primary Health Care', *British Medical Journal*, 305 (1992), 601; WHO, Regional Office for Europe, *Draft General Practice Profile—Sweden* (Copenhagen: WHO 1995), 2.

with lower health-care costs, better levels in specific indicators of health in the population, and greater satisfaction with health services.

Continuity

Such statements of the ideal as 'personal responsibility for providing continuing care for his/her patients'[67] do not reveal the wide variety of views about what the maintenance of continuity entails in practice.

In the UK, Denmark, and the Netherlands, the doctor's continuing 'longitudinal' responsibility results from the registration of each person with a named doctor who is legally required to provide twenty-four-hour cover, either personally or through a deputy. But such longitudinal responsibility does not in itself guarantee a valuable relationship between doctor and patient. It may or may not be characterized by what is better called 'personal continuity'.[68]

Continuity, whether longitudinal or personal, has been liable to dilution as group practice has developed. Some doctors believe that personal continuity, which is valued most by elderly patients, who like to count on seeing the same doctor on every occasion, is the ideal. Others believe that the essence of continuity is preserved if there is passage of information between different members of the health-care team through the medical record, whether written or computerized.[69]

In reality, these different interpretations of what is needed for continuity of care are likely to be found within each of the countries under consideration. They inevitably result in different degrees of one-to-one contact, familiarity, trust, and differences in the doctor's knowledge of a patient's past history, and the sense of personal responsibility.[70] Different degrees of continuity within practices have been shown to correlate with, for instance, compliance with treatment, the number and duration of hospital admissions, time saving, patient and doctor satisfaction.[71]

[67] WONCA, The Role of the General Practitioner/Family Physician, 2.

[68] P. Hjortdahl and G. K. Freeman 'What Future for Continuity of Care in General Practice?', *British Medical Journal*, 314 (1997), 1870–3.

[69] G. K. Freeman and S. C. Richards, 'How much Personal Care in Four Group Practices?', *British Medical Journal*, 301 (1990), 1028–30

[70] P. Hjortdahl and C. F. Borchgrevinck, 'Continuity of Care: Influence of General Practitioners' Knowledge about their Patients on Use of Resources in Consultations', *British Medical Journal*, 303 (1991), 1181–4.

[71] P. R. A. Ettlinger and G. K. Freeman, 'General Practice Compliance Study: Is it Worth being a Family Doctor?', *British Medical Journal*, 232 (1981), 1192–4; J. L. Alpert, L. S. Robertson, J. Kosa, M. Heagarty, and R. J. Haggerty, 'Delivery of Health Care for Children: Report of an Experiment', *Pediatrics*, 57 (1976), 917–30; P. Hjordtahl and E. Laerum, 'Continuity of Care in General Practice: Effect on Patient Satisfaction', *British Medical Journal*, 304 (1992), 1287–90; J. H. Wasson, A. E. Sauvigne, R. P. Mogielnicki, W. G. Frey, C. H. Sox, C. Gaudette, and A. Rockwell, 'Continuity of Outpatient Medical Care in Elderly Men: A Randomised Trial', *Journal of the American Medical Association*, 252 (1984), 2413–17; R. Baker and J. Streatfield, 'What Type of Practice do Patients Prefer? Exploration of Practice Characteristics Influencing Patient Satisfaction', *British Journal of General Practice*, 45 (1995), 654–9.

A number of factors are likely to influence continuity—for instance, the growth of group practice. Continuity of care is most easily achieved in single-handed general practice. The proportion of single-handed practitioners has declined in all the countries described in this chapter, but the absolute levels have varied widely. In the UK (and in Sweden, where only 5 per cent of general practitioners were single-handed in 1990) one finds the lowest levels of single-handed practice and the largest groups (for the UK see Fig. D1). Many other countries have far more single-handed practitioners. In France, for example, 90 per cent were single-handed in 1965, 70 per cent in 1995. In Denmark 68 per cent were single-handed in 1968, 32 per cent in 1995. In 1995, 58 per cent were single-handed in the Netherlands, and 65 per cent in Germany.

Another factor of importance for continuity is the efficiency with which medical records are transferred when a patient changes his or her primary-care doctor, usually as a result of moving to a new home in a new area, which people in developed countries have been doing more often than they used to do; indeed many people now expect to move several times in a working lifetime. Likewise, the process of referral to secondary care and social-care agencies is of importance for continuity because, the greater the freedom of access to secondary care, the greater the risk of failures in communication and coordination between different agents.

Comprehensiveness

The line between primary care, on the one hand, and secondary care and care by other agencies, on the other, has never been fixed and immutable. In all countries it has changed with time. But there are also quite wide traditional differences between countries in what is considered to be the content, or comprehensiveness, of primary care.

For instance, in the UK, childbirth (or at least intra-partum care) has moved steadily between 1950 and the 1990s from a large proportion of home births conducted by general practitioners and midwives to hospital care for virtually all deliveries (see Chapter 4), and this has happened at roughly the same rate in almost all developed countries. But the Netherlands is the famous exception. There, home deliveries by independent midwives have persisted at a much higher level than elsewhere. Now, in the 1990s, home deliveries by independent midwives still account for about a third of the total. Even in the Netherlands, however, home deliveries by midwives are being replaced partly by hospital deliveries, but mostly by deliveries by midwives in clinics in which the mother usually stays overnight and then goes back home the day after delivery.

There are considerable differences in the care of children. In the UK, Denmark, and the Netherlands most of the care of children is in the hands of the same doctor—the general practitioner—who looks after the rest of the family. The alternative is care by paediatricians working mainly or entirely outside hospitals, as is common in the USA. In this matter, France and Germany occupy an intermediate position; for example, routine surveillance and immunizations in France are usually carried out by paediatricians, while general practitioners deal with those illnesses that do not require the care of hospital paediatric departments. Increasing reluctance to remove children to hospital, except when essential, is not confined to the UK.

There have been attempts, particularly in the USA, to make primary care technically more comprehensive by grouping together doctors with different specialist trainings in the same local facility, directly accessible to patients. The number of all types of group quadrupled between 1965 and 1988; among them, the percentage of single speciality groups rose from 54 per cent in 1975 to 71 per cent in 1988.[72] The same principle was adopted widely in Sweden (and Finland) after the Second World War. But it was abandoned in both countries in the 1970s, in favour of beginning again to train generalists who would, when necessary, refer patients to specialists concentrated at the secondary level.[73]

Another aspect of the comprehensiveness of primary care is the care of populations—in other words, public health. In the UK this has traditionally been in the hands of public-health physicians. The recent trend to integrate disease prevention and health promotion within primary care has not been reflected in all the countries here discussed. The concept of a practice population, implying a responsibility to study and respond to its health needs, also recent, has long been familiar in Sweden.[74]

Such extension of responsibility is one of several reasons why primary care has become a task for groups which include not only doctors but also nurses, public-health nurses, and social workers, with help from secretarial staff and computerization. The concept of teamwork in primary care is widely interpreted and variously implemented at present within all the countries under consideration, despite advocacy by governments. It has taken hold most firmly in Sweden, the UK (and Finland).

In more recent role definitions of the general doctor working in primary care, the duty is included of integrating physical with psychological and social factors in considerations about health and illness. This reflects overall a gradual change of attitude and increased understanding among both the public and health professionals since the Second World War. But change of behaviour still requires that these aspects are given sufficient priority and sufficient time in consultations (as do the preventive aspects also). The UK is not the only country where hurry in consultations has troubled both patients and doctors. The positive relationship which has been shown here between the attention

[72] P. L. Havlicek, *Prepaid Groups in the US: A Survey of Practice Characteristics* (Chicago, 1990).
[73] Rudebeck, 'General Practice'.
[74] As in Finland, Norway, Portugal, and Spain, where general practice and primary care have been combined in remote districts.

TABLE 11.2 *General practitioners' working patterns, various countries, 1992–1995*

Country and year	Average number of minutes usually allocated per appointment	Number of consultations in an average working week	Number of hours worked per week
UK	8.5	128	42
Netherlands (1995)	10	142	46
Denmark (1995)	13.5	98	43
Sweden (1995)	24.7	100	42
France (1995)	20.7	82	54
Germany (West) (1995)	13	200	54
Canada (1992)	15	140	45
USA (1992)	14	134	48–53

Sources: WHO, Regional Office for Europe, Department of Health Services, Primary Health Care Unit, *Draft General Practice Profiles* (Copenhagen, 1995); D. Fleming (project leader), *The European Study of Referrals from Primary to Secondary Care* (COMAC/HSR. Occasional Paper 56, London: RCGP, 1992); J. Fry and J. Horder, *Primary Care in an International Context* (London: Nuffield Provincial Hospitals Trust, 1994).

paid to these aspects and the mean length of consultations seems likely to apply in other countries too.[75]

Table 11.2 shows mean consultation lengths for the countries discussed here.

Coordination

The need for coordination has arisen more and more often as advances in technology have added to the repertoire of effective treatments and as the proportion of elderly people in all developed countries has increased. One in three patients over the age of 65 brings more than one problem to consultations with general practitioners. Multiple problems may interact, and there may be adverse reactions between different drugs prescribed for different disorders. Coordination is essential, even for the single-handed doctor, but failure is more likely to occur in a large partnership or multiprofessional team if information is not recorded and passed on. Failure is yet more likely in those countries where patients are free to consult more than one primary-care doctor on one day and there is no contact between them. When a primary-care group exceeds three or four members, a different need arises. Small organizations need to be managed if they are to work efficiently. A new profession—that of practice

[75] D. C. Morrell, M. E. Evans, R. W. Morris, and M. O. Roland, '"The Five Minute" Consultation: Effect of Time Constraint on Clinical Content and Patient Satisfaction', *British Medical Journal*, 292 (1986), 870–3; J. G. R. Howie, A. M. D. Porter, D. J. Heaney, and J. L. Hopton, 'Long to Short Consultation Ratio: A Proxy Measure of Quality of Care for General Practice', *British Journal of General Practice*, 41 (1991), 48–54.

manager—has grown up in the last twenty-five years, particularly in Canada, the UK, and the USA, so that doctors and nurses can devote maximal time to clinical work.

Coordination is equally crucial if there is a need for referral to a specialist or hospital or social agency. The tradition of referral and referral back is not as widely maintained in all the other countries as it is in the UK. It is breached more frequently where there is direct access to specialists by patients or where the system of payment of specialists gives a financial advantage if the care of the patient is retained by them. Medical records held by patients themselves, introduced very recently in France for people over the age of 65, offer one method of dealing with this aspect of coordination.

Education

From the original position that general practice, alone among the branches of medicine, needed no specific training, the second half of the century has seen a change, in one country after another, whereby this is being provided after qualification. All countries of the EU are committed since 1986 to a minimum of two years' training for this purpose, partly in hospital, partly in a selected practice. In most countries, including the USA, hospital experience predominates. Germany makes provision for four years of hospital posts, Finland for six years. These lengths are exceptional, but they are not obligatory in either country. Three and a half years are obligatory in Denmark, of which at least six months must be spent in a training practice. The Netherlands has recently required that half its obligatory three years should be spent in training practices (the UK equivalent is only one-third).

Several countries now offer diplomas as a voluntary end point of postgraduate training. All provide widespread opportunities for continuing refresher education, but only the USA has so far organized re-accreditation every five years, at least for those family physicians who are members of their Academy.

The introduction of a specific training has been paralleled by the inclusion of general practice as a significant contribution to the training of students before qualification. But there are large differences among these countries in the speed and completeness with which this change has come about. For example, all medical schools in the Netherlands had a professorial department by 1966, and all in Denmark by 1974. Although the earliest of all such departments was established in Edinburgh in 1963, it was not until 1996 that this objective was finally met throughout the whole of the UK. It is still far from achievement in France and Germany, where the formal barriers to the acceptance of general practitioners in senior teaching posts have proved hard to overcome (both countries lack a strong national academic organization comparable to the Colleges or Academies of general practice formed in all the other countries under consideration except Sweden).

In most countries, throughout this half-century, general practice has been the preferred choice of career for fewer medical students than subsequently enter this branch. (This applies particularly to countries where general practitioners are paid for each item of service.[76]) A notable exception was the UK between 1970 and 1990, when this branch advanced as first career choice for final-year medical students from 29 per cent to 45 per cent.[77] Prejudice against a generalist career persists in Germany and in France, where the best student examination results routinely open a royal route through the best hospital appointments, in preparation for a specialist career.

Pay and workload

In all the countries in question physicians have been among the most highly paid members of society. This has contrasted sharply with the situation of doctors doing similar work in the countries of Eastern Europe before 1990. General practitioners have been less well paid than specialists. Nevertheless, despite some diminution in recent years affecting all types of doctor in most developed countries, they have still been earning twice to three times the average national wage (Fig. 11.4).

The basic forms of payment are a salary, a capitation payment (a fixed amount per patient per year, sometimes differentiated by age and/or by sex), and a fee for each service provided. General practitioners are salaried in Sweden and Finland; paid mainly by capitation in Denmark, Netherlands, the UK, and Italy; by fee-for-service in Canada, France, Germany, and Belgium. In the USA the traditional method has been fee-for-service, but, under the impact of managed care systems, only 31 per cent of family physicians were receiving only fee-for-service income in 1993. A larger number were receiving their income from a mixture of fees from private patients and contracts with some form of managed care system. Most countries have adopted a combination of methods.

General practitioners in the UK have also enjoyed lifelong security of employment, to a greater extent than most other professions. This is also true for other countries in which payment by capitation or salary has been accompanied by strict control of the entry to medical schools. Denmark and the Netherlands are examples. It has not been true for Belgium, France, Germany, Italy, or Spain, where, until recently, medical school entry has been relatively unrestricted. Freedom of entry has resulted in a high ratio of doctors to population, strong competition, and a significant level of medical unemployment.

General practitioners are usually less concerned about what is earned by their fellows in other countries than with the level of their own earnings

[76] Gervas, Fernandez, and Starfield, 'Primary Care'.
[77] J. Parkhouse, *Doctors' Careers: Aims and Experiences of Medical Graduates* (London, 1991).

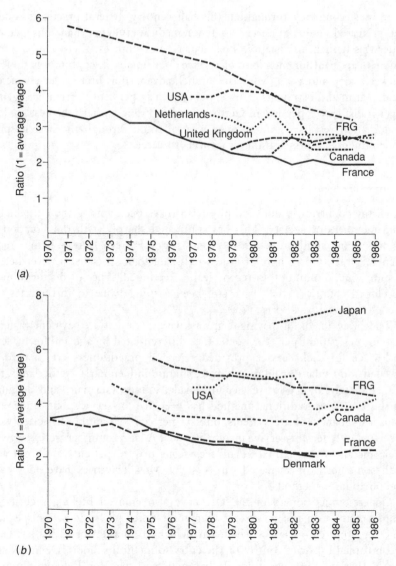

F IG. 11.4 Ratio of average net pre-tax income per physician to national average wage, various countries, 1970–1986

   (*a*) General practitioners
   (*b*) All physicians

Source: S. Sandier, 'Health Services Utilization and Physician Income Trends', in *Health Care Systems in Transition* (OECD Social Policy Studies, 7; Paris, 1990), 51, fig. 5.

compared with those of specialists and people in other professions. Pay differentials are particularly important in determining recruitment to different medical careers.

In the UK throughout the years covered by this chapter general practitioners have frequently complained of their load and the stress which seems to accompany it. If the relevant criterion was only hours of work per week, complaint would appear more justifiable in, for example, France, Germany, or the USA (countries in which competition is greater). However, Table 11.2 also shows that the UK has the highest number of visits (consultations) per week, except for the Netherlands, but also the shortest average duration of consultations.

Towards a strong primary-care orientation?

In the Alma Ata Declaration of 1978 the government of every nation accepted a requirement 'to devote a share of its resources to ensure that the public has access to a basic set of health services that first and foremost emphasize primary health care and to ensure an adequate supply of appropriately trained physicians and other health workers to provide these services'. Primary health care was defined as 'the central function and main focus of a country's health system'.[78] The two essential reasons for this agreement were that the costs of health care were rising in every country and that, despite this, essential needs were not being met.

The recurring theme in this chapter and in much of this volume has been about the balance of emphasis on the primary generalist or on the secondary specialist elements in a country's health system. But neither the balance of emphasis nor the direction of change in it has been the same in all the countries.

Since 1980 evidence has been put forward which clarifies the meaning of 'a strong primary-care orientation' and suggests that its strength in different countries can be assessed and compared. Maxwell proposed, in an early study of ten developed countries, that there was a negative correlation between the percentage of a country's gross national product spent on health care and the extent to which access to secondary specialist care was controlled by referral from a primary-care physician.[79] Starfield has more recently studied eleven developed countries and proposed specific features of a health system and of primary care within it which can act as indicators of the strength of a country's primary-care orientation.[80] Each of these features or indicators was given a

---

[78] WHO, *Alma Ata 1978*, 3.
[79] R. J. Maxwell, *Health and Wealth* (Lexington, Mass., 1981).
[80] B. Starfield, 'Is Primary Care Essential?', *Lancet*, 344 (1994), 1129–33. See also B. Starfield, *Primary Care: Concept, Evaluation, Policy* (New York, 1992); and US Institute of Medicine, *A Manpower Policy for Primary Health Care* (IOM Publication 78-02; Washington: National Academy of Sciences, 1978).

TABLE 11.3 *The strength of primary care, measured by the aggregation of certain features and characteristics to provide a means of comparison in various countries, 1994*

UK	1.7	Sweden	1.2
Denmark	1.5	Australia	1.1
Finland	1.5	Belgium	0.8
Netherlands	1.5	Germany (West)	0.5
Canada	1.2	USA	0.1

Note: The higher the score, the greater the strength of primary care.

Sources: Based on data from B. Starfield, 'Is Primary Care Essential?', *Lancet*, 344 (1994), 1129–33, and *Primary Care: Concept, Evaluation and Policy* (New York, 1994).

rating from one to three and countries were compared in respect of each. The ratings were then aggregated to provide a country's overall score and the scores compared. On this basis she found the strength of primary-care orientation varied in the manner shown in Table 11.3.[81] Starfield's scores, for European countries, receive strong confirmation from the European GP Task Profile Study.[82]

The importance of assessing and comparing the strength of primary-care orientation in different countries lies in the possibility of relating greater strength to fundamental outcomes of health care—evidence of improved health status, greater satisfaction with the service, and lower costs. Starfield was able to propose important correlations in all these three respects. Shi, in a very detailed study comparing all the states of the American Union, showed that the number of primary-care physicians (family practice, general internal medicine, and general paediatrics, combined) was significantly correlated with improving the life chances of the population, with reduced mortality, increased life expectancy, and improved childbirth outcome.[83]

Correlations do not necessarily indicate cause and effect. By themselves these studies might be seen to support in all countries a policy of strengthening primary care in the balance with secondary and tertiary care, but lower mortality, better health, and the cost of services are all subject to other important influences—socio-economic, life style, and demographic. Primary care must be seen in a very broad context.

The information in this chapter about other countries is limited for reasons

[81] Starfield's criteria and ratings are supported by Fry and Horder, in a study of twelve developed countries, using a similar approach (J. Fry and J. P. Horder, *Primary Health Care in an International Context* (London, 1994)).

[82] W. G. W. Boerma, J. van der Zee, and D. M. Fleming, 'Service Profiles of General Practitioners in Europe', *British Journal of General Practice*, 47 (1997), 481–6.

[83] L. Shi, 'Primary Care, Specialty Care, and Life Chances', *International Journal of Health Services*, 24 (1994), 431–58.

explained at the start. Nevertheless it may not be widely known that it is only Denmark and the Netherlands—and to a lesser extent Canada—which, hitherto, have had a system close to that in the UK. At the other end of the scale, the USA, as far as primary care is concerned, least resembles it. France, Germany, and Sweden occupy an intermediate position. The degree to which there has been convergence or divergence overall between systems during this half-century must remain a matter of opinion. The evidence collected in this chapter, although it includes many instances of convergence, does not point uniformly in that direction.

12

Conclusion

JOHN HORDER

In all the chapters of this volume, in which different writers have discussed different aspects of general practice and primary care under the NHS, a single underlying theme can be found, expressed sometimes overtly, sometimes by implication. This is that there has been, since the end of the Second World War, a revival—a renaissance—in this part of the service, after a period of stagnation.

In this concluding chapter this theme will be treated as a hypothesis which needs critical review in the light of the evidence that has been assembled. Such review is particularly important, because a majority, although not all, of the writers have been actively involved in the developments which they describe. This personal involvement is, of course, a gain which might have been neglected until it was too late, but the risk of bias is obvious.

The evidence of stagnation

No significant developments occurred in the organization of general practice (and few in its clinical work) between the First and Second World Wars. The proposals of the Dawson Report (1920) for health centres in which general practitioners would work in groups alongside other professionals had been very far-sighted, but there was not a single example of the intended pattern until after 1948, and then few until much later.

Although it was intended that the new NHS should be 'general-practice led', the largest effort and the most money were put, in the earliest years, into the development of the hospital service. Much had been learnt from wartime experience in the Emergency Medical Service and from clinical advances rapidly developed under the impact of war. Hospitals were now seen as the future place for developing the increasing promise of specialized medical and surgical care for acute and life-threatening illnesses.

Hospitals, with their attached medical schools, were also the site of all education for medical students. Furthermore, they were the site of postgraduate training, but only for all types of hospital specialist practice. In the circumstances of the time, such specialist training and experience under supervision could last from five to fifteen years before appointment to a career post (and this seemed to justify the assumption, commonly held at the time, that all specialists were not only 'consultants', but also better doctors in all respects). Finally, hospitals were among the most important sites for medical research.

The growing contributions and prestige of specialized medicine, its monopoly of undergraduate training (which then included the whole formal training for intending general practitioners), and its dominance over medical research, development, and institutions, made an increasing contrast with the general practice of the time. For that half of the profession there was no formal training after qualification (until 1953, when a year of junior hospital appointments became obligatory before registration with the state—the 'pre-registration year'). The role of general practice was usually seen as the care of patients and of illnesses which did not qualify for care in hospital. The phrase 'just a signpost to hospital' was often heard. More than one authoritative figure proposed that general practice might have no future, given the complexity and rapid development of medical knowledge and skills, except perhaps in remote rural districts. This view seemed to be supported by the realization that general practitioners were fast disappearing in the USA and some Scandinavian countries.

These were sufficient, basic reasons for threatening the morale of general practitioners (and it is surprising that not all were disheartened). But there were other reasons, less fundamental, more immediate. The new service was creating major changes for a conservative profession and it had been opposed by the profession's leaders. The first experience of it was alarming—a sharp increase in demand from a population more than half of which was experiencing free access to general medical care for the first time. There were lesser reasons for discontent, but by 1952 disappointment with pay had become a major one.

Of the three surveys of general practice carried out between 1948 and 1954 (Collings, Hadfield, Taylor), the first, by Collings, has been quoted in most chapters of this volume, because of its dramatically critical nature. It is clear from the other two surveys that he concentrated on one part of the whole picture. The whole picture, then as throughout this half-century, was of standards of practice which varied greatly, not just, for example, between town and country, but literally from practice to practice (and indeed even within the practice of one doctor, since failures in one aspect would frequently be accompanied by high quality in another). Taylor intentionally described the best ones and those that were already making innovations. His book makes clear that stagnation was occurring in a national structure which still maintained basic elements of strength from its long tradition, and was already acquiring new ones from the recent changes. Of these, the registration of almost the whole population with general medical practitioners and access to them without payment at the time of consultation were the most far-reaching.

The evidence of revival

It might be expected that the ideal form of evidence about revival should be sought in the results of care by general practitioners—results in terms of improved health of patients and population and in the satisfaction of both patients and doctors. It might also be expected that there would be information about such results which could be compared at different points during the half-century in question.

There is indeed evidence of very important changes during these years in such basic indicators of health as expectation of life or infant mortality. But these have resulted, of course, from an interaction of influences, some attributable to the NHS as a whole, but more still to developments outside it—for instance in nutrition, housing, education, social security, or full employment. Within the NHS the control and near-disappearance of, for example, infections such as diphtheria, poliomyelitis, whooping cough, and measles, through immunization, might seem attributable to the work of doctors and nurses in primary care. Moreover, the results are quantified in epidemiological statistics which are comparable over the years. But even here we must recognize a collaborative effort with scientists who developed the means and with government and the public-health service.

Since 1950 general practitioners have become capable of treating many other disorders successfully, as described by Loudon and Drury in Chapter 4 in this volume. The credit must again be given first to those who devised and developed the methods of treatment which could be carried out later in the setting of primary care. Although a stronger general practice has proved capable of applying new methods of diagnosis and treatment, the roots of greater success are too widely spread for this achievement to rate as clear evidence of revival in one part of the service. Objective comparisons at different points in time about the population's health and satisfaction with health care, which are relevant to the question of revival, can be found, but they are limited in number. They will be included in the historical account of developments which now follows. This will be divided into the three periods proposed in the chapters by Bosanquet and Salisbury.

In the first period, 1948–66, two new contributions to the strength of general practice from the new NHS have already been mentioned—free access at the time of use for the whole population, and registration on a general practitioner's list of patients (with the potential for a single lifelong record of health and illness). At least as important for the revival of general practice and primary care was the pre-existing tradition of referral when specialist advice or care was needed (and of referral back when the need ended). This sustained characteristic of the health system in this country contrasts with what is found in most comparable countries, where direct access to specialists is permitted or customary. Its relevance to both the subsequent development and status of general practice and to the low cost of the whole service through control of the gateway to specialist and hospital care has become increasingly clear. Its absence in certain other countries has proved to be a major barrier to strengthening primary care.

The foundation of the College of General Practitioners (1952) was a fundamental step, without which the revival of general practice would have been very unlikely. Linking what was at first a relatively small group of enthusiasts and innovators, the vision of its founders, John Hunt most notably, was to revive this branch of the profession through effort from within, using education and research as the leading methods. From now on general practitioners would be responsible for their own thinking, instead of relying on others.

Within four years the College, working with the General Register Office, had organized a large national study of illnesses for which patients consulted general practitioners. Such coordinated research by a large and scattered group of doctors could not have taken place in the absence of a national network such as the College now provided. Within fifteen years the College had taken the initiative in planning a special postgraduate training, coordinating the first experimental training schemes in different parts of the UK, and exerting crucial influence on the Royal Commission on Medical Education (1968), which declared its confidence in the future of general practice and recommended a period of five years of part-time training after the pre-registration year, properly resourced. Meanwhile, the first professorship in general practice (in the world) was set up in the University of Edinburgh (1963).

The Family Doctor Charter (1966) can be seen as the start of the second period (1966–90). It was the joint achievement of the General Medical Services Committee of the BMA and the Minister of Health, Kenneth Robinson. It brought to an end a system of paying doctors which discouraged care of high quality, it provided loans for building better premises, and it subsidized the employment of secretaries and nurses in practices. It is largely regarded as the beginning of a period of twenty years or more in which general practice began to flourish in this country, but it must be seen in context. As Bosanquet and Salisbury point out, the developments in practice organization which now occurred came about because of the combined effect of economic incentives, the emerging culture of general practice, and evolving social expectations and political imperatives.

Once this more acceptable contract was in place, the existence of the Doctors' and Dentists' Review Body removed the need for the confrontations over pay which had been such a big feature of the period before 1965 and had contributed to low morale.

Important evidence of revival at this time was an upturn in recruitment, based on a steady increase in the percentage of senior medical students and newly qualified doctors making general practice their first choice of career (from a level of 26 per cent in 1961 to 44 per cent in 1983). This increase did not occur in any other comparable country. At the same time, the gap between the career-long earnings of general practitioners and the average earnings of all specialists was narrowing. Equally significant was the rapid growth in published research and in the number of books now, for the first time, devoted to the subject of general practice. By the end of the 1970s most medical schools included the subject as a routine part of the undergraduate curriculum, and vocational training schemes had been created across the whole of the UK. Morale was high.

Information of particular relevance to the question of revival is to be found in the two national studies of Ann Cartwright, carried out in 1964 and 1977 (the second with Robert Anderson), many of the data being comparable. The information—derived from interviews with a representative national sample of 836 patients (1977) and questionnaires to a high proportion of their own doctors—is partly descriptive and partly quantitative. It is concerned essentially with the satisfaction of both the patients and their doctors with the NHS. In so far as a number of comparisons between the two studies were made, the results were disappointing. 'Improvements might have been not only hoped for but expected. In fact experiences and views had changed remarkably little. This is in spite of what might be seen as a considerable increase in investment of both money and manpower in general practice.'

Changes due to the 1966 Charter had been in place for ten years when the second study was made. During these ten years, however, as the authors point out, the expectations of both patients and doctors had risen. Even if actual improvements had occurred, they might by then have been taken for granted by both sides. But it was significant that there was no drop in the percentage of consultations that general practitioners felt to be trivial, inappropriate, or unnecessary—an observation which throws light on the relationship between doctors and patients, and which correlates with certain other observations indicating standards of practice.

Practitioners who enjoy their work see fewer consultations as trivial and are more likely to regard it as appropriate for patients to consult them about problems in their family lives. In the second study it was found, against expectation, that fewer doctors thought this appropriate. Given also a reduction in home visiting, there seemed to be two ways in which doctors were retreating from more intimate contacts with their patients. The main improvement between 1964 and 1977, as seen by the writers, was that patients were becoming not only more knowledgeable, but also more willing to criticize their doctor and to question what was said.

These two studies, long since acknowledged as models of their kind, do not fit easily with the widespread view that general practice took a leap forward between 1970 and 1990. Less comprehensive enquiries (i.e. a variety of opinion polls) about patient satisfaction have consistently presented a more optimistic picture overall, with criticism in details. Some of the criticisms are to be found in every poll and are still made, for example about the sense of hurry in consultations, despite the fact that the average duration of consultations has nearly doubled over thirty years.

Since 1980 three years of specific ('vocational') training after registration has been obligatory by Act of Parliament for all doctors wishing to become 'principals' under the NHS. The training has become increasingly rigorous and highly organized. The majority have also elected to take the examination for membership of the Royal College. It would be difficult to imagine that these changes have been without effect, particularly in improving technical capability.

The steady development of partnerships and group practices has certainly brought important benefits to doctors. For patients there have been both advantages and disadvantages, the latter particularly in loss of personal continuity with a particular doctor in practices which do not make a special effort to foster this.

Rightly or wrongly, during the later 1980s general practice, now renamed 'primary care' to emphasize its collaborative nature with other health professions, was praised as the 'jewel in the crown of the National Health Service'. But complacency and self-satisfaction were short-lived. A government driven by a set of beliefs at variance with those on which the NHS had been based and enjoying an overwhelming majority in Parliament, after much vacillation, introduced major changes in a new contract for general practitioners and in the White Paper 'Working for Patients', the latter without any consultation with the health professions.

This brings us to the third period, 1990 to the present. General practice had always been called the lynchpin or cornerstone of the NHS by successive governments, but such statements were usually received with scepticism by practitioners. It was only about 1980 that the proportion of state funding devoted to primary care ('general medical services') began to rise, though not dramatically. But the multiple and major innovations introduced by the government between 1988 and 1993 have, among many other effects, produced changes in the balance of power between the primary generalist and the secondary specialist parts of the service which go further than the slogan 'a primary-care-led service'. Both fundholding and the role of general practitioners in commissioning secondary care have changed a balance which had already lost much of its earlier hierarchical quality and become one based on complementary responsibilities and mutual respect. It is, therefore, entirely paradoxical that morale and recruitment have suffered a dramatic drop since 1990—a situation strangely reminiscent of the 1950s. The drop in recruitment, so far most apparent in applications to vocational training schemes, is likely to be the more serious problem, if only because the reactions to change of those already in practice have not all been adverse. Doctors seem to be divided between those who wish to devote all their energies to the direct care of individual patients and others who welcome the managerial tasks which belong to group practice and more especially to fundholding.

The increased responsibilities now placed on general practice and primary care must be attributed chiefly to economic pressures in the face of international competition for markets, an ageing population at home, and health-care costs which seem to rise inexorably in all countries because of technical advances and rising expectations. But, without the developments described in this volume, this part of the service would have been entirely unable to cope with its present and likely future load.

Looking back over the whole of this period since the start of the NHS, we might agree on the verdict that general practice in the UK has indeed undergone a marked revival, against expectation, after a long period of relative stagnation in which the impressive gains in specialized medicine seemed to leave no room for the medical generalist. It is impossible to single out any year, or any single event, as the starting point of the revival, but it was becoming visible to most observers soon after the mid-1960s.

Until very recently there was little evidence of a parallel revival in all but a few other Western countries. Now, however, there is a growing recognition of the need for generalists alongside specialists in all developed countries, because it is in the very nature of specialization to subdivide, fragment, and require new expenditure. While change and fragmentation has characterized specialized medicine, the definition of the generalist's role in medical care has scarcely needed to change, because it is both basic and flexible—to provide a single point of access, breadth and comprehensiveness, continuity, coordination, and advocacy, in illness and health.

Yet, change is in the air, for the general practitioner as well as for the specialist. It would have been easier to write this conclusion if general practice and primary care had entered a period of stability from which we could look back calmly, with an analytical eye, at what has been achieved, and what still needs to be done. But we are writing in the spring of 1997 and are only too conscious that this decade has seen more proposals for radical changes—all contributing to a sense of uncertainty—than any similar period since the NHS began. We cannot possibly attempt to forecast the future. But we can say that, if judgements of quality in health care can be divided between its technical and its interpersonal aspects, the revival of general practice during the last thirty or so years has been most obvious in the former. Erosion of the tradition of personal care is now a real danger, and its preservation is one of the great challenges we face in these times of uncertainty and confusion over the future direction of the NHS and of general practice within it.

APPENDIX A

Demography

Changes in the demographic structure of the population obviously affect the planned provision of medical services and the spectrum of disorders treated in medical practice. Fig. A1 shows the increase in the total population since 1951, the rise in fertility to a peak in the 1960s (the 'baby boom'), followed by a fall to some of the lowest levels seen in this or the previous century, and the crude death rate. Figs. A2 and A3 show the well-known increase in the elderly, the increase being much more marked in women. By the end of the twentieth century, it is likely that a fifth of all females will be aged 65 and over, while the proportion of males in the same age group is likely to be about 16 per cent. Fig. A3 shows the increase in life expectancy over the last 150 years, expressed as the number of survivors at various ages of 10,000 born alive at various times. The large contribution to life expectancy due to the reduction in infant and child mortality is clear.

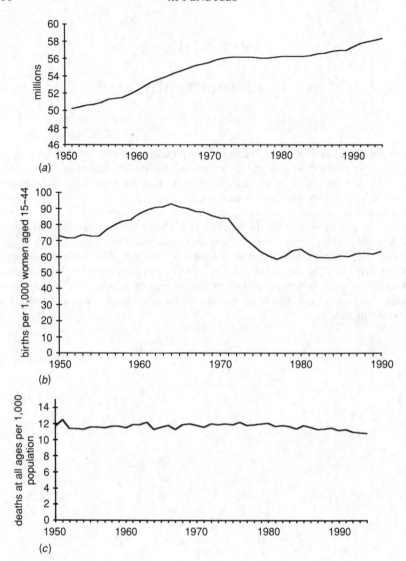

FIG. A1 Population changes, UK, 1950–1994
  (a) Population
  (b) Fertility rate
  (c) Crude death rate

Sources: Registrar General's Statistical Reviews (1950–94); OPCS, Mortality Statistics (1950–94).

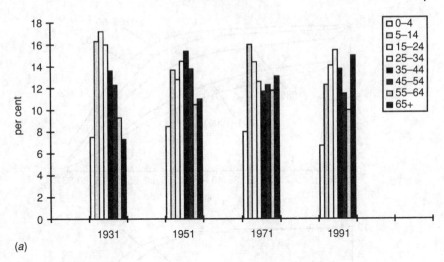

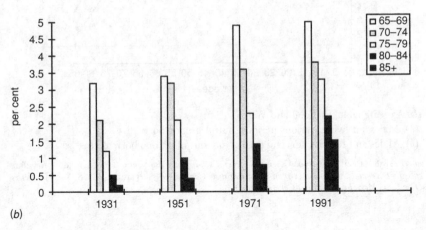

FIG. A2 Population of certain age groups, England and Wales, 1931, 1951, 1971, and 1991

(a) All ages

(b) Population 65+

Source: Registrar General's Statistical Reviews (1931–91).

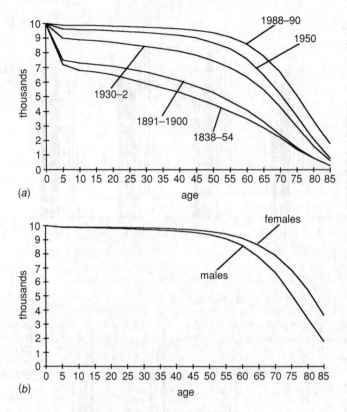

FIG. A3 Life table, England and Wales
(a) Males surviving, various periods, out of 10,000 born alive
(b) Males and females surviving, 1988–90, out of 10,000 born alive

Sources: 1838–54 and 1891–1900: *Registrar General's Decennial Supplement* (1901); 1930–2: *Registrar General's Decennial Supplement* (1931); 1950: *Registrar General's Reports* (1951); OPCS, *Surveys, Series DH1 no. 24, Mortality Statistics, General* (1990).

APPENDIX B

Mortality and Morbidity

While the crude death rate has altered little during the time of the NHS, there have been striking differences in age-specific and cause-specific mortality rates. Figures and tables in this appendix show that there has been a marked decline in deaths due to infective diseases, including tuberculosis, in deaths from respiratory diseases, and most strikingly in the indicators of maternal and child health: perinatal, infant and child mortality, and in maternal mortality. Infant mortality is measured as the number of deaths per 1,000 births. It is split into two parts: neonatal mortality (death in the first 28 days) and post-neonatal (death from 29 days to the end of the first year). Perinatal mortality is stillbirths + deaths in the first week of life, per 1,000 births. The maternal mortality rate (strictly a ratio rather than a rate) is the number of deaths related to pregnancy, labour, or the post-natal period (six weeks after delivery). It used to be expressed as the number of maternal deaths per 1,000 births, but it is usually expressed today as the number of deaths per 100,000 births because maternal deaths have become so rare. Table B7 shows that 'cot deaths' (Sudden Infant Death Syndrome), a syndrome which was not recognized in 1950, has now become the most common cause of post-neonatal mortality, whereas the leading causes of post-neonatal mortality in the 1950s were infective disorders.

Data on morbidity (morbidity being illness as opposed to death) are less easy to obtain than mortality data, but there is no doubt that there have been profound changes in the spectrum of diseases between 1950 and the 1990s. Some diseases have become less common, or have virtually disappeared. Others have become more common and a few entirely new diseases have appeared. Table 4.1 shows these changes. Morbidity tables in this appendix include changes in the incidence of certain infectious diseases which are notifiable under the Infectious Diseases Act (for example, diphtheria and poliomyelitis), and changes in the prevalence and age-distribution of chronic illness which forms such a large part of the work of general practice today.

The use of the logarithmic scale

In most of the figures the scale on the Y (vertical) axis is arithmetic, but in a few it is logarithmic. The logarithmic scale is useful where several trends whose absolute value is widely different are shown in the same graph, and where one is comparing *rates of change* over time, or rates of change in two or more separate entities. Fig. B1, which shows the decline in infant and child mortality, is an example. When these two values are plotted on an arithmetic scale it looks as if infant mortality fell much more steeply between 1931–5 and 1986–90 than child mortality. This false perception occurs because the number of child deaths are small compared to infant deaths. When plotted on a logarithmic scale, falls (or rises) of two or more values which occur at the same relative *rate* are seen as parallel lines, regardless of their absolute values and one is able to see that infant and child mortality fell at much the same rate. Likewise, Fig. B2, which shows the decline in maternal mortality, is plotted on an arithmetic scale and suggests that the *rate* of decline in maternal mortality after 1935 was very steep until 1950, after which the fall continued but at a declining rate. If maternal mortality is plotted using a logarithmic scale, however, the fall from 1935 to the 1980s is virtually a straight line, showing the unexpected feature that maternal mortality has declined at virtually the same rate, year after year, for a period of over fifty years.

TABLE B1 *Changes in the mortality rates in certain selected common causes of death, England and Wales, 1940–1990* (deaths per million population)

ICD Groups		1940	1950	1960	1970	1980	1990
I	Infectious and parasitic diseases	1,009	470	123	72	46	48
II	Neoplasms	1,820	1,945	2,180	2,390	2,619	2,846
VII	Diseases of the circulatory system	3,950	4,241	4,340	5,942	5,498	5,103
VIII	Diseases of the respiratory system	2,270	1,264	1,274	1,259	1,642	1,201
IX	Diseases of the digestive system	567	380	299	274	332	362
XV	Perinatal mortality[a]	57.7	37.4	32.8	23.5	13.3	8.1
XVII (ex VII)	Violence, accidents, and poisonings	1,083	431	505	462	434	569
	Suicide	113	102	112	80	87	76

Notes: The ninth revision of the International Classification of Disease (ICD) of 1975 came into operation in 1979. The data for 1980 and 1990 are not strictly comparable with the data for 1940–70, and the change accounts for the apparent discontinuities.

[a] Perinatal mortality rate = the number of stillbirths + the number of deaths in the first week of life, per 1,000 live births.

Sources: OPCS, *Surveys, Series DH2* (various years); perinatal mortality: A. Macfarlane and M. Mugford, *Birth Counts* (London: HMSO, 1984), ii, table A3.4.

TABLE B2 *Deaths from certain selected causes, by age, England and Wales, 1990* (deaths per 100,000 population)

Cause of death	0–24	25–44	45–64	65–74	75+
Male					
All causes	88	132	920	3,870	10,833
Ischaemic heart disease	0	19	325	1,138	2,959
Cerebrovascular disease	1	4	48	304	1,307
Cancer of lung	0	3	105	455	707
Pneumonia	1	3	10	61	622
Cancer of prostate	0	0	12	117	414
Cancer of colon	0	1	22	88	189
Bronchitis, emphysema, and asthma	1	1	13	86	239
Cancer of stomach	0	1	21	92	179
Diabetes mellitus	0	1	9	46	159
Motor vehicle traffic accidents	15	14	10	14	30
Cancer of rectum	0	1	14	53	107
Cancer of oesophagus	0	1	17	56	85
Cancer of bladder	0	0	10	50	144
Cancer of pancreas	0	1	15	50	92
Suicide	5	17	15	14	19
Ulcer of stomach and duodenum	0	0	6	27	92
Parkinson's disease	0	0	1	22	139
Atherosclerosis	0	0	1	10	87
Chronic liver disease and cirrhosis	0	3	14	21	18
Female					
All causes	52	76	560	2,189	8,223
Ischaemic heart disease	0	3	97	571	2,000
Cerebrovascular disease	0	4	35	232	1,439
Pneumonia	1	1	6	43	664
Cancer of female breast	0	12	79	135	218
Cancer of lung	0	2	47	164	165
Cancer of colon	0	2	18	64	151
Diabetes mellitus	0	1	8	37	130
Bronchitis, emphysema, and asthma	1	1	10	35	80
Cancer of stomach	0	1	7	33	94
Cancer of pancreas	0	0	11	38	68
Cancer of rectum	0	1	8	25	60
Atherosclerosis	0	0	1	6	107
Ulcer of stomach and duodenum	0	0	3	17	74
Cancer of oesophagus	0	0	6	22	51
Parkinson's disease	0	0	1	11	70
Cancer of bladder	0	0	3	16	44
Chronic liver disease and cirrhosis	0	2	10	15	12
Motor vehicle traffic accidents	4	3	4	9	17
Suicide	1	4	5	6	6

Source: OHE, *Compendium of Statistics* (8th edn., 1992), table 1.18.

TABLE B3 *Leading causes of death, by sex, England and Wales, 1901* (deaths per million population)

Cause of death	Rate	Cause of death	Rate
Males		*Females*	
All causes	18,192	All causes	15,777
Tuberculosis, all forms	2,094	Tuberculosis, all forms	1,550
Heart disease, all forms	1,445	Heart disease, all forms	1,520
Bronchitis	1,389	Bronchitis	1,352
Pneumonia	1,377	Old age	1,019
Diarrhoeal diseases	1,009	Cancer, all forms[a]	987
Old age	835	Pneumonia	910
Atrophy, debility[b]	706	Diarrhoeal diseases	894
Cancer, all forms[a]	693	Cerebral vascular disease[c]	771
Cerebral vascular disease[c]	692	Atrophy, debility[b]	518
Premature birth	665	Premature birth	483
Convulsions[b]	628	Convulsions[b]	465
Chronic Bright's disease	333	Whooping cough	335
Whooping cough	291	Diphtheria	269
Diphtheria	278	Chronic Bright's disease	246
Violent deaths from vehicles and horses	147	Violent deaths from vehicles and horses	23
Suicide	148	Suicide	48

Note: Apart from the last two categories (which are included for comparative purposes), all diseases and disease categories which caused more than 5,000 deaths in 1901 are included in this table.

   [a] Categories: carcinoma, sarcoma, cancer and malignant disease.

   [b] A very large majority of these were deaths in early childhood and infancy, mostly under age 1.

   [c] Categories: cerebral haemorrhage, cerebral embolism, apoplexy, and hemiplegia.

Source: *Registrar General's Report for 1901*, tables, pp. 137–51.

TABLE B4 *Leading causes of death, by sex, England and Wales, 1941–1951* (deaths per million population)

Cause of death	Rate	Cause of death	Rate
Males		*Females*	
All causes	15,692	All causes	11,810
Coronary artery disease	1,588	Other myocardial degeneration[a]	1,965
Other myocardial degeneration[a]	1,555	Cerebrovascular disease[b]	1,590
Cerebrovascular disease[b]	1,188	Coronary artery disease	855
Bronchitis	830	Hypertensive disease	480
Tuberculosis, all forms	469	Bronchitis	472
Pneumonia	453	Pneumonia	390
Hypertensive disease	445	Cancer of breast	350
Cancer of stomach	379	Cancer of stomach	284
Cancer of lung	350	Chronic rheumatic heart disease	270
General arteriosclerosis	259	Tuberculosis, all forms	267
Cancer of colon	204	General arteriosclerosis	260
Chronic rheumatic heart disease	181	Cancer of colon	257
Nephritis and nephrosis	162	Cancer of uterus	183
Motor vehicle accidents	151	Nephritis and nephrosis	152
Cancer of prostate	146	Cancer of ovary	110
Suicide	136	Cancer of lung	61
Gastroenteritis of infants[c]	971	Suicide	70
		Motor vehicle accidents	46
		Gastroenteritis of infants[c]	624

[a] Broadly speaking this category contained heart disease other than rheumatic and coronary artery heart disease.

[b] This consists of two categories—1 cerebral haemorrhage, and 2 cerebral thrombosis and embolism—which have been combined for comparative purposes.

[c] Deaths between 4 weeks and 2 years expressed as rates per million aged under 2 years.

Source: *Registrar General's Statistical Review for the Year 1951*, table 8, pp. 43–57.

TABLE B5 *Leading causes of death by sex, England and Wales, 1990* (deaths per million population)

Cause of death	Rate	Cause of death	Rate
Males		*Females*	
All causes	10,106	All causes	9,917
Ischaemic heart disease	3,046	Ischaemic heart disease	2,316
Malignant disease of lung	911	Cerebrovascular disease	1,391
Cerebrovascular disease	877	Pneumonia	531
Pneumonia	313	Malignant disease of breast	510
Malignant disease of prostate	287	Malignant disease of lung	411
Malignant disease of colon	200	Malignant disease of colon	223
Chronic bronchitis and emphysema[a]	199	Senile and presenile psychoses[b]	221
Malignant neoplasm of stomach	197	Diabetes mellitus	156
Motor vehicle accidents	140	Malignant neoplasm of ovary	154
Diabetes mellitus	125	Chronic bronchitis and emphysema[a]	125
Malignant neoplasm of oesophagus	122	Malignant neoplasm of stomach	124
Malignant neoplasm of rectum	120	Malignant neoplasm of uterus	121
Malignant neoplasm of bladder	120	Malignant neoplasm of pancreas	116
Suicide	117	Malignant neoplasm of rectum	90
Malignant neoplasm of pancreas	114	Malignant neoplasm of oesophagus	77
Senile and presenile psychoses[b]	98	Parkinson's Disease	65
Parkinson's disease	73	Leukaemia	59
Leukaemia	71	Malignant neoplasm of bladder	57
Chronic liver disease and cirrhosis	67	Motor vehicle accidents	54
		Chronic liver disease and cirrhosis	54
		Suicide	36

[a] Bronchitis, chronic and unspecified, emphysema, and asthma (490–3).

[b] Senile and presenile organic psychotic conditions (290)—largely Alzheimer's disease.

Source: OPCS, *Surveys, Series DH2 no. 17, Mortality Statistics by Cause* (1990).

TABLE B6 *Deaths within certain age groups, England and Wales, 1896–1990* (age-specific death rates per 1,000 population)

Age group	1896–1900	1921–5	1946–50	1970	1990
All ages	17.7	12.1	11.8	11.8	11.1
0–1	156	76	36	18	8
1–4	23.6	10.2	1.8	0.7	0.4
5–9	4.1	2.5	0.8	0.3	0.2
10–14	2.4	1.7	0.6	0.3	0.2
15–19	3.5	2.6	1.2	0.6	0.5
20–24	4.5	3.3	1.6	0.7	0.6
25–34	6.0	3.8	1.8	0.8	0.7
35–44	10.1	5.7	2.9	2.0	1.4
45–54	16.2	10.1	6.9	5.7	3.8
55–64	30.5	21.6	17.1	15.3	11.4
65–74	62.9	51.1	41.9	38.3	29.4
75–84	133.8	121.8	103.5	88.5	71.0
85+	267.7	251.4	219.3	216.3	162.7

Source: OPCS, *Surveys, Series DH1 no. 25* (1990), table 2.

TABLE B7 *Leading causes of neonatal, post-neonatal, and infant mortality, England and Wales, 1950 and 1990* (death rates per 100,000 live births)

Cause of death	Neonatal mortality	Post-neonatal mortality	Infant mortality
1950			
All causes	1,853	1,133	2,986
Immaturity*	986	24	1,010
Pneumonia and bronchitis	125	412	537
Congenital malformations	270	166	436
Asphyxia and atelectasis	326	9	335
Injury at birth	258	3	261
Gastro-enteritis	14	152	166
Whooping cough	0.5	39	46
Tuberculosis	1	17	18
Meningococcal meningitis	0.1	9	10
Measles	0.1	9	10
1990			
All causes	455	330	785
Congenital abnormalities	132	51	183
Prematurity	143	18	161
Sudden Infant Death Syndrome (cot deaths)	—	148	148
Non-infectious respiratory disease	117	—	117
Birth asphyxia	34	—	34
Diseases of the respiratory system	—	29	29
Slow fetal growth and malnutrition	—	18	18
Birth trauma	16	—	16
Infectious and parasitic diseases	—	14	14
All external injuries and poisoning	—	13	13
(motor vehicle accidents)	—	(2.1)	(2.1)
(accidental falls)	—	(1)	(1)
(homicide)	—		(0.8)
(other violence)	—	(2.7)	(2.7)
Metabolic and immunity disorders	—	6.3	6.3

Notes: Neonatal mortality consists of deaths in the first 4 weeks of life per 1,000 live births. Post-neonatal mortality consists of deaths from the end of the first 4 weeks to the end of the first year per 1,000 live births. Infant mortality is neonatal deaths + post-neonatal deaths. Thus the infant mortality rate in 1950 was 1,853 + 1,133 = 2,986 per 100,000 live births, or, as it is usually expressed, 30 per 1,000 live births; and in 1990 it was 455 + 330 = 785 per 100,000 live births or 7.8 per 1,000 live births.

  * This included the categories 'Immaturity' and 'Immaturity associated with diseases of early infancy'.

Sources: 1950: *Registrar General's Statistical Review for 1950*, table 28; 1990: OPCS, *Surveys, Series DH6 no. 4, Mortality Statistics, Childhood* (1990).

TABLE B8 *Long-standing ('chronic') illness, by selected conditions, in various age groups, Great Britain, 1989* (per 1,000 reporting)

Illness	0–15	16–44	45–64	64–74	75+
Arthritis and rheumatism					
male	0	14	72	108	181
female	0	25	129	211	282
Back problems					
male	0	37	67	44	24
female	1	33	46	28	37
Other bone and joint problems					
male	12	36	43	71	67
female	8	20	29	48	107
Hypertension					
male	0	4	50	77	44
female	0	6	63	102	93
Heart attack					
male	0	2	46	100	79
female	0	1	24	64	65
Other heart complaints					
male	6	4	31	51	50
female	0	7	21	36	73
Stroke					
male	0	0	10	30	48
female	0	1	4	15	40
Asthma					
male	70	34	26	25	21
female	46	34	30	29	24
Bronchitis and emphysema					
male	3	3	15	34	46
female	1	5	14	24	32
Hay fever					
male	13	18	4	2	0
female	7	14	3	2	2
Other respiratory complaints					
male	13	12	19	44	53
female	13	9	13	25	37

Source: OPCS, Social Survey Division, *General Household Survey* (1990).

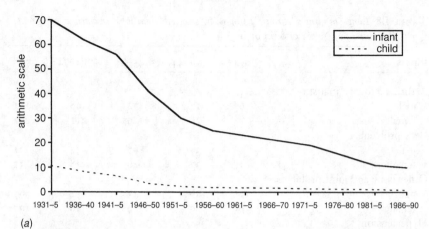

(a)

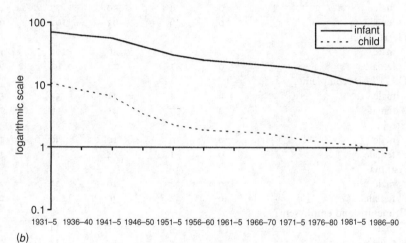

(b)

FIG. B1 Male infant and child mortality, England and Wales, 1931–1990
  (a) Arithmetic scale
  (b) Logarithmic scale

Note: infant mortality: deaths under 1 year per 1,000 live births; child mortality: deaths per 1,000 population aged 1–4.

Source: OPCS, *Surveys, Series DH1 no. 25* (1990), table 2.

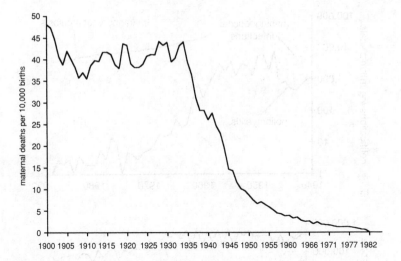

FIG. B2 Maternal mortality, England and Wales, 1900–1982

Sources: *Annual Reports and Statistical Reviews* for England and Wales (1900–20); A. Macfarlane and M. Mugford, *Birth Counts* (London: HMSO, 1984), ii, table A10.2.

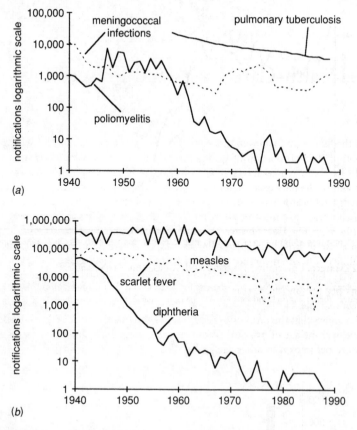

FIG. B3 Annual notifications of infectious diseases, England and Wales, 1940–1990
    (a) Cases of pulmonary tuberculosis, meningococcal infections,* and poliomyelitis
    (paralytic)†
    (b) Cases of diphtheria, scarlet fever, and measles

  * Notifiable as 'meningococcal infections' until 1969, and thereafter as 'acute meningitis'.
  † Notifiable as 'poliomyelitis' unitl 1949 and thereafter as two categories, 'acute poliomyelitis (paralytic)' and 'acute poliomyelitis (non-paralytic)'. The notifications of 'acute poliomyelitis (paralytic)'
have been used after 1950.

Source: DHSS, *Health and Personal Social Services Statistics for England* (various years).

APPENDIX C

Health-Care Costs and Prescribing

Most of the figures and tables in this section speak for themselves, but a few points are worth noting. The proportion of health expenditure spent on various services within the NHS has been remarkably stable, with the rise in administrative costs since the 1970s as almost the only exception (Table C1). As far as international comparisons are concerned, total health expenditure expressed as a percentage of GDP has risen in all Western countries, but most of all in the USA where it appears to be running out of control (fig. C2). The UK, however, has one of the lowest rates of expenditure. There has been a rise in private health insurance—especially since 1970–80—although the comparability of health insurance schemes in different countries is questionable (Tables C3 and C4). Likewise the wide variation between countries in the number of prescriptions per person (fig. C3) is also open to the criticism that the data may not be strictly comparable.

Fig. C1 shows that the rates of expenditure for the two extremes of life—births and for people over the age of 75—are almost the same per person, and far in excess of the expenditure per person in other age groups.

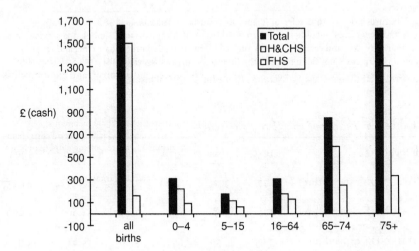

FIG. C1 Estimated NHS gross expenditure per person in certain age groups, by category, England, 1993/4

Note: Categories are (1) total NHS expenditure; (2) total spent on hospital and community health services (H&CHS); and (3) total spent on family health services (FHS).

Source: OHE, *Compendium of Statistics* (9th edn., 1995), table 2.11.

TABLE C1 *The proportion of NHS gross expenditure spent on various services, 1950–1995* (%)

Service	1950	1955	1960	1965	1970	1975	1980	1985	1990	1995
Hospital services	54.9	57.1	57.2	60.4	65.4	62.0	60.0	57.1	53.0	54.2
General-practitioner services	10.1	10.2	10.0	7.8	8.7	6.5	6.3	7.3	8.1	8.4
Community health services[b]	7.8	8.9	9.1	10.3	7.1[a]	6.1	6.1	6.4	8.4	8.6
Pharmaceutical services	8.4	9.5	10.1	11.1	10.2	8.5	9.4	10.1	10.3	11.2
General dental services	9.9	6.2	6.3	5.1	5.0	4.1	3.8	4.2	4.1	4.0
Ophthalmic services	5.2	2.5	2.0	1.6	1.4	1.4	1.0	0.9	0.5	0.6
Other Services[c]	3.8	5.4	5.3	3.7	2.4	11.2	13.0	14.1	15.7	13.0

Note: Data for 1995 are estimates.

[a] In 1969 certain local health authority services were transferred from the NHS to the Social Services.

[b] Figures prior to 1974 refer to former local-authority services.

[c] 'Other services' include headquarters and central administration, ambulance services, mass radiography, etc., and certain centrally funded items such as laboratory, vaccine, and research and development costs not falling within the finance of any one service.

Source: OHE, *Compendium of Statistics* (9th edn., 1995), table 2.16.

TABLE C2 *The cost of the NHS, 1950–1995*

Expenditure	1950	1960	1970	1980	1990	1995
Total NHS expenditure (£m.)	477	902	2,040	11,915	28,534	41,457
Total NHS expenditure at 1949 prices (£m.)	477	588	919	1,417	1,860	2,209
Total NHS expenditure (as % of GDP)	3.65	3.50	3.94	5.16	5.24	5.93
Total NHS expenditure per head of population (£)	10	17	37	212	503	709

Note: Data for 1995 are estimates.

Source: OHE, *Compendium of Statistics* (9th edn., 1995), table 2.7.

TABLE C3 *Private health-care expenditure, UK, 1955–1993*

Year	Persons insured (1,000 s)	Persons insured per 1,000 UK population	Benefits paid (£m.)
1955	585	11.5	2
1960	995	19.0	4
1965	1,445	26.6	8
1970	1,982	35.6	17
1975	2,315	41.2	46
1980	3,577	63.5	128
1985	5,057	89.3	456
1990	6,625	115.4	975
1993	6,580	113.1	1,250

Note: A large majority of persons in the UK who hold private medical insurance do so for hospital treatment only and receive general-practice care under the NHS.

Source: OHE, *Compendium of Statistics* (9th edn., 1995), table 2.22.

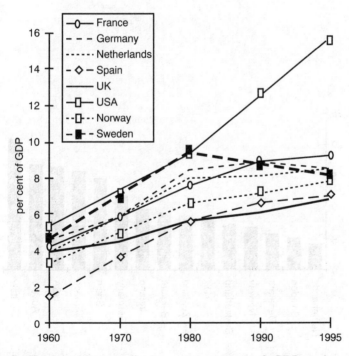

FIG. C2 Total health expenditure as a percentage of GDP, various countries, 1960–1995

Note: Data for 1995 are estimates.

Source: OHE, *Compendium of Statistics* (9th edn., 1995), table 2.3.

TABLE C4 *Private health-care expenditure per person in various countries, 1960–1992* (£ cash)

Country	1960	1970	1980	1992	Country	1960	1970	1980	1992
USA	41	96	274	1,010	Netherlands	10	10	104	243
Switzerland	7	26	161	604	Italy	2	6	45	310
Canada	25	35	88	337	Sweden	9	18	45	187
Austria	4	16	108	417	Denmark	2	11	56	186
Germany	8	23	119	397	Belgium	6	6	57	116
Japan	2	11	75	341	New Zealand	5	10	36	104
Australia	15	32	126	252	UK	3	5	25	114
France	9	17	85	314	Ireland	2	5	39	120
					Norway	3	5	7	43

Source: OHE, *Compendium of Statistics* (9th edn., 1995), table 2.24.

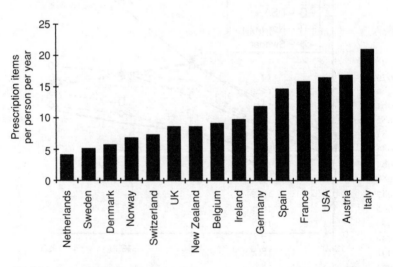

FIG. C3 Number of prescription items per person per year, various countries, various years

Note: Austria, Spain, Germany, New Zealand, and Switzerland for 1989; France for 1992; UK for 1993.

Source: OHE, *Compendium of Statistics* (9th edn., 1995), fig. 4.14.

TABLE C5 *Annual number of NHS prescriptions, UK, 1949–1994*

Year	Total number of NHS prescriptions (m.)	Prescriptions per head of population	Prescriptions per head of population (1949 = 100)
1949	225.1	4.5	100
1955	254.6	5.0	111
1960	247.9	4.7	105
1965	278.9	5.1	114
1970	306.0	5.5	122
1975	346.2	6.2	137
1980	374.0	6.6	147
1985	393.1	6.9	154
1990	446.6	7.8	173
1994	520.7	8.9	198

Source: OHE, *Compendium of Statistics* (9th edn., 1995), table 4.26.

TABLE C6 *Prescription items for the elderly and children under 16, England, 1978–1993*

Year	Number of prescription items per person			Percentage of total prescription items by age	
	Total	Elderly[a]	Under 16	Elderly[a]	Under 16
1978	6.6	12.2	3.4	32	12
1979	6.6	12.5	3.2	33	11
1980	6.5	13.2	3.5	36	12
1981	6.4	13.3	3.5	37	12
1982	6.7	13.4	4.0	36	13
1983	6.7	13.9	3.9	37	12
1984	6.8	14.3	3.9	38	12
1985	7.3	15.8	4.3	39	12
1986	7.4	16.3	4.1	40	11
1987	7.6	16.8	4.3	40	11
1988	7.4	16.3	4.3	41	12
1989	7.4	16.8	4.3	42	12
1990	7.6	17.5	4.2	42	11
1991	7.7	18.2	4.4	43	11
1992	8.0	18.9	4.4	43	11
1993	8.3	19.8	4.8	44	12

[a] Men aged 65 and over, women aged 60 and over.

Source: OHE, *Compendium of Statistics* (9th edn., 1995), table 4.27.

APPENDIX D

Clinical Practice

The final appendix is the one most directly related to general practice. Thus it shows the change in the ratio of general practitioners to population (Table D1), the number of general practitioners in various categories (Table D2), the striking change in the size of partnerships (Fig. D1), and the rise in the number of female general practitioners (Table D3). Trends in the place of consultation are demonstrated in Tables D4 and D5, and changes in the workload of general practitioners are shown in Table D6. Comparisons of the expansion in numbers of general practitioners and hospital doctors are shown in Table D7, and trends in the number of hospital in-patients and outpatients are shown in Fig. D2 and Table D8. The final table, D9, shows the percentage of births which take place in NHS hospitals and in general-practitioner maternity units.

TABLE D1 *Number of registered resident population ('list size') per unrestricted general practitioner, UK, 1951–1995*

Year	Number of population per general practitioner
1951	2,492
1956	2,282
1961	2,239
1966	2,360
1971	2,330
1976	2,215
1981	2,050
1986	1,881
1991	1,812
1993	1,799
1995	1,782

Note: Data for 1995 are estimates.

Source: OHE, *Compendium of Statistics* (9th edn., 1995), table 4.11.

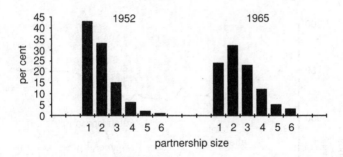

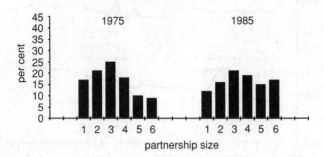

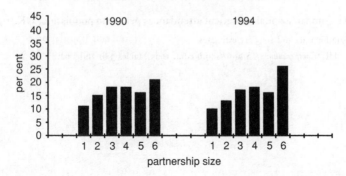

Fɪɢ. Dɪ Percentage distribution of unrestricted general practitioners by partnership size, 1952–1994

Sources: DHSS, *Health and Personal Social Services Statistics* (various years); OHE, *Compendium of Statistics* (9th edn., 1995), table 4.16.

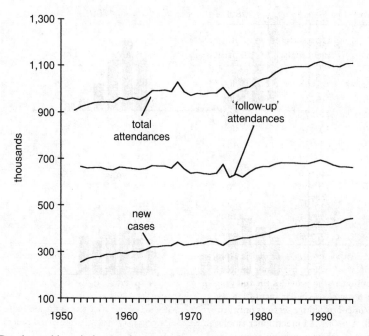

FIG. D2 Annual hospital outpatient attendances per 1,000 population, UK, 1951–1995

Note: Data for 1994 and 1995 are estimates.

Source: OHE, *Compendium of Statistics* (9th edn., 1995), tables 3.61 and 3.62.

TABLE D2 *Number of general practitioners, England and Wales, 1952–1995*

Year	Unrestricted principals	Restricted principals	Assistants	Trainees	All GPs
1952	17,568	896	1,689	309	20,162
1956	19,145	806	1,546	368	21,865
1961	20,175	701	1,141	201	22,218
1966	19,832	609	740	121	21,302
1971	20,633	431	602	244	21,910
1976	21,837	314	419	819	23,389
1981	22,100	294	395	932	23,721
1986	26,009	163	262	1,814	28,248
1991	27,197	139	447	1,777	29,560
1993	27,991	149	517	1,653	30,310
1995[a]	28,474	146	624	1,606	30,850

Note: An *unrestricted principal* is a practitioner who provides the full range of general medical services and whose list is not limited to any group of persons. A *restricted principal* is either a practitioner who provides the full range of medical services but whose list is limited to the staff of a hospital or similar institution, or a practitioner who provides maternity medical services and/or contraceptive services only. An *assistant* is a practitioner who acts as an assistant to a principal. A *trainee* is a practitioner employed for the purposes of training in general practice and in respect of whom a training grant is paid.

[a] Data for 1995 are estimates.

Source: OHE, *Compendium of Statistics* (9th edn., 1995), table 4.9.

TABLE D3 *The rise in the number of female general practitioners, England, 1965–1993* (%)

Year	Total number of male and female general practitioners	Female general practitioners (%)
1965	21,489	10
1970	21,709	12
1975	23,125	14
1980	25,160	18
1985	27,889	21
1990	29,323	25
1993	30,310	29

Note: General practitioners include unrestricted principals, restricted principals, assistants, and trainees.

Source: DHSS, *Health and Personal Social Services Statistics for England* (various years).

TABLE D4 *Trends in place of consultation by general practitioners, 1971–1990*

Year	Surgery or health centre (%)	Home (%)	Telephone (%)	Numbers interviewed: (base = 100%)
1971	73	22	4	5,031
1976	76	19	5	4,300
1982	78	16	6	4,417
1988	81	13	7	4,151
1990	83	10	7	5,023

Source: OPCS Social Survey Division, *General Household Survey 1990* (London, 1992), table 5.5.

TABLE D5 *Trends in place of consultation by general practitioners, by age group, 1990*

Age groups	Surgery or health centre (%)	Home (%)	Telephone (%)	Numbers interviewed: (base = 100%)
0–4	80	12	7	544
5–15	84	8	8	496
16–44	88	5	7	1,898
45–64	87	6	7	1,123
65+	68	24	8	962

Source: OPCS Social Survey Division, *General Household Survey 1990* (London, 1992), table 5.6.

TABLE D6 *The average number of consultations with an NHS general practitioner per year according to age, all persons, England, 1972–1990*

Age group	1972	1976	1979	1981	1983	1985	1987	1989	1990
0–4	4	4	5	6	7	7	8	8	8
5–15	2	2	2	3	3	3	4	3	4
16–44	4	3	4	4	4	4	4	4	5
45–64	4	3	4	4	4	4	5	5	5
65–74	4	4	5	4	6	5	6	6	6
75+	7	5	7	6	7	6	7	7	7
All ages	4	3	4	4	4	4	5	5	5

Source: OPCS Social Survey Division, *General Household Survey, 1990* (London, 1992), table 5.3.

TABLE D7 *Numbers of NHS medical staff, England and Wales, 1951–1993*

Year	NHS hospital staff[a]	Hospital consultants[b]	Unrestricted general practitioners
1951	14,777	3,488[b]	17,135
1961	20,345	5,322[c]	20,175
1971	28,852	8,273	20,633
1981	41,464	12,397	23,701
1991	52,423	16,263	27,333
1993	55,254	17,103	27,991
Percentage increase 1951–93	274	390	63

[a] Data are for the UK.
[b] Data are for 1949.
[c] Data are for 1959.

Source: DHSS, *Health and Personal Social Service Statistics* (1993).

TABLE D8 *NHS hospital discharges and deaths in different parts of the UK, 1951–1991* (thousands)

Year	England and Wales	Scotland	N. Ireland	UK
1951	3,259	443	104	3,806
1961	4,269	583	155	5,007
1971	5,494	728	219	6,441
1981	6,135	793	249	7,177
1991	8,001	912	274	9,187
Percentage increase 1951–1991	145	106	163	141

Note: The term most commonly used for discharges and deaths is 'admission as in-patients'. The two are not precisely the same, but both are measures of the quantity of in-patient hospital care.

Source: OHE, *Compendium of Statistics* (9th edn., 1995), table 3.19.

TABLE D9 *The distribution of births, England and Wales, 1959–1985* (%)

Year	Births in NHS hospitals	Births in 'isolated' GP maternity units	Home births and births in private hospitals
1959	60.7	0.45	38.85
1965	69.3	0.46	30.24
1970	84.7	0.64	14.66
1975	95.0	0.74	4.26
1980	97.5	0.46	2.04
1985	97.8	0.33	1.87

Note: A survey in 1988 of GP maternity units in England and Wales, to which not all units replied, found that 134 'integrated' units (GP units within a consultant maternity hospital) undertook 42% of GP unit deliveries. A further twenty-nine were 'alongside' units (units which had close links with a consultant maternity hospital), which undertook 31% of GP unit deliveries. These deliveries in the 'integrated' and 'alongside' GP units are included in column 1 of the table. The figures in column 2 refer solely to the 'isolated' GP maternity units, which undertook only 27% of GP unit deliveries. The survey suggested that in the late 1980s GP maternity units as a whole were responsible for about 6% of all deliveries in England and Wales, but data in Chapter 4 suggest that the true figure may be closer to 9%. (See L. F. P. Smith and D. Jewell, 'Contribution of General Practitioners to Hospital Care in Maternity Units in England and Wales', *British Medical Journal* (1991), i. 13–16.)

Source: DHSS, *Health and Personal Social Services Statistics for England* (1993).

Index

Note 1: general practice, National Health Service, and primary care have not been indexed as main entries as they appear throughout the text.
Note 2: The chronology has not been indexed.
Note 3: United Kingdom has only been indexed where it appears on statistical charts.